Frederick Brown

The Embrace of Unreason

Frederick Brown is the author of several award-winning books, including *For the Soul of France*; *Flaubert*, a National Book Critics Circle Award finalist; and *Zola*, one of *The New York Times* best books of the year. Brown has twice been the recipient of both Guggenheim and National Endowment for the Humanities fellowships. He lives in New York City.

The Embrace of Unreason

The
EMBRACE
of
UNREASON

France, 1914–1940

Frederick Brown

ANCHOR BOOKS
A Division of Random House LLC
New York

An earlier version of chapter four was first published as "The Battle for Joan" in
The Hudson Review, Vol. LXV, No. 3 (Autumn 2012).

All images are reprinted courtesy of Getty Images with the exception of images on
pages 204 and 227 from a private collection.

The Cataloging-in-Publication Data is on file at the Library of Congress.

Anchor Books Trade Paperback ISBN: 978-0-307-74236-0
eBook ISBN: 978-0-385-35163-8

Book design by Maggie Hinders

www.anchorbooks.com

Printed in the United States of America
10 9 8 7 6 5 4 3 2 1

To Ruth Lurie Kozodoy and Paul Dolan
And in memory of my dear friend Joseph Frank

Contents

Prologue

Until recent times, the French political imagination was disposed to associate its dogmas and enthusiasms with the symbol of the tree. In 1792, revolutionaries at war with monarchical Europe planted *"arbres de la liberté"* in towns and villages throughout the country, taking their cue from the American patriots who had rallied for independence at a famous elm near the Boston Common. Among the hundreds that dotted Paris (mostly poplars, which grew quickly and had the further advantage of deriving etymologically from the Latin *populus*), one was planted within view of the royal palace in a ceremony over which the king himself presided, under duress. It was cut down several years later, not long after Louis XVI had been guillotined, despite the chief judge's pronouncement at Louis's trial that "the tree of liberty grows only when watered by the blood of tyrants." Otherwise, cutting down a liberty tree under the new dispensation was tantamount to profaning the host under the old regime and punished accordingly. When a villager felled one in the Vaucluse, sixty-three neighbors who concealed his identity paid the forfeit, exemplifying Robespierre's notorious oxymoron, "the despotism of liberty." They were killed, their houses were burned, and their fields were salted.

As the Revolution understood freedom to be a universal birthright, liberty trees did not require native soil. They grew in land conquered by the Republic beyond the Rhine and, abroad, in the Caribbean colonies, where their proximity to slave markets before the abolition of slavery, in 1794, was noted by one derisive observer.*

Far from preserving the original character of trees planted under revolutionary auspices, Napoleon, who came out of the Revolution,

---

* Slavery was restored in 1802 by the Consulate, under Napoleon.

allowed them to survive as "*arbres Napoléon*" while discouraging ceremonies that glorified the advent of liberty. They numbered at least sixty thousand when Louis XVIII mounted the throne of a restored monarchy. Seen thenceforth as culpable mementos of a hiatus in the the Bourbon succession, liberty trees were harvested for firewood or furniture.

With the overthrow of Louis-Philippe in 1848 and the establishment of the Second Republic, maypoles reappeared in plantings that surpassed the exuberance of eighteenth-century celebrations. "The plantings had multiplied a hundredfold," wrote a chronicler. "They were to be seen at all the markets, squares, quays, gardens, intersections, and even in the courtyards of public institutions, at the Prefecture of Police, at the Opéra, etc. Patriotic songs, religious ceremonies, speeches, music, the national guard, acclamations, flowers, ribbons, the discharge of weapons, the curious crowd made for a lively spectacle." As Louis XVI had been pressed into service in the early 1790s, so now Victor Hugo, deputy mayor of the 9th arrondissement, presided over the planting of a poplar on the Place des Vosges, where he resided. Priests were invited to water saplings with their silver aspergillums.

Those thousands of well-watered saplings were given no nourishment once the Second Republic was overthrown by the future Napoleon III, in 1851. They withered during the Second Empire, but their right-wing analogue sprang to life several decades later, after the Franco-Prussian War of 1870 to 1871, not in a material sense but as a trope signifying national and racial authenticity. Of paramount importance was the publication in 1897 of *Les Déracinés* (The Uprooted), a novel that follows seven young Lorrainers torn from their cultural roots and sent into the world as existential waifs by a teacher of philosophy pledged to Kantian universals. "Alas, Lorraine undertook a great enterprise," wrote Maurice Barrès, who had made his name not only as a novelist but as a politician militantly championing the would-be dictator General Georges Boulanger. "She deported a certain number of her sons from Neufchâteau, from Nomeny, from Custines, from Varennes, so that they might rise to a superior ideal. The thought was that by elevating the seven young Lorrainers from their native grounds to France, and even to humanity, they would be brought closer to reason. . . . Did those who directed this emigration realize that they had charge of souls? Did they perceive the dangerous gravity of their act? They couldn't 'replant' the uprooted in congenial earth. Not knowing whether they wanted to make them citizens of humanity or Frenchmen of France, they evicted them from sturdy, age-old homes and let the denless cubs fend for themselves. From their natural order, humble perhaps but social, they blundered into anarchy, into mortal disorder." The soul, which thrived on necessity rather than freedom and owed its consecration to forebears buried in the soil of one's homeland, could not be transplanted. It was rooted rather than intellectual, organic rather than abstract, collective rather than individual. It was the pith that showed intelligence to be "a very small thing on the surface of ourselves." It was to Frenchmen what derelict country churches were in the secular, bourgeois state to *la France profonde*.

Its virtue lent itself to many of the evils of the twentieth century. In novels, essays, and articles, the prolific Barrès did much to shape opinion during the Dreyfus Affair and the war of 1914–1918, expounding the view as eloquently as any of his ideological confrères that diasporic Jews with shallow roots were susceptible of treason, glorifying the brotherhood of men in trenches, consecrating the blood they shed on fields shorn of trees, and generally reviling the Enlightenment. These were not his pieties alone. They became the accepted wisdom of the Right and echoed across the decades, from war to war. In the seventeenth century, Blaise Pascal had observed ironically, "What is truth on one side of the Pyrenees is error on the other." But in 1940 Marshal Pétain, justifying his pact with Hitler and the invention of a satellite state in the face of de Gaulle's exhortations from England to resist, assured his compatriots without a trace of irony that the soil on which he stood like a deeply rooted tree vouched for his authority: "The earth does not lie; it will be your refuge."

Suffice it to say that unreason had its apostles on the Far Left as well as the Far Right after the catastrophe of World War I, in every intellectual community that regarded "salvation" as the supreme goal of the human community. That will be the subject of other chapters.

· PART ONE ·

CHAPTER I

The Coming of War

Nothing collapses more quickly than civilization during crises
like this one [the Revolution of June 1848]; lost in three weeks
is the accomplishment of centuries. Civilization, life itself, is
something learned and invented. Bear this truth well in mind:
Inventas aut qui vitam excoluere per artes. After several years
of peace men forget it all too easily. They come to believe that
culture is innate, that it is identical with *nature.* But savagery is
always lurking two steps away, and it regains a foothold as soon
as one stumbles.

—SAINTE-BEUVE, quoted by George Eliot in
Impressions of Theophrastus Such

W ord that Archduke Francis Ferdinand, heir to the Hapsburg
throne, had been shot dead in Sarajevo by a nineteen-year-old
Serb named Gavrilo Princip made front-page news in Paris on June 28,
1914. People were shocked. But to Frenchmen, who regarded Serbia,
if they claimed to know anything about her, as the primitive under-
belly of Europe, where peasants dug houses under hillsides, where pigs
driven by swineherds armed to the teeth outnumbered people, and
where Tumult was a house god, the assassination seemed very much
in character. They would have readily agreed with Edmund Spencer,
who toured European Turkey in 1850, that "the Servian [*sic*] is both
by principle and inclination a man of war." Was Serbia not constantly
breathing fire at the two empires—Ottoman Turkey to the south and
Austria-Hungary to the north—that still held fragments of the pen-

insula in their dying grasp? Had she not just fought two Balkan wars and won them both? Could she ever forget the Greater Serbia she once was or stop aspiring to be the prow of an independent South Slav confederation?

Still vivid in European memory were the gruesome circumstances under which King Alexander of the Obrenović dynasty, a feckless monarch given by turns to cringing and terrorizing, had been overthrown eleven years earlier. On June 11, 1903, in the dead of night, some twenty or thirty military officers, one of whom, "Apis," was to play a prominent role in the assassination of Archduke Ferdinand, had surrounded the royal residence with artillery and a regiment of troops. Henchmen doing palace duty let them in, and the slaughter began. Dozens of guards died. Queen Draga and Alexander were flushed out of a hidden alcove in their bedchamber and killed three times over. The conspirators riddled them with bullets, disemboweled them with swords, and threw them out the window. A similar fate awaited cabinet officers, including the prime minister. Belgrade rejoiced. Newspapers compared Alexander to Nero. Flags flew, fanfares blared, people paraded in the rain, and measures were taken to summon home from Geneva Peter Karageorgević, scion of the Obrenović's rival clan, who became King Peter.

An American journalist, possibly drawing on the evolutionary theories of Lamarck, proposed in the *New York Times* that as the character of races showed most clearly during "moments of excitement," when inborn nature rose to the surface, defenestration had to be a racial characteristic of Slavs. The reason for this, he continued, should be sought in the ancestral habits of "Russians, Poles, Servians, Sorbs, Polabians, Croats, Cassubes, Wends, Lusatians," and other "forest-dwelling tribes."

French correspondents may not have been quite so baldly racial in their accounts, but almost all laid emphasis on the outlandishness of the assassination, implying that Serbia cut an archaic or Asian figure in the community of civilized European nations. "The assassination of King Alexander of Serbia, following a military conspiracy, is one of those tragic events the shame of which one hoped would not visit our modern age," declared *Le Petit Parisien*. "The horror of it surpasses that of an isolated murder. And one would have thought that we in Europe were unlikely ever again to witness a military coup d'état of the kind that once took place in ancient Rome, when emperors were proclaimed over the corpses of their predecessors." *Le Matin* referred to the extinction of the Obrenović dynasty as one of the most frightful tragedies yet recorded in the history of mankind. Characteristic of revolution in Balkan countries, it observed, was their particular "savagery" and "barbarity." *Le Gaulois* noted that although five hundred years under Turkey's yoke could not but leave its mark, it was still surprising to learn that the barbaric traditions honored by the Ottomans had been applied with such exuberance "in a Christian country." Free within her own cramped borders since 1878, when the European powers pronounced it independent in the Treaty of Berlin, Orthodox Serbia hardly impinged on French consciousness (except, in certain quarters, as a virgin ripe for industrial development). One journalist assigned to the French Ministry of Foreign Affairs heard a high official maintain, after Alexander's assassination, that no more attention need be given to the tragic event than to items from the police blotter reported under the rubric of *faits divers*. It was irrelevant to France. "The Serbs change government in their own idiosyncratic ways," the official declared. "That's their business, not ours. Once the new regime has constituted itself, it will seek recognition from the Powers, and obtain it. I say again, we have no reason to interfere in the internal affairs of other countries. Others may; let them speak, or get involved."

Eleven years later, the assassination of Archduke Ferdinand at Sarajevo inspired something of the same indifference. Strictly speaking, it too was an internal affair, as Austria had arbitrarily annexed Bosnia-Herzegovina, with her large Serb population, in 1908. To be sure, there were strong grounds for believing that the plot had been hatched in Belgrade by Unification or Death, a clandestine organization of fanatical patriots also known as the Black Hand, which reached into court circles. Certainly, Vienna believed it. And lurking behind that belief was the suspicion that Russia, the guardian spirit of Balkan Pan-Slavism, had had foreknowledge of the event. But most French— indeed, most Europeans—assumed that even if Austria took drastic measures, she would quickly crush Serbia's ill-equipped army in a war confined to that cramped corner of the continent. So it was that Winston Churchill could write, in *The World Crisis*, that an exceptional tranquillity prevailed in Europe during the spring and summer of 1914, when he attended to England's relentless naval competition with Germany as first lord of the Admiralty. "There had been a score of opportunities had anyone wished to make war. Germany seemed, with us, to be set on peace." In July 1914, Paris was more deserted than tranquil. Sun scorched the city, heat waves rose from its streets, and a steamy mist veiled the sky. Working-class crowds found refreshment on Sundays in the *guinguettes* of the valley of the Marne. All who could afford it flocked to the seacoast after Bastille Day, or to spas such as Aix-les-Bains, where, according to *Le Figaro,* everything augured well: "Never has the season been more elegant, more attractive, more carefree. Never have nobler, more radiant guests graced the flower-lined walks and shady groves, the fragrant terraces, the sparkling salons of the Grand Cercle and the Villa des Fleurs. One can easily believe that the very heart of high society is present here." On the front page of its July 15 issue, *Le Figaro* promised readers acquainted with Marcel Proust a long excerpt from the second volume of "that great and beautiful book," *Du Côté de chez Swann.*

The *grand monde* at Aix-les-Bains did not include France's president and premier. On July 16, Raymond Poincaré and Premier René Viviani (who was also minister of foreign affairs) boarded the battleship *Le France* at Dunkirk for a state visit to Russia. They pondered Austria's intentions with "a shade of anxiety," according to Poincaré, but otherwise enjoyed the leisurely, four-day cruise. And such anxiety as they felt may have been dispelled once *Le France* anchored at Kronstadt. Guns boomed an imperial salute, bands played "La Marseillaise," pleasure craft swarmed around the French squadron, and Czar Nicholas welcomed his ally aboard the yacht *Alexandria* before depositing Poincaré and his entourage at the vast palace complex of Peterhof. A banquet held for them there on July 20 quite outshone Aix-les-Bains. France's ambassador, Maurice Paléologue, remembered gorgeous uniforms and finery, in the midst of which Poincaré's plain black frock coat looked like a republican smudge. While fountains played outside, precious jewels of every description made "a blaze of fire and flame" inside the Empress Elizabeth room. Politics waited until the following day, when, still at Peterhof, the czar and the president reviewed seriatim questions of moment on Europe's diplomatic agenda. It was agreed that the Great Powers should meet sometime that year to set matters right in the Balkans.

On July 21, diplomats attended a banquet at the Winter Palace. President Poincaré exchanged pleasantries with the German ambas-

Raymond Poincaré, 1860–1934, three times premier, and president of France from 1913 to 1920.

sador, Count Friedrich von Pourtalès, who spoke of plans to visit his French relatives at Castellane. In conversation with Sir George Buchanan, Poincaré pressed the need for transforming Britain's entente with France and Russia into a tighter military alliance. He chatted up Baron Motono of Japan and the Marquis de Carlotti of Italy. Alone among members of the diplomatic corps unresponsive to the president's salutations was Austria's ambassador, Count Frigyes Szapáry. Poincaré asked him about Serbia only to be told, cryptically, that the judicial inquiry into the circumstances of Ferdinand's assassination was "under way." Their brief encounter ended with Poincaré hoping that punishment of the assassins would not be inflicted upon an entire nation and Szapáry uttering (in Poincaré's recollection) "commonplace assurances as to the inoffensive character of Austrian policy." Poincaré's memoirs make no mention of striking workers staging a huge demonstration on the streets of St. Petersburg.

The "shade of anxiety" Poincaré had felt before reaching Russia now turned a shade darker, but not yet dark enough to spoil his delight in the vivid color of imperial pageantry. On July 22, at Krasnoye Selo, he saw sixty thousand troops drawn up in serried ranks for a prayer service attended by the czar, the czarina, the czarevitch, grand dukes, grand duchesses, and ladies of Petersburg society crowding the stands under white parasols. The next day he and Viviani watched that army march across a vast parade ground to the strains of "Le Régiment de Sambre et Meuse" and "La Marche Lorraine" (Poincaré came from Lorraine). At a final banquet, this one on board *Le France,* the president concluded his toast to Nicholas by declaring that their two countries shared "the same ideal of peace in strength, honor, and self-respect." It proved to be a sinister valediction.

Poincaré's diplomatic tour was not yet over. After departing St. Petersburg on the evening of July 23, *Le France* charted a course toward Stockholm, Copenhagen, and Christiania (now Oslo). The vessel was in the Gulf of Finland when word came that Austria had handed Serbia an ultimatum to be answered within forty-eight hours. Poincaré knew less than he wanted of its contents, as wireless messages (which may have been jammed) were fragmentary and garbled. Austria's ultimatum remained unread at Stockholm, as he and Viviani continued their Scandinavian tour ignorant of demands that Serbia could not possibly accept without forfeiting her sovereignty. Thus, the French ship of state was rudderless. Not until July 26, at the behest of colleagues whose desperate wire reached *Le France* intact, did the president and the premier decide to sail straight for home. The next morning they received a telegram in which Maurice Paléologue reported from Petersburg that Russia

> had decided *in principle* to mobilize the thirteen army corps which are in the event destined to operate against Austria. This mobilization will only be made effective and public if the Austro-Hungarian Government means to bring armed pressure to bear on Serbia. Secret preparations will, however, commence already today. If the mobilization is ordered, the thirteen corps will immediately be concentrated on the Galician frontier, but they will not take the offensive, in order to leave Germany a pretext not to invoke the *casus foederis* immediately. . . . Russian opinion affirms her determination not to let Serbia be attacked.*

By then French who read their newspapers closely may have been better informed than Poincaré and Viviani. According to *Le Figaro,* the Russian minister of war had proclaimed in a long, detailed speech

---

* *Casus foederis* describes a situation in which the terms of an alliance come into play. A country may be compelled to declare war, for example, if its ally is attacked.

at Krasnoye Selo that his country was prepared for war. *Le Matin* enlarged upon this bulletin. Sergey Sazonov, Russia's foreign minister, maintained that the community of views between France and Russia was impeccable.

Had Poincaré been at his post three days earlier, in time to make a difference, would he have challenged the perfect community of views alleged by Sazonov? Would he, who had fought in 1913 for passage of a law extending obligatory military service from two years to three, have vigorously opposed the lethal system of alliances suddenly whipping its coils around Europe? Did the eloquent Lorrainer, who had spoken of "honor" and "self-respect" in his toast to Czar Nicholas, lean more toward revanchism* than an "ideal of peace" or conceive that ideal as Germany's peaceful cession of the French provinces it had annexed after the Franco-Prussian War of 1870–71? What moved him to tears, when he and Viviani finally stepped ashore at Dunkirk on July 29, hours after Austria had declared war against Serbia, was the "unanimity of patriotic resolution" he perceived in crowds of workmen standing on the jetty, the quays, and along the railroad tracks.

What moved him beyond tears was the reception he and Viviani received in Paris, where nationalist ideologues, about whom more will be said, had been declaiming the notion that war was a sacrament destined to save France's soul and restore wholeness to a mutilated country—that collective sacrifice would be the supreme tonic for moral fatigue. Assembled at the Gare du Nord were ministers, prefects, senators, and deputies. Several thousand members of the right-wing Ligue des Patriotes, led by its president, Maurice Barrès, followed Poincaré's open carriage across Paris, singing "La Marseillaise." Crowds along the route hailed the president with vivats to France, to the Republic, to the army, to Poincaré himself. "Never have I felt so overwhelmed," he wrote. "Never have I found it more difficult, morally and physically, to maintain an impassive bearing. Greatness, simplicity, enthusiasm, seriousness, all combined to render the welcome unbelievable and infinitely beautiful. Here was a united France. Political quarrels were forgotten."

---

* "Revanchism," or "revengism," was the term for a political agenda based on the abiding desire to gain revenge for the military defeat of 1870–71 and recapture Alsace and Lorraine.

An account of this jubilant reception appeared on the front page of the mass-circulation daily *Le Petit Parisien*. But *Le Temps* did not even mention the president's return to the Élysée Palace. A roving reporter observed that Paris looked its customary self: "no disorder, no panic." Except for more clients than usual queuing up at banks to exchange notes for gold, litter remaining on the boulevards from pro-Serbian demonstrations held a day or two earlier, more brokers selling off stock in Russian railroads, more pedestrians pausing to read news dispatches posted outside major establishments, and specialty clothiers doing a boom business in officers' uniforms, "one would not think that grave events impended." *Le Figaro* felt confident that the French lawn-tennis team, which had departed for St. Petersburg, would "carry the French colors in triumph" across Russia, from Moscow to Vladivostok. And front-page news in July 1914 was not the distant mobilization of armies but the trial of Madame Henriette Caillaux.

Henriette Caillaux's husband, Joseph Caillaux, had figured prominently in French politics since 1899, serving in four cabinets as finance minister, presiding over a fifth, and chairing the Radical Party. In 1914, he hoped that the premiership, a seat seldom warmed for long by its occupants during the Third Republic, would soon be his again. But Caillaux had made enemies, and his private life exposed him to ridicule. Georges Clemenceau was a vehement foe. Another was Gaston Calmette, the editor of *Le Figaro*. When love letters Caillaux had written thirteen years earlier, during an adulterous affair with Henriette (who became his second wife), were made available to Calmette, he dared publish one on the front page of the March 13 issue. Madame Caillaux visited him at the paper, drew a pistol from within her fur muff, and shot him six times—"because," she said to stunned employees, "there is no longer any justice in France."

As it turned out, French justice bent over backward for her. At her trial, which opened on July 21 in High Court, she was defended by Fernand Labori, the lawyer who had defended Émile Zola against charges of libel after the publication of "J'accuse." It lasted until July 28 and during that week held the French public spellbound. Newspapers, in Paris and the provinces alike, drove a thriving trade with stenographic accounts of the testimony and partisan portraits of the witnesses. Madame Caillaux's wardrobe loomed larger than the fate of nations. On page 1, journalists examined at length the issue of legal responsibility in a crime of passion.

On July 29, large crowds gathered at the Palais de Justice for the verdict. In his summation, Labori, anticipating what came to be known as the "Union Sacrée," implored the jury to visit its anger on France's external enemies rather than on Madame Caillaux, to "proceed united as one . . . toward the perils that threaten us." The jury may have taken his plea to heart. It acquitted the murderess, and in so doing wrote the perfect denouement to a play from which neither the press nor the public could yet tear itself away. Henriette Caillaux's acquittal inspired more intense coverage, more angry debate, more threats to the life of her husband. She walked free; her enthralled audience stayed put.

Louis-Ferdinand Céline, the novelist and physician, who once observed that most people don't die until the last minute, was old enough in 1914 to remember how far minds still were, late in July, from thoughts of the abyss yawning just ahead. On July 25, Serbia agreed to almost all the outlandish stipulations set forth in Austria's ultimatum. Austria, assured by Kaiser Wilhelm that Germany would honor its alliance if Russia should join the fray, demanded unconditional acceptance. A proposal by the British foreign minister, Sir Edward Grey, that the ambassadors of France, England, and Italy convene to find a diplomatic solution went unheeded. He then urged Germany to mediate the quarrel. Chancellor Theobald von Bethmann Hollweg equivocated in the absence of the kaiser, who had not allowed ominous portents to interfere with his midsummer cruise aboard the imperial yacht *Hohenzollern*. On July 28, Wilhelm, home after three weeks at sea, proposed an expedient enabling Austria to take action without forcing Russia to mobilize. Serbia had indeed met the wishes of the Danubian monarchy, but the promises it made on paper would be worthless until translated into deeds. "The Serbs are Orientals, therefore liars, deceitful, and master hands at temporizing," Wilhem asserted. "In order that these fine promises may become truth and fact, the exercise of *douce violence* [gentle violence] will be necessary. This will best be done by Austria's occupying Belgrade as *security* for the enforcement and execution of the promises and remaining there until the demands are *actually* carried out. This is also necessary in order to give an outward *satisfaction d'honneur* to the army which has for a third time been mobilized *to no purpose,* an appearance of success in the eyes of the rest of the world and enable it to have at least the consciousness of having stood on foreign soil." The Austrian war party led by Foreign Minister Leopold Berchtold would thus be placated and the conflict "localized."

No matter. Berchtold would ultimately have his way. Austria declared war on Serbia that same day, July 28. Russia, to whose "generous Slav heart" Serbia had appealed for support three days earlier, mobilized troops along her border with the Austrian province of Galicia. Meanwhile, General Joseph Joffre, France's chief of staff, advised the Russian military attaché that his country was fully prepared to do everything expected of a loyal ally. The besetting fear of tactical advantages and surprise attacks, which dictated military strategy throughout Europe, set in motion a monstrously reflexive sequence of events. "My thoughts were utterly pessimistic," Maurice Paléologue wrote in his diary on July 27. "Whatever I did to fight them they always brought me back to the one conclusion—war. The hour for combinations and diplomatic artifices had gone. . . . Individual initiative existed no longer; there was no longer any human will capable of withstanding the automatic mechanism of the forces let loose. We diplomats had lost all influence on the course of events." On July 29, Austria bombarded Belgrade. At the request of the kaiser, whose chief of staff, Helmuth von Moltke, predicted that the embroilment of other nations would result in civilized Europe being torn apart, Czar Nicholas suspended an order for general mobilization, but eleventh-hour diplomacy failed.* Austria kept bombarding; Nicholas took the crucial step of reinstating his order; France acquiesced in Russia's mobilization; England waffled; and Germany, whose generals wanted as much time as possible to implement the revised Schlieffen Plan and invade neutral Belgium, threatened. Like gamblers guessing and bluffing in a game played for mortal stakes, European leaders spent late July frantically wondering who would be the first Great Power to withdraw, or the first to attack. War may have been inevitable, in their minds, but who would incur the blame of declaring it?

In Paris, the voice protesting most eloquently against the alliance

---

* Moltke shared Paléologue's feeling of inevitability: "This is the way things will and must develop, unless, one might almost say, a miracle takes place to prevent at the eleventh hour a war which will annihilate the civilization of almost the whole of Europe for decades to come. Germany does not want to bring about this terrible war. But the German Government knows that it would fatally wound the deeply rooted sentiment of allied loyalty, one of the finest traits of the German spirit, and place itself at variance with all the feelings of its people."

that tied France to Russia's foreign policy and made her a partner in the maneuvers of czarist government belonged to Jean Jaurès, leader of the French Socialist Party. From the rostrum of the Chamber of Deputies, where he represented the Tarn region, and in the paper *L'Humanité*, which he had founded with Aristide Briand in 1904, Jaurès denounced revanchists, unreconstructed anti-Dreyfusards, and apostles of animal drive. On January 22, 1914, at a memorial service for his colleague Francis de Pressensé, he exhorted students in the audience to reject the preachers of "vitalism" and ignore the "reactionary dilettantes" who had made it their credo.

> Today you are told: act, always act! But what is action without thought? It is the barbarism born of inertia. You are told: brush aside the party of peace; it saps your courage! But I tell you that to stand for peace today is to wage the most heroic of battles. . . . Defy those who warn you against what they call "system"! Defy those who urge you to abandon your intelligence for instinct and intuition!

An article Jaurès published in *L'Humanité* six months later sounded the keynote of innumerable speeches and essays: "If all of Europe does not understand that the true strength of States no longer resides in the pride of conquest and the brutality of oppression but in the respect for liberties, in the concern with justice and peace, the East of Europe will remain a slaughterhouse in which the blood of the butchered will mingle with that of their butchers." By mid-July, when the SFIO (French Section of the Workers' International) held its annual congress, everyone with eyes to see knew that the whole continent might become that slaughterhouse. Jaurès argued zealously, and in vain, for a general strike. On July 25, the day Austria rejected Serbia's reply to her ultimatum, he delivered his last speech on French soil, at a political rally near Lyon, incriminating French imperialism, Austria's crude ambition, and Russia's "devious policy." Only the masses could save Europe from ruin. "Think of what it would mean for Europe. . . . What a massacre, what devastation, what barbarism! That is why I still fervently hope that we can prevent the catastrophe."

Even after Germany issued a proclamation anticipating war (the *Kriegsgefahr Zustand*) on July 31, Jaurès continued to hope against hope that disaster could be averted. There was no more time for ponderation and rallies, but the leader, with his sights set on a full meeting

Jean Jaurès, 1859–1914, leader of the French Socialist Party and cofounder of its daily newspaper *L'Humanité*. Clara Malraux, née Goldschmidt, was his neighbor in the early 1900s and wrote of him: "What did I know of this gentleman when, at the age of six, I was confronted with him, with his broad beard like dark parsley, with his arms and their sweeping gestures, and his close attention that was as if you were being given a present? I was struck by the fine ring of his voice, but hardly at all by his southern accent. He was short, rather thick-set, and both brisk and heavy at the same time" (Clara Malraux in *Memoirs*).

of the International to be held in Paris on August 9, didn't know it. On July 31, he primed himself to write a manifesto demanding once again France's repudiation of her entente with Russia; denouncing the machinations of the czar's ambassador, Alexander Izvolsky; and urging upon lackluster ministers a Franco-German rapprochement. He might have wanted to reiterate what his German colleague Hugo Haase had recently declared in Brussels:

> The ultimatum sent to Servia must be regarded as a provocation to long-desired war. As you know, Servia's answer was so conciliatory in tone that if Austria had had the honest desire peace could have been brought about. Austria wanted war. The most fearful thing about it all is that this criminal sport may deluge all Europe with blood.

He would likely have written it had his hand not been stayed by Fate in the person of a twenty-nine-year-old drifter suffering from delusions of grandeur and crazed by the patriotic demonology of rabid nationalists. On Friday, July 31, as the last week of peace drew to a close, Jaurès sat down to dinner at a café near *L'Humanité* in Montmartre. Raoul Villain approached him from behind and blew his brains out. Jaurès was fifty-four. Whereas Henriette Caillaux's crime anesthetized the public, Villain's shot woke them up.* The war that ultimately left Europe in shambles came as a bolt from the blue to many people. Events may have overtaken everyone, including men in power, but it did not help that newspaper publishers who squeezed as much print as possible out of Henriette Caillaux had consigned diplomatic dispatches to relative obscurity. Midway through July, when the government issued orders for the recall of soldiers on leave, the press was strongly advised to keep mum. "Care must be taken to avoid being conspicuous about measures likely to alarm the public," declared the minister of the interior. Fearful of pacifist rallies, the War Ministry made "silence and discretion" its watchwords.

The government was all too successful. Its strategy did more than disarm most pacifists. It gave wings to the myth that the Teuton was a predator with an insatiable appetite for French innocence. Suddenly set upon during her midsummer repose, France had done nothing to invite aggression, or to suggest that forty-three years of peace weighed heavily on her. This construction of events found almost immediate purchase in the national psyche. Surprise begot indignation, and indignation led to a wave of bellicose patriotism that swept through the country in the early days of August. Bishops, pastors, financiers, and factory workers all joined in the chorus of outraged virtue. "All civilized people will pay homage to the loyalty, to the dignity of our attitude," declared the bishop of La Rochelle. A prefect reported that everyone in the region he administered, the Var, understood that "the conflict became inevitable despite France's best efforts to promote peace." The mayor of a small town, following his party's line, assigned

---

* Like Henriette Caillaux, Villain was acquitted, but only after spending the entire war in prison. His trial took place in March 1919. The defense attorney, Alexandre Zévaès, addressed the jurors as follows: "Your sentence will have no political significance. It will be a verdict of pardon and forgetfulness effacing our prewar hatreds." In *L'Humanité*, Marcel Cachin asked what the true meaning of the jury's "lamentable gesture" may have been. "Perhaps it meant to affirm that . . . the real assassin [the warmongering demagogues], who had found a mere instrument in Villain, was not in court, that they didn't want to incarcerate the poor stooge who, on a day of lunacy, had held the revolver that killed our friend. Or perhaps this jury of Parisian bourgeois privately approved of his abominable act. We are told that the verdict was reached quickly."

the principal cause of the conflict to "the criminal maneuvers of imperialism" but exonerated France, which had "sought to bring about a peaceful solution." Departmental archives, from Savoie to the Charente, abound in irate commentary, often recorded by schoolteachers: "This Wilhelm, who has the gall to provoke all nations, must be a barbarian. He deserves to die"; "Germany has long been spoiling for war"; "War had to erupt, since Germany has wanted it forever and at all costs." The racial cant of a Maurice Barrès or his friend Charles Maurras (leader of the royalist movement L'Action Française) was echoed at the village level in references to Germany as the "ancestral" enemy, the "hereditary" enemy, the "eternal" enemy.

Socialists were another matter. Had Villain missed his mark on July 31, Jaurès would have lived to see comrades who had only recently been standard-bearers of antimilitarism rallying around the flag—as he himself intended to do if all else failed—and conferring the virtue of revolutionary evangelism upon their newfound ardor. When France had been besieged by Austria and her allies in 1792–93, had she not, in her victorious retaliation, brought Enlightenment to the benighted Europe of kings and autocracies? Patriotism displaced internationalism in pronouncements—patriotism construed not as an expression of xenophobic intolerance but as internationalism in another guise. (Many Germans, notably Hugo Haase in the Reichstag, were professing their love of country just as ardently across the Rhine). Jean Longuet, Karl Marx's grandson, declared on August 2 during a rally at the Salle Wagram:

> If France is invaded, how could Socialists not be the first to defend the France of the Revolution and of Democracy, the France of the Encyclopédie, of 1793, of June 1848, the France of Pressensé, of Jaurès? They know that in doing so they will be reviving the motto of '93: "Peace for the world's peoples! War against its kings!"

Four years later, when Socialists were reciting mea culpas over 1,385,000 French graves, including that of Jean Jaurès's only son, a steadfast antimilitarist named Ludovic-Oscar Frossard, who had nothing to repent of, reviewed the enthusiasms of 1914 from a sober perspective. "The truth of the matter is," he declared at a union congress,

> that if we had wished to resist [as he in fact had done] on July 31, 1914, we would have been swept away by the torrent of chauvinism surging

through the country. The truth is, and one must have the courage to admit it, that one cannot stage a general strike without strikers; there can be no insurrection without insurrectionists. Even if we had tried to apply the resolutions of our union congress, we would have been repulsed by those same laboring masses who, now weary of the war, reproach us for not having acted back then. Comrades, we did nothing, because we could do nothing.

The occasion was not appropriate to air another truth, that many who might have stood firmer in the chauvinist tide lost their footing with Jaurès's departure. The "great tribune" had been the Socialists' backbone and compass.*

On the morning of August 4, Raymond Poincaré, René Viviani, ministers, senators, and fellow deputies, including Maurice Barrès, president of the ultranationalist Ligue des Patriotes, gathered with leaders in Passy, where Jaurès had lived, to deliver eulogies over his coffin. A large crowd had come at the behest of the CGT,† which promised that the funeral ceremony would be the ultimate demonstration of pacifist vigor.

But what they heard, for the most part, on the day after Germany declared war against France and only hours after a German army violated Belgian neutrality, were orations posthumously enlisting Jaurès in the cause of national solidarity. "At this tomb, on which the most passionate of men lies inanimate," declared Premier Viviani, "I summon all French to reconcile their differences, to unite and achieve supreme concord. The great tribune, if he could rise, trembling, would express himself no differently." Édouard Vaillant, a venerable Socialist who had fled France after the 1871 Commune of Paris, had lived abroad until 1880 (when Communards received amnesty), and had fought the good fight since 1893 as a deputy fiercely opposed to national armies, projected his support of the government through Jaurès. "What he would say, how he would advise us, if he were present?" he asked. "He would say that at this moment, when, facing the

---

* After the Zimmerwald Conference of 1915, at which Lenin organized opposition to the "imperialist war," he wrote the pamphlet *Socialism and War,* denouncing Socialists who collaborated with their national governments as "social-chauvinists."

† The Confédération Générale du Travail—a large confederation of unions.

prospect of a general catastrophe, all the forces of barbarism, all the powers of imperialist militarism are being unleashed against us, we must not lose our internationalist faith, nor even allow it to slacken. He would recommend poise. He would have us bear in mind the battles that will follow the great battle now upon us, and remember that afterward we shall have to contend with the spirit of militarist reaction that may vanquish the victor. That is what he would tell us. . . . So, let us swear to do our duty, for our Fatherland, for the Republic, for the Revolution." Equally confident that Jaurès would have wanted workers to do their duty in a war justified as an Armageddon-like contest against imperialism was Léon Jouhaux, secretary-general of the CGT.* Others followed, making similar pledges of allegiance, much to the satisfaction of Maurice Barrès, whose seat in the National Assembly had placed him, ideologically, at the farthest remove from Jean Jaurès.

Jean Jaurès's funeral cortège proceeding from Passy to the Gare d'Orléans on August 4, 1914.

---

* Jouhaux delivered a feeble palinode after the war, in 1918, at the thirteenth congress of the CGT. "What was the psychological phenomenon, so to speak, that oriented my thought in the direction it took?" he asked, referring to his eulogy at Jaurès's funeral. "I'm hard put to say what it was. There are circumstances in the life of a man that make him evoke more or less forcefully thoughts that seemed foreign to him but which are the baggage of traditions he carries within himself. Perhaps I lived one of those moments." His capitulation to the war effort was, he implied, attributable to the martial impulse of his revolutionary unconscious. On the Right and Left, the unconscious was invoked for good and ill, as a responsible party.

In 1924, Jaurès's remains were interred near Zola's in the Panthéon. Until then he lay buried at Carmaux in the Tarn valley, his birthplace. On August 4, 1914, thousands of Parisians lined the streets to bid him farewell as the funeral cortège wended its way from Passy, along the Avenue Henri Martin, past the Trocadéro, to the Place de la Concorde, and thence to the Gare d'Orléans for the long train voyage south. Later that day, fellow deputies who normally sat on either side of him in the National Assembly commemorated his absence by leaving the bench empty. They had reconvened there after the funeral to hear the government rally France and prescribe measures needed in defense of the homeland.

Poincaré declared that France had been the object of a brutal, premeditated aggression; that for forty years the French, in repressing their desire for "legitimate reparations," had set an example of an impeccably peaceful, conciliatory nation, had pulled France up by her bootstraps and used her renewed strength "to advance progress and the good of humanity." France's heroic sons, charged with defending her, would present the picture of a "sacred union." No mortal enemy could pry apart the brotherhood. They would stand "as one" in their patriotic faith and their "indignation against the aggressor."

Premier Viviani, in a much longer address reviewing the events of recent European history, bestowed upon France the virtues of a medieval knight. She was "*sans peur et sans reproche*" (fearless and irreproachable). She was the guardian of liberty at war with the powers of night. "Under siege," he declaimed, "are the freedoms of which France, her friends and allies are proud to be the defenders. They are what is at stake; everything else is a pretext." Lest France's foes think the less of her as a physical force for prizing peace, piety, and enlightenment above military prowess, Viviani insisted that virtue was not without the strength to wield a mighty sword.

A strong, free people who uphold an age-old ideal and are indissolubly one in safeguarding its existence; a democracy which has been able to discipline its military effort and did not fear, during this past year, to increase the weight of it to match neighboring armaments; an armed nation fighting for its own life and the independence of Europe—that is the spectacle we honorably offer witnesses to this formidable struggle. . . . France has often proved, in less favorable conditions, that she is a most redoubtable adversary when she fights for liberty and justice, as is the case now.

The Gallic cock at its most combative, clawing back the two provinces ceded to Germany in 1871, after the Franco-Prussian War. *"Enfin!"*—At last!—expresses the sentiments of revanchists, zealots bent on avenging their loss.

Ovations punctuated every sentence. Newspapers across the political spectrum describe a revival meeting rather than a parliamentary session, and conservative reporters found nothing but glory in this anomalous communion. Where parties—each with more than one mind of its own—had traditionally wrangled, here politicians exemplified the "Union Sacrée." Now that Parliament had ceased to be a forum for cranky debate, the institution was at last "worthy of France," opined *Le Figaro*. And the French could now be French, imbued with common ideals of brotherhood, salvation, and sacrifice. It was as if war, under a Republic forever teetering at the brink, abolished the threat of revolution. Older deputies exempt from military service embraced younger ones. Spectators in the galleries applauded. It was great theater, according to a journalist reporting for *Le Figaro*. After the last words had been spoken, people filed silently out of the hall in which had occurred "one of the grandest, most beautiful things that we veteran observers of party strife have ever been privileged to witness."

In Berlin, where only two members of the German Reichstag had voted against war credits, Kaiser Wilhelm said, "Henceforth I know no parties; I know only Germans."

· · ·

September 1914. An Englishwoman offering cigarettes to a grateful cuirassier.

No one rejoiced more exuberantly than Maurice Barrès, a militant in party warfare since 1889. This Lorrainer gave full voice to his belief that blood was needed to reconsecrate France, to regenerate it, to liberate the energy held in thrall by arid philosophy, to do everything Jaurès had condemned as "vitalism." For Barrès, the curtain had fallen on individual consciousness. August 4, 1914, was a day on which true Frenchmen, practicing Catholics and lapsed alike, could not tell God's blessing from the warm sun. "Even if it involves the awful lessons of battle," proclaimed Barrès, "I've wanted nothing more than for Frenchmen to unite around the great ideas of our race. So they have. Blood has not yet rained upon our nation and war has already made us [at the Assembly] feel its regenerative powers. It is a resurrection."

The army—whose prestige, Barrès and others felt, ought to have taken precedence over considerations of justice for one wretched soul, Alfred Dreyfus had been grievously insulted; but war would set France straight. The celebrants prophesied in chorus that a decadent nation would regain its health once released from the drear monotony—the *horrible quotidien*—of peacetime. Fire, mortal danger, and the common enemy would enforce a collective truth. At the front, disparate elements would fuse into the "organic" society so loathsome to Kant-besotted intellectuals, for whom France's honor had depended upon the exculpation of a Jew. Men suddenly plucked out of civilian life and thrown together in their hundred thousands

August 1914. Departing for the front.

would not suffer from anomie. On the contrary, the battlefield would seat them in their Frenchness. Those who died would die as martyrs to the cause of national rebirth.

Almost everywhere, religious fervor sounded the call to arms along with bellicose patriotism, ignoring Pope Benedict XV's effort to reconcile the warring parties. "The task of Christians consists in preparing, stimulating, hastening, in the bosom of our Churches first of all, then of all our people, a government of repentance and of faith," declared one eminent ecclesiastic. Joan of Arc rode again. Church joined state in the sacred union, the sacredness of which rested upon the moral certainty that France stood for civilization and Germany for barbarism. Barrès called the Germans "Orientals," soon to be vulgarized as "Huns."*

---

* A young soldier writing from the front formulated a German version of the received idea: "We know full well that we are fighting for the German idea of the world, that we are defending German feeling against Asiatic barbarism and Latin indifference."

CHAPTER 2

The Making of a Xenophobe

Maurice Barrès [was] one of the most influential writers of
contemporary France. Few young men drawn to a career in
letters between the 1880s and the eve of World War I escaped his
power of seduction.

—MICHEL WINOCK in *Le Siècle des Intellectuels*

If M. Barrès had not lived, if he had not written books, his
age would be different and so would we. I don't see any
contemporary in France who has exerted, through literature,
comparable or equal influence. Like Voltaire and Chateaubriand,
he has created not the temporary scaffolding of a system but
something more intimately bound up with our lives: a new
attitude, a new cast of mind and sensibility.

—LÉON BLUM in *La Revue Blanche,* November 15, 1897

Friends and foes might have agreed that moral certainty was at
home in Maurice Barrès, who unabashedly spoke of wanting
to "educate" and "illustrate" the sensibility of his generation. The
National Assembly gave him political heft after 1889 as an elected deputy from Nancy, but more important for a writer prolific even by the
standards of his age was the printed page. Between the 1880s and the
1920s—throughout the would-be coup d'état of General Boulanger,
the Panama Scandal, the Dreyfus Affair, the parliamentary debate
over the separation of church and state, the war—he filled a hundred
volumes with essays, chronicles, and fiction that expound his successive enthusiasms.

The name Barrès, which derives from the Auvergnat word for a palisaded bastion, was well suited to this man, whose exclusionary creed rooted Frenchness in the soil and bound it to the dead. It's as if his patronymic shaped his ends. He was born eight years before the war of 1870–71, when Prussian troops overran Lorraine and occupied his native town of Charmes-sur-Moselle, fifteen miles south of Nancy. A grandfather from the Auvergne, Jean-Baptiste Barrès, who had served in Napoleon's army, married the daughter of a tanner in Charmes, settled there, bought land, and produced one child before his young wife died. Brought up motherless, Jean-Auguste Barrès entered a loftier circle of provincial society in 1859 by marrying Claire Luxer, the daughter of a rich pharmacist. They, in turn, had two children, Anne-Marie and Auguste-Maurice.

To all appearances, Maurice's childhood was that of a serious boy securely ensconced in a privileged little world over which the fifteenth-century Église Saint-Nicolas spread its mantle. He was taught to write by Sisters of the Christian Doctrine. He sang in the church choir. He learned his catechism. He fixed his mind every Sunday at mass on the stained-glass image of three skeletons lecturing three carefree young gentlemen. He enjoyed, albeit timidly, the ritual antics of Holy Week.*

A complement to religious instruction—salutary in several ways— was Walter Scott's *Richard Coeur de Lion en Palestine (The Talisman)*, all twenty-six chapters of which his mother had read to him when, at age five, he lay bedridden with typhoid fever. "At this moment," he reminisced in his *Cahiers*, "my imagination seizes on several ravishing figures that will always inhabit me. The damsels, who are angels, the Orient: they slept in the depths of my mind, along with the harmony of my young mother's voice, until reawakened during adolescence." Other Waverley novels followed. Secretly exploring his parents' library, he discovered books quite beyond his ken but the more pertinent for being inaccessible—Jean Cabanis's *On the Relations Between the Physi-*

---

* One ritual was called "Killing Pilate," during which the choirboys, after hearing a rattle announce the end of lamentations, were permitted to run amok for a few minutes and beat each other over the head with clogs and prayer books. Another was called "Killing the Jew." Shopkeepers or country peddlers impersonated members of the "race," while children danced around them chanting, "*Le juif errant / La corde aux dents / Le couteau et le canif / Pour couper la tête au juif!*" (With rope between one's teeth, a butcher knife in hand, and a pocket knife in reserve, to cut off the head of the wandering Jew).

cal and Moral Aspects of Man, for example. Later, in correspondence with her son, Claire would recommend the articles of Jean Charcot's student Alfred Binet.*

One of Barrès's fondest memories was of excursions east from Charmes to the medieval ruins of Andlau and west to Sion-Vaudémont, a pilgrimage site in the Vosges Mountains, where Celts and Gallo-Romans had worshipped their gods before Christianity displaced them. Perched high above thirty other villages in a wide swath of countryside extending almost to Joan of Arc's birthplace, it retained vestiges of the citadel demolished during the seventeenth century, when France absorbed Lorraine. For Maurice, who returned to it at every age, like an eagle to its first aerie, and wrote about it lyrically, Vaudémont would always be "*la colline inspirée.*"†

In childhood, those trips to the hilltop may have offered a reprieve from the mystifying inhibitions of home life. He remembered his father spending much of the day alone rolling cigarettes and reading Virgil, or playing piquet at the neighborhood café. A frail, taciturn man who collected enough rent from inherited property to employ his time as he saw fit, Auguste had few words for his family. He was kind but remote. Claire Barrès, tormented by migraines, which conjugal life did not alleviate, took to residing almost year-round among bourgeois ladies awaiting surgery or diagnosed as "neurasthenic" in a rest home at Strasbourg. Ministered to by nuns of the Soeurs de la Toussaint order, she became an absentee to her two children, though Auguste left one or the other with her for brief sojourns when he visited Strasbourg. Maurice, who never forgot the sight of wimpled sisters flitting down long corridors, sometimes said—as if in wishful thinking—that he was raised in a hospice. "I liked sorrow."

His mother was restored to him, at the expense of his motherland, when war with Germany broke out in July 1870. All of Charmes crowded the train station under a broiling sun to cheer recruits headed for the front, many of them obviously drunk, with shouts of "On to Berlin!" Days later, the sober and the drunk lay dead en masse near

---

* Binet wrote prolifically in the field of developmental psychology. He is famous for inventing the IQ test.

† A monument of Romanesque inspiration called "*le monument Barrès*" was erected in Vaudémont in 1928, with money raised by public subscription. It stands fifty feet high, on the brow of the hill.

towns whose names became synonymous with catastrophic defeat: Froeschwiller-Woerth, Forbach, Wissembourg. By August 10 the Germans had surrounded Strasbourg. On August 14, they entered Nancy. French soldiers trooped through Charmes hour after hour, beating a retreat in steady rain and camping wherever night overtook them. Charmésiens who had cheered them at the station a few weeks earlier now visited their muddy bivouacs. "It was an immense and squalid confusion," wrote Barrès. Alsace and Lorraine were essentially lost after two weeks of fighting.

Compelled to supply tons of bread, rice, and meat to the German army based at the nearby village of Chamagne, Charmes had already been severely taxed when, on October 14, two battalions descended on the town with orders demanding that each landlord billet as many men as he had windows in his house. Barrès's parents were fortunate: the quartermaster assigned them only one soldier, a Bavarian. They were additionally fortunate in not being taken hostage, having their house burned down, or suffering any of the lesser indignities meted out at random as punishment for attacks on German patrols. Not so lucky were their relatives, one of whose fingers were chopped off with a saber. During the winter of 1871–72, Maurice's maternal grandfather, Charles Luxer, traveled on a hostage wagon to Germany, where he contracted pneumonia and died.

The Treaty of Frankfurt, whose draconian terms France formally accepted on May 10, 1871, may have worked to Maurice's advantage. Sent out of harm's way when Charmes was overrun, the boy came home after some months to a family more convivial for including a foreigner under its roof. In the division of Lorraine mapped out at Frankfurt, the southern Moselle valley, including Charmes and Nancy, remained French. But the treaty stipulated that French territory should continue to be occupied by imperial troops until France paid Germany the enormous ransom of 5 billion francs. It would take France more than two years to raise that sum. Until then Maurice had the company of the Bavarian, who often walked him to school in full dress.

Photographs of Maurice at age eight show a miniature version of the haughty, ascetic figure Barrès cut in later years. One boyhood friend later recalled that whenever classmates ran wild he assumed a "resigned, ironical air," opened a book, and divorced himself from the scene. Rough-and-tumble play alarmed him. But the primary school, where not much was taught or learned, had at least the virtue of being in Charmes and thus releasing him to his family every day. That arrangement changed in his eleventh year. On July 27, 1873, the German garrison paraded through town for the last time. Church bells rang jubilantly. Three months later Maurice himself left Charmes, dejectedly, to enter a Catholic boarding school at Malgranges, near Nancy.

Although parents could visit with their children every Saturday, Barrès remembered feeling cast away, and alone, in a world that discredited every reason he had ever had to love himself. The son and grandson of small-town notables now found himself snubbed. The bookish boy who, unlike his new peers, had never conjugated *amare* was given to understand that some knowledge of Latin separated the wheat from the chaff. And in the little gray suit chosen for him by Claire—complete with baggy knee pants, a high, starched collar, and buttoned boots—he inspired as much ridicule as Charles Bovary entering a Rouen schoolroom fresh from the countryside in yellow trousers too short to cover his blue socks. "Rambunctious kids were taken aback by his distinguished air, and made imbecilic remarks about his attire," wrote a sympathetic witness. Worse awaited him in class. Where teachers set their pupils examples of insensitivity, one outstanding sadist hung a board around the boy's neck listing his spelling errors. There were other incidents, all vividly remembered fifty years later. At eleven, Maurice cried himself to sleep every night in a cold dormitory room (virile discomfort *à l'anglaise* being the rule especially in pensions for the well-heeled) and found consolation in prayer, reciting David's seven psalms of penitence.

The sense of being unassimilable—a pariah at worst, a Triton among the minnows at best—went deep. It pervaded all his dogmas and enthusiasms. Whether glorifying egoism in novels he wrote during the 1880s or exalting the collective unconscious thereafter, Barrès would never cease to feel isolated. At Malgranges, life became tolerable but never much more than that. The school compelled him to exchange his incongruous wardrobe for a smart blue uniform. Several boys befriended him. His mother learned, with apparent satisfaction, that he had played the part of the Virgin Mary in a play. After several years of application to Greek and Latin, he earned honorable mentions. And novels by Dumas, Hugo, Erckmann-Chatrian, and George Sand peopled his imagination with characters who made the dearth of close companionship less painful. What he couldn't do yet, for lack of a proper model, was invent himself. "Was I to become a likeness of my schoolmates?" he wrote in his memoirs. "I couldn't have done it even if I hadn't been repelled by the idea. Too weak, too timid, prodigiously imaginative, desirous of another world. But what world? I had no model for what I unconsciously aspired to be. My predestined journey interested no one, was suspected by no one, neither by masters, nor my parents, nor myself."

At the Nancy lycée, which he entered in 1877, his private syllabus came to include works reflecting not only an appetite for literary adventure but a more subtle respect for the anguish that set him apart. One can only suppose that Pascal's *Pensées,* Baudelaire's *Les Fleurs du Mal,* and Flaubert's *Salammbô* dignified his isolation, each in its own way. Did he see himself as the vexed unbeliever whom Pascal challenges to wager on God? Did the adolescent "desirous of another world" discover a kindred spirit in the author of *"N'importe où hors du monde"*? Did he identify with Flaubert's lovelorn hero Matho, who, leading a revolt of mercenaries against Carthage, moves from camp to camp around the besieged citadel more like a Romantic outcast bewitched by the beauty hidden behind its walls than a generalissimo? His literary affinities all spoke of the unconsummated and the unattainable.

As well as a home for those affinities, Maurice found a mentor to help him furnish it with philosophy. During his final year of lycée he met Professor Auguste Burdeau, who, since his arrival at Nancy five years earlier from Paris's elite École Normale Supérieure, had galvanized the school. For bright boys stifled by a faculty of timeservers, his presence was charismatic. He lectured fluently on Herbert Spencer, on Schopenhauer, on the great Hellenist Louis Ménard, on Hugo, on a hundred works outside the canonical program, but above all on Kant. The fact that the government had honored him for courage under fire during the Franco-Prussian War added luster to his erudition. Several months of Burdeau's tutelage marked Maurice forever. "Those who did not begin their studies in the aftermath of the war will no doubt be disconcerted by the prelude to *Les Déracinés,*" a literary critic wrote in 1908, referring to the novel in which Barrès portrays Burdeau as Paul Bouteiller. "The fact of the matter is, however, that that generation of lycée students was fascinated by professors of philosophy. Bouteiller is not an exception; he is a type. Erudite, curious, and self-assured young masters succeeded the sober, solid Cartesians of the old regime and the somnolent Cousinians of mid-century France.

They were as grave as Germans, as ardent as apostles. The vague and passionate way they had of teaching philosophy conferred upon it the seriousness of a religion."* Barrès himself later wrote that Burdeau was "the first superior man" he had encountered. "Well, if not superior," he added, begrudging him the full compliment, "at any rate a man of energetic will, bent on high attainment. . . . He had what it took to dazzle a callow youth."

Burdeau eventually fell victim to Maurice's conviction that the intellectual paragon, far from enlightening his disciples, had estranged them from their vital core with Kantian universals. By 1880 Maurice was already warming to the idea popularized by Hippolyte Taine, among others, that "race" and "milieu" explained more of human truth than pure reason. Still, not everything broke when Burdeau fell. Barrès would never lose respect for the master's ability to bend an audience to his will. He may have loved sorrow. He also loved eloquence, high pulpits, and Napoleon.

When Maurice graduated from lycée, Auguste Barrès, who stood on heights only as a tourist, insisted that his son follow a pedestrian path by studying law in Nancy and practicing it in Lorraine, where well-trained *notaires* were sparse.† Maurice did as bidden, with nothing to console him but the knowledge that a friend from lycée named Stanislas de Guaita would likewise be sacrificing Paris and literature on the altar of bourgeois convention. Stanislas, who was blond, robust, extroverted, born to two aristocratic lines, and in all these respects Maurice's foil, had bonded with him.

In law school Maurice distinguished himself almost from the first as a chronic absentee. Hours that should have been spent at stultifying lectures on the Roman code were instead devoted to reading poetry. Stanislas introduced him to Émile Zola's *Rougon-Macquart,* and Zola led him to works upon which literary naturalism based its claim to scientific authority. He was omnivorous, making great meals of Michelet's history of France, political theory, Schopenhauer (about whom

---

* By Cousinians, the author, Henri Brémond (an ex-Jesuit and a friend of Barrès's), refers to followers of Victor Cousin, who championed a philosophical system called eclecticism, the cardinal principle of which is that truth lies in the conglomeration of partial truths distilled from various philosophies. Eclecticism greatly influenced American transcendentalists and during the 1850s and '60s became the established teaching in French lycées.

† The *notaire*'s domain was voluntary private civil law.

Burdeau wrote), anything on Napoleon, modern fiction, physiology, Goethe, Mickiewicz, and Philip Sidney.

It wasn't long before he moved from taking private notes to writing omnibus reviews for a local paper, *Le Journal de la Meurthe et des Vosges,* in which Stanislas had preceded him. Under the rubric "Échos de la Librairie," he cast his net wide, with strategic praise for useful authors, among them Louise Ackermann, a poet whose Paris salon provided an audience for her verse. Maurice's compliments won him an invitation, and in October 1881 he took advantage of it, hoping that Madame Ackermann would bolster his fantasies of literary elevation. She did. He chatted up Anatole France. He discussed poetry with poets whose work he knew by heart. He spied eighty-year-old Victor Hugo at the Senate library. He placed an article in a literary weekly of note (*La Jeune France,* to which he soon became a regular contributor). Claire Barrès, his staunch champion and close reader, rejoiced. "You were born with a caul," she declared.* But success only validated Maurice's belief that a protective hood was the reward for assiduous courtship. "When one wants to *arrive,* when one is far from Paris and unknown, . . . when one has been told about the futile hours spent outside the doors of newspapers, reviews," he wrote to Auguste Vacquerie, an old associate of Victor Hugo's, whom he met through Louise Ackermann, "one dreams of a little word of recommendation reaching some editor on whose desk blotter one's essay or study lies dormant."

At the Paris Law School, Maurice did little work to good effect, cramming for examinations and passing them. Trouble didn't really brew until his second year. He began to loathe the prospect of a professional career for which he felt no calling. It lay in the middle of the road like a coiled snake. But more acutely distressing was his competition with Stanislas de Guaita for the favors of Guaita's mistress. All at once, Maurice suffered a humiliating rebuff and the (temporary) loss of his boon companion. Was there a connection between this betrayal and his estrangement from Professor Burdeau? Was he intent on defending an imperiled sense of self by challenging his revered teacher's intellectual eminence and disputing Stanislas's feminine conquest? Whatever the cause, the result was obvious. Maurice moped. Claire

---

* The caul is the thin, filmy membrane, or amnion, sometimes covering a newborn's head. It was thought to be a good omen, that the child born with one was destined for greatness.

Barrès, convinced that his childhood bout with typhoid fever continued to undermine her son, took him to the thermal resort of Bex, in Switzerland. There, doubts about his talent joined doubts about everything else. Beset by migraines, like his mother, he wondered whether he was mad or an idiot.

But he may have been secretly resourceful. Maurice's condition had the hallmarks of a flight into illness, with depression ultimately making the best case for suspending or abandoning the course prescribed by Auguste Barrès. Doctors agreed that his "brain cells" would need a sabbatical of six months or a year to "reform themselves." His father, who continued to rate a secure livelihood in law above any alternative, stood firm, which meant that Maurice enjoyed no respite from his dilemma when he convalesced at home after returning from Switzerland. He prepared for law examinations to be held in November 1882, even as clandestine projects ran through his head helter-skelter: a weekly magazine, a novel inspired by his blighted love affair, a Taine-like study of the seventeenth-century poet Saint-Amant and his times, a long article on Anatole France, who had become famous with the recent publication of *Le Crime de Sylvestre Bonnard*. Maurice spent every spare moment reading. "The important thing," he wrote to a friend named Léon Sorg, "is *one's Self*. Well, I hope to perfect myself this year." Had his friends Léon Sorg and Stanislas (with whom he had reconciled) not left Nancy for Paris, Maurice might have submitted to a schizoid arrangement, "perfecting" himself under cover of filial piety. Letters in which Léon described the greenness of intellectual and artistic pasture in the Latin Quarter was a powerful lure. Auguste Barrès would not hear talk of Paris, but what finally swayed him was a conversation with Albert Collignon, a professor of rhetoric at the Nancy lycée, whom his former student had enlisted to plead on his behalf. Father and son struck a bargain: Maurice could live in the capital with an allowance, provided he complete his law studies there.

Stanislas, Léon, and four other compatriots welcomed him at the Gare de l'Est when he arrived in January 1883.

Some years later, Barrès recalled the experience of moving to Paris through the character of Sturel in *Les Déracinés*. "The young king of the universe!" he wrote. "Those first days were overwhelming. He loved the cold, which pinched him into believing that this beautiful, wholly new life was not a dream. His young, fresh mouth was open to shout his happiness, and savored the air. It wasn't Paris but solitude that possessed him. A solitude more intoxicating than love." Like Balzac's Lucien de Rubempré, Maurice came from the provinces with his family's blessings and at their expense to study law, but committed to dreams of literary glory. Unlike the hero of *Lost Illusions,* he realized his dreams and honored the family pact.

As for solitude, Maurice may have had in mind the absence of village eyes and of judgments interfering with the accomplishment of his "new life." Certainly there was not much solitude enjoyed or sought in Paris by the ambitious young man, who immediately reached out to writers he admired. The poet Leconte de Lisle, a leading light of the Parnassian movement, recalled that Maurice appeared at his studio unannounced on the very day he set foot in the Latin Quarter. After *La Jeune France* published his long essay on Anatole France, France invited him to dinner. One such event led to another, and Maurice followed every lead, like a spider hectically spinning its web around fireflies. At brasseries frequented by literati he made his presence known. It was difficult not to notice him. Lanky and elegant, dark-skinned, with a long, beaky nose, large, heavy-lidded eyes, a fringe of mustache, and a lock of black hair draped over his right temple—where it remained for the next forty years—he cut an odd figure, at once remote and nonchalantly familiar. Having very little published work to show for himself, he seemed bent on illustrating in person the Parnassian ideal of marmoreal eloquence. What struck people were his settled opinions about literature and almost everything else, pronounced in a nasal voice. Rachilde, who coedited the review *Mercure de France,* found him somber and conceited, "very much the prince of shadows." Anatole France may have had something of the same impression. "Who are you, anyway?" he asked Maurice at their dinner. It isn't known how a twenty-one-year-old in the throes of self-invention, whose smugness cloaked a multitude of demons, might have answered the question. "Why did I want Paris and the life of a writer?" he later recalled. "No very strong and clear reason, an orientation as determined as a bird's but no reasonable reason, no clear idea of my future, not even a work plan. It was slender and invincible. . . . It didn't really transcend the idea of celebrity."

By 1884 Maurice had a diploma from the École de Droit. By 1885 he also had some literary baggage in the form of articles, chronicles, and short stories. They didn't amount to celebrity, but they did attract some notice. Opinion lined up for and against him, seldom on neutral ground. To Juliette Adam, the editor of *La Nouvelle Revue,* who rejected a story entitled "Les Héroïsmes Superflus," about the triumph of fanatical Christianity over Hellenic culture in fourth century Alexandria, he was a precious pup captivated by the sadistic eroticism of Flaubert's *Salammbô* and the erudite pageantry of *La Tentation de Saint-Antoine.** To poets he dismissed with one swipe in a review for *La Minerve,* he was the executioner who quipped as he killed: "I have concluded that French poetry in 1885 resembles nothing so much as a duck that keeps on running after its head has been chopped off. It no longer quacks. It has no perceptible direction. But it does run well." The provocations that made him obnoxious to some ingratiated him with others. His prose was mannered but supple and original enough to captivate young Marcel Proust ten years later.

Impatiently waiting upon the judgment of editors, Maurice took matters into his own hands and founded a review. It was not unusual for ambitious young writers to do so in fin-de-siècle Paris. Little reviews abounded. When Maurice launched *Taches d'Encre* (Ink Spots) on November 5, 1884, with help from Claire Barrès, it became one of the 130 or more that lived the life of mayflies during the 1880s. Readers were warned that it would appear every month for only one year and have only one contributor—himself.

As far as its life span is concerned, his warning was excessively optimistic. The first issue contained an essay entitled "Baudelaire's Madness," a short story set in revolutionary times, a review defending high German culture against the animadversions of a popular Germanophobe, and miscellaneous remarks about books, authors, and literary life. The second issue contained a similar assortment. But after four monthly offerings of almost fifty pages each to a short and dwindling list of subscribers, the review ceased publication. Barrès wrote its epitaph twenty-one years later: "Raising funds, finding a publisher, recruiting subscribers, and engaging readers are a rough gauntlet. One needs energy to climb staircases all over Paris, and resilience to keep knocking on doors that slam shut! For a young man who has literary ambitions, the founding and directing of a little review is an excellent apprenticeship; it cannot fail to teach him these two essential truths:

---

* Barrès included it in his first novel, *Sous l'Oeil des Barbares.*

1) that money is almost omnipotent; 2) that the literary industry is an industry of beggars." If he was as alert as other provincials—Flaubert and Zola, for example—to the opinion of hometown readers, a report from Claire Barrès that their fellow Charmésiens took umbrage at his irreverence, his pervasive sarcasm, and especially his defense of German culture might not have displeased him. What one Parisian reviewer praised as "strange" and "sickly" in his prose and another as suavely contrarian was all that Charmes-sur-Moselle associated with big-city decadence. On the Left Bank, however, *Taches d'Encre* made him a more conspicuous figure.

Maurice also frequented the Right Bank, at night more often than by day, and the Butte Montmartre rather than the fashionable west end. To provincial bourgeois, nothing could have been more decadent than his nocturnal rambles. Slumming had become all the rage among toffs and adventurous young ladies of the upper class. Snobbery in this inverted form challenged its initiates to visit dangerous neighborhoods on the Butte—"apache territory"—and risk assault by hooligans or rub against the unwashed at cabarets like Le Chat Noir and subject themselves to Aristide Bruant's musical taunts at Le Mirliton.* Maurice, on the other hand, wanted to penetrate the tragic strangeness, as he put it, of Paris's lower depths.

Befriending natives of the Château Rouge district comported with his excursions into the *bas fonds* of the human psyche. Although Maurice never met the celebrated neurologist Jean Charcot, during a visit home he witnessed hypnosis as practiced by a local pharmacist on epileptics and hysterics, of whom there was apparently no lack in Charmes. "You wouldn't believe what I see every day," he wrote to his friend Léon Sorg. "It's frightening. It turns all one's ideas about life upside down." In Paris, where young Sigmund Freud had been a near neighbor between 1883 and 1885, Maurice attended Dr. Benjamin Ball's lectures on morbid psychology at the Sainte-Anne asylum (founded twenty-two years earlier, under Napoleon III, to replace the city madhouse). When *Le Voltaire,* a prominent newspaper of the political Left, signed him up for freelance articles, he devoted his first one to the new discipline of psychiatry. It must have gratified

---

* Inverted snobbery took elaborate forms, one example being a costume ball at which guests, many of them titled, had to dress as characters in *L'Assommoir,* Zola's novel about life in a slum neighborhood of Paris.

his anxious mother, who in their correspondence had often recommended literature on disorders of the mind—Théodule Ribot's work, for example. Ribot was a professor of experimental psychology at the Collège de France and the author of *Diseases of Memory* and *Diseases of the Will*. His magnum opus, *Heredity: A Psychological Study*, appeared in 1885.

Maurice may have hoped to gain from Dr. Ball's lectures a better understanding of friends who had veered off the road they'd once traveled together into a dark woods, above all Stanislas de Guaita. It was indirectly through Maurice that Guaita met Sâr Mérodack Péladan (born Joséphin Péladan), a black-bearded occultist often seen swanning around the Latin Quarter in a velvet tunic with leg-o'-mutton sleeves, a jabot, tan gauntlets, and doeskin shoes.* Guaita became Péladan's disciple after embracing the idea that magic of the ancient Near East held the key to mankind's salvation. Together they founded a school called the "Kabbalist order of the Rosicrucians." In due course Guaita, heavily addicted to morphine (as were other of Maurice's friends), would spend more time at the family château, applying Kabbalist exegesis to the Hebrew Bible, than in Paris.

The demise of *Taches d'Encre* did not leave Maurice idle. He had visited Bayreuth the year before and paid homage to Wagner, the idol of the day, in *Le Journal Illustré*.† He published book reviews in Anatole France's *Les Lettres et les Arts Illustrés,* a Paris chronicle in *La Vie Moderne,* and cultural commentary in other magazines (sometimes under the pseudonym "Oblique") and thus eked out enough money, with his father's allowance, to cover expenses when he left the Latin Quarter for a larger flat near Clichy, around the corner from Émile Zola's town house.

How to become self-sufficient was the question. By 1886, Auguste Barrès had despaired of his son ever practicing notarial law. The family tried, without success, to secure him gainful employment in the Senate or the Chamber of Deputies—a clerkship of the sort that

---

* On occasion Maurice himself cut an extravagant figure, sporting lilac-colored pants. But the pants didn't fit, figuratively speaking; he came to eschew company that prized extravagance for its own sake and weary mandarins, as he described the Symbolists, who played "complicated literary games."

† On the verge of World War I, he noted in his *Cahiers:* "I see how it was Wagner who dominated our youth." Sâr Péladan appeared at Bayreuth wearing a burnoose and hoping to meet Siegfried and Winifred Wagner, but he was not granted an audience.

Young Maurice Barrès in a pose and in attire appopriate to the author of *Le Culte du Moi.*

hadn't prevented well-known writers from pouring out stories and novels after a day at the office. Maurice's emotional state complicated matters. Though he had made a modest name for himself, it hadn't dispelled his doubts. As fast as he ran, depression stayed hard on his heels and, whenever it caught up, robbed the seemingly impervious ironist of all self-confidence. By turns lofty and morose, the prophet of a new era and the superfluous man, he claimed to be suffering from a disease known to psychiatrists of the day as "cerebral anemia." Others called it infirmity of purpose. The remedy for it, his family agreed, was winter in Italy.

Maurice spent two successive winters in Italy. What he remembered most vividly of the first—besides a collection of German metaphysical studies available to guests at the hotel he occupied in Lucerne, en route to Milan—was the numbing cold. More agreeably memorable was his second voyage, in 1887. It began with a fortnight touring Venice and being enraptured by all he saw there: Tiepolos in the Accademia; canals flowing between escutcheoned walls; Palladio's

San Giorgio Maggiore; a January sun slanting over faded red facades.
These conjured up Baudelaire's image of Beauty as a "dream of stone,"
and every parcel of his soul, he wrote, was "fortified, transformed."
Thinking that this aesthete's Jerusalem might have occasioned a new
birth, he left Venice happier than ever, or happy for the first time,
though perhaps not noticeably so to writers he met during the next
stage of his journey, in Florence. There he moved in the company
of Anglo-American expatriates. A letter of recommendation from the
French novelist Paul Bourget prompted Henry James to offer Barrès lunch at a restaurant on Via Tornabuoni. Through James, he met
Robert Browning and Violet Paget (alias Vernon Lee), the Renaissance scholar and author of supernatural tales. He studied Italian; he
read a history of the Risorgimento; he took long walks, as much for
the pleasure of gazing at young Italian women as of admiring "the
artistic glories of the public place"; and he wondered how much longer it would take him to find purchase in a world whose rewards he
coveted. "When, then, will I be done with these slow preparations of
my life?"

In one sense Maurice was the eternal initiate, toeing the margin of
life while posing as an exemplar of personal authenticity. In another
sense he entered the public arena with dramatic pirouettes. A year
after his Italian awakening, he published *Sous l'Oeil des Barbares*
(Under Barbarian Eyes), the first installment of a trilogy whose appeal
to disaffected French youth was such that literary journalists dubbed
him "prince de la jeunesse." Barrès would soon become a name to be
reckoned with.*

The title of the trilogy, *Le Culte du Moi* (Cult of the Self), was not
only a lure but a caveat to readers expecting a plot and realistically
portrayed characters. Cut from the same cloth as *Taches d'Encre*, the
work of a sole contributor, *Sous l'Oeil des Barbares* follows a loner,
Philippe, through mazes of abstraction and emotion from his school
days (when his pariahdom begins), to Paris (where money talks and
hypocrisy rules), to enlightenment, to prostration, and finally to
prayer. His "rebirth" takes place when a kind of ecstatic agnosia that

---

* Barrès owed his modest renown less to *Sous l'Oeil des Barbares* than to an imaginary
dialogue, published in pamphlet form, with the famous author of *Vie de Jésus*, Ernest
Renan. Readers mistook it for reportage. Renan's son challenged Barrès to a duel for putting words in his father's mouth. This brouhaha called attention to *Sous l'Oeil* and to the
second volume of the trilogy, *Un Homme Libre*.

Barrès describes as "love of love" replaces his nebulous involvement with nameless women. At night, in a garret high above Paris, the sensible world disappears and Philippe finds himself transported by indefinable images. He has no limits. The universe penetrates him. He is all beings. "His was a virgin consciousness, a new world innocent of ends and causes, in which the myriad bonds that tie us to people and to things fall slack, and where the mundane dramas playing through our heads are merely a spectacle."

What will happen at daybreak, Barrès asks, when his hero rejoins the "non-Self"—the world over which "barbarians" enforce their moral ascendancy? What will colleagues accustomed to seeing him strive for mediocre goals and squander himself in trivial pursuits make of his transformation? Will social commerce dull the "sublime influence" of that nocturnal trance? Will he conform? "Not at all," writes Barrès. "This night celebrates the resurrection of his soul. He is Self. He is the passage through which ideas and images proceed solemnly. He trembles with haste. Will he live long enough to feel, think, try everything that stirs him about people moving across the centuries?"*

The question is posed by a man for whom limits are anathema, as they were for Barrès. While undoing the "myriad bonds" that make him a hostage to society, his alter ego embraces all of humanity. Rejecting the cant of barbarians, who dress themselves for the social masquerade of everyday life in "formulas rented from the reigning costumer," Philippe resolves to name things and assign values as he sees fit.

In a preface written for a later edition, Barrès defended himself against critics who decried his anarchical skepticism:

[It's not that we're heroic]. Our lack of heroism is such that we would, if we could, adjust to the conventions of social life and even accept the

---

* The conflict between selfhood and philistine society had a chorus of voices in fin-de-siècle Europe. William Butler Yeats was thirty-six and in the throes of occultism when he noted, "The borders of our minds are ever-shifting, . . . and many minds can flow into one another, as it were, and create or reveal a single mind, a single energy" (1901). Later, in his autobiography, he recounted his own inner flight from the world of rational barbarians. The religious myths of his childhood having been stolen from him by those "detestable" glorifiers of science, John Tyndall and Thomas Huxley, he created for himself "a new religion, almost an infallible church, of poetic tradition . . . passed on from generation to generation by poets and painters, with some help from philosophers and theologians."

strange lexicon in which you have defined, to your advantage, the just and the unjust, duties and merits. We have to smile, for a smile is the only thing that enables us to swallow so many toads. Soldiers, magistrates, moralists, educators—though we are powerless to swim against the current sweeping us downriver all together, . . . don't expect us to take seriously the duties you prescribe and sentiments that haven't cost you a tear.

Readers who feel at odds with the "order of the world" are assured that the only tangible reality is the Self. It is a fortress to be defended against "strangers," against "Barbarians," against the myth that the world outside is something more solid than a canvas for one's imagination. But if withdrawal fosters lucidity, will it not also result in the torpor from which Philippe prays to be delivered at the end of *Sous l'Oeil*? Free he may be, but free for what? "It is said of the man of genius, that his work enlarges him; this is equally true of every analyst of the Self," Barrès continues.

The modern young man suffers from lack of energy and self-ignorance. . . . May he learn to know himself. When he does, he will identify his genuine curiosities, he will go where instinct points and discover his truth. . . . He will acquire reserves of energy from this discipline and an admirable capacity to feel.

He will also acquire the ability to combine with like-minded souls.

Only when the fortress of the Self has been secured can it surrender to the "man of energy" or the "man of genius," introducing a new religion. "Indeed, we would be delighted if someone furnished us with convictions." The narrator's final words are addressed imploringly to the "master" who will guide him in life, "be you axiom, religion, or prince of men."

Like those Romantics for whom "energy" was a human endowment far more consequential than reason or piety, he made the word his battle cry. Acquaintances wondered how Barrès the militant nationalist had suddenly come to supplant Barrès the aesthete. Henry James, for one, distrusted him. But in fact his nationalism followed logically from the central argument of *Le Culte du Moi*. It was only a matter of expanding the Self to coincide with France, of viewing France as a fortress under siege by barbarians (the *non-Moi* in one guise or another), and of joining the fray should history present a triumphant embodiment of the nation's instinctual life.*

History complied. Until 1888, Barrès had been more or less unconcerned with the vicissitudes of the Third Republic. One year later, he abandoned his stance of antisocial *dégagement;* when a general named Boulanger emerged as a political force threatening the Republic itself, he threw in his lot with him and stood for election to the Chamber of Deputies on a Boulangist platform.

Georges Boulanger had graduated from the elite military academy of Saint-Cyr in 1857 and had risen quickly in the ranks after distinguishing himself (with serious wounds to prove it) in the colonial wars: at Robecchetto, during Napoleon III's Italian campaign, and in the invasion launched on May 21, 1871, to recapture Paris from the Communards. By June 1880, when a liberal government amnestied surviving insurgents, Boulanger's role in the brutal repression known as *la semaine sanglante* (bloody week) had largely been forgotten. Indeed, he had become a protégé of Léon Gambetta, the republican eminence chiefly responsible for legislation granting amnesty. In Boulanger Gambetta found, or thought he had found, that rarest of birds: a high-ranking cavalry officer with great panache and apparent sympathy for the common man. Gambetta did what he could (before his death in 1882) to promote Boulanger's career. Georges Clemenceau, Boulanger's fellow Breton, did likewise. Appointed inspector of infantry, then commander of the expeditionary force in Tunisia, Boulanger was given a ministerial portfolio in 1886 and as war minister made himself immensely popular, instituting reforms that benefited the ordinary recruit.

If Boulanger came to embody the *furor Gallicae*—France bold and triumphant—the occasion that engraved his popular image was the military review at Longchamp on Bastille Day 1886. He prepared for it by acquiring a magnificent black horse that showed his person and his horsemanship to great advantage. Frock-coated, top-hatted government leaders were lost in a sea of more than a hundred thousand

---

* Barrès still preferred to think of himself as a "cosmopolite." In *Les Taches d'Encre* he declared, "We have intellectual fathers in all countries" and praised the virtue of "intellectual hospitality." That door would close when the word "cosmopolite" became synonymous with "Jew."

spectators and shouts of "*Vive Boulanger!*" "*Vive l'armée!*" drowned out "*Vive la République*" as the general, white plumes fluttering, cantered around the racetrack. Boulanger, not the president of the Republic, was the cynosure of all eyes. And when the review ended, far more people than a police cordon could restrain mobbed their idol. Long before this glorification, Clemenceau had begun to doubt the wisdom of fostering Boulanger's career. "There's something about you that appeals to the crowd," he warned. "That's the temptation. That's the danger I want you to guard against." He might as well have asked Zephyr to guard against blowing. The born actor in a star role on France's most prominent stage could not resist playing it for all its worth. Being "offensive-minded" was his passionate motto. While it thrilled the masses, it unnerved his political confrères, and unnerved them all the more when monarchist newspapers seized upon one of Boulanger's more provocative speeches to warn that under a republic, France was riding for another fall. In Berlin, Otto von Bismarck argued the same. "We have to fear an attack by France, though whether it will come in ten days or ten years is a question I cannot answer," he told the Reichstag. "If Napoleon III went to war with us in 1870 chiefly because he believed that this would strengthen his power within his country, why should not such a man as General Boulanger, if he came to power, do the same?"

Boulanger's new cognomen, General Revenge, voiced the dream of a national Second Coming. The Ligue des Patriotes, an organization whose membership dwelled fanatically on the deliverance of Alsace and Lorraine from German hands, formed up behind him. Its founder, Paul Déroulède, became Boulanger's knight-errant. Known for his patriotic poems, his duels, and his monomaniacal oratory, Déroulède traveled the length and breadth of France beating a drumroll of revanchism. "Throughout the whole of my journey," he told a large crowd that gathered at the Gare du Nord to welcome him home after one tour, "the name of a single man, the name of a brave soldier, has been my touchstone. It is the name of the supreme head of our army, the name of General Boulanger!" Thanks to photogravure, images could now be turned out en masse, and the image of Boulanger swamped France. Framed chromolithographs hung in town houses and taverns and mayors' offices. A memento industry reproduced his image on dinner plates, on pottery, as sculpted pipe bowls, on soap, on shoehorns.

This enthusiasm was by no means universal, least of all among moderates in the Chamber of Deputies, who constituted a majority. It alarmed them that Boulanger, far from being the passive object of hero worship, played to the passions he roused, and that his rich friends swayed opinion makers with well-placed largesse. They saw Boulanger's immense popularity as a dark shadow cast upon the Republic itself. One prominent liberal, Jules Ferry, wrote to a colleague that France's neighbors, even the most benevolent, would never trust a government inclined to look away when its chief of staff publicly flirted with civil and military demagogy: "The renown he craves, his verbal imprudences, the fantasies aired around him . . . have unleashed in the German press and public a bellicosity of which we should take careful note."

Since mayhem might have resulted if Boulanger were dismissed outright, moderates devised a Machiavellian strategy. They would bring down the otherwise acceptable prime minister, René Goblet, on some extraneous issue and thus make way for a new cabinet, from which Boulanger could be excluded with relative impunity. It meant sacrificing the bathwater to get rid of an unwanted baby. And so it came to pass. Dropped from the new cabinet, Boulanger was instead made commander of the Thirteenth Army Corps, based in Clermont-Ferrand in south-central France, an assignment tantamount to exile.

His departure proved an occasion for mob protest as hysterical as the jubilation on Bastille Day one year earlier. Thousands gathered outside the Gare de Lyon. Protesters nearly unhorsed Boulanger's carriage and gave the police all they could handle until reinforcements arrived; then gendarmes cleared a path through the crowd as the general, in civilian dress, held his top hat high for everyone to see. Inside, the police encountered thousands more, thronging the great hall, barricading platforms, standing four deep on coaches, on girders, on canopies. Scrawled across a locomotive was the newly coined slogan "*Il reviendra!*" But it seemed the general would never leave. At length, Boulanger, besieged in a train compartment, was hustled over to his private coach. Maniacs lying on the railroad tracks like prostrate dervishes waiting to be trodden underfoot by the Holy Litter had been removed, and the train began its run south.

While Boulanger marked time in Clermont-Ferrand, Boulangism marched forward and continued to raise alarms. Jules Ferry, who recognized the revolutionary impetus of revanchism in what was fast becoming a widespread movement, deplored its brutish character: "For some time we have been witnessing the development of a species of patriotism hitherto unknown in France. It is a noisy, despicable creed that seeks not to unify and appease but to set citizens against one another." What distressed him was not nationalist sentiment per se but the tribal character of Boulangist nationalism, its Robespierrian exploitation of patriotic virtue, its intense xenophobia, its spurning of individual judgment and quasi-religious allegiance to a leader, its clamorous irrationalism. Where the new ethos prevailed, Montesquieu's humanist oath—"If I knew something useful to my family but prejudicial to my country, I would endeavor to forget it; if I knew something useful to my country but harmful to Europe, or useful to Europe but harmful to the human race, I would reject it as a crime"—spelled treason. Indeed, Ferry, the consummate liberal, was, by Boulangist lights, more "foreign" than the Austrian demagogue Georg von Schönerer, whose nationalist association, the Verein der Deutschen Volkspartei, founded in 1881, had much in common with French populism. Warmongering hung a light veil over hatred of one's bourgeois compatriots.

The conviction upon which Boulangism thrived—that France needed a hero to clean house—was greatly strengthened in September 1887 by a scandal. It began, like the play illustrating Eugène Scribe's dictum "Great effects from small causes," with two trollops quarreling over a dress, and it ended three months later with Jules Grévy, president of the Republic, resigning from office. What came to light that autumn was the existence of an influential ring trafficking in decorations awarded by the state. Implicated were three generals, one of whom had been financially ruined six years earlier in a bank crash. Their confessions led investigators to Daniel Wilson, a prominent deputy who resided at the Élysée Palace with his wife, President Grévy's daughter. Wilson had used his strategic position to raise revenue for his newspapers, selling membership in the Legion of Honor to well-connected nouveaux riches who wanted their mercantile success consecrated with a ribbon or rosette.

Confusion, which had assisted Boulanger more than once, would favor him again during the parliamentary embroilment surrounding Grévy's resignation. Among presidential candidates, Jules Ferry enjoyed an advantage in intellect and character, but Ferry was anathema to almost every party except his own, the opportunist republican faction: to the Right for having secularized institutional life, to left-wing Radicals for having expanded a colonial empire that benefited financial and industrial interests, to Boulangists for having disparaged Boulanger, and to nationalists altogether for having enjoyed excessively cordial relations with Bismarck. Moreover, intellect and character were not prerequisites for the presidency. Neither parliamentarians who wanted a figurehead nor anti-parliamentarians who wanted a savior insisted on greatness. Inoffensiveness was bound to emerge the victor from this scrum, and so it did in the person of Sadi Carnot, whose chief claim to fame was his family name. Elected president by the National Assembly on December 3, 1887, Carnot invited another reputable moderate to serve as prime minister. With the political landscape thus cleared of tall trees, a Parisian horizon opened for Boulanger.

December 1887 and January 1888 played out like the phantasmagoria of Saint Anthony's temptations. Malcontents right and left viewed Boulanger as the charismatic partner who would dance them into power. He was a soldier, pure and simple, he insisted. But the soldier, being all things to all men, welcomed all comers. Like disparate elements of an army advancing in the dark, Bonapartists, royalists, and radical republicans pretended not to notice who their allies were, or to forget and forgive until the regime they despised had been routed by the hero they embraced.

A pivotal event in the hero's career lay at hand. Boulanger had two self-styled impresarios, one being Count Arthur Dillon, a financier of low repute who sported a title of dubious authenticity, and the other a journalist, Georges Thiébaud, who had arranged a meeting between Boulanger and Napoleon's nephew Jérôme Bonaparte. In February 1888, on the eve of seven by-elections, Thiébaud launched a publicity campaign urging voters to make Boulanger their write-in candidate. Fifty-five thousand people heeded him. The repercussions in Paris were immediate. Asked to explain himself, Boulanger assured General Logerot, minister of war, that his military duties occupied him to the exclusion of everything else. The secret service had meanwhile intercepted letters that proved Boulanger's political activity. Having been unlawfully gathered, they could not be used against him, but another, admissible infraction supplied Logerot with all the evidence he needed: Boulanger had made three unauthorized trips to Paris, in disguise. Logerot suspended him from active service. On March 26, a council of inquiry took the next step and discharged him. Boulanger, who must on some level have regarded his electoral victory as a celebrity poll, was shocked.

Thus began his brief, flamboyant political career. Boulangists— Maurice Barrès among them—stood ready with a platform based on three words; their slogan, "*Dissolution, révision, constituante,*" signified that Parliament should be dissolved, a new assembly elected, and the constitution revised. Scarcely a week after his victory in a region he had never visited, Boulanger set out to campaign in the industrial northeast, where, three years earlier, Zola had taken notes for his great saga of proletarian hell, *Germinal.* The flag was waved and Parliament thrashed. "You are called upon to decide whether or not a great nation such as ours can place its confidence in callow men who imagine that suppressing defense will eliminate war," Boulanger declared. And again: "Even Parliament is frightened by the results of its inaction. It pretends to be rousing itself but doesn't fool anyone. . . . For the impotence with which the legislative assembly is afflicted, there is only one solution: dissolution of the Chamber, revision of the Constitution."

Although Boulanger's rhetoric was plebiscitary rather than evangelical, it made any rally a revival meeting. He addressed the abject misery of his audience but also spoke to a yearning that transcended material interests. For many people, he embodied "the Way." Ferry had noted as much in 1887. Eight years later, the social psychologist Gustave Le Bon used Boulangism to exemplify what he called "the religious instinct" of crowds. "Today, most great soul-conquerors no longer have altars, but they still have statues or images, and the cult surrounding them is not notably different from that accorded their predecessors," Le Bon wrote in *La Psychologie des Foules.* "Any study of the philosophy of history should begin with this fundamental point, that for crowds one is either a god or one is nothing." Could anyone still believe that reason had firmly gained the upper hand of superstition? He continued:

> In its endless struggle with reason, emotion has never been vanquished. To be sure, crowds will no longer put up with talk about divinity and religion, in the name of which they were held in bondage; but they have never possessed so many fetishes, and the old divinities have never had so many statues and altars raised in their honor. Those who in recent years have studied the popular movement known as

Boulangism have seen with what ease the religious instinct of crowds can spring to life again. There wasn't a country inn that didn't possess the hero's portrait. He was credited with the power of remedying all injustices and all evils, and thousands of men would have immolated themselves for him.

As with all popular creeds, Le Bon observed, Boulangism was shielded against contradiction by religious sentiment. It wasn't Le Bon but Barrès who wrote, "[Boulanger's] program is of no importance; it is in his person that one has faith. His presence touches hearts, warms them, better than any text. One wishes to let him rule because one is confident that in all circumstances he will feel as the nation does."

Boulanger won the north handily, in what one moderate called an "inexplicable vertigo that gripped the masses and left no room for rational thought." Now representing a populous, industrial region, he planned to take his new seat four days later, on April 10, 1888. A landau (resembling "a harlot's carriage," wrote the Russian ambassador) fetched him at the Hôtel du Louvre. Drawn by two magnificent bays with green-and-red cockades pinned behind their ears, it circled the obelisk on the Place de la Concorde to the acclaim of a large crowd and continued past mounted soldiers guarding the bridge. Déroulède accompanied Boulanger as far as the Palais Bourbon, where ladies had packed the gallery. At that inaugural session, Boulanger said nothing. When the prime minister declared that Parliament should postpone debate on constitutional change until time had allayed suspicions that the issue might be a monarchist snare or a cloak for dictatorship, Boulanger held fire. On April 27, three hundred acolytes, all prinked with carnations, met to celebrate their new party, the Comité Républicain de Protestation Nationale (abbreviated to Comité National), at one of Paris's most fashionable restaurants. Presiding over them was their leader, who exhorted Frenchmen to join him in creating an "open, liberal Republic." Opponents on the left might have responded with a version of Voltaire's famous quip about the Holy Roman Empire, that it was neither holy, nor Roman, nor an empire.

Maurice Barrès did not attend the celebration on April 27. He was revisiting Venice for the third time. But he raised his glass with an article entitled "M. le Général Boulanger et la Nouvelle Génération." Boulanger's political inauguration was a ray of hope for France, he wrote, claiming to speak for "thousands of young people stifled by vulgarity." Savants and artists who had met the general found him not only "infinitely seductive" but keenly aware of their work, unlike the "brutally ignorant" men in power. And unlike the latter, he loved the common man. It was to be hoped that his charismatic presence would discipline the "stupid free-thinkers" who indulged their passion for intrigue and bickering in the National Assembly. Parliamentary institutions repelled Barrès. He made no secret of it.

And yet, with Boulanger's blessing, he decided to run for office from Nancy in the fall of 1889, as the official candidate of the Comité National. "For any man of action constantly goaded by appetites," he declared, "life is a constant state of war." The platform on which he ran was Boulangist in its emphasis on constitutional reform, but with an anti-Semitic slant influenced by the demographics of eastern France, where many Jews resided. He was not anti-Jewish, he protested, only the advocate of countrymen being disloyally exploited. Implicitly, Jews were not countrymen but foreigners and disloyal. His first legislative campaign thus prefigured his anti-Dreyfusism.*

The odds against Barrès were steep. Even if his potential constituents, few of whom read books, had read the second novel of his trilogy, *Un Homme Libre,* in which Lorraine is seen to be his genetic crib, they might have regarded the tall, slim, suspiciously well-groomed twenty-seven-year-old speaking Parisian French through his nose as a carpetbagger.

Against all odds, Barrès, whose family hadn't been able to help him secure a modest clerkship in the Chamber of Deputies five years earlier, entered the chamber as a full-fledged deputy. "The thing I relished about my adversaries was the energy of their insults. No healthier milieu. The delightful brawls of September and October! . . . That's where I came to love life. Raw instinct!" he wrote. And elsewhere: "The violence of approbation and disapprobation was a tonic. I relished the instinctive pleasure of being in a herd." Friends were astonished that someone who personified hauteur and archness could have stooped to fighting in the vulgar guise of a Boulangist. How did he reconcile his pugilism with his annual pilgrimages to Venice or the pleasure of afternoons spent in the atelier of Jacques-Émile Blanche, Paris's foremost society portraitist?

Anatole France concluded that Barrès had perpetrated a hoax on

---

* His anti-Semitism may not have been unrelated to an abortive love affair in 1887 with Madeleine Deslandes, whose mother belonged to the wealthy Jewish banking family of Oppenheim.

the voters of Nancy. Others thought the same. Had they known him since childhood, however, they might have guessed that he was avenging himself on the boy who'd shied away from playground havoc. "Instinct," "energy," "temperament," "animality," "roots," "soul," "unconscious" became core words in the vocabulary of an ideologue at war with himself—or with the culture of which he was a particularly refined product. Interviewed soon after his election by the newspaper *Le Matin,* he stated that his political life would be devoted to the defense of democratic ideas and the principle of authority. "My temperament carries me in that direction. I have always celebrated the instincts, generosity, whatever else constitutes the soul of the populace. I also revere the intelligence oriented toward a leader chosen by popular instinct."* The larger irony was that his Kantian professor of philosophy at the Nancy lycée, Auguste Burdeau, had been elected to the Chamber of Deputies from Lyon four years earlier, and sat to the left of his proto-Fascist student.

The largest irony was that Boulanger no longer sat in the chamber and no longer resided in France. On June 4, 1888, several months after his election from the north, he had presented his brief for constitutional revision to fellow deputies. What they heard was not so much a carefully reasoned argument as a catalog of ambiguous measures. He denounced the regime in the strongest possible terms but otherwise spoke by rote, like a man going through the motions of parliamentary discourse. Openly contemptuous of him was Prime Minister Charles Floquet, who declared that young Napoleon returning from a victorious campaign had not addressed the Council of Five Hundred as haughtily as Boulanger did the Chamber of Deputies. What deeds authorized his impudence?

Undaunted, Boulanger mounted the tribune again five weeks later to demand that a stale, impotent, unrepresentative legislature be dissolved and new elections held before the World's Fair of 1889. Once again, Floquet refuted him, mocking the pretensions to open, liberal government of a man who had spent more time in "sacristies" and "princes' antechambers" than in republican forums.

---

* In *Un Homme Libre,* the sequel to *Sous l'Oeil des Barbares,* Philippe, after liberating his Self from society, proceeds systematically to reengage the world on his own terms. Barrès describes this exertion as "the effort of instinct to realize itself," or as an embrace of the collective unconscious. "In expanding, the Self merges with the Unconscious, not to be swallowed up by it and disappear but to feed upon the inexhaustible forces of humanity."

Boulanger's secret pact with the monarchist party, which underwrote his campaigns, did not embarrass him. He resigned his seat in high dudgeon and, declaring that his honor had been impugned, challenged Floquet to a duel.

Floquet accepted the challenge. The combatants met on July 13. No one imagined that the feisty, potbellied, bowlegged fifty-nine-year-old prime minister would gain the upper hand, but he did, and buried the point of his foil in Boulanger's neck.

Instead of deflating Boulanger, the wound earned him political kudos. Humiliated at the hands of the bourgeois establishment as France had been humiliated at the hands of Germany, the general could still do no wrong. Five months later, a by election to fill a Paris seat provided the springboard for his leap into the heartland of republican strength. Electioneering began in mid-January 1889. Republicans had chosen a candidate, Édouard Jacques, whose joviality made him acceptable to most factions. The posters that had littered provincial towns in Boulanger's previous campaign now plastered the capital. To approach the Orangerie was to encounter Boulanger's face on the flanks of the lions overlooking the Place de la Concorde. To enter the Opéra was to see his name stenciled on the steps. Boulanger stumped neighborhoods rich and poor, running with the hares and hunting with the hounds. Often accompanied by Paul Déroulède, he had the full support of the militaristic Ligue des Patriotes. To radical republicans he spoke as a radical. Catholic clergy embraced him despite the misgivings of their prelates. The Comte de Paris waffled, but royalist papers uniformly endorsed him. And indispensable to the movement was a large population of the generally disaffected.

On July 27, Boulanger garnered far more votes than Jacques. In the dead of winter, crowds chanting, "*Vive Boulanger!*" filled the Boulevard des Italiens, the Place de la Concorde, the Boulevard Saint-Michel. Workers who had streamed down from Montmartre joined well-groomed gentlemen from the *beaux quartiers*. Trumpets blared "La Marseillaise" outside the offices of *L'Intransigeant* while royalists at *Le Gaulois* prepared to toast the future restoration.

Election results reached Boulanger at Durand's restaurant on the Place de la Madeleine, where his patroness, the immensely rich Duchesse d'Uzès, presided over one banquet table and his herald, Paul Déroulède over another. News of a landslide, the prodigal flow of champagne, thousands outside shouting, "*À l'Élysée!*" made thoughts of a coup d'état suddenly thinkable. Boulanger's entourage believed that a march on the presidential palace could be accomplished without serious opposition from gendarmes, the Republican Guard, or regiments garrisoned in Paris. Déroulède urged Boulanger to wait until the morning, when his Ligue des Patriotes would have assembled twenty thousand strong at the Palais Bourbon. Boulanger himself fought shy of danger, arguing that regimes born of coups d'état died of original sin, and that in any event he stood to gain power legally six months later, at the general election. In Nancy, Maurice Barrès was jubilant.

Well acquainted with the lawyerish adages that recommended obliquity over direct confrontation, Minister of the Interior Ernest Constans, a seasoned veteran of political infighting, attacked Boulanger's flank with a legal maneuver that justified the dissolution of the Ligue des Patriotes. Then, through agents planted in the Boulangist Comité National, Constans spread rumors that the general himself would soon be indicted on charges of plotting to subvert the legally constituted government, hoping to scare him out of France before holding a trial whose outcome he could not predict. Constans knew his man. After a brief interval, during which Boulanger's dual privy councils—royalist here, republican there—asked themselves in feverish debate whether he would lead more effectively from exile or from prison, he arranged to flee with his mistress, Marguerite de Bonnemains. On April 1, they boarded a train at the Gare du Nord, and two hours later crossed into Belgium.

They moved from Brussels to London and finally to the isle of Jersey. Although Boulanger was reelected in absentia to the Chamber of Deputies on September 22, 1889, his party was crushed everywhere except in major cities, and he, having proved useless as a stalking horse for his royalist allies, found himself disavowed by them. "General Boulanger didn't deceive us," wrote one. "It was we who deceived ourselves. Boulangism is failed Bonapartism. To succeed it needs a Bonaparte, and Boulanger as Bonaparte was a figment of the popular imagination."

During the four years he represented Nancy, Barrès, unnerved perhaps by Burdeau's presence, seldom rose to speak or question ministers. He observed debate from his bench at the Palais Bourbon and voiced his opinions in print, as a prolific contributor to *La Presse, Le Courrier de l'Est,* and *Le Figaro,* commenting on not only political issues of the moment but literary events. While monarchists and Bonapartists who had hoped that Boulangism would answer their dreams of restoration abandoned the general, Barrès stood firm. On November 8, 1889, he joined two dozen fellow loyalists on the isle of Jersey, Boulanger's new sanctuary, to formulate a legislative program. But toasting Boulanger in a dining hall decked with tricolor flags was their first and last collective act. After hours of equivocation, they agreed on nothing. Barrès despaired. Three days later, Boulanger issued his "Manifesto to the French Nation." To anyone listening, it must have sounded like a voice from beyond the grave. The wraith of his party struggled on for another season, until April 1890, and breathed its last in Paris's municipal elections.

Boulanger's mistress, Marguerite de Bonnemains, died the following year, in Brussels. The woman whose companionship had been his refuge from the dangers and impostures of public life was now the absence that left him homeless. Sitting beside her empty deathbed and placing flowers at her tomb were the chief rituals of his day. During the last week of September 1891, he put his affairs in order. On the thirtieth he took a coach to the Ixelles Cemetery in Brussels, sat with his back against Marguerite's tombstone, and committed suicide.

Several months before Boulanger shot himself, one of his apostates published an article in *Le Figaro* revealing what he knew of the general's political, financial, and sexual transgressions. By then, Barrès had become convinced that Boulangism could not survive as a movement (or he as its representative) unless it yoked nationalist ardor to Socialist ideals. In an open letter addressing his working-class constituents, he glorified brotherhood and solidarity: "You are isolated laborers toiling in salt mines and soda-works. Grasp the hands of fellow laborers, your brothers, and despite your wretched wages and endless fatigue, you will dominate the world." In a more public forum, *Le Figaro,* he confessed that he envied his forefathers who had witnessed four revolutions in half a century, and that Boulanger had blighted his hopes of witnessing a fifth before his thirtieth year. Greatly to be lamented, he wrote, was the general's insufficient genius as a hypnotist.

CHAPTER 3

The Nightingale of the Carnage

No longer is there beauty except in battle. Everything that
deserves the title of masterpiece has an aggressive character.

—FILIPPO MARINETTI, "Fondation et Manifeste du Futurisme,"
in *Le Figaro*, February 20, 1909

There I am in a temple, in a sacred place where something
sublime, timeless is taking place, the consummate miracle,
the great invisible power meeting puny man. [Our soldiers]
saw the burning bush. And in evoking this great biblical
image . . . I don't mean to say that these supernatural favors
are reserved for believers. Whatever their rational and reasoned
attitude may be toward mystery and dogmas, whatever their
prejudices, the moment they enter the heroic zone, our soldiers
find themselves in a religious zone. . . . On these heights, God,
fatherland, devotion, sacrifice, forgetfulness of self, all these
great summonses intermingle.

—MAURICE BARRÈS, overlooking the battlefield of Vimy in 1916

Boulanger fell, but a bust of Caesar on Barrès's mantelpiece stayed
put and a portrait of Napoleon hung on the wall. After July
1891 these presided over a household that included his bride, the
eighteen-year-old Paule Couche, who came from a bourgeois family
of high functionaries generally ill-disposed to Boulangism, scornful of
journalists, and alarmed by her interest in art and literature. Paule had
set her cap for Barrès seven months earlier, when, under the auspices

of the Philotechnic Association, he had introduced Molière's *Tartuffe* at the Odéon theater with a lecture on "the Jesuit spirit." And he had responded to the devout, willful adolescent as decisively as he could. The courtship resulted in a marriage whose binding force was said to be affection rather than convenience or passion. What one knows for certain is that they were well matched in their oppositeness—he being the author of *Le Culte du Moi* and she the spouse who, when asked for biographical details some years later, answered, "Madame Barrès really doesn't exist; I have always had a keen sense of the relative importance of individuals, thus of the self-effacement that befits me."

The wedding took place in a church near the Latin Quarter. Present were Gaston Calmette of *Le Figaro,* Leconte de Lisle, Anatole France, Raymond Poincaré (a fellow deputy, soon to become minister of education and fine arts), Félix Faure (president of the Republic during the Dreyfus Affair), the right-wing polemicist Léon Daudet (Alphonse's son), and Stanislas de Guaita.

Paule and Maurice—she as fair as he was swarthy—spent their honeymoon in Bavaria, at the Bayreuth Festival, visiting King Louis's temple of Walhalla near Regensburg and touring Louis's picture-book castles.*

Barrès's term had not yet expired when the Chamber of Deputies became a scene of tumult that fortified his anti-parliamentarianism and revived hopes that a fifth revolution might take place before his thirtieth year. The spark to tinder was a scandal associated with the Panama Canal Company. The great dig had begun in 1880 and since then had encountered one daunting obstacle after another, unbeknownst to shareholders receiving false reports of progress authorized by the company's president, Ferdinand de Lesseps, builder of the Suez Canal. In truth, investors who had subscribed to the great man's belief that a sea-level trench like the Suez could be dug across Panama were

---

* In *Degeneration* (1892), Max Nordau observed of the Wagner cult prevalent throughout Europe, "The pilgrimage to Bayreuth became a mark of aristocracy, and an appreciation of Wagner's music, in spite of his nationality, was regarded as evidence of intellectual preeminence. . . . It was with [*Parsifal*] that Wagner chiefly triumphed among his non-German admirers. Listening to it . . . has become the religious act of all those who wish to receive the Communion in musical form."

coming to realize that, after years of futile excavation, nothing flowed between the Atlantic and Pacific but mud and money.

In 1887, Gustave Eiffel was hired to redesign the canal with locks, but it was too late. Thenceforth, attention shifted from the pestilential swamp of Panama to a financial morass in Paris. On March 1, 1888, de Lesseps formally announced that the company would need 600 million francs to complete work by July 1890. When yet another bond issue—the sixth since 1882—yielded only thirty-five million, authorization from the government to lure investors with lottery bonds was strenuously sought. Thousands signed a petition. Five major newspapers—on the canal company payroll, as the public would soon learn—rallied around it. Financiers lobbied. Eiffel displayed his model locks. None of this swayed the prime minister. But in the legislature, where opinion was divided, more and more deputies—also on the company payroll, as it turned out—began to favor a lottery. Some supporters cited the example of the Suez Canal in arguing that a year before that magnificent project reached fruition, "experts" had declared it futile. Others claimed to speak for small investors whose financial well-being was at stake.

In June 1888, the Chamber of Deputies passed a law authorizing lottery bonds, but the public, having heard about the company's woes, did not invest. Only a third of the bonds issued were sold, and on June 29 de Lesseps attributed this latest, definitive fiasco to a conspiracy. With the whole edifice of Panama collapsing around him, he continued to put a Micawberish gloss on things. The canal would open in July 1890, he assured shareholders in August 1889.

Six months later (shortly after Barrès began his term in the Assembly), the Panama Canal Company was no more. On February 4, 1890, the civil court of the Seine pronounced its dissolution, ordering the company to be liquidated. Its books were audited by a chartered accountant named Henri Rossignol, whose report cast suspicion on certain individuals and financial practices, paving the way for a more detailed inquiry and a trial that exposed a viper's nest to public view.

The numbers were damning. An exorbitant proportion of the funds raised by the company had been squandered on commissions to underwriters responsible for placing stocks and bonds. Rossignol noted that the relationship between services rendered and commissions charged became, with each successive issue, progressively more tenuous.

Added to these enormities were the sums disbursed to Baron

Jacques de Reinach, de Lesseps's personal financial adviser. The son of a German-Jewish financier with European connections, and a Frenchman by choice, Reinach exemplified the internationalist of anti-Semitic lore. In 1863, when he was twenty-three, he and a brother-in-law had founded the investment bank of Kohn, Reinach & Co., which had prospered. Through his nephew Joseph Reinach, who had been Léon Gambetta's protégé and had succeeded him as director of the newspaper *La République Française,* Baron Jacques mingled with leaders of the moderate-left republican majority, the so-called opportunists. This appellation, which was intended to describe the party's political pragmatism, came, in Reinach's salon, to signify its venality. Many "opportunists" made it known that they had their price, and pledges of support for the Panama bond lottery were secured with a portion of the millions in Reinach's account.

Opportunists and radicals had been on the opposite side of many fences, but lucre established a community of opinion when it came to voting on Panama bond issues, and the associate through whom Reinach swayed Clemenceau's Radical Party was a strange figure named Cornelius Herz. Like Reinach, Herz had German-Jewish parents. The "doctor," as he liked to be called (having acquired a dubious medical degree from a school in Chicago), had covered his tracks well. Everyone knew him, but no one knew much about him. "I've never witnessed a stranger phenomenon," the columnist Joseph Montet wrote in *Le Gaulois* years after the Panama Scandal. "His importance was something specific yet elusive. . . . In the spheres of industry, finance, and politics, everyone reckoned with him. . . . Through a cunningly devised web of associations and friendships, he exercised influence everywhere, from ministerial offices to the inner councils of government."

Most mystifying was Herz's hold over Reinach, who treated him with uncharacteristic deference. The terms of a contact drawn up between Herz and the Panama Canal Company in 1886 through Reinach were remarkably generous. De Lesseps agreed that Herz should receive 10 million francs for wielding his influence in parliamentary circles if the Assembly approved a lottery bond.

In June 1891, a minister of justice assigned the Panama affair to a sluggish magistrate, but in February 1892, Parliament, having received numerous petitions, instructed the government to act "swiftly and energetically." A new prime minister, Émile Loubet, took office in February; his minister of justice was less solicitous for the well-being of compromised colleagues than his predecessor, and in September the attorney general, Jules Quesnay de Beaurepaire, concluded that the state should prosecute Panama Canal Company executives. At that point, Loubet panicked—a trial would almost certainly implicate three members of his cabinet—and implored Quesnay de Beaurepaire to reverse his decision, arguing that the Republic itself was in danger. The same position was taken by the president of the Republic, Sadi Carnot, whom an anarchist would assassinate two years later. "The principal participants of the regime . . . thought it natural that in a liberal political system, regulated by haggling and blackmail, the roost should be ruled by traffickers who knew the exact price of consciences and already possessed a stock of receipts," Maurice Barrès wrote several years later. "Dominated by fear, an endemic illness at the Palais Bourbon, they concluded that it would be best, in the interests of good social order, not to inspect the sewer into which the excrement of parliamentarianism is flushed."

By October 1892, much of the waste had already been exposed in a series of articles featured on the front page of *La Libre Parole,* the newspaper Édouard Drumont (already famous for his best-selling anti-Semitic harangue entitled *La France Juive*) had launched in April 1892 with the motto *"La France aux Français"*—France for the French. Written pseudonymously by a banker named Ferdinand Martin, who had formerly drummed up business for Panama lottery bonds, "Les Dessous du Panama" struck terror into the hearts of all concerned. "Thanks to the hospitality of *La Libre Parole,* the only newspaper independent enough to allow an attack against the Golden Calf of yesterday, I shall state impartially, for the benefit of shareholders, what I saw and noted each day, either at the isthmus of Panama itself or in Paris," he wrote in the September 6 issue.

Martin's last article appeared on September 16. Weeks passed before *La Libre Parole* served up more scandal, and this time the disclosures came from an entirely unexpected source: Baron Jacques de Reinach. Although cited only once by Martin, Reinach lived in fear of all-out assault. To ward off Drumont's blows, he offered him the names of several deputies whose votes had been bought. *La Libre Parole* honored its agreement, but another paper, *La Cocarde,* which would appoint Barrès its director in 1894, was not pledged to the conspiracy of silence and aimed its full battery of execration at Reinach. On November

19, 1892, the minister of justice informed Parliament that five men, including Ferdinand de Lesseps and Gustave Eiffel, faced charges of fraud. Later that day, Reinach, accompanied by Clemenceau and the minister of finance, visited Cornelius Herz, who, for reasons not clear, had been leaking prejudicial information to the right-wing press. They begged him to desist. He refused. The next morning Reinach was found dead in his mansion, having suffered a cerebral hemorrhage (according to the official report) or, more likely, killed himself. "Baron Jacques de Reinach," wrote Barrès, "calls to mind those large rats that swallow the bait, then go behind a paneled wall to die. Their rotting cadaver poisons the poisoner. One must tear down half the house to get at it. That is what enraged Frenchmen proceeded to do."

The drama unfolded simultaneously on many stages: in the Palais Bourbon, where denunciations flew like cawing crows across the Assembly chamber and suspect deputies were stripped of immunity; before an enlarged board of inquiry appointed by Parliament; in the courts; and on a field outside Paris, where Clemenceau, who avoided prosecution but lost his seat in the 1893 elections, dueled the Boulangist standard-bearer Paul Déroulède, who invited Barrès to act as his second. De Lesseps was sentenced to five years in prison and Gustave Eiffel to two and a half. Freed on appeal in June, Eiffel was compelled the following year to reimburse Panama bondholders 10 million francs. In due course, the High Court of Appeals annulled de Lesseps's sentence. He was in his dotage by then and died in 1894.

There were sinners enough to keep magistrates well occupied for years. The sordid tale of Panama illustrated, if nothing else, the democracy of greed. But anti-republican papers intent on exploiting public rage wanted a satanic malefactor into whom all sinfulness could be cast, and three men prominently embroiled in the scandal justified their choice of the Jew. *La Libre Parole* (along with prominent Socialists) declared Panama to have been a "Jewish disaster" in an article with that name. Tribunals and investigative committees would pass judgment on one French culprit or another, declared *La Libre Parole*, but no matter: Jews were behind it all. The Jew was the puppet master.

It seems that all of Jewry, high and low, congregated beneath the udder of this cow. In the disaster that cost so many French their savings and so many good deputies their reputations, one encounters Jews wherever one turns. They were the authors of this foul mess. It was they who organized the siege of consciences, who finally strangled the enterprise. And while they divvy up the fruit of their rapine with impunity, the unfortunate administrators of the Society, Lesseps first of all, are being dragged before tribunals.

The author challenged any man capable of seeing beyond his political prejudices to deny that the collapse of the venture was "a flagrant instant of the Jewish peril to which we have so often drawn attention."

The Panama affair confirmed Barrès in the belief that the soul of France could not long endure parliamentary government. It also prepared the ground for a view of French society hospitable to the xenophobia preached by Drumont and others. Barrès's earlier writing did not distinguish him from Socialists such as Jaurès, who, before the Dreyfus Affair, equated Jewry and capital. A more vehement Barrès emerged in 1894, one year after losing his bid for reelection, when he became director of the Parisian daily *La Cocarde* and honored Drumont in his first editorial as a "combination moralist and historian" whose exposés were "a very important element in the social history of this age." Having recruited collaborators who did not often see eye to eye, he herded them all together on a platform of comprehensive recrimination.* Odious were industrial society, the centralized state, high finance, a traditional curriculum imprisoning schoolchildren, Jews, the Enlightenment, parliamentarianism, and specifically his old philosopher professor Auguste Burdeau, who had meanwhile become president of the Chamber of Deputies. Barrès would soon be heard sanctifying "the earth and the dead," but, as his editorial manifesto suggested, not all French earth and not all its inhabitants were eligible for his benediction. He set aside plots of unhallowed ground for "barbarians," meaning, above all, bourgeois rationalists convicted of squelching the instinctual life of the young. "They continue to impose their conception of the Universe and of the social order upon us," he wrote. "Their system no longer has anything whatever to do with our real nature. They oppress us and prevent us from being ourselves."

Ideologically, the most important name associated with Barrès at

---

* Fifty years later, Charles Maurras, one of Barrès's young collaborators, recollected, "The paper's tendencies were indefinable and even contradictory in the extreme. Not a trace of doctrinal unity. But one great rallying point: the man, I won't say the chief, because he never took the trouble to command, but the admired, adored, loved man who served as the funnel of this whirlwind. One was 'barrésien': that meant everything in those days."

La Cocarde was that of Jules Soury, professor of "physiological psychology" at the Sorbonne. Soury's magnum opus, *Le Système Nerveux Central,* is a monograph almost two thousand pages long tracing the history of Western thought as it applied to man's central nervous system. But he wrote much else besides and wandered into other fields, always with "physiological psychology" as his compass. About human nature, race, society, and politics he abounded in theories, which Barrès, who attended Soury's lectures between 1893 and 1897, recorded as gospel. This was a threshold that skepticism never crossed. General Boulanger may have been—as long as his hypnotic influence lasted—the mortal embodiment of Barresian nationalism. Soury, on the other hand, provided Barrès with a conceptual framework apparent in the formulation of almost everything he wrote after the mid-1890s, when, as he lost elections and attended funerals (Stanislas de Guaita's among others), the future looked bleak.

Soury's worldview was predicated upon a determinism that held everything of nature and humankind to be governed by "iron laws" irreconcilable with free will, individual reason, or moral being. In Freudian terms, the ego counted for nothing while the id—a collective version of it—had acquired transcendent status. And over this quasi-scientific dogma, like the Idea reflected in Plato's cave, fell the distorted shadow of Charles Darwin. What identifies humans, according to Soury, are "hereditary instincts" born of "useful variations mechanically acquired during the many phases of their long struggle for existence." By natural selection, ancestral habits become organic traits, making the individual the impersonal specimen of an ethnic personality. Soury might have embellished his argument with Arthur Rimbaud's famous solecism "I is another." Instead he looked to the well-known Austrian physiologist Sigmund Exner: "How is this conscious self related to that other self, impersonal in a way, which Exner designates by the neuter pronoun 'it' in this sentence: 'Es denkt in mir' [It thinks in me]? The 'thinking It,' unknown to the 'thinking I,' determines the nature of our feelings and our ideas and predestines our vocations." No longer on speaking terms are "cogito" and "sum." What makes us who we fundamentally are is as unrelated to intellect and consciousness in Soury's scheme as the operations of original sin are inaccessible to reason in Augustinian theology. We are our dead forebears' living puppets. They think through us. Our nerves, which encode their gestures, habits, and "hereditary reactions," are the strings they pull from beyond the grave. Soury continued: "Ethnic and national traits born of age-old variations, which distinguish the Frenchman of France from the foreigner, are not metaphors but phenomena as real as our neurons, the only elements of our anatomy that never renew themselves in an individual's lifetime, that endure without proliferating."

Subverted from without by the introduction of foreigners and mined from within by the prevalence of ideas foreign to her nature, France the colonial power was herself a country possessed, in Soury's view. Preachers of "peace, fraternity, and human solidarity" had spawned degenerate cosmopolites. The influence of Jews, Protestants, and Freemasons made itself felt in the self-forgetfulness—the *"oubli de soi"*—afflicting the secular Republic. And this loss or abuse of identity extended to the borders of France, which had become porous. The argument was not new. Alexandre Dumas fils had presented something like it in the preface to *The Lady of the Camellias* fifty years earlier, where society's ills were blamed on "the invasion of women from abroad, the glorification of courtesans, the daily trainload of exotic mores that enter the city on every line, hastening local degenerations." By 1936, the foreign horde would be seen as an invasion of Jews who had elected a coreligionary to high office.

For Soury as well, the modern world promised alienation, with international railroad lines replacing the ganglia of organic France—*la France profonde*—whose nature was inherently rural, inward, and bellicose. Doomsday impended unless France armed herself for war, he would declare in the aftermath of the Dreyfus Affair, vowing never to exculpate the Jewish traitor. Salvation lay in "eternal war, the source of all superior life, the wellspring of all progress on earth."* Published in 1902—the year Zola died and Barrès bundled his own professions of anti-Dreyfusism into a volume—Soury's *Campagne Nationaliste* was appallingly prophetic.

I have faith in the regenerative virtue of steel and fire for peoples who are fallen, debased, resigned to having a history no longer; if they die in the process, so much the better! They are thus saved from them-

---

* In 1911, with the publication of *Germany and the Next War,* the great German military historian, Friedrich von Bernhardi, declared that war and conquest are a biological necessity, echoing Heinrich von Treitschke.

selves, from the shame of surviving. Above all, we must continue the interrupted duel, recommence the age-old struggle against our Germanic brothers, our hereditary enemies, who are destined perhaps in coming centuries to master the Gauls, but with whom it is a duty and a joy, an heroic joy, to fight for the sake of fighting!

In the 1890s, Soury anticipated the fatal dictum of European general staffs in 1914. A Frenchman must always attack if he means to conquer. "So forward!" he exhorted. "To the Rhine this time, across the territory of Helvetians and the fields of Flanders."

Still straddling nationalism and Socialism, but more mindful of race than social justice, Barrès turned Soury's dogma to account in lectures, in *Le Figaro*, in pamphlets, and in *Le Roman de l'Énergie Nationale*, a trilogy for which he did extensive research on Boulanger and the Panama Scandal. Volume 1, entitled *Les Déracinés* (The Uprooted), was serialized by *La Revue de Paris* between May and August 1897. It opens in Nancy, where seven young Lorrainers destined to set out on different paths, all leading to Paris and all but three to bad ends, fall under the spell of a philosophy professor named Bouteiller, whose encyclopedic mind flies in wide circles but nests in the work of Immanuel Kant. What becomes of them individually once they graduate matters less here than the general harm Barrès attributes to Bouteiller's pact with the devil of Kantian universalism. The professor is described as "the modern national spirit" personified, relating "humanity's dreams" and divulging "the world's laws" to a class of entranced students whose roots in Lorraine are deemed irrelevant. "He preached the truth according to his master. The world is so much wax on which our mind, which perceives the world in light of certain abstract categories—space, time, causality—impresses its seal." Gifted teacher though he is, only at the peril of his pupils can he ignore the land that shaped them: "Does [Bouteiller] not recognize special needs, manners and mores that call for tolerance, qualities or defects that can be put to good use?" A multitude of indefinable cultural traits influence the young Lorrainers in their judgment and reasoning. Were the Kantian to give them their due, the spontaneity and range of human energy would gain by it. Instead, he uproots his followers, tearing them from the soil and the social group to which they are attached by every fiber of their being, and resettling them in a Germany of abstract reason.

The Dreyfus Affair, which truly became an affair with the publication of Zola's "J'accuse" several months after *Les Déracinés* appeared, was a pivotal event for Barrès. It completed his radicalization. By 1902 he looked back at *Le Culte du Moi* as a youthful delusion. Relegating the "I" of that work to his nineteenth-century past, he entered the twentieth century pledged so single-mindedly to the principle of a collective unconscious or a "thinking It" that certain rebarbative passages in *Scènes et Doctrines du Nationalisme* parrot Jules Soury almost word for word. "The sands gave way beneath me as I scrutinized the 'Self' after the fashion of novelists, and I descended deeper, ever deeper until I found firm footing in the collectivity," he wrote.

> The individual! His intelligence, his ability to grasp the laws of the universe! We must reject all that. We are not the masters of the thoughts born in us. They do not originate in our intelligence; they are ways of reacting that translate very old physiological dispositions. How we judge and reason depends on the milieu in which we are immersed. Human reason is so bound to the past that we all walk in the steps of our predecessors. There are no personal ideas; even the rarest notions, the most abstract judgments, the most self-infatuated metaphysical sophisms are general modes of feeling, to be found in all organically kindred beings exposed to the same images. . . . We continue our parents. . . . They think and speak in us. The whole cortège of descendants constitutes a single being.

Was the dogmatic fervor with which Barrès embraced Lorraine and the collective identity of his forefathers proportionate to the loneliness of the schoolboy who still inhabited him and to the son whose father seldom spoke at all, except to propose alien ambitions? These were ghosts best kept under lock and key, or projected into a scapegoat. "Jews," he wrote in *Scènes et Doctrines*, "have no fatherland in the sense we ascribe to that word. For us, the fatherland is the soil of ancestors, the earth of our dead. For them, it is wherever they find their greatest interest. Thus, their 'intellectuals' conclude famously that 'the fatherland is an idea,' the idea being whichever one serves them best—for example, that nationality is a prejudice to be overcome, that military honor reeks of blood, that we must disarm (and leave money in charge)."

· · ·

Word of a Jewish captain named Dreyfus facing a court-martial for treason reached Barrès in November 1894, when he was still editor in chief of *La Cocarde*. In his initial response he declared that the man, if found guilty, should be shot for treason rather than for the "innate wrong" of being "an Israelite," but no sooner did the army try Dreyfus behind closed doors with bogus evidence and render its verdict than Barrès baptized him Judas and entered the camp that blamed Dreyfus's treason as well as the skulduggery of Panama on a Jewish "Syndicate." His gall earned him a prominent place among journalists invited to witness Dreyfus's public mortification in the courtyard of the École Militaire. He recalled that at the stroke of nine, a mounted general drew his sword and commands were shouted, whereupon four gunners marched toward the middle of the square, escorting Dreyfus and a helmeted officer of gigantic stature delegated to tear off his braid, pluck out his buttons, and break his sword. "[Dreyfus] walked with a firm step, holding his chin high and his left hand on the pummel of his saber. . . . This sinister group stopped only a few paces from the general, who sat frozen in his saddle. The four artillerymen stepped backward, the court clerk spoke, the rigid silhouette didn't budge, except to raise an arm and loudly proclaim his innocence. . . . Until then, Judas had been a small, motionless clew battered by all the winds of hatred."

Elevated from a verdict rendered in a military courtroom to the status of biblical villainy, Dreyfus's treason was placed beyond the reach of facts proving his innocence. When inconvenient evidence came to light, Barrès dismissed it as the confabulation of "the Syndicate." Judas was eternally Judas. The Dreyfus case was a res judicata, a case adjudicated once and for all.

Not until Clemenceau's paper *L'Aurore* published Zola's "J'accuse," on January 13, 1898, did Barrès give further consideration to the matter of Dreyfus's alleged treason. The open letter electrified France. Around this manifesto gathered the disparate energies that became a coherent Dreyfusard movement, and almost instantly Zola acquired the political role urged upon him five years earlier, when he was finishing *Les Rougon-Macquart*. "The party of justice had been born," declared Joseph Reinach. "Dreyfusism was reinvigorated" . . . "We could feel the confidence boil and rise within us," wrote Léon Blum, who called "J'Accuse" a polemical text of "imperishable beauty." High-minded youths—students at the École Normale Supérieure, young writers associated with the avant-garde literary magazine *La Revue Blanche*, young Socialists alienated by official party doctrine—sprang forward in response to this clarion call and marshaled signatures, among them Anatole France's, for a "Protest of Intellectuals" (giving that nineteenth-century term its full, modern sense for the first time). During the following weeks their numbers multiplied, along with the protests. "We the undersigned," read one, which appeared in *L'Aurore* on January 16, "struck by the irregularities in the Dreyfus trial of 1894 and by the mystery surrounding Commandant Esterhazy's trial, persuaded furthermore that the whole nation is concerned with the maintenance of legal guarantees, which are the citizen's sole protection in a free country, astonished by the search of Lieutenant Colonel Picquart's residence and by other, no less illegal searches visited upon that officer . . . demand that the Chamber uphold the legal guarantees of citizens against all arbitrary conduct." After that, readers of *L'Aurore* seldom opened the paper without encountering statements of this kind or collective tributes. On February 2, a group of writers, artists, and scientists lauded Zola's "noble, militant attitude" even as they promised support "in the name of justice and truth." On February 6 support came from attorneys who offered him heartfelt thanks "for service rendered to the cause of Law, which touches all civilized nations." On his editorial rostrum Clemenceau declared, "It redounds to the honor of thinking men that they have bestirred themselves before everyone else. Not a negligible thing. In the great movements of public opinion, one doesn't often see men of pure intellectual labor occupy the front rank."

Barrès issued a swift rejoinder to the protest of intellectuals. Currying favor with the working class, he dismissed signatories of the Dreyfusard protests as "aristocrats of thought." A "demi-culture," he wrote, was prepared to destroy instinct but not to substitute conscience for it. So-called intellectuals who no longer marched spontaneously in step with their "natural group" were the "destructive dross" of society's effort to form an elite. Later, Barrès resumed his chronic denunciation of Burdeau (under the fictional guise of Bouteiller): "(B.) is at once an intellectual and an instrument of deracination, whose realm of malfeasance expanded when he left teaching for politics. There is an epigram of Goethe which goes: 'Every enthusiast should be crucified at the age of thirty. Once a dupe comes to know the real world, he becomes a rascal.' My Bouteiller, who spoke only of sacrificing everything to justice, would gladly have preferred, along with our Kantian intellectuals, that society be destroyed than that one miscarriage of justice be countenanced." It served Barrès's purpose to suggest that their humanistic absolutism was of German inspiration. He could have blamed it on Montesquieu or Voltaire.

Barrès seldom allowed facts to interfere with a settled opinion. When, in 1899, Dreyfus was brought back from Devil's Island to be court-martialed again, on appeal, Barrès joined the international throng of journalists at Rennes and stayed there for a month, recording the trial for *Le Journal* and portraying its cast of characters in unabashedly partisan terms. When military judges upheld the guilty verdict, Barrès wrote, "Let us rejoice. . . . Contrary to the government's wishes, public morality and national salvation demanded the condemnation of a traitor exploited by a political faction." When the president of the Republic immediately pardoned Dreyfus, Barrès railed. When Zola died, in 1902, he debated with himself whether to attend the funeral as a respectful mourner or as the leader of a nationalist demonstration. When the government exonerated Dreyfus, in 1906, Barrès, once again a deputy, mounted the podium to praise General Auguste Mercier, a central figure in the conspiracy against Dreyfus. And when, in 1908, the legislature voted to rebury Zola's remains in the Panthéon, Barrès voted against his civil consecration.

Barrès had had his own consecration of sorts two years earlier, when elected to a seat in the Académie Française. Had he counted his blessings, there would have been much else to be thankful for. That same year, 1906, he won election to the Chamber of Deputies from Paris. By then, his son, named Philippe after the hero of *Le Culte du Moi*, was ten years old and thriving. What he had apparently never felt for his complaisant wife he experienced (to his ultimate chagrin) with the poet Anna de Noailles. As a writer, he had gifted young admirers. And as a lover of the sorrowful, he found a lost cause in tottery country churches starved of government funds after the separation of church and state in 1905, Native Frenchmen living under laws imposed by a secular republic had an *inborn* government inseparable from "Catholicity." "The laws of our mind won't comply with the whims of legislators," he wrote in *La Grande Pitié des Églises de France*. "We Lorrainers have been set upon by two hostile bands: Prussians who are destroying our language, and sectarians [the government in power] who would destroy our religion, that is, the language of our sensibility." In 1914 he succeeded Paul Déroulède as president of La Ligue des Patriotes.*

---

* The Ligue des Patriotes is not to be confused with La Ligue de la Patrie Française. Barrès had also been a director of the latter but resigned from it in 1901.

War was as therapeutic for depressed spirits as it was for economic stagnation. If Barrès wanted, above all, a reprieve from tedium and from himself, salvation came on August 4, 1914, when the bell tolled an end to creeping tomorrows.* A new day had dawned. In the hundreds of "chroniques" he wrote between 1914 and 1918, he made it known, with frequent obeisances to self-sacrifice, that bourgeois France had entered the era of heroes and saints. Where years had been mere time, hours were now apocalyptic. "At this moment, the fullness of which will surely spread over all the days of our life," he wrote in *L'Écho de Paris* on September 13, 1914, after the German army advancing toward Paris had been repulsed at the Marne, "a single thought animates us: 'What hideous beings are these assassins we have on the run! The French soul is superior to them. And although things may have appeared otherwise in recent weeks, we are still charged, after so much sacrifice and bloodshed, with the lofty task [of saving the world].' " It pleased him to report that France's sacred flame had not after all been extinguished by a "learned, skeptical age." Still alive in his countrymen, under the mass of textbooks and scholarly editions churned out year after year, was a marvelous "primitive" bent on winning back the lost provinces, on dispelling the pall of inferiority that had hung over France since her defeat in 1870–71, on "cleaning French thought of Germanism," on restoring to preeminence "the sentiment of honor and the idea of self-sacrifice." In France, 1914 had brought forth a generation whose heroism revived the spirit of Joan of Arc. Well might Germans wanting models for the virtues they exalted hallow the King of the Vandals in their temple of Walhalla, but France, wrote Barrès, marched to war with the chivalrous sentiments that had armed her God-sent maiden. "While the Germans deify disloyalty and cruelty, and—licensed by their ideal—propose to crush the weak and enslave the world, let us assemble around a virgin who was val-

---

* On August 5, an infantry officer reported from one of Paris's railroad stations, where crowds had gathered to see off soldiers departing for the front: "At six in the morning, without any signal, the train slowly steamed out of the station. At that moment, quite spontaneously, like a smoldering fire suddenly erupting into roaring flames, an immense clamor arose as the *Marseillaise* burst from a thousand throats. All the men were standing at the train windows, waving their képis. From the track quais and the neighboring trains, the crowds waved back . . . , behind every barrier, and at every window along the road. Cries of 'Vive la France! Vive l'armée!' could be heard everywhere, while people waved handkerchiefs and hats. The women were throwing kisses and heaped flowers on our convoy. The young men shouted *Au revoir! À bientôt!* "

POUR RAISONS.........
STRATÉGIQUES ; ENTRÉE TRIOMPHALE
_A PARIS ... AJOURNÉE.

In September 1914, a French army fortified by five thousand reserves transported to the front in Paris taxicabs launched a surprise attack on German infantry pouring into France from Belgium and stopped them at the Marne, forty kilometers from Paris. General Alexander von Kluck retreated and dug in, initiating trench warfare. The ironic caption reads: "The triumphant entry into Paris deferred . . . for strategic reasons."

iant, good, righteous, and self-sacrificing to the core of her being." In December 1914, the erstwhile Wagnerian, or Wagnerian *malgré lui,* proposed an annual national holiday in Joan's honor.* As we shall see, he was not the first to do so.

Barrès toured the ravaged countryside of the Marne valley five days after the German army had retreated to high ground beyond the Aisne and dug trenches. In subsequent years he visited the front as often as he could, up and down the line. The Comité du Secours National, responsible for providing embattled civilians with basic necessities, sponsored his trip to Lorraine in November 1914. He returned to Lorraine in April 1915 and looped through the valleys of the Meurthe and the Mortagne from Lunéville to Nancy, where German shells burst a few miles away. The property in Charmes, which had become his in 1901 when his mother died (three years after her

---

* Barrès's efforts on Joan's behalf did not come to fruition until 1920, two years after the war.

Maurice Barrès visiting the front with several other dignitaries.

husband), had been deliberately shorn of trees that had blocked the aim of French riflemen but remained otherwise intact. Also shorn was the densely wooded countryside outside town, at the Charmes Gap, where General Noël de Castelnau had repulsed Prince Rupprecht of Bavaria in a ferocious battle waged between August 23 and August 26, 1914. In June, Barrès traveled farther north, to fields near Arras scored with half-abandoned trenches, strewn with barbed wire, and pocked with shell holes. Everything lay in ruins. Thousands had died there even before General Robert Nivelle's strategy for breaking through the German lines doomed tens of thousands more on the chalky ridge of the Chemin des Dames in 1917. What Barrès saw and felt in June did not pass his lips when, on October 11, 1915, he bade farewell to his nineteen-year-old son. Bound for a regiment of armored cavalry under heavy fire in Champagne, Philippe, who had earned a lieutenantcy at Saint-Cyr, was, according to his father, "radiantly happy." (He survived the war, twice wounded, with commendations for bravery.)

Neither did the horror of what Barrès saw find its way into print. He exercised a self-censorship that lightened the task of government functionaries who closely vetted every issue of every paper. Being san-

French trench diggers.

guine was more important than keeping readers of *L'Écho de Paris* informed. "I am reproached for my optimism, for my confidence," he noted in March 1917. "Well yes, I am fully confident! . . . Every article I write speaks of my certainty that we are not to be conquered." But optimism in the service of patriotism colored everything he wrote, even notes not intended for immediate publication. About life at the northern front he wrote:

> These soldiers coming and going in the trenches and access corri-
> dors as in a walled town, these dug-outs where candles gutter and the
> cadaverous odor of catacombs, of misery exhaled by lives lived in such
> close quarters create an atmosphere in which physical anguish mingles
> with emotional distress. Then the soul girds itself. Each of these men
> feels subordinated, wretched, a mere straw near the furnace, but with
> incredible vibrancy of inner life. Ah! How alive are the hearts!

Readers were assured that half-buried soldiers yearning for the family hearth found their consolation in the source of their misery, in the
trench itself, with comrades who formed a collective soul stronger than
the individual. Born in the trenches, he wrote, was "a new being—the
combat unit." The larger the unit, the braver its constituents. "A regiment is a new being. The commanding officer is its head; the men are
its muscles; the cadre is its nervous system." If it worked as it should,

it moved autonomously, without commands but always in accordance with the will of the leader and "the spirit of the war."*

So much for trenches. Unlike his young compatriots underground, Barrès was free to stand above the mêlée when it suited him. Looking out toward Flanders from a hilltop not far from Arras, like the hero of *Sous l'Oeil des Barbares* contemplating the barbarians below from his Paris garret, he waxed lyrical.

> One could spend hours looking at this battlefield: hours following the story of our splendid efforts to smash the eight army corps the Germans brought in one after another and recapture the Vimy heights, which would have opened to us the plain of Lens; hours catching sight of our projectiles being launched with a sudden flash from beneath shelters arranged for artillery pieces here and there across the countryside; and then, far off, the cloud of their explosion in enemy ranks. It is an immense symphony which, strangely, inspires less horror of its abominations than respect and admiration for these men who know how to die. It seems as if a mystery were taking place beneath our very eyes in this corner of the earth.

His morbid paean, which resonates with the image of music emanating from a rotting corpse in Baudelaire's *Les Fleurs du Mal,* abundantly justifies the title "nightingale of the carnage" bestowed upon him by Romain Rolland. There was carnage galore at Vimy, where generals—one of whom, Philippe Pétain, gained a brief foothold on the summit—sent wave after wave of infantry uphill into German machine-gun fire. The corpses of men "who knew how to die" piled up along the Artois front in May 1915.† Many more fell four months

---

* After the war, Georges Valois, an early member of the the Action Française movement, who began political life as an anarcho-syndicalist and ultimately moved into the neighborhood of Italian Fascism, propagated the idea of a corporate state to be led by an elite of war veterans.

  In Germany, a Nazi prominent in the early years of the movement asserted, "Only by understanding the *Fronterlebnis* [front experience] can one understand National Socialism." Another declared, "National Socialism is, in its truest meaning, the domain of the Front." And in Italy, Mussolini spoke of *trincerocrazia,* "trenchocracy," as the model for Italian society led by a Fascist elite.

† Barrès liked to quote the remark Napoleon was supposed to have made after reading Goethe's *Werther:* "On doit vouloir vivre et savoir mourir" (One must want to live and know how to die).

A charge of French infantry during World War I.

later on the ridge angling across Champagne toward Lorraine at its southeastern extremity. In command once again was Philippe Pétain, who deployed a thousand heavy cannons. Some regiments, according to John Keegan, attacked "with colors unfurled and the brass and drums of their bands in the front trench." Barrès's son arrived soon after the climactic moment of fighting, when an odor of chlorine gas still hung in the air and Germany still held the heights. At no point did French troops gain more than two miles of ground, paying for them with 144,000 casualties. A soldier named Louis Mairet wrote from the front, "It is preposterous to talk about reason when unreason holds sway. Despite everything it is necessary that the struggle continue until one of the two parties surrenders."

In April 1917, an ill-conceived attempt to break through German entrenchments not far from Champagne, along the Aisne River, resulted not only in defeat—with legions dying on a muddy slope beneath a ridge road whose genteel name, the Chemin des Dames, came to signify futile bloodshed—but in mutiny. "Acts of collective indiscipline" is how the army described the refusal of thirty or forty thousand men to risk their lives until something was done about the suffering endured in the trenches.* Pétain, the new army chief of staff,

---

* About suffering in the trenches, one historian writes: "*Le Crapouillot,* the only trench paper whose title still exists, described the hardship caused by the cold thus: '[To appreci-

A surviving mural in the bombed-out market hall of Ypres.

took measures that some colleagues found excessively lenient. Reforms were introduced, and order was restored before Germany (which had its own desertions) could exploit the strike.* Courts-martial were held. Though 629 mutineers were condemned to death, fewer than one in ten were executed.

---

ate it] you need to have remained for six days and six nights of this winter sitting tight, your belly frozen, your arms hanging loosely, your hands and feet numb, you need to have felt despair, convinced that nothing could ever thaw you out again.' Rain was even worse than the cold. According to *L'Horizon* this simple word encapsulates all the horror experienced by a soldier during a campaign. 'To sum up, the only thing which made me really feel wretched during the war was the rain.' Rain led inevitably to the formation of the infamous mud in the trenches which became cesspits where stagnant water mingled with earth from the crumbling parapets. This liquid mass sometimes came up to knee-level. 'Sticky, liquid mud,' 'oily tide,' 'an enormous octopus with vile slaver dripping from its mouth,' these are the terms used by the fighting men in their newspapers to conjure up the scourge of the mud. 'Hell is not fire' affirms *La Mitraille,* 'it would not be the worst form of suffering. The real hell is the mud.'"

Some historians have argued that even the mutineers, for the most part, did not question the patriotic justification of the war, or the messianic mission imputed to it (it was called "la fin des fins," the war to end all wars), only the way it was being waged.

* The reforms included better food and shelter, plus more regular and longer leaves.

Barrès laid blame for the mutiny on unnamed officials raising false hopes that the war would be of short duration, on German agents demoralizing the home front and infiltrating the front lines, on the Russian Revolution of February 1917, and on the prospect of French Socialists endorsing a pacifist manifesto at a conference of the Second International to be held in Stockholm (the conference never took place; no manifesto was ever issued). "The maneuvers of German agents" in Stockholm would distract France from the business at hand, he wrote in his chronicle of June 1. "We must reinforce government authority, maintain and strengthen still further our martial spirit. It would be a huge mistake to let Slav mysticism mingle with our martial spirit and dispossess our government of the right that belongs to it alone." Nothing made him question the solidarity he attributed to men in the trenches: neither reports that peasants speaking thick patois could hardly make themselves understood, nor the persistence of class resentments, nor "the collective acts of indiscipline," which may in fact have best expressed his ideal of brotherhood. Letters from officers and ordinary soldiers who, after three years of unspeakable deprivation, still "considered one another brothers fighting for the same cause" urged him to air their grievances. This he did, and fully, but always with the caveat that France must not flinch on the verge of reaping the rewards for her "courage," her "good sense," and her highest virtue: energy. "It isn't because they are fighting the good fight that the French have commanded world admiration; it is because they are fighting with sublime energy."

Furthermore, the Americans had already arrived and would soon lighten the burden borne by war-weary veterans.* Hadn't President Wilson declared that his country wanted its share of "the privilege of sacrifice"? This declaration was to be repeated every day like a mantra, Barrès wrote in *L'Écho de Paris* on June 10, 1917.

When guns fell silent on the western front seventeen months later with the signing of an armistice agreement at Compiègne, Barrès felt the satisfaction of life coming full circle. He had been born early enough to remember German troops strutting through Charmes-sur-Moselle and lived long enough to see that humiliation avenged. Now that

---

* The draft age in France was eighteen to forty-nine.

The halt and the lame being decorated in the courtyard of the Invalides.

Metz and Strasbourg had been reconquered, France would make her influence felt east to the Rhine in "a beautiful marriage of French and Celto-Rhenish thought," he asserted. Always more disposed to glorify the dead than to love the living, he celebrated the restoration of France's integrity at cemeteries in Alsace and Lorraine. He might have been heard to recite Horace's line *"Dulce et decorum est pro patria mori."**

Barrès was an official witness to the ceremonial repatriation of Strasbourg by French troops on November 26, 1918. Spectators had arrived from the countryside in horse-drawn calèches. Women wore costumes that evoked Alsace of yore. Every scrap of red, white, and blue cloth became a flag. Trumpets blared and drums rolled as gorgeously uniformed spahis and Zouaves paraded past a reviewing stand on which seven or eight generals flanked Marshal Pétain. Later, an enormous crowd gathered on a square in front of city hall to hear the marshal proclaim that France's task of restoring the beautiful provinces ravished by Germany had been accomplished, that right and justice had triumphed. Thousands sang "La Marseillaise" before moving toward Notre Dame de Strasbourg, the great cathedral beloved of Goethe, where the archpriest embraced Pétain and led him down a nave draped with republican flags and royal oriflammes for a "Te

---

* *Dulce et decorum est pro patria mori*—It is sweet and fitting to die for one's country—provides the title of a powerful antiwar poem by Wilfred Owen, who denounces it as "the old lie."

Deum" of thanksgiving. Barrès exulted in the marriage of church and army. Never would he forget, he declared, how the marshal of France and the eldest of the canons walked hand in hand, like a child with his father. "The holy familiarity, the inexpressible simplicity of heroism! Organ music swelled, light crowned the cortège of infantrymen, voices scaled up to heaven, everyone sobbed. The immense multitude loved and thanked those who had fallen in battle and their families, and united them in spirit to the surviving sons of France. All the war dead and all the survivors filled the nave, which for once happily contained a soul worthy of its beauty."

After the war, when Joan of Arc was canonized, Barrès, arguing that her sainthood reflected upon the holiness of every French warrior, resumed his campaign to honor her with a national holiday.* The marriage of church and army may have been sanctified, but it remained for France herself, fourteen years after the official separation of church and state, to celebrate, in Joan, the French soul. "Joan of Arc . . . obeyed an impulse of the unconscious when she obeyed what is not reasonable," he wrote. "It is not reasonable for a woman to want to command an army. . . . It was a vital surge, a dream . . . , [the upwelling] of profound forces." Joan exemplified the truth by which he set store, as an apostle of Jules Soury's, that "intelligence is a very small thing on the surface of ourselves." In June 1920, the Chamber of Deputies decided without debate that Joan of Arc be given a feast day.

Gratifying though it was for Barrès, the victory did nothing to silence his private demons. Kept at bay by the boom and brass of war, they returned afterward with a vengeance. "I don't long to be young again but to be someone else, someone other than my spent self." It had always been thus, and the "cult of the self" prefigured that of the virgin warrior.

---

* In public and private, Barrès heralded the transcendent virtue of *poilus,* foot soldiers dead and alive. "France's churches need saints. . . . They are to be found in the trenches. For the Christian every day of our armed struggle renews the passion of Christ," he noted in 1916.

CHAPTER 4

The Battle for Joan

Since the eighteenth century, Joan of Arc had ridden under every political color. For militant royalists and Catholics, she bore the cross of Lorraine and the oriflamme of French kings; for anticlericals who did not want it forgotten that the church had burned her at the stake, she memorialized religious hypocrisy; for republicans who associated her victory over the English with the triumphant campaign of revolutionaries against the monarchical regimes invading France in 1792, she hoisted the flag of freedom. Joan came into her own as the darling of rival cults after Waterloo, when a resurgent church called upon her to wield Napoleon's fallen sword against France's own revolutionary past.

In due course, historians dismissive of the supernatural but sworn to the Romantic idea of heroes and heroines embodying a collective identity dated the birth of the nation to Joan's advent. Like the Semitic scholar Ernest Renan, who caused outrage with his *Vie de Jésus* by denying Jesus Christ's divinity, the historian Jules Michelet portrayed Joan in his *Histoire de France* (1855–67) not as a heaven-sent emissary but as a luminous patriot from France's peasant heartland. "This living enigma, this mysterious creature whom everyone considers supernatural, this angel or demon who wouldn't have surprised some people if she had flown away one day, was a young woman, a wingless girl fastened to a mortal body, who suffered and died a frightful death!" he wrote. Elsewhere, he exhorted, "Always remember, Frenchmen, that our nation was born of a woman's heart, of her tenderness and tears, of the blood she shed for us." During the 1840s, his disciple

Jules Quicherat brought to light, in five octavo volumes, with much erudite commentary, the complete archival record of Joan's trials, thus contributing greatly to her humanization. A professor of philosophy named Joseph Fabre subsequently translated all five volumes from Latin into French.

Undaunted by this scholarship was Bishop Félix Dupanloup of Orléans, a magisterial figure in the French episcopate, who, two decades after Quicherat published his magnum opus, petitioned Pius IX to recognize the miraculous nature of Joan's deeds and dignify her appropriately. There were several reasons to urge her beatification in 1867. During the summer of that year, a widely read liberal newspaper, *Le Siècle,* rallied groups in opposition to Napoleon III with plans for a monument honoring Voltaire. Beatifying Joan would be the church's rejoinder. It would lead people who had distanced themselves from religion in desperate times to see that "Christian sanctity informs patriotic and civic virtues they admire." Furthermore, the bishop argued, a pro Gallic gesture by Pius was certain to thwart French republicans demanding the withdrawal of the French auxiliary force garrisoned in Rome for the pope's protection since 1848.

But Joan was not to be beatified until 1909. In 1870, events dismissed all thought of it. Soon after the Franco-Prussian War broke out, France recalled its Roman garrison. (A Piedmontese-led army then entered Rome, installing Victor Emmanuel II as king of a united Italy and confining Pius IX—Pio Nono—to the compound now called Vatican City).* By January 1871, when an armistice agreement with Prussia was negotiated, 150,000 French soldiers had been killed. In March, left-wing insurgents dead set against the armistice and scornful of the provisional government, with its conservative country

---

* Since 1866 Otto von Bismarck, the Prussian prime minister, whose grand design was to forge a German empire in the heat of war, with Wilhelm of Prussia as its sovereign, had been carefully devising a casus belli against France. History abetted him when the Spanish throne fell vacant. Bismarck persuaded King Wilhelm's relative Prince Leopold of Hohenzollern to present his candidacy, knowing full well that France could not allow itself to be pinned between two of that family. Leopold subsequently withdrew his bid at Wilhelm's urging, but his gesture did not mollify France's foreign miniser, the Duc de Gramont, who insisted that Leopold should never again be allowed to come forward. Wilhelm refused, and the matter might have rested there had Bismarck not made the refusal sound contemptuous by mischievously editing a telegram from Wilhelm to Napoleon III. Inflamed by the press, which generally denounced Prussia's "slap in the face," Frenchmen mobbed the streets of Paris. On July 14, 1870, an order to mobilize was issued.

squires wanting peace at all costs, had proclaimed Paris an independent commune. A new French army raised by the government, which now met in Versailles, having moved north from its seat of exile in Bordeaux, besieged the capital. On May 21 it broke through the gates and crushed the rebellion. During one week in which French were slaughtered by fellow French—the so-called *semaine sanglante*—blood colored the Seine red and fires blazed out of control, including one that left city hall, with all its civil records, a smoldering shell.

Among other equestrian statues that sprang up around Paris after the war, like dreams in stone and bronze of the victory that had eluded flesh and bone, was Emmanuel Frémiet's figure of Joan of Arc on the Place des Pyramides, opposite the Tuileries.

Although she held high the battle flag of French kings, this Joan was not born of deeply sectarian feeling. Jules Simon, the liberal minister responsible for commissioning it, had had in mind a monument to national consensus. The statue would stand where it could best express France's valor and resilience, looking south beyond the rubble of a royal palace burned during the "bloody week."

On both banks of the Seine, three more Joans joined Frémiet's before World War I, but Frémiet's gilded bronze beauty would remain *prima inter pares*. Hundreds attended its unveiling in 1874. With or without votive tributes, every political creed was represented. "Everyone had something to say about [the recent war]," a police observer reported. "One individual shouted that Garibaldi was nothing but a brigand, whereupon others made him retreat."* Republicans confronted monarchists, tempers flared, and a ceremony on which officialdom kept close watch, lest it offend Bismarck only fifteen months after the German army of occupation had left France, ended with gendarmes dispersing the crowd.

By 1878, the republicans, who had won a substantial majority in elections held the previous year, were setting their mark on public life. The legislature, no longer fearful of convening amid the incendiary populace, would reoccupy the Palais Bourbon—its traditional seat in Paris. "La Marseillaise" would become the national anthem

---

* Garibaldi was a military hero of the Italian Risorgimento and a mortal enemy of the pope, against whose armies he had led bands of volunteers. After Napoleon III's abdication, he declared his support for the Government of National Defense and even commanded a volunteer army against the Germans in the Vosges Mountains.

and July 14 national independence day. The Église Sainte-Geneviève would become a Panthéon dedicated to "great men of the fatherland," and a government program facetiously referred to as "statuemania" would populate the capital with republican paragons. Streets would be named or renamed. Education would soon be made "free, compulsory, and secular," but a secular bias already imbued new schoolbooks, particularly the one most widely assigned to children learning French history and geography, *Le Tour de la France par Deux Enfants: Devoir et Patrie.* In it Joan is portrayed as a sublime innocent who "thought" she heard voices commanding her rather than as a supernaturally guided instrument of salvation. The verb "thought," implying doubt, was to be a terrible bone of contention between schoolmasters and village priests.*

Beaten back by a force that took proprietary liberties with time and space, Catholic royalists made their stand at Frémiet's statue, treating the square over which Joan cast a shadow as consecrated ground. Rituals of the Left demanded counterrituals, and in 1878 the Right laid plans to commemorate Joan's martyrdom on May 30. A more symbolically pointed month than May 1878 can hardly be imagined, for it also marked the centenary of Voltaire's death. Voltaire, whom the church anathematized, had in fact lauded Joan in the *Dictionnaire Philosophique.* But his revilers knew him only as the author of *La Pucelle d'Orléans,* a mock-heroic poem in which Joan, besieged on all sides by lustful males, including the donkey she rides, is hard-pressed to preserve her virginity. Rumor had it that freethinkers, after a commemorative ceremony at Voltaire's statue on the Place Monge, planned to march across town and taunt devotees as they proceeded from a mass at Notre Dame to the Place des Pyramides. With such lively prospects of an ideological clash marring the Universal Exposition of 1878, which had just opened, the police intervened. There would be no mourners for Joan, nor wreaths, nor royal fleurs-de-lis discreetly sewn into the border of tricolor flags, like fingers crossed under the table to nullify a public oath. The entire ceremony was forbidden, and gen-

---

* Three million copies of *Le Tour de la France* were sold within the first ten years of publication and six million by the end of the century. There were many more readers than that, as children often used copies purchased by their school. *The Catholic Encyclopedia* states, "It was at the age of thirteen-and-a-half, in the summer of 1425, that Joan first became conscious of that manifestation, whose supernatural character it would now be rash to question, which she afterwards came to call her 'voices' or her 'counsel.' "

darmes guarded against clandestine tributes. "This prohibition will enter the annals of French history," a Catholic newspaper exclaimed. "Let it be noted that in May 1878, paying homage to the heroine who saved the country and died a martyr was deemed a public danger by the government. Let it also be noted that what provoked the measure was fear of Voltaire's godless disciples, who, on that day, honored him, much to the delight of the Prussians who had just crushed us!"

Several days earlier, *La Lanterne,* an aggressively anticlerical paper, had also supported a commemoration, for its own quite different reasons. It was high time, the commentator wrote, that the church doused with tears of penitence the fire it had lit under Joan's feet after her inquisition.

> Better late than never, and today's clericals are well advised to make due apology at the feet of that glorious girl whom clericals of yester-year so piously burned. As for us, we can only applaud this demonstration and we urge all republicans to lay wreaths bearing the following inscription: "To Joan of Lorraine, To the French heroine, To the victim of clericalism."*

Irony was lost on the devout ladies who formed the Jeanne d'Arc Committee. Cheated of the ceremony that their president, the Duchesse de Chevreuse, had organized in Paris, they betook themselves to Domrémy, Joan's native village in Lorraine, with fifty crates of wreaths originally intended to festoon Joan and her mount. To no avail. The republican subprefect vetoed a procession through the village.

The conflict festered, with would-be healers of the Left proposing ineffective balms every few years. In 1884, Joseph Fabre—the translator of Joan's trial records—had resigned his professorship at the University of Bordeaux, written *The Liberators; or, Civic Heroism in Action,* entered the National Assembly as a senator, and now urged "believers and free-thinkers alike" to celebrate their civic duties every year on a holiday for Joan of Arc. Was this "daughter of the People" not, after all, as much a liberator as Harmodius, Brutus, Cato, and Washington? Whether or not her mission had been dictated to her

---

* Pierre Cauchon, a French bishop and strong partisan of English interests in France at the end of the Hundred Years' War, was instrumental in convincing the Burgundians, who had captured Joan, to surrender her to the English. He then presided over her trial.

by voices, had it not also sprung from the heart? Conservatives, many of whom smelled a Rousseau or Robespierre in Fabre and an attempt to exorcise the nation's Catholic past in his proposed bill, would have none of it.

The idea of a commemorative day was not taken up again in great earnest until 1894. In January of that year the Sacred Congregation of Rites dubbed Joan "Venerable," thus launching her toward beatification and sainthood. Leo XIII had meanwhile shown himself to be a different kind of pope. In the encyclical *Rerum Novarum* he inveighed against the iniquity of capitalist greed and called upon industrial economies to develop a social conscience. Another papal pronouncement advised French Catholics that they could in good conscience swear allegiance to a republic whose revolutionary antecedents were drenched in blood, provided it abide by "Christian, civilized" principles. The altar need not be absolutely wedded to the throne.

What came to be called the "Ralliement"—hostile Catholics rallying to the Republic, with papal blessings—boded well for a patriotic festival in Joan's name and honor. At Vaucouleurs, where a national monument was to rise, the local bishop laid the first stone with fighting words: "Like her, let us say to those who dare threaten us, wherever they come from, and no matter that they come a million strong, let us say to them: never will you lay hold of this beautiful country of France."* Raymond Poincaré, the future prime minister, who was then minister of public instruction and fine arts, celebrated Joan's universality: "She was the dawn of the Fatherland. . . . She soars above parties, she is the prisoner of no sect, no group, no school. . . . Every one of us has the same right and the same duty to admire and love her, for she embodies and resumes what is common to our feelings as French of all parties: our inalterable devotion to the homeland and our passion for national independence." It was appropriate that she have star billing on Patriots' Day.

But before long, the idol was dragged off her horse into the bastions of anachronistic royalism and militant Catholicism. The Bourbon pretender warned that while memories of "the great liberator" belonged to all Frenchmen, "sectarians" threatened to strip her of her "supernat-

---

* It was to the commander of a military bastion at Vaucouleurs, Robert de Baudricourt, that Joan spoke of her message and presented a demand for troops to raise the siege of Orléans.

A Joan of Arc born to sanctify the cult of energy. Jules Roulleau's monumental statue in Chinon.

ural mission" and deny the royalist and Catholic character she herself ascribed to it. "Jehanne leads us to the king," one of his champions, General de Charette, declared at a royalist rally in April. Catholic orders, notably the Assumptionists, whose newspaper reached every presbytery in France, were no less determined to preserve her sanctity. It was a special mark of God's favor, *La Croix* told its readers, that He heard "the popular outcry" for a day celebrating "God's envoy" and chose thus to raise patriotic Frenchmen from their despondency. The church, and Assumptionists in particular, who built the Sacré-Coeur in Paris as a penitential monument after the Franco-Prussian War, had been blaming France's defeat on its wicked ways. Now they preached reparation. France was presented with a golden opportunity to make amends for ignoring Joan's example and forgetting the divine mission assigned to her. On May 8, the canon of the Sacré-Coeur prayed that the memory of her victory over the English at Orléans in 1429 inspire a victory over Freemasons and their ilk. "May you disappear forever, century of Revolution, and sleep in your historic sepulchre with dishonor, amidst the wreckage you have left behind. . . . Christians, let us advance toward the twentieth century as Joan of Arc advanced toward the English, under the banner of the King of Heaven."

Word having reached the War Ministry that army officers in full dress were a conspicuous presence at religious ceremonies honoring Joan, an executive memorandum instructed soldiers to leave their uniforms at home.* Alarmed by the zeal of their "tenebrous enemies," Freemasons declared that the church sought to "strangle our young national festival," the better to promote another, which would celebrate neither Joan of Arc nor the fatherland but "only the spirit of clerical domination and perhaps, alas, monarchical ideas." On May 30, the anniversary of her death, Freemasons laid a commemorative wreath "to Joan of Arc, relapsed heretic, abandoned by royalty and burned by the Church," at the foot of her statue on the Place des Pyramides. Flailed with canes and umbrellas, they were rescued by gendarmes as the crowd chanted, "Long live Jeanne!," "Down with Freemasons!," and "Down with Jews!"

The skirmish on the Place des Pyramides foreshadowed the parliamentary debates of June. Right and Left faced off with acrimony in Parliament. Republicans who had been well disposed to Fabre's proposal now shied away from it lest Patriots' Day become a Catholic festival and, given the church's genius for pageantry, eclipse July 14. It failed again.

The belief shared by many of those Republicans that royalists, right-wing nationalists, and Catholics who argued away the church's complicity in the death of their heroine were capable of shaping her to any purpose or bias was fortified several years later, during the Dreyfus Affair. In 1894, shortly before Dreyfus's first court-martial, Père Pie de Langogne, the future bishop of Corinth, improved his chances of elevation by exclaiming, "How twisted and Tartuffe-like, how cynical are these Jewish or Jew-tainted fulminations against the pathetic bishop of Beauvais! Spurned by the Church, Pierre Cauchon was actually the enemies' own agent." Joan was more insistently dragged into the campaign against Jews, and Freemasons became more prominent as the case for Dreyfus's guilt began to unravel. Could an army of facts marshaled in his defense hold their ground against the mute testimony of a mythic figure? Cries of "Long live Joan of Arc! Down

---

* No such concern banished military pomp in a celebration of Joan's venerableness at the Church of St. Vincent de Paul on Twenty-third Street in Manhattan. "The presence of soldiery in full uniform gave a quasi-military character to the ceremonies," reported the *New York Times* on November 26, 1894. "Detachments from the Bataillon Français, the Grenadiers Rochambeau, and the Garde Lafayette were stationed in the centre aisle. The parishioners walked through a lane of glistening bayonets to their pews. . . . At times, above the chanting of the mass, would ring out the sharp orders of the commanding officers, followed by the rattle of the rifles upon the stone floor."

with the Jews!" were heard at May assemblies on the Place des Pyramides. The double exclamation was stamped on neighborhood walls and insinuated into the minds of worshippers attending solemn high mass on the anniversary of Joan's victory over the English at Orléans. "Yesterday, while the Germans were celebrating the twenty-fifth anniversary of the Treaty of Frankfurt [ending the Franco-Prussian War], thousands thronged Notre Dame Cathedral to honor the liberator of the Fatherland," *Le Gaulois* reported on May 8, 1896. "Père Monsabré ascended the pulpit at 4 o'clock. He declared that he had had a kind of vision while pondering the first lines of his sermon. He thought he saw the archangel Saint Michael showing him Joan in a suit of shining armor emblazoned with the word 'Patriotism.'" The contrast between French victory at Orléans and German jubilation in Frankfurt rang consonant bells during the Dreyfus Affair, for mention of Frankfurt evoked not only the surrender of Alsace-Lorraine but the tentacular influence of the Rothschilds, who were inevitably stigmatized in the xenophobic press as "*les banquiers de Francfort.*" Suggesting that the forces arrayed against Joan combined Germans, diasporic Jews, and international capital would have been in character for *Le Gaulois.*

On other occasions and wherever the opportunity presented itself, anti-Dreyfusards did more than insinuate. A case in point was Godefroy Cavaignac, a former minister of war, speaking at a banquet three weeks before the High Court of Appeals granted Dreyfus a new trial. Cavaignac defended the honor of the besmirched army and the integrity of the Republic against foreign financiers. "I am most anxious that democracies heed the danger posed by the unforeseen alliance between cosmopolitan finance and parties accustomed to fighting it," he said.

> Foreign capital doesn't repudiate its essence when it joins the fray [on Dreyfus's side] so ardently, and it isn't pledged to the cause of justice and truth just because it represents itself as being indifferent to material gain. By demonstrating the innocence of a condemned man, it means to prove that money is the master. And the day this will have been demonstrated, the day the golden calf reigns supreme over all other authorities, we may still have the material form and appearance of a republican regime, but the Republic will no longer have its life, its strength, its grandeur.

La Croix reported that an investigative committee appointed by the czar had exposed a network of vastly rich Russian Jews pledging money to thwart the proper course of justice in Dreyfus's retrial. Dreyfus's pardon and ultimate exoneration did not end the war against subversive opinion, much less diminish Joan's stature. In 1904, implacable zealots found another villain in the person of Amédée Thalamas, a history professor at the Lycée Condorcet.* What Thalamas taught, or a parodic version of it, was reported to the monarchist deputy Georges Berry, who notified the minister of public instruction, Pierre Chaumié, who flinched. Thalamas was said to have cast doubt on the role of divine intercession at the Battle of Orléans and proposed to analyze England's politics in their fifteenth-century context rather than portray them as an expression of transcendent evil. This complaint (even discounting the contention of students or colleagues that he had called Joan a slut) sufficed to provoke demonstrations, parliamentary outrage, a duel, a press campaign, and, finally, a public reprimand from Chaumié. Physically thrashed by the "Camelots du Roi"—cane-wielding ruffians pledged to Charles Maurras's reactionary movement L'Action Française, who hawked its newspaper—Thalamas was transferred to another school.† The left-wing majority criticized Chaumié for giving way to the Right, but the minister made no excuses. "[He] replied that the professor unquestionably showed lack of tact," according to the *Montreal Gazette.* "It was not advisable . . . to address the boys with the same freedom as adult students. The punishment of the offender, he said further, would remind the professor of the necessity of respecting public opinion. The minister concluded with a eulogy of Joan of Arc and a promise to maintain the political neutrality of the schools."

Thalamas was an obvious stand-in for Dreyfus. And his alleged

---

* Among Condorcet's most distinguished alumni was Marcel Proust.

† The thrashing took place in an amphitheater of the Sorbonne, where Thalamas was lecturing. Camelots du Roi also staged campaigns against Jewish lecturers and the dean of the faculty. Anti-Semitism was written into the oath taken by inductees: "I pledge myself to fight against every republican regime. The republican spirit disorganises national defense and favors religious influences directly hostile to traditional Catholicism. A regime that is French must be restored to France. Our only future lies, therefore in the Monarch, as it is personified in the heir of the forty kings who, for a thousand years, made France. Only the Monarchy ensures public safety and, in its responsibility for order, prevents the public evils that anti-Semitism and nationalism denounce."

Dignitaries paying homage to Joan of Arc at her statue on the Place des Pyramides in Paris, July 14, 1912.

indiscretion was largely an excuse to stage once again the mystery play featuring Jewry and the virgin warrior as eternal antagonists. When royalists summoned by Charles Maurras held a rally for Joan of Arc on December 15, 1904, Édouard Drumont, who could not attend, alluded only to Dreyfus in his letter of apology. "You know my ideas and those of my friends," wrote Drumont, France's preeminent anti-Semite. "You also know by what name we call the Enemy in our midst, who has replaced the English invader of the fifteenth century and who hopes to subjugate us with the corrupting power of gold, as the brutal English hoped to do so at swordpoint. This Enemy is the Jew and the Freemason. I don't want to belabor the point today, I simply want to join you in shouting: 'Long live France! Glory to Joan of Arc!'" The letter was read aloud. Celebrants echoed his exclamations and added two more: "Down with the Jews! Down with the Freemasons!"

The battle raged on at Joan's statue. Masons laid wreaths bearing the inscription "To Joan of Arc, who was burned by priests," and Catholics countered with "To Joan of Arc, whom the Catholic Church has the courage to honor despite the error of the bishops."

In December 1908, three years after the liberal Assembly voted to separate church and state, two years after Dreyfus's guilty verdict was quashed by a Court of Appeal, and the same year Émile Zola's remains were transferred to the Panthéon, Pius X beatified Joan, along with seventeenth-century French missionaries killed in China. It gave him particular pleasure, he declared, that thirty-six men and one woman whose lives testified to the power of divine intercession came from a country that had denied its inherent Catholicism. Hopeful that a divine hand would one day guide home the prodigal "first daughter of the Church," he exhorted French prelates at the ceremony to remember what he called Joan's last words: "Long live Christ and the King of France." Pius added "the King of France." Witnesses to the burning had heard her appeal only to Jesus.

Pius's exhortation did not help Barrès, Maurras, or the like-minded patriots bent on instituting an official Joan of Arc day. In 1912, with Premier Poincaré favoring the idea, a legislative committee recommended that the Assembly act upon it, but to no avail. War broke out two years later and, according to Catholic papers, inspired pilgrimages of supplication to Joan's iconic landmarks. In December 1914, soon after the remarkable feat of French troops supported by reserves urgently driven to the front in six hundred requisitioned taxicabs beating back a massive German army forty miles from Paris, Maurice Barrès reintroduced Joseph Fabre's thirty-year-old bill. It was the ideal moment to celebrate Joan of Arc's miracle.* "Yesterday we seemed capable of admiring it and commenting upon it, but not of renewing it," he declared in the Chamber of Deputies.

> Today, the treasures of the race appear. There is a gushing forth of underground springs, a flowering of the noblest virtues, a spreading of wings. Joan of Arc is eternal. The virgin of Orléans, the Phoenix of the Gauls, rises from the ashes. Let us seize the moment. All circumstances have combined to make it a sacred moment. Our very alliances are propitious.

---

* The "taxis de la Marne" became the stuff of legend. France suffered 250,000 casualties in the first battle of the Marne, and Germany almost as many.

With some historical revisionism of the sort Catholics practiced on the subject of Joan's burning, Barrès arranged to have her take a fraternal view of the English.

> Yesterday, in his magnificent tribute to the glory of France, Rudyard Kipling, England's poet laureate, sang: "Yoked in knowledge and remorse, now we come to rest, / Laughing at old villainies that Time has turned to jest; / Pardoning old necessities no pardon can efface— / That undying sin we shared in Rouen market-place." But there is more: Joan of Arc wanted us to be able to collaborate. We must remember today that the generous young girl's dream was that French and English ride together in defense of Christianity once France had been delivered and peace restored. . . . The warrior virgin, even as she shows us how to repel the invader, shows the universe the heroic and benevolent face of French valor.

On May 16, 1915, one of the largest crowds ever to gather on the Place des Pyramides honored Joan of Arc. Floral tributes piled high around her statue, including a very conspicuous one from the English delegation. *Le Temps* declared that the centuries had long since worn away pride and rancor: "At the feet of Joan of Arc, who is adored wherever dream governs movement, we can in good faith call the English our brothers." In an article published the following day, Barrès quoted Joan's lines in *Henry VI* to demonstrate that even Shakespeare, no lover of the French, acknowledged her nobility. Barrès had been moved by the sight of a "supernatural" or "superhuman" spirit animating the multitude on the Place des Pyramides. "Once again Joan is winning the battle which, in her lifetime and since her death, she has had to wage against artful men bent on impeding her eternal mission."

France's Pyrrhic victory in 1918 set the stage for the divine and civil consummation that Joan's various advocates had long been urging upon church and state. The wartime truce had not yet succumbed to party politics when, on April 14, 1920, Barrès proposed one more time that the Assembly give Joan of Arc her day. She was, he said, a heroine compatible with every piety and temperament. Thus, royalists had her to thank for consecrating the son of Saint Louis according to Gallican rites at Reims; Catholics could pray to the martyr; scorners of the supernatural would have found a bantering, down-to-earth country girl inside the mystic; and Socialists could look upon the Joan who proclaimed that she had been sent by God to console the abject as a kindred spirit. In short, she enshrined the ideal of the Union Sacrée.

Some political observers thought that the Vatican, with which France had broken diplomatic relations fifteen years earlier, seriously compromised the bill's chances of passage by canonizing Joan on May 16.* More than fifteen thousand French pilgrims crowded Saint Peter's Basilica, where panels illustrated miracles with which the new saint was credited. A trainload of legislators came from Paris. Sixty-nine French bishops and six cardinals attended. A former minister of foreign affairs, Gabriel Hanotaux, represented France as ambassador extraordinary. Pope Benedict XV made May 30 Joan's feast day.

Despite the resistance of anticlericals who feared that Joan's sanctification would tell against the best interests of the Republic, the Assembly agreed upon a secular holiday in her honor, the "fête de la patrie," to be celebrated on the Sunday after the first Tuesday in May.

The first such celebration was grandly staged in Orléans and in Paris at the Place des Pyramides. Detachments of the Paris garrison lined the Rue de Rivoli, holding back a large crowd. Generals and high government officials assembled around the gilded statue. Tricolor flags flapped in a stiff wind. A flourish of trumpets and a rendition of "La Marseillaise" announced the minister of the interior, Pierre Marraud, who evoked (in a speech sadly reminiscent of the subprefect's in *Madame Bovary*) the high, traditional virtues being commemorated under the aegis of a luminous Frenchwoman. "Alas, how many Frenchmen suffered a glorious martyrdom in sacrificing their lives for their country! But not in vain were all our national energies harnessed during the ordeal. Not in vain did a single thought guide our concordant wills during those four years. Now we share an abundance of joys and griefs: the beneficent, sweet union can bear fruit. France is instinctively waiting for the occasion and the signal." The signal was thereupon given for an interminable parade of soldiers, bemedaled veterans, the halt and the lame, youth groups, patriotic leagues. Great care had been taken throughout to avoid offending the susceptibilities of the English. Joan, said the minister, would have loved them "just as we all do now."

While Pierre Marraud rejoiced in the beneficent union born of

---

* When President Loubet visited King Victor Emmanuel III very early in the century, Benedict XV's reactionary predecessor, Pius X, chose not to meet him. Relations deteriorated. The law of separation between church and state in 1905 was denounced by Pius and led to a break in diplomatic relations. They were resumed in May 1921.

war and the bishop of Verdun sang the praises of Joan to a nave full of civil and military eminences at Notre Dame Cathedral,* an enormous demonstration was building just beyond the city wall (for Paris still had a wall and custom gates). Workers in their thousands gathered on the slopes of the Chapeau Rouge outside Pré-Saint-Gervais to hear fuglemen denounce war, its profiteers, and the connivance of the "sword and the aspergillum." Speakers reached back across a deep abyss to the memory of Jean Jaurès standing before a crowd on that same hill denouncing war in the summer of 1914. Revolution flared off their tongues, and red flags, of which there were a multitude, moved toward the fortifications. Hundreds of mounted police and foot guards confronted them at the Saint-Gervais gate. Demonstrators threw stones; the armed force charged with sidearms loaded, truncheons in hand, and bayonets fixed. "There was considerable disorder today in Paris and in other places during the celebration of the anniversary of the lifting of the siege of Orleans by Joan of Arc in 1429," the *New York Times* reported on May 9. "Fourteen policemen and twenty-three Communists were wounded, and many arrests were made when Communists tried to enter the gates of Paris in protest against the celebration. There was hand-to-hand fighting between the demonstrators and mounted guards. . . . The disorder continued for several hours, during which time there was considerable shooting and the hurling of missiles from the walls of the fortifications. . . . Shouts of 'Down with war' were frequently heard." According to *L'Humanité,* one person was killed and more than fifty wounded.

Readers of other French newspapers might not have known that a demonstration with violent consequences had even taken place. It went unreported, or was summarily dismissed as the mischief of extramural delinquents. Paris's "red belt" was not alone in violating the sacred union. A number of cities refused to bear the cost of a celebration. There were protest marches at Brest. The deputy mayor of Limoges led a red-flag parade of several thousand persons through the streets.

But Joan of Arc's colors, white and blue, flew almost everywhere. And American warships anchored off Cherbourg fired salutes in honor of the heroine. Writing his last article about her, a frail Maurice

---

* The bishop portrayed her as "a model for Christian youth, a model of the virtues that characterize the good citizen and true patriot, a model of resignation to the sacrifices everyone is called upon to make in life."

Barrès, who had only three more years to live, exhorted humanity, celebrating the triumph of civilization, to hold high Joan's standard and to plant it at the Rhine. For Barrès, civilization, and humanity, had well-defined borders.

As for Joan's fate during the 1920s and '30s, right-wing ideologues of various stripes clasped her to their collective bosom. "Our daughter of the fields was not a democrat," declared Charles Maurras. "By bending to the natural order of the French kingdom, Joan judged that the supernatural purposes her voices conveyed from heaven were being fulfilled. In all earthly matters, she went straight to the essential thing, which was the prompt establishment of central authority and its swift recognition throughout the country. This national heroine was not the heroine of democracy." Divorced from the Republic, she rose to greater prominence than ever under the Vichy regime, riding pillion with the octogenarian chief of a satellite state. Between 1941 and 1944, on every Joan of Arc Day, Pétain dutifully reviewed elements of the French Metropolitan Army at Vichy's Monument to the Dead. He eulogized the "martyr to national unity," proceeded in full uniform to the Église Saint-Louis for a solemn mass, and sat beside the papal nuncio. Joan's cult took a fundamentalist turn. The archenemy was no longer Germany but England, once again.

CHAPTER 5

Royalism's Deaf Troubadour

L'Action Française has acquired broad influence in French thought. You are a patriarch, already. One can see in outline the historical chapter written and filled by our generation.

—BARRÈS to Maurras, December 1920

Civilization is an effort to reduce violence to an *ultima ratio*. Direct action reverses the order and makes violence the first option or, rather, the only one.

—ORTEGA Y GASSET

As president of the Ligue des Patriotes, Maurice Barrès often had occasion to join forces with Charles Maurras, leader of the royalist movement L'Action Française, who contributed in no small measure to the brutalization of French political life between the world wars. *Barrésien* and *maurrassien* both denoted programmatic xenophobia. Unlike Barrès, Maurras lived long enough to see several of his prominent young followers gravitate toward Fascism, to hail the Vichy regime, to be convicted after World War II of "complicity with the enemy," and to spend his last years in prison.

The cult of a virgin savior—indeed, the Neo-Romantic penchant in conservative circles for all things medieval—reflected a fortress-France nationalism whose mission was not only to protect the fatherland from external hordes but to defend the cohesive social organism against subversive change. What went by the name of progress loomed ahead even more menacingly than Germany. "[This worldview] oriented itself toward the interior, toward the past," wrote the historian Michel Winock.

> It directed its antagonism first and foremost against the democratic and liberal regime, the "Jewish, Masonic Republic," but discernible beneath the political agenda was a spiritual reaction against decadence by people who understood the defense of French interests to be that of a completed civilization at war with the new mobility of things and beings.

"Completed civilization" is a key phrase. It calls to mind the opprobrium heaped on Impressionist pictures for spurning the historical and biblical themes favored by juries at the annual *Salon*. Art that lacked "*fini*" (high finish) was not art but the defiling of consecrated space by alien eyes. Napoleon III arranged to have paintings deemed unworthy of state recognition—most famously Manet's *Déjeuner sur l'Herbe*—displayed, like freaks in a side show, at an alternate exhibition indelicately called *Le Salon des Refusés*. The name had great symbolic resonance. Nationalists of the kind Winock describes would have welcomed a Salon des Refusés for every manifestation of the modern intellect and sensibility, from a government inclined to place time itself in quarantine and enforce principles as retrograde as Pius IX's *Syllabus of Errors*. No one illustrated this disposition more obstinately than Charles Maurras.

In 1923, André Gide observed of the fifty-five-year-old Maurras, who had begun to lose his hearing at age fourteen, that he was "a deaf man as England is an island nation—whence his strength." Goethe's aphorism "What doesn't kill me makes me stronger" suited him just as well.

Intensely proud of his ability to store "auditory memories," Maurras could still, in old age, hear his first teacher reciting Casimir Delavigne's passionately patriotic poem "La Mort de Jeanne d'Arc." Elementary school was the École du Sacré-Coeur in Martigues, a town situated on the canal linking a large brackish lake, the Étang de Berre, to the Mediterranean. Natives earned their living from the sea, spoke Provençal more fluently than French, and, unlike boisterous Marseillais, twenty miles away, looked askance at the Third Republic taking its first, uncertain steps after the Franco-Prussian War. Maurras's mother, Marie, who came from a seafaring family with relatives planted on distant shores, was Provençal born and bred, although apt to treat Provençal as a vulgar patois unwelcome in the household. Her father had commanded a frigate in the fleet that repulsed Ottoman line-of-battle ships at Navarino during the Bourbon Restoration and had fought under Louis-Philippe's third son, the Prince de Joinville (famous for bringing Napoleon's ashes back from Saint Helena). In retirement he served as mayor of Martigues. Not so venturesome was the Maurras clan. Its generations had been collecting taxes in the lower Rhône valley since the early eighteenth century. Jean Maurras, the last of his name to do so, married late and fathered Charles at fifty-seven, in 1868. What little is known about him suggests that he was rather more fun-loving than his young wife. But fun didn't run free in the Maurras household, as Marie, who supervised her family's spiritual welfare, left nothing to chance. Except La Fontaine's fables, only Bible stories passed for entertainment. By the time Charles entered the École du Sacré-Coeur, where history meant *histoire sainte,* his mother had thoroughly schooled him in both Testaments.

Still, there were excursions to the coast and to the lush valley of the Huveaune River, which flowed seaward from the Provençal hills. Maurras remembered Martigues's island suburb sitting on the canal like a white gull, long days threaded with gold, church bells ringing the Angelus, lapping waves, a warmhearted nanny from the Dauphiné, and himself a pampered child—pampered the more for having entered the world after the death of a two-year-old brother. Another brother, Joseph, arrived in 1872.

At five, Maurras, the future royalist who dreamed of restoring the ancien régime, was shaken by a domestic upheaval that ended the unbroken succession of golden days, creating a "before" and an "after." In 1874, his father died.

Two years later, Marie Maurras, ambitious for Charles, moved her small family from Martigues to Aix-en-Provence and enrolled him in the cathedral school. If her hope was that Greek and Latin would purge him of everything primitive or provincial, she did not reckon with the need, in a fatherless boy, to find anchors wherever he could. Marie spurned Provençal as peasant jargon, but when Charles discovered Frédéric Mistral's poetry, he embraced the movement to restore classical Occitan, and eventually became a powerful advocate.

Its restoration agreed with his idea of France as it had been before eighteenth-century Jacobins cast a net of bureaucratic uniformity over *la France profonde*—the organic hinterland and its regional cultures. Marie Maurras found Charles's scholarship worth the scrimping. Every year he brought home prizes for excellence in Latin, French, and religious instruction. It was an unusual child who fell in love with Racine at age twelve, and priests noted the phenomenon. Fortunately for all concerned, the decision of an aggressively secularizing minister of education to close schools run by "unauthorized" religious orders did not affect the Collège Catholique, a diocesan establishment. Maurras would always remember the day in June 1880 when three thousand soldiers descended upon Aix to maintain order, or to restore it should the expulsion of Jesuits excite resistance, in this town whose traditionally conservative population had swollen since 1871 with the arrival of refugees from the surrendered provinces of Alsace and Lorraine. Charles's first teacher at the Collège Catholique, and his neighbors, were all Lorrainers.

Charles had hardly begun to heal from one catastrophic loss than tragedy struck again. In 1882, at the age of fourteen, he went deaf. The deafness was not complete; nor would it ever be. But a malady baffling every doctor consulted—and there were many—drove home the feeling that nature had wronged him, that he stood outside the human species in an occluded head. What future could he have among men? Attending naval college and following his heroic grandfather to sea were unthinkable. What *present* could he enjoy among barely audible schoolmates and teachers? "The most cherished voices were henceforth heard only as a murmur devoid of meaning," he later wrote. "No one can portray this state who has not experienced it. You'd think that a tragic silence envelops the sufferer, but nothing is falser. On the contrary one is assailed within oneself by a storm of cries, of hummings and of moans, which overmaster one."

An incident that took place during the summer of that fatal year at the Maurras house outside Martigues, which Marie never sold, bears upon his response to these tormenting questions. Five ancient cypresses separated the house from an orchard whose owner regarded them as an abomination depriving his fruit trees of light and sending their roots into his soil. Charles argued that they should be cut down. He argued the case so well, in fact, that his mother, who was desperately short of funds, conceded. "What evil demon made me plead for the enemy and produce sophistries that ultimately, to my eternal shame, met with success. . . . I can still see the pink flesh of their sap-wood bleeding between the foliage. . . . No sooner had the last trunk fallen than I felt pangs of conscience, and a desire to repair the irreparable." Later on, he may have come to believe that his forceful brief was dictated by anger at the irreparable in himself. He had assaulted five patriarchal shoots of nature before turning his rage against his own defective being. It was then, in 1882 or not long afterward, that he tried to hang himself with a cloth tied to the hasp of a window.

What didn't kill him made him stronger, though not right away and not without the support of a remarkable priest from the cathedral school. Upon learning about Charles's disability, Abbé Jean-Baptiste Penon, who was known in the diocese as a superior classical scholar, offered to tutor the boy and to shepherd him through his troubled adolescence. This he did for three years. Charles's salvation was his thrice-weekly lessons at home or at a local seminary with Penon. The young priest assigned him long passages of Homer, Virgil, and Horace. Together they steeped themselves in French classical theater. Penon introduced him to Sainte-Beuve. He deferred to Charles's love of Musset and Baudelaire. They read histories of France by writers of different ideological persuasions. Most important was philosophy. For Charles, days began and ended with Plato, Aristotle, Lucretius, Aquinas, Hume, Kant, Berkeley, Schopenhauer, and Hippolyte Taine. The self-destructive rage that had afflicted him at fourteen waxed into a fever of philosophical speculation. Penon kept faith with him even when the boy, after studying Pascal at his mentor's behest, announced that religious belief was a lost cause. The *Pensées* had shaken young Maurras. As much as "the silence of infinite spaces" frightened Pascal, a silent universe answerable to a cryptic God repelled the boy. Pascal conceived of Creation as a sphere whose center is everywhere and circumference nowhere; the world for which Charles yearned would be as centered as the solar system. Writing to Penon during a school retreat at Le Tholonet (near one of Paul Cézanne's favorite perches below Mont Sainte-Victoire), he quoted these lines from Shakespeare's *Troilus and Cressida*:

> The heavens themselves, the planets, and this center
> Observe degree, priority, and place,
> Insisture, course, proportion, season, form,

> Office, and custom, in all line of order
> And therefore is the glorious planet Sol,
> In noble eminence enthroned and sphered
> Amidst the other, whose med'cinable eye
> Corrects the influence of planets evil,
> And posts, like the commandment of a king,
> Sans check, to good and bad.

The words are spoken at sea by Ulysses to Agamemnon and followed by the warning that "mutiny," "plagues," "portents," a "raging of waters," and a "shaking of the earth" supervene when "planets in evil mixture to disorder wander." He was sixteen. It was 1884. His inner life, he told Penon, felt like "a carnival of the mind, the heart, and the senses."

The sun shone less brightly in Paris's Latin Quarter, where Marie Maurras arrived a year later with sons in tow, Charles having passed the baccalaureate exam and Joseph being admitted to a lycée for the intellectually gifted. Charles would pursue his studies at the Sorbonne, hoping that France's best physicians could help him hear. Penon, who encouraged the move lest his talented student languish in the backwater of Aix-en-Provence, saw him off.

Charles's deafness defeated the specialists. It soon became apparent that modern medicine had no cure for his malady. This conclusion put an end to any prospect of university studies.* He spent his days reading at the Bibliothèque Sainte-Geneviève and taking solitary walks. What to do? The question might have gone unanswered if not for his loyal Provençal mentors. Furnished with recommendations from Penon and another teacher at the Collège Catholique, Charles wrote a ten-page review of a 930-page conspectus of Western philosophy for a Thomist periodical called the *Annales de Philosophie Chrétienne*. Even longer reviews followed. Its director was so impressed that he assigned the seventeen-year-old a book column in another journal under his direction, *L'Instruction Publique*. France's sluggish economy appears not to have slowed the outpouring of literature, histories, and philosophical treatises: they gave Charles enough material for seventy columns in three years. There was more. *La Réforme Sociale,* a

---

* Not that the physicians didn't do their utmost. They resorted to catheters and tar vapor, among other formidable procedures.

fortnightly of Catholic inspiration founded by Frédéric Le Play and named after his quasi-feudal reformist movement, welcomed Charles, who, undaunted by the challenge of having to write intelligibly about social economics, became a regular contributor.* The Maurras family scraped by on what he earned and on rent from a tenant in Martigues.

Charles remained deeply ambivalent in the matter of religion. Unable to embrace the church or to purchase security outside it, he unburdened himself to Penon: "In spite of weaknesses, I feel an inexpressible need to attach myself to something firm. I have found what appear to be principles of solidity in human science, but when I clutch them, I bloody my hands on their rough surface." The more philosophy he read, the more phantasmagoric the world became. "Questions without answers, tangled and contradictory. One thing is certain: the question exists and one must resolve it in order to feel happy." Penon insisted that Charles's longing for invincible selfhood could be satisfied only one way. The heartfelt observance of religious duties was imperative: "You must perceive Jesus Christ as a live presence rather than a remote sovereign, and reserve several minutes of the day for Him, as you would for a friend. The means are very simple. Read the Gospel without commentary; especially Saint Luke or Saint John: a chapter a day. . . . If one passage leaves you cold and distracted, another will transport you." What led to religious conviction, he said, was the heart, not mathematical proof—Aristotle's "truth prior to predication." Knowing the young man to be afflicted with feelings of "anguish" and "moral emptiness" dampened the pleasure he took in his success. He wrote, "I shall never resign myself to seeing you torn from these beliefs, these practices for which your intelligence and your heart are so well suited, and which alone give life its true meaning."

---

* The Catholic Encyclopedia describes as follows the principal reforms proposed by Le Play: "(a) the observance of the Decalogue; (b) public worship—on this point Le Play . . . expresses his fear that the concordatory regime in France will produce a Church of bureaucrats, and dreams of a liberty such as exists in America for the Church of France; (c) testamentary freedom, which according to him distinguishes peoples of vigorous expansion while the compulsory division of inheritances is the system of conquered races and inferior classes. It is only, he asserts, under the former system that *familles-souches* can develop, which are established on the soil and are not afraid of being prolific; (d) legislation punishing seduction and permitting the investigation of paternity; (e) institutions founded by large land owners or industrial leaders to uplift the condition of the workman. Le Play feared the intervention of the State in the labour system and considered that the State should encourage the social authorities to exercise what he calls 'patronage,' and should reward the heads of industry who founded philanthropic institutions; (f) liberty of instruction, i.e. freedom from State control; (g) decentralization in the State."

Between 1886 and 1891, Maurras published 169 articles in *La Réforme Sociale* and as many in a Catholic daily called *L'Observateur Français*.* Penon marveled at his fecundity. But he would just as certainly have frowned upon the un-Catholic company the young man began to keep. That Maurras kept any company at all was the result of an impromptu visit from three young poets whose work he had praised. Undeterred by his protestations of deafness, they introduced him to the profane neighborhood of cafés at his doorstep. Before long, he became fluent in Latin Quarter argot and seasoned his prose with it. He cultivated an unkempt appearance and bad manners. He read Émile Zola's novels and people's palms. He described this world as *la brousse*—the bush—and its feminine fauna as a "veritable nation" of the unhappily married, the separated, and the divorced. In short, he spent several seasons visiting a place walled off from him since adolescence by deafness, philosophy, and religion. The bush was "delicious," he wrote. But it was uninhabitable. Its offerings were a mixed blessing, depriving him of weight even as it liberated him from gravity.

Maurras turned twenty on April 20, 1888. He would always remember the year, not so much for that reason as for his encounter with the twenty-five-year-old Maurice Barrès, in whom he immediately recognized a more sympathetic confidant than Jean-Baptiste Penon. *Sous l'Oeil des Barbares*, which he reviewed in *L'Observateur Français*, was the link. His political idiom may not have been Barrès's, nor were their barbarians identical, but the narrative of a struggle between the Self and non-Self rang loud and clear. "At the time," he later recalled, "I was dwelling almost obsessively on an idea of the English historian Macaulay, who thought that our civilization would perish, not at the hands of invaders from without, like the Roman, but of internal barbarians, 'barbarians from below,' as he put it: our Communards, our Socialists, our plebs." Their first exchange of letters struck a more personal note. "I must admit that *Sous l'Oeil des Barbares* enthralled me," Maurras wrote on November 4, 1888. "I have lived fragments of that life. And where our sensibilities differ, the analysis is so painfully close to the bone that one can imagine oneself suffering in your place. It is an overflowing of egoistic sympathy."

The sentence in *Sous l'Oeil des Barbares* that resonated with Maurras more than any other was the hero's ultimate supplication: "Oh master, you alone [can point the way], if you exist somewhere—whether you

---

* *L'Observateur Français* was the official organ of the Vatican in France.

be an axiom, a religion, or a prince of men." Despite their differences, he and Barrès recognized in each other the believer manqué yearning for salvation. Unable to feel "whole," authentic, or centered without a transcendent guide, they made gospel of Hippolyte Taine's materialist formula: *race, milieu, moment.* Individualism was their common bane. Selfhood resided not in one's unique history but in a sameness Taine likened to that of the leaves of a tree. It was ordained by one's race, one's cultural milieu, one's moment in time. It was "organic." And the organic self postulated the existence of an alien "other" bent on invading and uprooting.

A year after the two met, Barrès decided that Georges Boulanger was a "prince of men" and ran for political office under the general's banner. Maurras, on the other hand, had yet to raise the flag of white lilies. He concerned himself now with literature more than politics or philosophy, letting his ties with Catholic publications go slack. Even so, the literary program to which he subscribed as a founding member of the *école romane* (the Roman school) and an enthusiast of Provençal poetry foreshadowed his politics. The term "Roman" encapsulated the idea that France's genius belonged to the Mediterranean or Greco-Latin tradition, which had been perverted by Romanticism and its decadent offspring. Barrès praised the new school in *Le Figaro* of July 4, 1892, for reviving French literature of the past rather than following the crowd to authors whom the Roman school collectively dubbed "Nordic" (Tolstoy, Dostoyevsky, Ibsen); in the article, "The Quarrel of Nationalists and Cosmopolites," he applied those polarities to literature before they became the obsessive dialectic of his political thinking. Maurras, for his part, published a pamphlet entitled *Barbarians and Romans.*

What Maurras wrote about politics at that moment foreshadowed the nationalist sentiments with which he championed France's military establishment during the Dreyfus Affair. As important to him as classical fixity in the chaos of "isms" born of Romantic license was the virtue of one voice in the fractiousness of the Republic. To rise from its slough, France would have to end parliamentary squabbling. "Action" and "energy" were what she wanted. The word "action" became a shibboleth whose political insinuations were destined to inform French consciousness in the twentieth century. Thus, Maurras could despise the Revolution of 1789 yet sympathize with the Terror of 1793, for among Jacobins, the pale cast of thought never sicklied over the native hue of resolution. "Passion, willfulness, desire led to immediate gratification. Words were acts. The memory of those times casts a jaundiced light on our own; nowadays, thoughts have great trouble merely becoming spoken or written words, and actions get so tangled in verbiage that any well-bred mind disdains them, and abandons them to the mediocre."

Political debate became more relevant several years later, when parliamentary proceedings of the pale, sickly sort gave way to ideological warfare, allowing no middle ground for doubt or decorum. By 1890, Maurras was already hailing Édouard Drumont, the author of the recently published book *La France Juive.* "In Drumont's work there are pages, paragraphs, notes whose haughty impertinence reminds one of Saint Simon," he wrote in *L'Observateur Français.* "But that is not where his glory lies. His glory lies in having opened a career for men of action, for the audacious." In 1894, a remark by Barrès about Jews being well established in the Midi provoked a sharp response: "You persist in confusing one or two confined districts of the Gard region with the whole Midi. That is an error for which Alphonse Daudet is responsible." Maurras went on to say that the city of Nîmes did indeed swarm with Jews, Protestants, and Oriental hucksters, but that Nîmes was a "race" apart—dull-witted, "thick blooded," loudmouthed, and given to much gesticulation. "Moreover, it is sly and perfidious. . . . Nîmes is a story of shame. Bear in mind, however, that the entire Midi scorns these people. You won't find anyone like them elsewhere in our region, except perhaps in Cahors, which is a former ghetto." Maurras habitually described foreigners resident in France—all Jews included—as "*métèques,*" giving a pejorative twist to a word of Greek origin.*

When they had set matters straight, Barrès invited Maurras to write for *La Cocarde,* whose editorial direction he assumed with a tip of the hat to Édouard Drumont. Drumont, in turn, had launched his own newspaper, *La Libre Parole,* at the height of the Panama Scandal, with revelations of knavery in Parliament and his ears pricked for scandals to come. In 1894, readers were informed that a court-martial held behind closed doors had tried an unnamed officer accused of passing military secrets to Germany.

It was in the nature of things that the traitor should be Jewish. Cast

---

* The Greek *metoikos* simply meant a foreigner in residence or someone who has changed residence—often merchants and financiers. In its pejorative sense it became one of Maurras's principal contributions to xenophobic jargon of the twentieth century.

in a stock role waiting to be filled by opportune candidates, Dreyfus was treasonous long before treason was committed. His court-martial had not yet taken place when Maurras declared that Jews were "the scourge of nations," subversion being their "natural métier."* Loyal only to their own kind, they could not understand that the integrity of the social organism must prevail over the guilt or innocence of an individual, that judicial rectitude must always defer to "la raison d'état."

Like most people, Maurras saw no reason to question the rightness of Dreyfus's conviction until evidence came to light that fraudulent documents had been placed in his dossier and Émile Zola published an indictment of the general staff on the front page of *L'Aurore* in January 1898. Only then did Maurras join the fray, vehemently contending that the affair would never have become an affair if an ignorant populace hadn't been harangued by partisan tongues. Where pandemonium reigned, one voice, in the person of a king, could have settled accounts. "There was no one to say to deputies toeing a party line, 'I am neither this administration nor that one, I am neither Jewry, nor the Protestant Consistory, nor the Catholic Church. I embody the race that made France French. In the name of that race and that fatherland, all this muck must be carted away,'" he wrote. The French, he claimed, dreamed not so much of justice as of "public salvation," which compelled them to reorganize political life around a supreme arbiter. Judeo-Protestant individualism was the villain.

Maurras's commanding moment came after the imprisonment and suicide on August 31, 1898, of Colonel Hubert Henry, who had forged documents used to incriminate Alfred Dreyfus. With the conspiracy against Dreyfus unraveling, Maurras argued, in a series of seven articles entitled "First Blood," that Henry's mischief, reprehensible though it may have been by conventional standards, ought to be judged as the necessary means to a virtuous end. Far from blackening the forger, the forgeries illuminated his heroic character. Henry lied in the interest of "national salvation" and "public order." He lied to tell the truth. And at the end he sacrificed himself for the greater good, spilling his blood magnanimously. His was patriotic gore. "Every sacred drop . . . still runs warm wherever the heart of the nation beats," Maurras apostrophized.

---

* None of this, he noted, compromised his admiration for Heine and Disraeli.

We should have waved your bloody tunic and the sullied blades down the boulevards; marched the coffin, hoisted the mortuary banner like a black flag. . . . But the national sentiment will awaken to triumph and avenge you. From the country's soil . . . there will soon rise monuments to expiate our cowardice. . . . In life as in death, you marched forward. Your unhappy forgery will be regarded as one of your best martial deeds.

Maurras's language did not fundamentally differ from that of Joseph de Maistre, who, a hundred years earlier, had enunciated the precept that "nations have a general overriding *soul* or character and a true moral unity which makes them what they are." Their happiness and power hinged on the stifling of "individual reason" and the vesting of absolute authority in "national dogmas, that is to say, useful prejudices."

From this conflict emerged L'Action Française, a movement whose founding prejudice was that Dreyfus could never be absolved of treason and that his unabsolvable guilt served the supremely useful purpose of restoring "national sentiment." More prominent than Maurras at the outset were Henri Vaugeois and Maurice Pujo, two young men united in the belief that liberal republicanism was sapping France's vital spirit. On July 10, 1899, they published the first issue of a slender bimonthly review, *Le Bulletin de L'Action Française.** In his manifesto, Vaugeois declared that "action" connoted "reaction," and he subsequently drove the point home in speeches, as at a banquet thrown by Maurras for Barrès during the Exposition of 1900. "All of us agree, I hope, on the morality, the legitimacy of iron. We have no hypocritically puritanical objections to it, do we? It seems to us that one has the right to save one's country despite itself. It seems to us that there have always been instances of virtuous violence in history, and that beating a sick man bloody is better than letting him rot." This was the mind-set that glorified Colonel Henry and only eight years later, in 1908, when L'Action Française attracted enough readers to justify a daily paper of the same name, organized the cadre of street hawkers called Camelots du Roi, who doubled as a paramilitary gang patrolling the student quarter with leaded canes.

The nickname "hawkers of the king" reflected the influence Charles

---

* "*Bulletin*" was soon changed to "*Revue.*"

Charles Maurras in 1903, at age thirty-five.

Maurras had come to exert upon the movement. Its founders agreed that France needed saving, but they couldn't define salvation. They had bugbears in common but no doctrine. That changed as soon as Maurras, with encouragement from colleagues who made light of his deafness, asserted himself. By 1904, activists were royalists echoing Maurras's disavowal of the Republic and his repudiation of its philosophical commitment to the rights of man. Salvation lay on the far side of 1789, in the France of monarchs, when rationalism had yet to undermine an organic nation and "cosmopolite" to become a French noun; when Money (almost always capitalized in Maurras's works and implicitly Jewish or Protestant) did not ventriloquize through a parliament; and when the rights of society still prevailed over the individualism propagated by eighteenth-century intellectuals. The Republic was feckless for speaking in many voices. With a multitude of centers and no circumference, it lent itself to the designs of other nations as surely as Dreyfus surrendered military secrets to Germany. "Dictateur et Roi," an essay written during the summer of 1899, dwells on the theme of identity and alienation. "M. de Bismarck undoubtedly foresaw several of our present woes when he did everything in his power to harness us to a republican system," wrote Maurras. The iron chancellor knew perfectly well that the strength of a state resides in its single-mindedness. "And since the Republican regime is nothing but the absence of a directing will and coherent thought at the center of power, he realized that such a regime profoundly divides the people who abandon themselves to it and condemns them to perpetual change."

Not unlike Jean-Jacques Rousseau, who, in his essay on the origin of languages, characterizes history as entropy, with the power and stamina of speakers in ancient forums devolving into the quarrelsome babble of modern assemblies, Maurras made "unity" his mantra. National selfhood was one resonant voice. It was kingship. "French unity, which is so solid that today it 'seems' spontaneous and natural, bespeaks the millennial designs of the French Royal House," he asserted. "Nature was content to make this unity possible, not necessary or ineluctable: our princes formed and fashioned it as an artist shapes his chosen material." Where Italy owed its unity to memories of Rome and England to its insularity, art and nature had combined to make France French. The Republic violated both.

The Republic further violated France by separating church and state in 1905, after the Dreyfus convulsion. To be sure, Maurras, although he invoked the country's basic "Catholicity," had long since ceased to commune or confess. And among practicing Catholics who had welcomed Pope Leo XIII's encyclical *Rerum Novarum* authorizing acceptance of the Republic, many found Maurras's argument for subjecting all other considerations to political expediency immoral. A liberal Catholic review, *Le Correspondant,* demanded answers to three questions—whether L'Action Française's "exclusive nationalism" and its "deep-rooted hostility to the democratic regime" could be reconciled with the "Christian doctrine of fraternity"; whether "the rigorously scientific observation of natural law" (i.e., Taine's "race, milieu, moment") espoused by L'Action Française did not imply the elimination of the supernatural; and what role the church would play in a restored monarchy. Several worried clerics wrote books characterizing Maurras's thought as pervasively Nietzschean, Machiavellian, or Comtean. "His idolatry of reason has made him disdainful of belief" was the indictment of an editor at *Le Correspondant.*

Maurras protested that he judged belief to be as natural to man as reason, and more necessary, even though he couldn't adjust his own mind to square with his judgment. Sympathetic clerics might have offered him the hope that Pascal's cryptic God offers a despairing seeker: "You wouldn't have sought Me if you hadn't already found Me." But better than belief, in their eyes, was his campaign to prevent the government from seizing derelict country churches and confiscating, auctioning, or destroying their contents.* He also drew praise from orthodox quarters by publishing in *L'Action Française* all eighty articles of Pius IX's memorable tirade against freedom of conscience, science, and the modern world—*The Syllabus of Errors*.† "Our institute," wrote the director of the St. Thomas Aquinas Institute in Aix, "wishing to recognize the services you have rendered the cause of truth by demonstrating that the principle of French nationality is instinct with Catholicism, and by choosing Pius IX's *Syllabus* as the basis for social reconstruction, elected you an honorary member at its session of April 12, 1907."

Blessings for Maurras as a believer in the inseparability of fatherland, religion, and society came from on high when Marie Maurras made a pilgrimage to Rome in 1911. Letters of recommendation secured her an audience with Pius X, who praised Charles for fighting the good fight. It cheered her. Pontifical favor (which would be denied Maurras the nonbeliever by Pius X's successor) was almost as heartwarming as the conversion she never ceased to urge upon him.‡

That year, three years before World War I, the good fight included debates in which L'Action Française joined battle with the Sorbonne, whose lecture halls were seen by parties of the Right as temples of republican proselytism. A witness to one such debate describes fifty Camelots du Roi armed with heavy canes forming a protective hedge

---

* The law of separation dealt many country parishes a severe blow, depriving them of state funds and rendering them incapable of maintaining their property. Another active campaigner was Maurice Barrès, who chronicled his efforts to rescue churches in *La Grande Pitié des Églises de France.*

A beneficiary of the dereliction of churches and abbeys was the American sculptor George Grey Barnard, who lived in Paris and collected medieval artifacts and architectural remnants. When he returned to New York, he housed his acquisitions in a building in Washington Heights. They became the main component of the Cloisters when John D. Rockefeller, Jr., bought them for New York's Metropolitan Museum of Art.

† The *Syllabus* was attached to his encyclical *Quanta Cura,* promulgated in 1864. Leo XIII, who succeeded Pius IX and preceded Pius X, was bracketed between reactionary popes.

‡ Maurras died forty-one years later clutching his mother's rosary.

at the foot of the stage. Loud applause greeted Maurras, "a young man, barely forty." He was of medium height, thin, and sporting his lifelong Vandyke, with "an air of authority, of keenness, of eminent distinction and something slightly sad and guarded." The witness saw "a hint of Richelieu" in him. He sat at a long table flanked by six confrères. Behind them stood two rows of friends, "like prelates behind fathers of the Church." All eyes were fixed on Maurras. The witness described "his head with its imperious profile held high, seductive in its insolence and youth, his brow careworn, furrowed, almost too wide for the diminishing oval of his bearded jaw." Barrès called him a "patriarch" several years later, after the war. He carefully groomed himself for the part.*

War was looming in 1911. A political crisis developed when a German gunboat docked at the Moroccan port of Agadir. This was viewed by England and France as a hostile gesture, challenging England's maritime dominion and France's occupation of Morocco. Germany did indeed feel that she had not received a fair share of African spoils and made her position known in negotiations that led to the Treaty of Fez. France surrendered the French Equatorial African colony of Middle Congo in exchange for Germany's recognition of her Moroccan protectorate.

Just as he had laid the blame for the entire Dreyfus Affair at the doorstep of a bickering National Assembly, so Maurras attributed France's surrender of Middle Congo to the absence of a coherent foreign policy, with ministers rotating through the Quai d'Orsay like horses on a carousel. Thenceforth, in *L'Action Française* and in lectures, Maurras concerned himself almost exclusively with the redemption of national honor. No one was more prolific of articles lamenting the unpreparedness of the army, denouncing Republican governments as pawns controlled by the same treasonous forces that had set Dreyfus free, calling attention to the omnipresence of spies, or generally beating the drums for war.

The drumbeat grew louder in 1913 during the weeks of parliamen-

---

* In his early thirties Maurras fell unrequitedly in love with a married countess, Madame de Lasalle-Beaufort, the mother of two children. There were several affairs before and after, but he remained a bachelor, unlike his brother Joseph, who fathered five children. Charles adopted three of them, the youngest a boy eight years old, when Joseph, a widower, died in Saigon. Joseph Maurras practiced medicine and wrote a medical column for *L'Action Française.*

tary debate over a proposal to lengthen compulsory military service.* Maurras hailed the three-year law as progress, but he credited royalty for its passage. "The lugubrious fact of the matter is," he wrote on July 21, "that neither our voices nor the sticks of the Camelots du Roi . . . would have sufficed to rouse the Republic of Dreyfus from its inertia." Agadir did it. The "republican world" would never have scrambled to its feet if not for the initiative taken by Emperor Wilhelm II— a Hohenzollern rather than a Capetian, but royalty all the same. In subsequent issues of *L'Action Française,* Maurras devoted his column to the generals who pressed the need for more troops at the National Assembly, applauding them at the expense of limp-wristed parliamentarians. Moved by the testimony of General Auguste Mercier, he asserted that there was nothing more eloquent in any language than the military order to charge: "I don't hesitate to express my admiration for a sick, crippled Garibaldi huddled inside a carriage but still managing to issue the command 'Advance, gentlemen!' to his band. Even more sublime was the injured Marshal de Saxe, carried to the front line on a litter, urging his troops forward not with words but with a simple gesture at the battle of Fontenoy [in 1745]."† General Paul Pau was made of the same stuff. He, too, exemplified the man of action whose plain language bespoke his virility. "General Pau's speech," Maurras wrote, "had the power of an act, a political act capable of changing views, feelings, and resolutions. . . . Parliamentarians are above all delicate old ladies sensitive to draughts. The masculine voice of General Pau stiffened their spine for several hours or weeks."‡

---

* For his efforts, Maurras received a steady flow of letters of gratitude from readers. "Monsieur Charles Maurras, he who will restore France's place in the front rank of world armies and thus save France from a Polish-like dismemberment. Homage and gratitude" came from a group of French officers. Another group of soldiers wrote, "In homage and with gratitude for your declaration of war against the Foreigner within." These letters and others were published on the front page of *L'Action Française,* February 12, 1913. The "royalist ladies and young women" of Saint-Étienne expressed their admiration for the "noble, courageous fashion in which you have defended the rights of Frenchmen against the Jewish oppressor."

† The Battle of Fontenoy was a major engagement in the War of the Austrian Succession; it pitted the forces of Holland, England, and Hanover against France. Saxe commanded the French army in the Netherlands.

‡ A year later, the Army of Alsace, under Pau's command, suffered a decisive defeat in the early weeks of World War I. General Joffre broke it up, assigned survivors to other corps, and sent Pau to St. Petersburg as France's representative at Russian General Headquarters— the Stavka.

Nothing is more beautiful, he went on, than some much debated idea stripped of everything but its necessary garments. The ancients knew it. Men of action enjoyed pride of place in the Athenian Pnyx and the Roman Forum.

A few days after shooting Jean Jaurès, Raoul Villain wrote to his brother, "So I have brought down the flag-bearer, the great traitor of the Three-Year Law, the furnace-mouth that swallowed all appeals from Alsace-Lorraine. I punished him, and my act was the symbol of a new day." Rumor had it that Villain was a Camelot du Roi or otherwise employed by L'Action Française, in whose rogues' gallery Jaurès figured prominently. Maurras, unlike Barrès's *maître à penser* Jules Soury and the anti-Semitic Comtesse de Martel de Janville (who wrote under the pen name "Gyp"), did not gloat over the assassination. But his memoir was a casuistic argument eulogizing the victim while condemning his thought, honoring a man who died in the service of "his faith" while execrating the faith. For some years, he wrote, the prospect of peace had been an illusion fostered by Jaurès, who believed that European nations were evolving toward unity. The opposite was true. If not for the chimera of a united Europe, France would have been better prepared for the imminent war. Soldiers would fall in the thousands because Jaurès had disarmed the nation with his oratory.*

Even so, dying for one's country was an enviable fate in Maurras's moral scheme of things. He said so on August 1 in an article entitled "National Duty." War, he declared, is a burden shared by all but borne for the most part by the happy few. "Fortunate are those whose hearts and arms enjoy the privilege of combat, of putting themselves in harm's way and smiting the enemy!" To be pitied were those left behind, "good Frenchmen born to shoulder arms but disqualified by some physical or mental condition." Mindful of all that they owe the air and soil of the fatherland, "they will wonder what price they can pay equivalent to the blood that their friends and brothers are going to shed. As for myself, I can hardly bear the thought of old colleagues departing for the supreme battle."

One sacrifice Maurras vowed to make on the home front was post-

---

* Many were judged at fault, not least of all Georges Picquart, the officer responsible for exposing the conspiracy against Dreyfus. Maurras accused him of lowering France's guard when he served as minister of war between 1906 and 1909, in Clemenceau's first cabinet.

poning his campaign for a monarchy. When France's salvation was at stake, he wrote, men were honor-bound to defend the Republic. He and his fellow royalists bent their energies to that patriotic end with a zeal fueled by their dedication to Dreyfus's guilt. Between 1914 and 1918, republicanism went largely undisputed in *L'Action Française*. But during those four years, the editors—above all Léon Daudet, Alphonse's elder son—waged war against defeatists and spies, collectively denounced as the "hidden foe."

CHAPTER 6

Spy Mania and Postwar Revenge

The truth is that espionage is an essentially German pursuit. In its chivalrous candor the French character does not lend itself to such skulduggery: we find it repugnant.

—*L'Information* (LYON), November 15, 1886

In Léon Daudet, who set out almost two years before the war to expose subversion, France's hydra-headed foe met its Hercules. Daudet lived for brawling and enlivened *L'Action Française,* of which he was editor in chief, with defamatory tirades. In article after article he cast suspicion on naturalized foreigners, unnatural Frenchmen, Jews, left-wing Russian exiles, and enterprises owned wholly or in part by Germans.

One such enterprise was Baedeker, whose roving cartographers were accused of tracking the disposition of troops on the pretext of updating French road maps. Another was Maggi, the Swiss food conglomerate known for its bouillon cubes, dehydrated soups, and milk. In January 1913, *L'Action Française* declared that German intelligence had been sheltering behind Maggi and colluding with high-level Parisian police officials. A torn memorandum said to have been found under a table at the brasserie Zimmer on the Place du Châtelet, where Charles Legrand, a Maggi executive, allegedly met Paul Guichard, a police commissioner supervising the city's central market, somehow turned up at *L'Action Française.* It listed sums that, in Daudet's indictment, could only refer to payments for classified information about official knowledge of German espionage in Paris. Legrand protested

Léon Daudet, Alphonse Daudet's son and Maurras's closest collaborator in the L'Action Française movement.

that the story was nonsense—that he had never met Guichard; that he was not Swiss but Norman; that he came from a family honored for its military service; that his signature on a typewritten document acquired by *L'Action Française* had been forged. Daudet shrugged his protests off: "Mystifications, forgeries—the usual cant of Dreyfus's defenders naturally flows from the pen of M. Legrand. Say what you will! We stand by our affirmations! *Maggi enterprises cloak a vast espionage network, and the police have been bribed to look the other way.*" Two days later, under the rubric "Jewish-German Espionage: Les Maggi at Strategic Points," the paper indicated that Maggi owned a huge warehouse at Mantes, with a private ferry to its dairy farms on an island in the Seine, which, should Germany declare war, would give prospective saboteurs easy access to a bridge connecting the main road from Paris to points west. Readers in the provinces lost no time informing Daudet of other Maggi farms and warehouses situated near other bridges whose strategic importance had been demonstrated forty-three years earlier, during the Franco-Prussian War. A precedent was thus established for the quantity of mail Daudet received after 1914 from civilian informants and soldiers suspicious of treason in the ranks. More tips reached him through an adjunct of L'Action Française, the Ligue de Guerre d'Appui, whose honorary president was that idol of unreconstructed anti-Dreyfusards General Auguste Mercier.

The threat of punishment did not silence Daudet. Risking fines and even imprisonment for libel only redounded to his virtue. The campaign against traitors intensified with his vilification of *Le Bonnet Rouge,* an anarchist newspaper that vehemently condemned the war. Its editor, Eugène Vigo, wrote under the pen name "Miguel Almereyda."* His favorite targets were Maurras and Barrès. In September 1916, Daudet announced that *L'Action Française* had received impeccable information from a high source of Vigo's involvement in an extensive spy ring. The source remained anonymous, which led some doubters to conclude that it was a fictive character (like "the veiled lady" conjured up by Esterhazy during the Dreyfus Affair) and others to speculate that it was someone in the know using *L'Action Française* as a cat's-paw to settle accounts with a political enemy while appearing to respect the "sacred union." Meanwhile, subscribers, whose number was to grow by leaps and bounds, enthusiastically joined Daudet's paranoid excursions.

Twelve years after the fact, *L'Action Française* published an article in which Maurras testified that the Vigo affair had begun with a visit he received on September 8, 1916, from Maurice Barrès acting as a messenger for his fellow Lorrainer President Raymond Poincaré. Barrès had previously visited Poincaré to complain about Vigo's vicious diatribes and about reports of *Le Bonnet Rouge* spreading defeatist propaganda among soldiers at the front. Poincaré nursed grievances of his own against Vigo, who had spent much of the first decade of the century in jail for theft, slander, the manufacture of explosives, and attempts at sabotage. According to French intelligence, Vigo the Catalan had been in Cartagena when a U-boat landed several German agents there. What could have attracted him to that city if not a clandestine rendezvous? The government lacked sufficient evidence to press charges, but nothing prevented it from airing its suspicions through a surrogate. Maurras and Daudet volunteered the services of L'Action Française and obtained more detailed information in subsequent meetings with Poincaré himself.†

---

* Vigo was of Catalan origin. Almereyda may have sounded Catalan but was apparently intended to be an acronym containing the words "la merde."

† Poincaré denied that these meetings ever took place. In April 1928, when Maurras published this *"témoignage,"* Poincaré was hoping to be reappointed prime minister, with a coalition cabinet. Barrès had died five years earlier.

Daudet now divided his prosecutorial efforts between Maggi and Vigo. In April 1917, when men were bleeding profusely at the Chemin des Dames or refusing to fight, Daudet blamed the slaughter and mutiny on the devil "defeatist." Vigo proceeded to sue him for libel. Before the trial, Daudet took the offensive in the pages of *L'Action Française,* referring to Vigo as "the ex-convict" and to *Le Bonnet Rouge* as Le Torchon (the Rag).

Had he not, by his own admission, gone to Saint-Sébastien—a hotbed of German espionage—in June 1916, passport number 11704—to found a "bilingual paper." One must note here that this trip coincided with the arrival in Cartagena of the submarine U-35—the famous German predator. Vigo, known as "Almereyda," claims that he couldn't have traveled from Saint-Sébastien to Cartagena in three days, which remains to be seen. At any rate, he was *spotted* in the neighborhood of Cartagena. Besides, a German agent could have brought a package or oral instructions from Cartagena to Saint-Sébastien, and that too must be looked into. One should note that when the German agent Gaston Routier tried to found a French pro-German newspaper in Madrid, the *Journal de la Paix,* Vigo rushed to his defense and, after Routier had been exposed, made the *first* public announcement that he had given up his criminal project. Would Vigo's paper in Saint-Sébastien have been the double of Routier's in Madrid? Only Prince Ratibor, Germany's ambassador to Spain, could enlighten us on the subject.

Also suspicious was the remarkable fact that the staff of "the Rag," all young enough to bear arms, had escaped military service. Only the influence of a higher-up could explain this collective exemption, and Daudet pointed a finger at the Radical minister of the interior, Louis-Jean Malvy.* Malvy, who allowed workers to demonstrate against the war with impunity, presented a wide target. Why had he not jailed Alphonse Merrheim, head of the steelworkers' union, for attending a congress of European Socialists two years earlier at Zimmerwald in Switzerland, which issued the proclamation "After one year of bloodshed, the imperialist character of the war has manifested itself more and more clearly; there is proof that it has its causes in the

---

* The full name of the party was Radical-Socialist. In the twentieth century its members were usually referred to as Radicals, though none were any longer politically radical.

imperialist and colonial politics of all governments, which will remain responsible for the unleashing of this carnage"?* And why had he not dissolved the General Confederation of Labor—the CGT—when munitions workers hampered the war effort with strikes in 1917?

Daudet's argument did not avail him in court. He was convicted of libel. But damages were a small price to pay for the exposés that greatly profited *L'Action Française.* Its circulation doubled and its editors continued their campaign against the enemy within, relying on information leaked by sympathizers in the Prefecture of Police, the Intelligence Agency, and the censorship and postal services. In May 1917, the arrest of Vigo's associate Émile Duval at the Swiss border with a very large check, the origins and purpose of which he could not readily explain, lent credence to the accusation that *Le Bonnet Rouge* was a German pawn. "I do not pretend to know all the financial resources of the defeatist campaign," Daudet wrote on July 8, "but those I cite here are certain, and will become evident." Among others, he cited a German-American "wheeler-dealer" known for his "shady schemes" and "the banker Rosenberg," formerly resident in Paris, who was said to have a direct line from his refuge in Zurich to the German General Staff in Berlin.

The turning point came on July 22, when Georges Clemenceau, no friend of *L'Action Française,* endorsed Daudet's campaign with a speech reviling anarchists and pacifists, Vigo and Malvy, in terms that endeared him momentarily to the right-wing press.† "He supported the nationalist thesis par excellence with singular bravura and flare, naming names with an audacity and bluntness seldom heard on the Senate floor," a conservative colleague wrote in *Le Figaro.* "Never has such vigorous speech been more necessary. Never has it been more opportune to say that at this moment treason and anarchy are twin sisters. . . . The former surrenders secrets to Germany, the latter seeks to make weapons drop from our hands. . . . They collaborate in producing pacifist propaganda." On August 7, the police arrested Vigo and Duval. Soon afterward, Malvy announced that daily attacks by the press compelled him to resign. Early in September, Vigo was found dead at Fresnes Prison, having hanged himself (with a shoelace,

---

* A splinter group led by Lenin called for revolution.

† Clemenceau, nicknamed "the Tiger," would have welcomed almost any pretext to discredit a significant rival in the Radical Party. During his tenure as prime minister, beginning in November 17, he helped bring Joseph Caillaux to book.

according to the official report) or been silenced by co-conspirators (in the opinion of *L'Action Française*). Malvy, a co-conspirator and murderer? On the basis of no evidence whatever, Daudet argued the case for treason in a personal letter to President Poincaré:

> M. Malvy is a traitor. For the last three years, with the complicity of M. Leymarie [his principal private secretary] and several others, he has betrayed the national defense. The proofs of this treason are overwhelming. It would take too long to state them. . . . M. Malvy has caused Germany to be exactly informed of all our military and diplomatic projects, particularly by the spy gang of the *Bonnet Rouge* and his friend Vigo . . . and by a certain Soutters, director of Maggi-Kub. This is how, to cite only one example, the German high command learned point by point the plan of attack on the Chemin des Dames . . . as soon as M. Malvy was admitted to the [cabinet's] War Committee. . . . Documents of indisputable authenticity also show the hand of Malvy and that of the Sûreté in the military mutinies and the tragic events of June 1917. . . . The only way to destroy the German plan is . . . to refer to a military tribunal the miserable creature by whom France has been handed over, bit by bit, to the enemy.

The government launched a criminal investigation. When Malvy demanded to know the charges against him, Premier Paul Painlevé—a brilliant mathematician but a premier sadly deficient in common sense—read Daudet's diatribe before the Chamber of Deputies. In the uproar that followed, France was seen at its most fissiparous, with Right and Left making a mockery of the "sacred union." Debate lasted for hours. "In this overexcited hall," one legislator complained, "we have argued on a question brought up by Léon Daudet. On one side a calumniator, a professional defamer, on the other the Chamber and the whole country. What is this person who can thus occupy the country's representatives for six hours? What is his importance? What is his power? I cannot find an explanation consistent with the dignity of this Assembly!"

While the High Court dismissed charges of treason against Malvy, it agreed that the former interior minister's lenient treatment of pacifists represented "*forfaiture*"—negligence or dereliction of duty—and exiled him from France for five years. Swept up in the purge was Joseph Caillaux, as outspoken as ever, who had repeatedly mounted the rostrum of the chamber to plead for armistice negotiations. He found himself stripped of parliamentary immunity at the request of the military governor of Paris, judged by the same tribunal that banished Malvy, and in February 1920, fifteen months after the war, sentenced to three years in prison.* Vigo's death did not call the hounds off *Le Bonnet Rouge.* Accused of treason for having a large, unexplained check in his possession at the Swiss border, Émile Duval was executed by a firing squad.

In the twilight of 1917, with missiles pulverizing huge armies at Passchendaele and Lenin's Bolsheviks seizing power in Petrograd, shadows fell everywhere. L'Action Française itself came under suspicion, not of treasonable relations with the enemy but of plotting a monarchist coup. Its newspaper was suspended for a week and its offices in five cities raided on October 27. Police searched the homes of Maurras, Daudet, Marius Plateau, and others. They harvested fifty guns, 250 loaded canes, enough brass knuckles and blackjacks to arm a squad of Camelots du Roi, files in which Plateau kept old plans for insurrection, and letters of allegiance to the movement from officers stationed near Paris in 1917. A left-wing commentator observed that union leaders caught with much less incriminating paraphernalia would have been jailed. Maurras, Daudet, and Plateau suffered no legal consequences.† Charges preferred against them were dismissed, as if the idea of a royalist coup were risible. Royalists didn't laugh, but even they could hardly deny that the "sacred union," for all its cracks, held together, like the shell of a religion to which dissident parties still paid lip service, under the high priesthood of Painlevé's successor, Georges Clemenceau.

Charles Maurras hewed to the belief that France would win the war only when she won the peace with a treaty dismembering Germany. Germans could not learn from defeat, he wrote. They are what they

---

* The indictment stated that Germany could count on Caillaux, throughout the war, to promote a "premature" peace agreement the terms of which would have been unfavorable to France. Testimony was given by the French mistress of a German spy, who claimed to be a carrier pigeon for correspondence between Caillaux and her lover. Caillaux was amnestied in 1925 and reelected to the chamber.

That Caillaux was the best financial mind in politics did not make him any friends when, as minister of finance during the war, he originated the tax on income in France.

† Journalists dubbed it "*le complot des panoplies.*" *Complot* is a plot or conspiracy, and *panoplie,* an ornamental display of weapons.

are—a people who had broken the moral bond that tied them to the rest of the civilized world, who sought a culture all their own and found their way to it in the glorification of their nature.* It behooved L'Action Française, which had disdained electoral politics, to constitute itself as a party and rally opinion against the spirit of clemency informing President Woodrow Wilson's speeches. To Charles Maurras, the League of Nations was a snare.

By the time its candidates ran in the elections of November 1919, the Versailles Peace Conference had, as Maurras's close associate Jacques Bainville put it, organized the perfect setup for eternal war. Declining an invitation to join the conservative coalition Bloc National, a coalition of conservative parties held together by fear of a Bolshevik revolution, L'Action Française drafted a platform that featured diplomatic recognition of the Vatican (which it helped achieve), measures to curb the immigration of all foreigners, greater incentives for the procreation of French babies, and smaller government.

L'Action Française won only one seat from Paris. But its Paris seat was filled by the voluminous Léon Daudet, who spoke louder than anyone else, interrupted his left-wing colleagues with peremptory accusations of treason, bullied the Bloc National, and in other ways as well exercised disproportionate influence on the chamber. Rumor had it that prefects were made and unmade at his behest. Ambitious functionaries enrolled their sons in the royalist party. With industry crippled by strikes in key sectors of the economy, conservatives who may have had nothing invested in the ideal of monarchy saw L'Action Française as a bulwark against revolution. To large cheering crowds (there were eight thousand present at the Salle Wagram in January 1922) Daudet railed indiscriminately against Bolshevism and "Anglo-German-Jewish" capital. *Le Temps* stated what had become quite obvious by 1922: "One can criticize, detest, or admire M. Daudet, but no one can deny that he is a power." When he and Maurras, marching under a large L'Action Française banner, led some hundreds of Camelots du Roi from the Place Saint-Augustin to the Place des Pyramides on Joan of Arc's civil feast day, they were gratified to hear themselves hailed by spectators along the route.

---

* "Their nature" presented a problem after the war in the form of children conceived by Frenchwomen who had been raped by German soldiers. There were those who characterized such children as genetic foes smuggled into France in French wombs and fated to corrupt the purity of the race. The issue was hotly debated.

Daudet's maneuvers helped to tilt the chamber against Aristide Briand in a confidence vote that abruptly ended his premiership in January 1922. Briand, the cofounder of *L'Humanité* with Jean Jaurès, had been one of the blacker beasts in the royalist bestiary even before tarring himself in 1921 by his willingness to reduce the sum total of Germany's indemnity.* *L'Action Française* wanted every punitive measure enforced *sine misericordia*. Maurras and Daudet rejoiced over Briand's fall and then again over the appointment of Raymond Poincaré as his successor—Poincaré being hospitable to their views in the realm of foreign policy. Reparations were a burning issue. The Weimar Republic, whose economy was stricken, had defaulted in its payments. No agreement could be reached by the Western Allies on an appropriate response. England and America favored a moratorium, while France and Belgium proposed to tighten the noose with sanctions. "Judging others by themselves, the English, who are blinded by their loyalty, have always thought that the Germans did not abide by their pledges inscribed in the Versailles Treaty because they had not frankly agreed to them," Poincaré wrote to the French ambassador in London. "We, on the contrary, believe that Germany, far from making the slightest effort to honor the peace treaty—has, indeed, always tried to escape her obligations—the reason being that she has not been convinced of her defeat. . . . We are also certain that Germany, as a nation, resigns herself to its pledge only under duress."

By "duress," Poincaré had in mind a military occupation of the industrial Rhineland, from which France could extract the mandated shipments of coal that Germany had failed to deliver. This would severely strain France's relations with England, but something of their

---

* In the course of a long, distinguished political career, which began in 1906, Briand held twenty-five ministerial portfolios and presided over eleven cabinets as premier. He was largely responsible for implementing the law separating church and state, but also, two decades later, for reestablishing diplomatic relations with the Vatican. He and Jaurès, who were of one mind in founding the French Socialist Party, parted ways before the war when Briand introduced legislation that led to a three-year draft. His principal achievement during the war was the close economic and military cooperation of the Allied powers. With the American secretary of state Frank Kellogg, he coauthored a manifesto in 1928—the Kellogg-Briand Pact—committing its fifty-seven signatories (the United States, France, the United Kingdom, Weimar Germany, Italy, and Japan among them) to renounce aggressive war as an instrument of national policy.

In the parliamentary muddle of the 1920s, ideologies were at a discount. Briand the maverick served as premier of a Chamber of Deputies with a conservative majority. Several years later, Poincaré the conservative served as premier of a leftist chamber. Though Radicals were not the only pragmatists, they were radical in this respect, if in no other.

Aristide Briand, 1862–1932, premier under Poincaré's presidency and coauthor, with Frank Kellogg, of a pact outlawing war as an instrument of national policy, for which both were awarded the Nobel Peace Prize.

historical antagonism had already begun to cloud the memory of wartime camaraderie. In the Chamber of Deputies, Léon Daudet cheered on Poincaré (who, four years earlier, had proposed that the Rhineland be wrested from Germany and placed under Allied military control). "Occupying the Ruhr valley certainly involves risks," he declared on December 15, 1922, "but so does every other option. There are risks in doing nothing, in granting a perpetual moratorium. M. Poincaré has no intention of granting one anyway, which is why my friends and I shall vote for him, should it come to a vote. We are indeed grateful to him for keeping his promises, for not calling up a class of recruits gratuitously, and for honoring the most important part of the Treaty of Versailles."

Daudet's speech was followed twelve days later by his lead article in *L'Action Française:* "We will know in a few hours or days whether the Poincaré government plans to occupy the Ruhr, a decision that will mark the present cabinet's collapse (if it decides against) or its victory and the victory of France (if for). We remind you that the question of the Ruhr was raised by *L'Action Française* right after the absurd Treaty of Versailles, as soon as it became perfectly clear that Germany did not intend to pay anything and, sooner or later, to take its revenge." Poincaré and Maurras had had a cordial correspondence since 1919, when Maurras, aware though he was that presidents under the Third Republic were little more than figureheads, urged him to protest Woodrow Wilson's presence at the Versailles Peace Conference and to represent France in place of Clemenceau.*

French troops marched on January 11, 1923, seizing as much of the Rhineland as was not already occupied, and most of its industrial wealth. They enforced reparations, but the blow to Germany, while it profited France materially, told against her in world opinion, all the more after March 31, when French soldiers gunned down resisting workers in the Krupp factory at Essen.† Sympathy began to shift toward the Weimar Republic, whose economy crumbled in a whirlwind of hyperinflation. National outrage united Germans in a "national unity front" reminiscent of the *Burgfrieden,* or civil truce, that had briefly effaced party lines in 1914. In Munich Adolf Hitler exploited the crisis to denounce left-wingers whose uprising in November 1918 had been, as he put it, the "stab in the back" that led to Germany's surrender and the establishment of the Weimar Republic. "The German rebirth is externally only possible when the criminals are faced with their responsibility and delivered to their just fate," he shouted to a packed audience of Nazi Party members at the cavernous Circus Krone in Munich on the day the French marched into the Ruhr. The real enemy was not France but compatriots who had rendered Germany defenseless before the onslaught of Marxism, democracy, parliamentarism, internationalism, and Jewish power.

L'Action Française had never enjoyed such prominence, both in and out of the National Assembly. It rented spacious quarters at 14 Rue

---

* Never forgotten by anti-Dreyfusards, among many other grudges, was Clemenceau's role in the publication of Zola's letter to the French president, accusing the military brass of a conspiracy to frame Dreyfus. As editor in chief of *L'Aurore,* it was he who splashed it over the front page and gave it the title "J'accuse."

† In the Ruhr, more than seventy thousand workers, most of them staging slowdowns, were evicted to provide living quarters for labor imported from France and Belgium; 130 civilians had been killed during the invasion.

de Rome, near the Gare Saint-Lazare. It had three hundred chapters distributed within ten zones, and thirty thousand dues-paying members. The circulation of *L'Action Française* hovered at one hundred thousand, but provincial papers eager to reprint Maurras, Daudet, and Bainville amplified its voice. Associated with it was a student bimonthly, *L'Étudiant Français,* whose contributors included young intellectuals destined to make their mark as scholars, men of letters, or traitors: Philippe Ariès, Claude Roy, Pierre Gaxotte, Raoul Girardet, and Robert Brasillach. A rural edition of the paper, *L'Action Française Agricole,* conveyed its message to farms and bistros in *la France profonde.* The movement sponsored a women's club for young royalist ladies. It organized lectures at its own institute and, of course, stood foursquare behind the Camelots du Roi, whose brawls with opponents of Poincaré's militarism made news in January 1923. Caning Communist demonstrators (who generally gave as good as they got) increased the royalists' popularity that month, when the chamber was preparing to strip Marcel Cachin, a Communist deputy and party founder, of his parliamentary immunity and try him for plotting to overthrow the government.*

January 1923 did not end until it proved to be even more ominously eventful, and by that time L'Action Française had begun its descent from the forum to the streets, reconceiving itself more as a movement animated by the vigilantism of its goons than as a party committed to the rough-and-tumble of republican politics. What took place at the headquarters of L'Action Française in the afternoon of January 22 quickened its descent. The day before, on January 21, a young woman had called on Léon Daudet at his home, claiming to have secrets from the terrorist underground. She was referred by Daudet's servant to his secretary on the Rue de Rome. She telephoned the latter and

---

* Marcel Cachin was a founder of the PCF (Parti Communiste Français). The case against him rested upon this letter, dated January 13, from the executive committee of the Third International: "In view of the extreme gravity of the situation in Europe, which threatens the working class with frightening new calamities, and as well the decisions taken by The Hague about strikes in time of war, the executive committee of the Third International . . . proposes that the French Communist Party immediately engage in talks with our representatives about common measures to be undertaken to prevent a new war. As representatives, the executive committee appoints: Clara Zetkin, Cachin, Neubold, and Radek. . . . We request that you send an immediate answer to Moscow and information through the German Communist Party, the French Communist Party, and the French CGTU [Confédération Générale du Travail Unitaire]."

conferred with him that evening in the presence of Marius Plateau, secretary-general of the Camelots du Roi. Her alleged information concerned plots being hatched by militant anarchists who had summarily expelled her from their cell. At home, under lock and key, she said, were documents that corroborated her story. She agreed to bring them the next day, and she showed up in the afternoon of January 22 at the appointed hour, empty-handed. (Daudet and Maurras, whom she had stalked that morning, were at a mass commemorating the 130th anniversary of Louis XVI's execution). After twenty minutes of conversation, Plateau led her to the door. Before he opened it, she pulled a revolver from her raincoat, shot him three times, and herself once. He died; she survived.

Questioned by detectives, the assassin identified herself as Germaine Berton, twenty years old, unemployed and supported by fellow anarchists. She would have preferred to assassinate Daudet, but Plateau served the purpose. Why Daudet? "I consider that he bore the heaviest burden of responsibility for the new war in the Ruhr. He is a man who has spent his life fighting the working class. I also hold him responsible for concocting the plots against Jaurès and, above all, Almereyda, leader of the young guard. I have done my duty." *Le Temps* reported that Germaine Berton had spent time in prison for assault and was thought to have been implicated in the delivery of a package bomb to the American ambassador one year earlier.

L'Action Française ran the headline "A German Bullet Killed Marius Plateau." It declared that the murder was the work of "Germano-Bolsheviks" infuriated by the French occupation of the Ruhr. The wheel had turned full circle. Grievously wounded at Vaux-sous-Fontenoy in 1914 and awarded the Croix de Guerre for heroic action, Plateau had now succumbed to the same enemy. The Great War was over, but Armaggedon remained to be fought. All "patriots" were invited to sign up at the offices of the paper and demonstrate with Camelots du Roi against agents of "Germany, the Soviet Union, and international finance." That night, at least seven Camelots—those who were caught—forcibly entered two left-wing newspapers and trashed everything, including the linotype machines. From then on, mounted police officers patrolled the newspaper district of lower Montmartre.

Four days later, on Paris's other bank, streets near the Champs de Mars swarmed with police marshaling the crowd that had gathered at the Église Saint-Pierre du Gros Caillou for Marius Plateau's funeral. Gathered inside the church was European aristocracy: the Duc de Luynes, representing the Duc d'Orléans, pretender to the throne; the Comte de Bourqueney, representing Queen Amélie of Portugal; Baron Tristan Lambert, representing the Duc de Vendôme; a pride of other titled lions. Behind them sat Plateau's colleagues and royalists in the National Assembly. Generals abounded. Journalists, students from the "*grandes écoles*," and wounded veterans spilled onto the Rue Saint-Dominique, where horses harnessed to carts piled high with wreaths awaited the funeral procession. Eulogizing Plateau at the Vaugirard cemetery, Bernard de Vesins, president of the Ligue de l'Action Française, called him the heart and soul of the Camelots du Roi. "In the street, in the dock, in prison, he set everyone an example by his energy, his abnegation, his good humor." The slender thesis that Plateau had been selected for martyrdom in the criminal underground of German agents who chose and armed Germaine Berton was padded with religio-patriotic verbiage reminiscent of the eulogies for Colonel Hubert Henry during the Dreyfus Affair. "They fingered him as a useful victim and armed the hand that assassinated him. The fact that he was killed for having served France confers a more sacred character upon our grief: our tears swear us to accomplish what Marius would have done if one of us had fallen in his place. . . . Miraculously saved during the war, he was destined by Providence to shed more blood for France. God claims the best among us, because the best have merited His eternal reward before the rest of us."

What Marius Plateau would certainly have done if one of them had fallen in his place was unleash the Camelots du Roi against those who hadn't shed tears, and, in fact, deputies of the Left were periodically mugged in the spring and summer of 1923. On May 31, they assaulted three well-known politicians scheduled to address fellow republicans protesting Poincaré's German policy. The three were beaten bloody and spattered with coal tar and printer's ink. A packet of dung was sent to a fourth. In scurrilous language, *L'Action Française* described the assaults as justice served in a nation whose dilatory courts had not yet tried Germaine Berton. Daudet explained that they were merely "warnings" or "moderate reprisals." They did not rise to the level of condign punishment. Cries of "French Fascism" in the chamber left him unphased.

In December, Germaine Berton was finally brought to trial. Her

Snapshots of the Surrealists (who took the liberty of including Picasso and Freud) garlanded around a mug shot of Germaine Berton, the assassin of Marius Plateau, a prominent member of L'Action Française. This display appeared in the first issue of *La Révolution Surréaliste,* December 1, 1924.

attorney, Henry Torrès, compared her to Charlotte Corday.* Appalled by a "Fascist" organization that spewed venom and ran riot with virtual impunity, she had aimed her weapon at the leader of a violent gang, not at the "glorious soldier." Torrès told the jurors that if Berton

---

* Charlotte Corday, a young Norman noblewoman, assassinated the Jacobin leader Jean-Paul Marat in 1793, at the height of the Terror.

were found guilty after Villain had walked free, they would judge Plateau's corpse more important than Jaurès's. It was a crime of passion.

The jury deliberated for only thirty-five minutes before reaching its verdict. Like Henriette Caillaux and Raoul Villain before her, she was acquitted of murder. *L'Action Française* declared the next morning, in its Christmas Day issue, that Plateau had been assassinated a second time, by eight bourgeois warped by anarchists who scorned all the values the bourgeoisie held dear.* Political murder had been legitimized. *L'Action Française* predicted that in due course the state would go further and bestow official honors upon sluts who killed heroes. Defenders of public order were therefore justified in administering justice as they saw fit. "While revolutionaries say the same thing," wrote the editors, "they neither do nor mean the same thing, for their violence is in the service of disorder rather than order, in the service of theft rather than property, in the service of anarchy rather than authority, of the foe rather than the fatherland."

Honors were indeed bestowed upon Germaine Berton, not by the state but by young artists and poets who flocked together in the name of "Surrealism" and, one year after Berton's trial, founded a review, *La Révolution Surréaliste,* the first issue of which pays homage to the murderess. Assembled around her mug shot, like children of a Lombrosian matriarch, are identity photos of the group (with Sigmund Freud and Picasso thrown in for good measure). The collective caption is a line from Baudelaire's preface to *Les Paradis Artificiels:* "Woman is the being who projects the deepest shade and the brightest light into our dreams."†

---

* The vote had been eight to four. Unanimity was not required under French law. What made the acquittal all the more embittering to Léon Daudet was the suicide several weeks earlier of his fourteen-year-old son, Philippe. The boy ran away from home, not for the first time, and, after trying to board a ship at Le Havre, returned to Paris. At the anarchist newspaper *Le Libertaire,* he told an editor, without identifying himself, that he was prepared to kill for the cause and, among possible victims, named his father. *Le Libertaire* gave him no encouragement. With the police in hot pursuit, Philippe, who had somehow acquired a pistol, blew his brains out in the backseat of a taxi. Daudet denounced first the Germans, then the police for having conspired to murder him and accused the taxi driver of being an accomplice. The taxi driver, Charles Bajot, sued him for slander and won. In 1925, Daudet was sentenced to five months in prison and ordered to pay a large fine. These punishments didn't stop his accusations.

† *"La femme est l'être qui projette la plus grande ombre ou la plus grande lumière dans nos rêves."*

· PART TWO ·

November 11, 1918. Silence descended on the front. That afternoon, Premier Georges Clemenceau entered the National Assembly at four o'clock to read the Armistice agreement, whose terms included the requirement that German troops evacuate France, Belgium, Luxembourg, and Alsace-Lorraine within a fortnight or face imprisonment. A rapturous crowd in the courtyard of the Palais Bourbon greeted the old man. Tens of thousands mobbed Paris's great squares, reveling as church bells tolled and artillery boomed. A multitude of Allied flags unfurled from windows all over the city, like glad rags draped over widow's weeds. Students paraded from the Latin Quarter to the Arc de Triomphe, dragging a captured German cannon and hurling derision at the kaiser, who was an exile in Holland by then. Clemenceau had no sooner read the fifty-fifth and final article of the agreement than legislators adjourned with a hearty rendition of "La Marseillaise."

In the trenches, reactions were often mixed. "News of the Armistice did not spark the enthusiasm one might have expected," wrote Adam Frantz, chief medical officer of the French army's Twenty-third Infantry Regiment. "Was it that four years of warfare had blunted all our feelings? Did men understand that success, however great, could never compensate for the atrocious losses we had suffered? Was it rather that in his unconscious wisdom the ordinary grunt realized that neither nations nor men would profit from the great, cruel lesson?"

Word of the Armistice was as baffling to those infantrymen as a sudden reprieve to lifers long removed from the outside world. "We did not cheer, but just stood, stunned and bewildered," wrote Sergeant Walter Sweet of the Monmouthshire Regiment, who heard a fellow survivor say, "To think that I shall not have to toddle among machine guns again and never hear another shell burst. It is simply unimaginable." What was to become of the soldiers in peacetime? "We have lived this life for so long. Now we shall have to start all over again." Colonel Thomas Gowenlock, an intelligence officer in the American First Division, observed that many soldiers believed the Armistice to be a ruse, or a restorative halt in a hundred years' war. There was no celebration on November 11. "As night came," he later recalled,

> the quietness, unearthly in its penetration, began to eat into their souls. The men sat around log fires, the first they had ever had at the front. They were trying to reassure themselves that there were no enemy batteries spying on them from the next hill and no German bombing planes approaching to blast them out of existence. They talked in low tones. They were nervous. After the long months of intense strain, of keying themselves up to the daily mortal danger, of thinking always in terms of war and the enemy, the abrupt release from it all was physical and psychological agony. Some suffered a total nervous collapse. . . . Some fell into an exhausted sleep. All were bewildered by the sudden meaninglessness of their existence as soldiers—and through their teeming memories paraded that swiftly moving cavalcade of Cantigny, Soissons, St. Mihiel, the Meuse-Argonne and Sedan. What was to come next? They did not know—and hardly cared. Their minds were numbed by the shock of peace. The past consumed their whole consciousness. The present did not exist and the future was inconceivable.

Having been "demobbed" and shipped back to England, Private John McCauley of the Second Border Regiment found himself swallowed up in the maelstrom of cheering crowds and blaring bands. "Such courage and nerve as I possessed were stolen from me on the blood-drenched plains of France," he wrote. "The trenches in Flanders helped make me a weakling. They sapped my courage, shattered my nerves and threw me back into a 'civilised' world broken in spirit and nerve. They might as well have taken my body, too."

Or at least his tongue, for McCauley was not alone in feeling

unable to communicate on any meaningful level with compatriots who had never visited that foreign country called the front,
where combatants divorced from civilization—Germans, French,
English, and Americans alike—shared a primitive language con-
jugating slaughter and mercy.* When Lance Corporal Thomas
Owen lay wounded in the rat-infested slime of a trench overrun by Germans, he was nursed by the enemy that had almost
killed him. "I cannot say how far I walked. I passed a first-aid
post in an old trench, but they waved me off despairingly. They
had too many to see to. Stretcher bearers passed me, carrying a
pole, with a blanket slung to it, and inside an agonized bundle
of broken humanity—blood trickling and dripping from the pen-
dulous blanket." At another first-aid station he fell into the arms
of a sad-eyed, black-bearded man who whispered, *"Armes Kind"*
(poor child), removed his tunic, leather jerkin, and cardigan, and
patched him up. "Truly the quality of mercy is not strained. I had
none of his tongue, nor he of mine, but he gave me a drink of warm
coffee from a flask, and his hands were as tender as a woman's as
he bandaged me. . . . A prisoner indeed; receiving succour from a
man whose countrymen I had blazed at in hate but a while ago."

Several months before the Armistice, nineteen-year-old Gustav
Regler, the future novelist and comrade of Arthur Koestler's, was
carried off a field of corpses near the Chemin des Dames and
woke up in Laon Cathedral, where the wounded lay side by side
on pallets lining the vast nave. It soon became apparent that his
physical wounds were more easily remedied than the psychological. Unable to talk, he was transported to a psychiatric hospital
in Germany, whose director, a Dr. Schomberg, took it upon himself to speak for him. The mute later quoted his spokesman in a
remarkable memoir entitled *The Owl of Minerva*. "I would like
to send you home but you don't want to go. If you did you'd be
able to speak. You want to go back to the front because you think
you're a deserter. And you want to stay here because you know

---

* "We seemed, as we moved up the road, to have left behind us the last link of the chain
which had connected us with civilisation. From now onward we were in a world apart,
where men moved openly only by night, where the scream and bursting of shells, and the
rifle fire, fitful and desultory, were the only interruptions to an unearthly silence—a desolate, scarred world, the playground of Death itself," wrote Corporal George Foley, Sixth
Somerset Light Infantry.

what the world looks like outside. You want to leave and not to leave. But you won't admit this to yourself, and so your tongue is crippled, because you can't say two such different things at the same time." There was no way back to the front, Schomberg continued. "This is a place from which one goes to a new life or else into total darkness. . . . You don't want to be a deserter? We are all deserters, all shams, more or less, throughout our lives. We lie to ourselves. Only one part of you despises war. I have read your diary. You will volunteer for other wars as senseless as this one. But so long as you remain here with me there is no war, and no laurels either. Only donkeys eat laurels."

Young André Breton, who was to confer, in the Surrealist movement, poetic dignity on the images and nightmares of the shell-shocked soldiers he attended as a male nurse at a psychiatric center near the Chemin des Dames and as a medical student at Paris's Val-de-Grâce hospital, mourned the loss of two voices in 1918. Only hours before the Armistice, Guillaume Apollinaire, a poet revered by the avant-garde, fell victim to the flu pandemic. Several months later, Breton received what proved to be letters of farewell from a beloved army friend named Jacques Vaché, for whose air of dandified invulnerability and murderous volleys of black humor he professed the greatest admiration. "Your letter finds me in a terrible slump," Vaché wrote on November 14, 1918. "I am empty of ideas and ring hollow, more than ever no doubt the unconscious recorder of many things, all balled up. . . . I'll leave the war quietly gaga, like one of those splendid village idiots, perhaps. . . . Dear friend, how am I to survive these last few months in uniform (I've been assured the war is over)? I'm really at my wits' end. What is more, THEY are distrustful. THEY suspect something. Will THEY lobotomize me while they still have me in their grasp?" In January 1919, Vaché—whom Breton portrayed forever after, idolatrously, as a cross between Beau Brummel and Arthur Rimbaud—overdosed on opium in a Brussels hotel room.

There was no generic equivalent in French to the English "shell shock" or the German *Kriegsneurose*. The language did not legitimate a psychiatric disorder that exempted the traumatized soldier from a holy war, a war waged in defense of civilization.

CHAPTER 7

Scars of the Trenches

While almost all French writers bowed to the law of this war
and made themselves its apologists, we, who were not yet old
enough to bear arms, or who reached that age only because the
murderous conflict lasted as long as it did, we spurned the Sacred
Union, which reached into the domains of thought and creation.

—Louis Aragon

Peace ruins people.

—Pierre Drieu La Rochelle

While Barrès, Maurras, and their confrères had sounded the
call to arms, like the graybeards in Giraudoux's *Tiger at
the Gates* who send young Trojans off to die for Helen, the future
standard-bearers of Surrealism fought for "Marianne." They survived
with wounds that never ceased to fester.

André Breton was a first-year medical student in 1916, writing
poems under Rimbaud's spell, when, as noted above, the army sent
him to a work at a psychiatric center within earshot of the front. It
was a brief internship but pivotal, not least because his exposure to the
panic attacks of traumatized soldiers coincided with his introduction
to the thought of Sigmund Freud.* In 1917, at the Val-de-Grâce hospi-

---

* The supervising psychiatrist had him read *La Psychanalyse des Névroses et des Psychoses*
by Drs. Régis and Hesnard, published in 1914. Freud's works had not yet been translated
into French.

André Breton, left, still in uniform, with Théodore Fraenkel, who participated in Dada japes after the war while attending medical school.

tal in Paris he encountered Louis Aragon, a medical student his own age who had returned from a tour of duty with the Croix de Guerre. On their days off, they took long walks through Paris (memorialized several years later in Aragon's strolling narrative *Le Paysan de Paris*) or made the rounds of literary haunts. Holding court at the Café de Flore on Boulevard Saint-Germain with a bandage wrapped over the hole that had been drilled in his skull to remove shrapnel, and surrounded by worshipful young writers, was the poet Guillaume Apollinaire.

In that circle, where Breton may have first heard the term "Surrealism," coined by Apollinaire, he met Philippe Soupault, a kindred soul recently invalided out of the army, who seized upon Breton's proposal that they conduct an experiment in what came to be known as "automatic writing" or, as Breton later defined it in the "Surrealist Manifesto," "the dictation of thought, free of any influence exercised by reason, heedless of all moral and esthetic concerns." The fruit of their collaboration was *Les Champs Magnétiques,* published in 1920. By then Breton cut the figure of a *chef de mouvement,* formulating his creed within the temporary confines of Dadaism. Other young men gravitated to him. There was Paul Éluard, whose first book of poems, *Le Devoir et l'Inquiétude,* had appeared in 1917, during the brief interlude between his release from a Swiss sanatorium for consumptives and his internment in a hospital for soldiers gassed at the front. There were also Robert Desnos, Georges Ribemont-Dessaignes, Roger Vitrac, Benjamin Péret, Jean Paulhan, Antonin Artaud, and Aragon's close friend Pierre Drieu La Rochelle, a thrice-wounded veteran of four campaigns from which he, too, emerged with the Croix de Guerre, but with one arm slightly shorter than the other. "War is my homeland," wrote Drieu. *"La guerre est ma patrie."* In large measure the same held true for all of them, and as well for a movement that put the camaraderie of a hallucinatory netherworld to poetic account. Surrealism, Breton proclaimed in the "Surrealist Manifesto" of 1924, was a prescription for rebirth of the spirit. It would work the magic that doctrinaires vested in nationhood and priests in communion. It would unlock the true life.

Fresh in the minds of these survivors was the ceaseless drumbeat of Barrès's wartime editorials and, most memorably, his assertion that a new being had been born in the trenches: the combat unit. They had their revenge in May 1921 when, with much hoopla, Breton presided over a mock trial of Barrès on a charge of "endangering the safety of the mind."* It was billed as a Dada event and held in the staid setting of the Salle des Sociétés Savantes on the Rue Danton. A full-sized dummy represented Barrès, who had ignored a summons to appear in person. Attorneys wore white surgeon's gowns and clerical birettas, red for the prosecution, black for the defense. Breton read a lengthy indictment; Aragon defended the accused; witnesses included Drieu La Rochelle, Tristan Tzara, and Giuseppe Ungaretti. The trial proceeded more or less soberly until Benjamin Péret marched into the hall wearing a German uniform and identifying himself as the Unknown Soldier (before being ordered out, in German).† Georges Ribemont-Dessaignes then delivered the prosecution's closing argument. Barrès's dubious succès d'estime would not in itself have warranted such treatment.

---

* The charge against Barrès implies that the Dada court was posing as a twentieth-century avatar of the Committee of General Security established during the First Republic to supervise the police and safeguard the Revolution. In 1793 it became a prime implement of the Terror.

† Conservative papers were outraged. "Everyone with a French soul will naturally be repelled by such baseness and foul abuse. . . . Another performance of the show may provoke something more than simple boos and anodyne hisses," wrote *La Presse*. A reviewer for *La Justice* suggested that hydrotherapy for Dadaists might be in order and that it was high time their identity papers be checked.

It wouldn't be worth a trial if it were only a matter of some amateur striving in old age to advance the glory of military men. The tip Barrès received for polishing their equipment might have appeased him once the gilt had worn off his academic nameplate and literary medals. We need not condemn this bourgeois attitude, this desire for both comfort and glory, for a situation that is celebrated with fanfares and alive with the sound of boots and talk of statues to be inaugurated. Dada would be more inclined to smile complaisantly at the parasitism, the hypocrisy of an arriviste who has arrived and even to sympathize with him for cleverly conning the public.

However, Ribemont-Dessaignes told the jury, there were the atrocious consequences of what Barrès had written between 1914 and 1918. When Barrès's prose is heard through one ear and through the other the din of catastrophes that universally constitute the heroic narrative of societies, it becomes apparent that his is a sinister game.

As an adolescent, Barrès offered a few homilies to children hobbled by social constraints. Then, one day, with an almost imperceptible shift in the axis of his lips, and a slightly different blink, he exhibited the anxious face of a . . . moralist who had located the basis of individual and collective morality in the honor of France, thus taking the narrowest possible view of the individual and society. This atheist changed the skin of his God. . . . As tolerant as we are of contradiction, we cannot suffer one that has led him to propagate a consummately dangerous, stupid, and vain gospel, to erect a monument to that most mortal of divinities: the Fatherland.

The jury voted for his execution.

It disappointed Ribemont-Dessaignes that some of his fellow iconoclasts—Louis Aragon, for example—could not unambivalently support the verdict. Aragon, the bastard son of a former police prefect, remembered that his adolescence had been cheered by lessons in moral anarchy drawn from Barrès's *Sous l'Oeil des Barbares* and *Un Homme Libre*. If present-day admirers of the accused bothered to read *Le Culte du Moi* more closely, Aragon argued, they would be as shocked as a pious parishioner discovering an obscene tattoo on the corpse of his confessor. What of his observation that "intelligence is a very small thing on the surface of ourselves"? Might that not have been a con-

Dada's mock trial of Maurice Barrès. Louls Aragon is at the far left, Breton third from the left, and Tristan Tzara next to him, dressed like the dummy representing Barrès, and about the same size.

genial slogan for his young judges? Even when they and Barrès situated true selfhood in very different realms—Barrès in the graveyard of venerated ancestors, Surrealists-to-be in the cradle of reawakened childhood—they were of one mind in prosecuting Reason as a subversive agent.

Another participant who declined invitations to condemn Barrès outright was Aragon's friend Pierre Drieu La Rochelle, who later called *Un Homme Libre* a masterpiece worthy of Montaigne's essays and Pascal's *Pensées*. The paths that he and Aragon would follow afterward, in the 1930s and 1940s—when politics oriented writers as fatefully as it had during the Dreyfus Affair—took them in opposite directions. Aragon became the poet laureate of French Stalinism. Drieu waffled between Communism and Fascism, ultimately pledged himself to the latter, and under Nazi rule directed France's leading literary journal, the *Nouvelle Revue Française*. Neither found accommodation in the middle ground of bourgeois values, or inner peace except in mortal combat.

Indirect light can be the most revealing. A page Drieu wrote in his diary many years after the event sheds light of that kind on his earlier self, the young man whom Ribemont-Dessaignes could not corner into testifying against Barrès in 1921. On September 11, 1939, Drieu attended a soirée at the home of Édouard Bourdet, director of

the Comédie Française.* Unhappy with the recent decision of officials, including Jean Giraudoux (who wore two hats, as a famous
playwright and as minister of information), to censor passages in his
autobiographical novel *Gilles,* he inveighed against a regime that subjected one writer to the political judgment of another. It being wartime and Bourdet also a high government functionary, Drieu won no
sympathy at the dinner table. But he got even in his diary. "To be sure,
Gilles is a ferocious indictment of the regime and above all of the way
its servants think," he wrote. "If Giraudoux and Bourdet read it, they
would feel personally impugned." Bourdet he described as frightfully
diminished—a much frailer man than the author who had bright-
ened Paris ten years earlier with his satirical comedies. His decline, in
Drieu's view, showed the depleting effects of peace. "To think that this
was an infantry officer in 1914. Peace ruins people." Giraudoux fares
no better in Drieu's journal. His novels and theater are dismissed as
specimens of the rhetorical ideals responsible for producing a literature
as unrelated to things of the world as Fabergé's confections or the
book "about nothing" that Flaubert dreamed of writing. He was born
to flourish in a Republic of effete mandarins. "Giraudoux regards the
events, the facts of life, as mere pretexts for deploying his system of
images and metaphors, which is a closed, immutable system." Had
anything changed, he might have asked, since the Franco-Prussian
catastrophe of 1870–71 when Ernest Renan declared that France's
malady was its need to speechify?

Running through Drieu's essays and fiction, like a dark thread without which the entire fabric would unravel, is the theme of decadence.
Early in life—though too late to witness the rise and fall of General
Boulanger—he fastened on to the idea that a hundred years of bourgeois dominance had unmanned the nation and that France had never
regained its virility after Waterloo. This perspective led him to invert
the saga of progress recited by many nineteenth-century historians

---

* Bourdet had been appointed to the directorship during the left-wing coalition called
the Front Populaire by Jean Zay, minister of education and fine arts, and Premier Léon
Blum. Both were Jewish and detested for that reason, among others. Zay—founder of the
Cannes film festival—was assassinated by Vichy militia in 1944. Blum was caught by the
Germans and sent to Buchenwald.
   Giraudoux entered the foreign service before World War I and resumed his career
afterward. He and Drieu could have met during the war, as both fought in the disastrous
Dardanelles campaign.

and statesmen. To Adolphe Thiers, for example, history was a dynastic ladder. "The father was a peasant, a factory worker, a merchant sailor," he wrote in *On Property*. "The son, assuming that a father was diligent and frugal, will be a farmer, a manufacturer, a ship's captain. The grandson will be a banker, a notary, a doctor, a lawyer, a prime minister perhaps. Thus do the generations rise, one above the other."* Where Thiers saw a pageant of the middle class ascending, Drieu La Rochelle saw a fall from heroic heights to the lowland of mercenaries shuffling behind the golden calf.

This was certainly the way he viewed the procession of generations in his own family. "La Rochelle" somehow attached itself to the patronymic "Drieu" in the 1790s, as a nom de guerre distinguishing Pierre's great-grandfather Jacques (who was Norman) from other soldiers named Drieu.† Jacques Drieu La Rochelle spent twenty-three years in uniform fighting first for the revolutionary government against the combined monarchies of Europe, then under Napoleon in many campaigns, but remained still vigorous enough, after losing a leg, to father three children. His son, Jacques *fils,* illustrated Thiers's paradigm of upward mobility. The owner of pharmacies in Avranches and Coutances, he thrived, professed political opinions that inspired a conservative government to appoint him justice of the peace, and, like the village pharmacist in *Madame Bovary,* might have been awarded the Legion of Honor if France hadn't taken a sharp turn to the left in the late 1870s.‡ Financial disaster followed hard upon political disappointment when an investment bank called the Union Générale crashed. To lure investors torn between piety and greed, its director, Eugène Bontoux, had presented himself as a Catholic knight joining battle with Jewish financial interests. Victims—among them Jacques fils—tended to cast blame for the crash not on Bontoux the speculator but on Rothschild the omnipotent.

True to Thiers's vision of bourgeois advancement, Jacques, despite

---

* Thiers rose very high indeed, first entering Paris as an obscure lawyer from Marseille, marrying into great wealth, playing a key role in the Revolution of 1830, attaining the premiership and, several decades later, the presidency of the Republic before exiting to occupy, offstage, the largest mausoleum in Père-Lachaise Cemetery.

† In fact, Jacques came from a village near Coutances in Normandy, not from the Atlantic seaport of La Rochelle.

‡ It will be recalled that Barrès's grandfather Charles Luxer was also a rich pharmacist.

his reverses, succeeded in putting his son Emmanuel through law school. It soon became apparent that Emmanuel, Pierre's father, was not cut out for the practice of law or for any other form of gainful employment; but the law degree, his good looks, and his fancy name served him well in the pursuit of dowered middle-class women. He married a lovely blonde named Eugénie Lefèvre in 1891. They settled near her parents in the neighborhood of the Gare du Nord. Their son and only child was born in 1893.

Recalling his childhood, which he did obsessively, Pierre Drieu La Rochelle pictured himself in somewhat the same way that Proust describes Marcel in *Du Côté de chez Swann,* as a delicately strung boy whose tears never prevented his beloved mother and remote father from abandoning him for nights on the town. Their neglect increased when Eugénie came to the realization that her husband was a philanderer looting her dowry to support a mistress and scrounging off Monsieur Lefèvre, who paid his son-in-law's debts lest the family lose face. Discord shattered the household. Pierre was seven or eight and the meek observer of fierce quarrels.

His salvation was the work of his maternal grandparents, Marie and Eugène, who regularly took him under their wing and as far as possible made up for the inconstancy of Eugénie and Emmanuel. Life with the Lefèvres had starch in it. The day proceeded according to plan. He and his grandmother—a robust, spirited lady—took long walks. They all ate together when his grandfather, a successful architect, returned from work, and after dinner they disposed themselves in the parlor for Madame Lefèvre's reading of tales by Jules Verne, Gustave Aimard, or Louis Boussenard. They took vacations in a rented villa every summer. Grandmother bought Pierre his first books. Under her tutelage and in a cosseted environment, the child who felt irrelevant at home was encouraged to adopt models of success, derring-do, and glory. "She counted on me to compensate her for her disappointments," Drieu later wrote in *L'État Civil.*

> Her instruction ran counter to that of the entire family. She spoke only of vigor and audacity; she warned me about being forced to bow and scrape if I didn't command respect physically. My least exertion would suffice to conquer men. Actually, she was quite ignorant of the world she shunned. In that milieu unfavorable to exalted fantasies, her élan dissolved into words. The same illness she scorned in others afflicted

her. She salted our walks with bellicose maxims, but if I happened to step a foot off the beaten path she would shriek, and call me back, the better to resume her dream of my adventurous future.

Having rebelled against her freethinking father by embracing religion and royalism, Marie managed to reconcile her heroic enthusiasms with her piety. But little devotion was expected of Pierre. If there were illustrated Bible stories in the house, images of the revolutionary wars and Napoleon's campaigns crowded them out. At home as well. "How often I sobbed over Raffet's somber lithograph of the last muster of Napoleon's Guard. . . . [Napoleon] was the only God I knew, the only God I saw with my own eyes." At the World's Fair of 1900, those young eyes would have traveled from the Grand Palais across the newly built Alexandre III Bridge to the resplendent dome of the Invalides, housing Napoleon's tomb. It was the centerpiece of the exposition.

Still, the church loomed large in Pierre's world, not so much a spiritual force as a political actor embroiled in the Dreyfus Affair. And it impressed itself upon him when the family moved to the fashionable west end of Paris, the Parc Monceau neighborhood, with its dense population of affluent *mondains* (living among Jewish bankers such as the Ephrussis and Camondos), who traditionally enrolled their children in schools run by religious orders.

A left-wing government had expelled the Jesuits from France in 1880. After 1902, Émile Combes's anticlerical administration denied almost all religious orders the right to teach, by way of punishing them for the actively partisan role they had played during the affair. Many more schools closed. This comprehensive purge was fat in the fire raging ever since the publication, in 1898, of "J'accuse," Zola's exposure of the military plot to frame the Jewish captain. People made no secret of their allegiances. Madame Lefèvre despised Zola.

The conservative upper crust were not absolutely condemned to have their sons attend public lycées, for Catholic schools stayed open.* In 1901 or 1902, Pierre, at his grandparents' expense, started his formal education at one such parochial school, Sainte-Marie de Monceau.

Drieu, who later portrayed himself as a "melancholic and unsociable" child, rarely smiling, had few fond memories of his school days.

---

* The neighborhood lycée was Condorcet, whose alumni included Henri Bergson, Stéphane Mallarmé, Thadée Natanson, Eugène Labiche, and Marcel Proust.

With no siblings or friends, a distraught mother, a scoffing father, and a self that lay prostrate or stood on Napoleonic stilts, he was ill-prepared to engage other boys at eye level. Least of all rich boys. The daily spectacle of pampered heirs in Eton collars and Lavallière cravats being collected after school by governesses or chauffeurs exacerbated the feeling that he came from a tatty world of debts and financial bickering. The occasional invitation for an afternoon *goûter* at the town house of a privileged classmate provided another opportunity for him to feel defeated and small.

That he received invitations at all is not something one might deduce from an autobiographical novel published in 1921, according to which the first few years of school were a nightmare. "During recess, I never played games for fear of betraying my clumsiness," he wrote. "It was all I could do to stand up in class and answer a question. I had no chums. I was ignored." Better ignored than noticed: fellow students looked past him unless some aberration of dress or manner made him an object of mockery. "My mother had bought me a red muffler. The color delighted me and I was proud of it. I arrive at school one day. A scamp points at me. I immediately shrink, capitulate to his judgment. At the behest of that little finger, which mechanically reacts to anything singular, like a railroad signal flashing danger, I conclude that the muffler is ugly, that its very smartness speaks to the unsightliness of my person. . . . I was miserable, repudiating myself, envying those happy children for being all alike and wallowing in their common certitude."

In 1905, at twelve, Drieu's long experience of solitude in a ménage à trois ended with the birth of his brother, Jean. The belated arrival, coinciding as it did with the onset of puberty, resulted in a radical change of demeanor. Drieu was reborn a brilliant student; his excellence inside the classroom served him well outside, where, by his own account, he manipulated school toughs with the verbal adroitness of a demagogue. Unlike the typical "brain," he exploited his intellectual prestige to become a pack leader, delighting in the power of self-invention. He who was slighted by his father now found that he could prevail upon others to follow him.

Not that he beguiled everyone, or felt any less a fraud for all the success of his ruses. Among his schoolmates were nonbelievers whose skepticism affected him more deeply than the credulousness of his clique. "There were two good students who always remained in a corner of the courtyard; they disdained the rowdiness," he wrote in *L'État Civil.*

They walked to and fro with their hands clasped behind their backs, sagaciously discussing their homework, telling each other stories, happy when the bell rang. They carried crosses. They were serenely self-possessed. From their corner they watched us frolic, shout, fight. We were obviously seen as vulgar jackanapes. . . . Despite my furious participation in the game, I was sensitive to their judgment. I didn't find it unjust. My self-allegiance was never complete enough to make me side with one or another of my personae. Friends and enemies alike always found me ready to betray myself. I suspected that the secret drama of my weakness was exposed. They realized that my exertions produced only a parody of strength.

After imploring the two solemn spectators to abandon their corner and join the fray, he and his comrades beat them up.

Drieu entered adolescence an irrepressible scamp, taunting teachers, talking dirty, flirting with girls, stalking women, and generally applying his talent to mischievous ends. Class uprisings were his tonic. Imbued with a sensation of "common strength," he invited the punishments—all short of expulsion—that Sainte-Marie de Monceau reserved for a brilliant bad boy.

At fifteen, Drieu organized himself differently. He turned into a serious reader, but without disavowing the upstart he had been. His literary and philosophical predilections conformed to his antic self, like a rich canvas stretched over a primitive frame. While still assigning people to categories according to their perceived strength or weakness, he found his worldview fleshed out in the works of Barrès and Nietzsche. *Thus Spake Zarathustra* (which his mother innocently agreed to buy for him) was a revelation. The words seemed to flow from his own pen even before he understood them, he wrote. And *Beyond Good and Evil,* where Nietzsche describes parliamentary government as embodying the virtues of the herd ("public spirit, benevolence, consideration, industriousness, moderation, modesty, indulgence, pity") and the higher happiness attained by "herd men" under a Napoleon, ensured young Drieu's affinity to the philosopher. "Energy" and "life affirmation" entered his vocabulary in tandem with "decadence" and "degeneration." During his penultimate year at Sainte-Marie de Monceau he also read Descartes, Schopenhauer, Hegel, Schelling, Fichte, Bergson, Hartmann, William James, the English neo-Hegelians, Darwin, and Spencer, burning the candle in a frenzy of lucubration. His *carnets,* which contain minute observations about himself, reflect the vexed soul of a hero worshipper bound up with a nihilist, or of an apostle of energy shackled to a boy "half in love with easeful death." Drieu no longer attended mass, despite appeals from his mother, who prayed for him at her bedside every night.

In 1908, Madame Lefèvre offered her fifteen-year-old grandson a summer abroad, with a clergyman's family at Shrewsbury, England (home of the boys' school immortalized by Samuel Butler in *The Way of All Flesh* as Roughborough). Drieu later called it a "pilgrimage," as if to say, in the spirit of Proust visiting Ruskin's Amiens, that he was visiting his spiritual home. Ultimately, however, the English experience may have had less to do with art or literature than with the construction of an identity that played well in snobbish circles on the Right Bank, where Anglophilia was endemic, and girded him against subversion from within. Tormented by feelings of inferiority, the tall, blond, blue-eyed Drieu managed to reconcile his Napoleonatry with the conviction that he had discovered the truth of his "Nordic" soul among Anglo-Saxons. And Oxford during the first or second of his two sojourns in England was where that truth fully revealed itself. "There, something gripped me," he wrote. "At first, it all seemed to be of a grandeur I couldn't have guessed from anything in my country. Its architecture was not as sublime as ours, but it had the singular virtue of accommodating modern times. The city honored the mind and body as sufficient wealth. A decorous fraternity united men and women. I was filled with revulsion and discouragement just thinking that I would soon have to return to Paris and study at the Sorbonne, which looked like a new suburban town hall, paltry, anonymous, exposed to all manner of noxious exhalations, lost amidst the monstrous concerns of a metropolis, and rub elbows with disheveled adolescents, soiled by their gross puberty, in whom youth rears like a wild horse because they lack the strength to harness it." When, in due course, he entered college, he might have been mistaken for a young English gentleman schooled bilingually in derision. He parted his hair down the middle, polished his shoes to a high shine, and wore tweeds (his lifelong uniform). "Strength" was now associated in his mind with sport and aristocratic self-restraint. That the Battle of Waterloo had been won on the playing fields of Eton impressed him as proverbial wisdom. Kipling's *Jungle Book* and Carlyle's *On Heroes, Hero-Worship, and the Heroic in History* joined Barrès's *Le Culte du Moi* and D'Annunzio's *The Flame of Life* in his syllabus of canonical texts. Wondering where to turn after Sainte-Marie de Monceau, Drieu enrolled in three schools: the École de Droit for law, the École Libre des Sciences Politiques (known as "Sciences Po") for foreign service, and the Sorbonne for a degree in English. His dilemma did not set him apart from other students slouching toward professional life. They, too, were daunted by the prospect of endless hours in the Palais de Justice, of an assignment to some remote consular post or exile to a provincial lycée. What did set him apart at Sciences Po were his modest circumstances.* André Jéramec, for example, with whom Drieu formed a close friendship, had all his needs attended to by seven servants in a vast apartment on the Boulevard Malesherbes. His father, Édouard, a graduate of the École Polytechnique, who had important political connections, presided over several companies, one of which monopolized Paris's hackney cabs. Not until they entered high school did André and his sister, Colette, learn that their parents were Jews who had never converted but had raised them as Catholics. This would not dissuade Drieu from marrying Colette during the war. Nor would it temper his anti-Semitism in later years.†

Events were drawing a curtain over the future. By 1913 Drieu had cast aside the Sorbonne and become a casual presence at law school. He immersed himself in history, without knowing to what practical purpose he could put it or whether history itself had run its course. He read Schopenhauer, argued that European civilization was spent, and demonstrated its decline by contracting gonorrhea in the brothels he patronized on his meager allowance. Nothing seemed certain or stable. In January 1913, during his last semester at Sciences Po, a creditor sued Drieu's profligate father. Word of it spread, resulting in bankruptcy and social disgrace.

One disaster paved the way for another. Drieu, who was expected to graduate near the top of his class, failed every part of his degree

---

* The Ministry of Foreign Affairs attracted children of the haute bourgeoisie and drew upon the École Libre des Sciences Politiques.

† His prewar notebook contains a prophecy: "There are two beings I shall spend my life trying to comprehend: woman and the Jew."

examination. No one wondered whether the fiasco had something to do with fear of success; but a fear of success, or of the path that success prescribed, was certainly implicated in the emotional havoc wrought by his father's bankruptcy. How could he have failed to anticipate that examiners would frown at essays phrased in the language of his cherished philosophers? He was reprimanded for distorting history to prove a theory—for spurning the etiquette of responsible scholarship and making prophetic assertions. "I revealed with brutal candor the strange, unusual knowledge I had acquired in my roving through the realm of unorthodox ideas," he wrote years later. "They wanted to punish the dangerous disorder of my mind and also bar me from a diplomatic career, which was wise, since my family was ruined, and . . . my timidity did not allow me to master feelings of social inferiority."

Suicide crossed his mind, as it would often again. Instead of throwing himself into the Seine, he decided to report for military service. André Jéramec, with whose family Drieu spent the summer at Pougues-les-Eaux, in Burgundy, joined him. In November 1913 they resigned from civilian life at the Pépinière casern near the Gare Saint-Lazare. The National Assembly had recently passed a law requiring conscripts to serve for three years. Drieu would serve more than five, André Jéramec less than one.

Drieu had a pneumatic history of pumping himself up and going flat. War favored bipolar extremes. On August 3, two days after general mobilization, he was a compassionate witness to the spectacle of a fellow soldier—a Breton peasant who spoke broken French—raging against the potentates who had torn him from his land and smashing his rifle. Three days later he was crossing Paris in a great tide of soldiers flowing from barracks all over the city and converging at the Gare du Nord. He carried *Thus Spake Zarathustra* in his knapsack.

Nietzsche remained in his knapsack during the bloody confrontation with Germans at Charleroi, where the French general staff, surprised by enemy troops wheeling into northeastern France through neutral Belgium, improvised a doomed defense. Drieu's regiment had nothing but knapsacks for protection and lay under them like tortoises in their shells as German machine-gun fire raked the fields of Flanders. When at last French artillery replied, a lieutenant ordered his men to charge. "I have known two or three formidable, unforgettable moments," Drieu wrote to a friend from a hospital bed.

At Charleroi, I heard a voice shout: forward, *bayonets fixed*! I was beside myself, bursting with passion. I adored my lieutenant, I would have liked to kiss the syphilitic corporal who opened his eyes (sleepy from the ignoble somnolence of peace) to the intoxicating call of glory. And the bugles. There were bugles. The trump of war sounded in my blood. At that moment, I belonged body and soul to my race charging through the centuries . . . toward the eternal idol of Power, of Grandeur. Then, afterward, childlike wails rising from the piles of dead and dying.

One of the innumerable corpses was André Jéramec, who disappeared on August 23, 1914. Drieu lost several more friends at Charleroi. He himself fell that day with shrapnel in his neck.

He wrote the above to a friend while recuperating from a second wound received two months later—farther south, at the front in Champagne, near Rheims, where, promoted to sergeant, he led a platoon over the top and across no-man's-land to the German trenches. But did he in fact qualify as a leader? he wondered anxiously. In one account of the battle he portrays himself as the young hero whose Gallic exuberance inspires older men under his command: "Only leaders count. A platoon is a troupe of tearful children." Elsewhere he confesses to having quailed before the enemy, as if fear were incompatible with courage under fire: "I too felt a wretched weakness inside; I wept for myself, I wished I had no pride, no remorse, nothing of the instinctual drive that illustrates our old History."*

In any event, the tedious vigils interrupted by episodes of mortal combat and followed by long convalescences tested his enthusiasm for war. After more than a year of military life, he had had enough of shuffling between muddy trenches and hospitals in which he lacked the time and privacy to make literary sense of his experience. His brain could not yet comply with the fantasy of holding a gun and a pen by turns, of being a soldier as Stendhal was a diplomat and Barrès a politician. It found more compelling alternatives in mania and depression. But things would change. In 1915, he began to write poems.

The war dragged on, transporting him to other hells. When men were asked to volunteer for service in the Dardanelles, Drieu joined

---

* It caused him no apparent discomfort to identify his instinctual drive as French, to have Nietzsche as his vade mecum, and to wish that he could continue the war in the stylish uniform of a British officer.

a polyglot regiment that shipped out from Marseille. By the time he returned, several months later, to a hospital at Toulon, his clinical profile included scabies, syphilis, and severe dysentery. He was alive, but all skin and bones after dawdling with the French force on Lemnos, a short hop across the Aegean from Gallipoli, where British and Australian troops were being slaughtered. For him, the ill-conceived campaign had been a dismal parody of the "voyage en Orient" ritually undertaken by nineteenth-century writers fleeing bourgeois Europe.* He wrote many letters to Colette Jéramec but later claimed to have been incommunicado. "No more family, no more worries about profession or money," he wrote in Le Voyage des Dardanelles. "No more vanity, no more future. If I have the courage to be unknown, I will push anonymity to the limit. . . . I was lost in the chaos, losing myself, drunk on perdition. Forgotten was my little bourgeois person."

He was not forgotten by the army, which needed everyone who could still stand (of whom only two came from his original regiment, he and the bugler) to man the Verdun fortifications. Frozen from a six-hour march, he arrived at the Thiaumont redoubt on February 21, 1916. German artillery had already begun a thunderous bombardment, lofting one hundred thousand shells across the Meuse River. On the third day one exploded near enough to render him temporarily deaf and to paralyze his right arm, which recovered movement after several operations on the ulnar nerve but never full feeling or its normal length. He was evacuated to a hospital at Bar-le-Duc, in Lorraine.

Wounds and illness suffered on four fronts earned him an exemption from duty at a fifth. He was thus vouchsafed the leisure to write about war, which he did in verse. Although a longing for self-extinction would always shadow Drieu, it did not prevent him, once reassigned to administrative duty, from submitting a poem to the editor of an important avant-garde literary magazine, Sic. More poems followed, seventeen all told, which found their way, through influential friends, to the desk of Gaston Gallimard, who agreed to publish them in a small edition under the title Interrogation (at the author's expense). The military authorities, who may have been satisfied that Drieu's belligerence compensated for expressions of fraternity with Germans entombed in trenches just as he was, allowed a small edition to pass through censorship. That Drieu glorified peace in the language of war undoubtedly worked to his advantage.

---

* Chateaubriand, Lamartine, Gautier, Flaubert, and Rimbaud, among many others.

Et nous saurons faire une Paix comme nous avons
Mené la Guerre.
Nous brandirons nos grues d'acier.
Avec du ciment armé nous dresserons le monument
*De notre Force.**

The prospect of turning swords against bourgeois institutions had greater appeal than the thought of beating them into plowshares. When, in later years, he came to embrace Fascism, *la force* would enjoy the same prominence in his political screed as *l'énergie* in Maurice Barrès's. All it needed in 1917 was a dogma befitting its shrines. Charleroi, Rheims, the Dardanelles, Verdun: those names resonated through Drieu like a drumbeat in his own savage procession. They spoke to a lifelong enchantment with death and martyrdom. "Violent death is the foundation of civilization, of the social contract, of all pacts," he wrote shortly after the war. "It is the only certitude. Among men, nothing is certain unless, at the end of their common undertaking, they are sure that they will risk death for whatever binds them, be it glory, lucre, love, despair, or one another."† A letter to Colette Jéramec dated July 7, 1918, sent her to Rupert Brooke's sonnet "Now, God be thanked who has matched us with His Hour," declaring that it captured the spirit of *Interrogation:*

> Now, God be thanked who has matched us with His Hour
> And caught our youth, and wakened us from sleeping
> With hand made sure, clear eye, and sharpened power,
> To turn, as swimmers into cleanness leaping,
> Glad from a world grown old and cold and weary,
> Leave the sick hearts that honor could not move,
> And half-men, with their dirty songs and dreary,
> And all the little emptiness of love!

---

* "And we shall make Peace as we made War. We shall wield our steel cranes. With reinforced concrete we shall raise the monument of our Strength." Elsewhere he described "*la force*" as "mother of all things"—"mère des choses."

† After the death of André Jéramec in 1914, Drieu wrote to Colette: "Those who have endured the suffering of months on the battlefield have often longed for death and regretted that they hadn't found it during the first engagement. . . . It helps to plunge into the swelling tide of one's race. I want to think about nothing but my minuscule place in the immense sacrifice we must make at the altar of our homeland to fend off the threat of annihilation."

After this, she could not have been surprised to learn that he detested Henri Barbusse's celebrated antiwar novel *Le Feu*. "I'm becoming very reactionary," he wrote. So long as France's eastern fields were killing fields, life had a solemnity utterly lacking in the goals and conventions of peacetime. War was a remedy for vapid dailiness.

And what of "all the little emptiness of love"? The battlefield had a Manichaean simplicity that he missed on the domestic front, where nothing was simple in his relationship with Colette, whom he had been courting after a fashion since 1913. The relationship, which led to their foredoomed marriage in 1917, was a story of ghosts in two haunted families. In 1884 Colette's mother, Gabrielle, had given birth to a son named Pierre, who promised to grow up tall and blond but died of meningitis at age four. With great difficulty, Gabrielle produced two more children, André in 1893 and Colette in 1896. Small, dark, and Semitic-looking, they embodied everything the would-be Aryan despised in herself and were treated accordingly. Gabrielle, who became a neurotic invalid, never ceased reminding her children of their ineptitude and physical disgrace.

If Colette saw in Drieu the handsome, blond brother idealized by her mother, Drieu may have succumbed to the opportunity of recapitulating his parents' *mésalliance*. Drieu would later write that he loved Colette for three months, platonically, during the summer of 1913 at Pougues-les-Eaux. That the Jéramecs considered a young man bearing the double stigma of academic failure and paternal bankruptcy ineligible for Colette's dowry only encouraged the romance. It was the summer before Drieu and André donned uniforms. The more deeply Colette fell in love, the more Drieu fought shy of it, ultimately leaving her, when war broke out, with nothing to embrace but a blond mirage. "Don't go crazy, I beg of you," he wrote to her by pneumatic dispatch on August 1, 1914. "Great events ask for dignity. Tell no one about us. All my ardor is reserved for war. Here at last is the test that will clarify my future for me. But we can no longer talk about love."

While war answered Drieu's dream of redemption, unrequited love gave wings to Colette's need to prove her capacity for devotion, especially after her brother's death. Neither could stop tormenting and consoling the other. When he was wounded, she arranged special medical care through the family's connection with Alexandre Millerand, minister of war. When he informed her that he had contracted syphilis, she scoffed at the idea that something so insignificant could come between them. "What is that, next to our affection? Pierre, how could you imagine for a second that I would flee? On the contrary, why not marry now? I would be so happy to live with you as brother and sister. Anyway, I must tell you, since it will perhaps soothe you, that I can't have children."* At his urging she read *Les Nourritures Terrestres,* André Gide's impeachment of the family and celebration of sensual freedom. She protested that she was indebted to Drieu for every bit of "beauty, goodness, and intelligence" in her soul.

Drieu could neither embrace Colette nor relinquish his hold over her. Families were the bane of his existence, but it weighed upon his conscience—it may even have outweighed his venality—that with the suicide of her depressed, grief-stricken father in December 1916, she desperately needed a man to lean on. Colette, in turn, would later claim that she married Drieu to save him from his demons. What seems certain is that they married each other's mortification when they wed in a ceremony at the town hall of the 17th arrondissement in August 1917. His parents did not attend. Drieu took leave from the desk job he had been given at army headquarters in Paris after his third injury, and the couple embarked on their *mariage blanc* (for such it appears to have been) in a sleeping car bound for the Côte d'Azur. Colette settled a small fortune on Drieu.†

They had no sooner returned to Paris than Drieu betrayed her with the forty-year-old wife of the famous actor-director Charles Dullin. It was his first passionate affair, he wrote—as passionate as his marriage was not, and the more so for Marcelle Dullin resembling his mother. However, the affair provided insufficient shelter from marriage, and in November 1917 he applied for service at the front, despite his feeble arm. The army assigned him to an American division in the Vosges Mountains as an interpreter. There he wrote poems about the strength and vitality of "soldiers from beyond the sea" while complaining to Colette about the difficulty of putting words on paper. "I am appalled by my past slothfulness, by all that I must learn. I don't know how to write. At the moment I am locked in a bitter struggle with my sentences. But the difficulty is passionately absorbing." He asked her to send him books by Socialist and monarchist writers.

---

* Colette bore two children in the 1930s.

† Some say 500,000 francs, or approximately $100,000 in 1917—the equivalent of almost $2 million in 2011; others say several hundred thousand dollars.

Pierre Drieu La Rochelle before World War I, arms folded, with André Jéramec,
his school friend, and André's sister, Colette, the uppermost figure, whom Drieu
married in 1917.

In 1918 the American division moved to Verdun, where Drieu spent
the last months of the war. He was discharged in March 1919.

The ornate apartment Colette and Drieu occupied after the war had
enough rooms in it for two people hiding from each other, and it was,
indeed, more often a scene of mutual evasion than of relentless mat-
rimonial conflict. But it was also hospitable to the larger world. Far
from shunning that world in Drieu's absence, Colette had enrolled in
medical school, almost completed work for the degree, and struck up
friendships with fellow students, one of whom, Louis Aragon, another
beau parleur, became Drieu's boon companion. She held receptions for
well-known poets, high-ranking diplomats, and publishers (Gaston
Gallimard and Bernard Grasset, who shared the honor of recogniz-
ing Proust's genius), during which Drieu, the presumed beneficiary
of her social exertions, was said to behave like an uninvited guest,

gazing abstractedly out the window. He felt at home nowhere but felt less marooned in the salon of Edmée de La Rochefoucauld, a young woman of letters and future suffragette as well as the bearer of an ancient title, or at Adrienne Monnier's bookstore on the Rue de l'Odéon, La Maison des Amis des Livres, chatting with Aragon, Breton, and Soupault.* There were serious conversations with a Communist friend from Sciences Po, Raymond Lefebvre, who never had time to convert him: on his way back from the Soviet Union in 1920, returning via Murmansk to elude the White Russian blockade, his boat disappeared.

In 1919, Drieu's fellow poets could think about little else but a review they were launching with help from Adrienne Monnier. They gave it an ambiguous title, *Littérature,* intending to echo the antiphrasis in Paul Verlaine's poem "Art Poétique," where "literature" signifies everything that true poetry is not (*"et tout le reste est littérature"*) or to trick subscribers in much the same way that the Dada movement lured the credulous public to its events with punning advertisements or false news.

Their kindred spirits were Arthur Rimbaud and Isidore Ducasse (Lautréamont) rather than Verlaine. Several years earlier, Breton had cocked a snook at aesthetic propriety in language reminiscent of Rimbaud's *Une Saison en Enfer.* "We are drawn to ageless, undreamt of, unimaginable little objects," he wrote, "the museum of a child raised in the wild, curios from insane asylums, . . . broken mechanical toys, steam organs." They loved what soon came to be known as "found objects"—objects valued for having no value, or for being prized by children and madmen, for being innocent of the culture that butchered millions while patenting the useful and insuring the beautiful. Poetry and art were to be found in trash cans and in the flea market rather than museums. "In old shop signs, in idiotic paintings, in the backdrops of circus performers," Rimbaud would have added.

But the ambiguity of *"littérature"* served a purpose. The journal's creators dared not dress in flaming red lest the well-bred modernists they needed to vouch for the seriousness of their enterprise take fright.

---

* Her bookstore was an international gathering place for writers, as was the review she launched in 1924, *Le Navire d'Argent.* She befriended and mentored Sylvia Beach, the young American expatriate who opened Shakespeare & Co. down the block and published James Joyce's *Ulysses* when no one else would. Drieu may have met Joyce's translator, Valéry Larbaud, at one bookstore or the other.

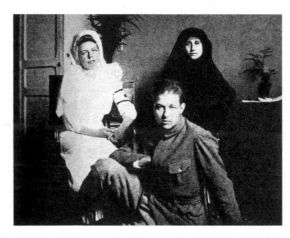

Pierre Drieu La Rochelle recovering from wounds suffered at Verdun. Dressed in black is Colette Jéramec.

Thus, André Gide, Léon-Paul Fargue, and Paul Valéry mingled with Aragon, Breton, and Drieu in the inaugural issue, conferring upon *Littérature* the imprimatur of a fin-de-siècle literary vanguard. Marcel Proust, who had just won the Goncourt Prize for *À l'Ombre des Jeunes Filles en Fleurs* and never abbreviated his opinions, wrote a twelve-page compliment. They were seen as heirs. Before them loomed the specter of careers.

Poetry and art were also to be found at the cinema, where the threesome of Breton, Aragon, and Soupault, with Drieu tagging along, found refuge from the thraldom of high culture in the exploits of a wildly popular villain named Fantômas. Exalted as "Master of Fright," "The Torturer," and "The Emperor of Crime," Fantômas, whose diabolical disguises match his ruthlessness, assumed the mantle of Balzac's Vautrin, of Maturin's Melmoth, of Byron's Manfred, of Ponson du Terrail's Rocambole, and, above all, of Lautréamont's Maldoror. At war with bourgeois mores, the future Surrealists fancied themselves denizens of the underworld before renaming it the unconscious. Crime prefigured nature. One act of terror would blow away the flimsy fortifications of a rational order.*

---

* Paris's monuments were subjected to terroristic revision in a game the Surrealists recorded for posterity. They proposed, for example, to cut the Panthéon in two and pull the halves one inch apart.

They also found refuge from high culture in the company of their cinematic heroines. "An entire generation's idea of the world was formed in the cinema and one film especially summed it up, a serial," Aragon wrote. "The young fell head over heels in love with Musidora, in *The Vampires*"—a hypnotized vamp who kills at the bidding of her lover. Musidora had a serious rival for their affections in Pearl White, the mindless, death-defying heroine of *The Perils of Pauline*.

That Surrealism belonged to the larger family of Romantic offspring was evident in its prenatal stage. The Romantic sensibility flourished after the bloodletting of World War I, as it had a hundred years earlier in the aftermath of the Revolution and the Napoleonic campaigns. With its penchant for the bizarre and the surprising, its contempt for bourgeois morality, its black humor, its glorification of evil genius, its language of rebirth, its messianism, its explorations of the erotic at the margin of death, the postwar literary generation envisaged a new human condition and succumbed to the ravages of a twentieth-century *mal de siècle.**

Breton and Aragon were chafing at their public sedateness when a small man named Tristan Tzara landed in their midst, like an imp from Pandemonium, and sparked the explosion of Dada in Paris. Born Samuel Rosenstock in Romania, Tzara had entered the University of Zurich during the war to study philosophy and found philosophy at a café among young habitués—mostly self-exiled Germans dodging military service or invalided out of the army—who spawned the Dada movement. Tzara made a name for himself beyond Zurich as the editor of reviews smuggled west across the battle line. "Dada means nothing," he wrote in a manifesto declaring war on the warring nations.

It was born of a need for independence, of distrust of the community. Those who belong to us retain their freedom. We acknowledge no theory. We have had enough of cubist and futurist academies, of laboratories of formal ideas. . . . We are spirits drunk on energy; we thrust pitchforks into flab.

The only literature Dada recognized, he continued, was the "necessary" utterance of "supreme egoism" leaping off the page in mixed

---

* In *Hope Against Hope,* Nadezhda Mandelstam recalls that "new" was used obsessively in daily conversation after the Revolution.

typeface, like the outrageous *blagues* of the great nineteenth-century actor Frédérick Lemaître, who inspired Daumier's Robert Macaire drawings.

> I tell you: there is no beginning and we do not tremble, we aren't sentimental. An angry wind, we shred the laundry of clouds and of prayers and prepare the great spectacle of disaster, fire, decomposition. Let us prepare to suppress mourning and replace tears with sirens blaring from one continent to another.

Reason and the belief that things can be explained rationally are the police force of authority. "Thought is a fine thing for philosophy," Tzara continued, "but it is relative. Psychoanalysis is a dangerous malady; it puts to sleep the anti-real penchants of man and systematizes the bourgeoisie. . . . I am against systems, the most acceptable system being that which has no principle." Morality was another weapon the abolition of which belonged to the Dada agenda.

> Morality will wither like every poisonous weed planted by the intelligence. . . . Let every man shout: there is a great destructive, negative project to be accomplished. Sweep everything clean. The selfhood of the individual will affirm itself after a world left to the devices of bandits, who destroy one another and destroy the centuries, is in shambles. Without goal or design, without organization: untamable madness, decomposition.

Dada, he concluded, encompasses a multitude of revulsions: for the family, for charity, for pity, for memory, for hierarchy and "social equation," for logic, for prophets, for the future. Like movements as far to the right of it as the mind could reach, it celebrated raw energy.

In January 1920, Breton, Aragon, and Soupault met Tzara at the apartment of the Franco-Spanish painter Francis Picabia, whose magazine *391* (published during the war in Barcelona, where French refugees found asylum) allied itself loosely with Tzara's six-page journal, *Dadaphone.** Old hands at nihilistic buffoonery, Tzara and Picabia prepared Dada's debut in Paris. Breton and Aragon rented a hall called

---

* Picabia, who had visited New York in 1913 to attend the Armory Show and had been given a solo exhibition by Alfred Stieglitz, named his journal after Gallery 291.

Opening of the Max Ernst exhibition at the Au Sans Pareil bookstore in May 1921. On top of the ladder is Philippe Soupault, holding an inverted Jacques Rigaut, who later served as the model for the drug-addicted, suicidal hero of Drieu's novel *Le Feu Follet*. Breton is on the right.

the Palais des Fêtes and engaged several actor friends to read Dada texts. Picabia and Tzara organized the program.

The Palais des Fêtes, on Rue Saint-Denis, was far removed from Left Bank literary circles. Flanked by two cinemas where Breton and Aragon had watched Fantômas, *Les Vampires*, and Chaplin films, the hall had been chosen for prankish and sentimental reasons. Located in a commercial neighborhood, it attracted merchants, who came hoping to learn more about France's financial crisis, for the event had been advertised in newspapers as a symposium entitled "La Crise du Change." *"Change"* could be understood to mean either "currency" or cultural and social change. The program opened with a lecture on Apollinaire. Puzzled jewelers and wigmakers who sat it out left soon afterward, as the evening descended from serious poetry to antics of the kind that had led to Tzara's arrest in Zurich. Drieu was present. He and Jean Cocteau read poems by Max Jacob and Pierre Reverdy before Breton came onstage with a canvas of Picabia's scrawls conspicuously entitled *L.H.O.O.Q.* The letters form, by their sounds, the sentence "Elle a chaud au cul."* Once it caught on, the audience—as much of it as remained—erupted, booing and stamping until a small orchestra calmed it down with the music of Satie.

The second act continued where the first had left off, but with no alloy of serious poetry and music. Preceded by a fanfare of rattles, Tzara announced that he would read his "latest work," which turned out to be a speech Léon Daudet had recently delivered to the National Assembly. Aragon and Breton drowned him out with bells, and members of the audience shouted, "Back to Zurich! To the gallows with him!" Juan Gris protested that he had been enlisted as a participant under false pretenses. He was not alone.

Other capers followed in quick succession. The May 1920 issue of *Littérature* carried thirty-two Dada manifestos, notifying subscribers and literary eminences who had originally sponsored it that it no longer operated within their understanding of literary modernism. On May 26, the Dada Festival was held in Paris's principal concert hall, the Salle Gaveau.

By then, the thirty-two manifestos notwithstanding, Tzara's French collaborators had already begun to distance themselves from him. "Every time a demonstration was foreseen—naturally by Tzara,

---

* "She has a hot ass."

A Dada tract, January 12, 1921, signed by Tristan Tzara, Max Ernst, Breton, Aragon, Man Ray, Francis Picabia, Paul Éluard, and Marcel Duchamp, among others. The title translates to "Dada moots everything. Dada knows everything. Dada spits everything out."

who never tired of them—Picabia would assemble us in his salon," wrote Breton, "[and] ask us, each in turn, to suggest ideas. The harvest became increasingly sparse." Dada continued fitfully. Tzara left Paris in July 1920 for the Balkans and returned in December, after a Dada Congress in Italy, to sabotage a lecture by Emilio Marinetti on tactilism. A concert of bruitist music met the same fate. Vacationing together in the Tyrol, Hans Arp, Max Ernst, and Tzara conceived a show called "Open Air Dada." In May 1921, Tzara reluctantly participated in Maurice Barrès's mock trial. Six months later, Picabia briefly distracted Paris from the very real trial of a serial killer with his painting *L'Oeil Cacodylate* at the Salon d'Automne (the *oeil cacodylate* being an eye surrounded by the comments and signatures of friends—like graffiti around a peephole inside a urinal, wrote one critic). Tzara broke with Picabia, or Picabia with Tzara, and, sooner or later, everybody with everybody else.

Drieu observed, as a supernumerary, the drama of large egos jos-

The Dada group assembled at the Church of Saint-Julien le Pauvre, staging one in a series of Dada "visits and excursions" to "places that really have no reason to exist."

tling for space at center stage of a Parisian sideshow. He followed where Aragon led, out of friendship or loneliness rather than conviction, and remained the fellow traveler when *Littérature,* having renounced Dada, found its true path in the practice of automatic writing.

He and Colette divorced in 1921, not bitterly. They became friends. Colette continued to socialize with their Surrealist acquaintances and practiced medicine.

CHAPTER 8

The Rapture of the Deep

On June 22, 1922, the *Almanach des Lettres Françaises et Étrangères* announced that *Littérature*, whose collaborators would thenceforth "devote themselves to Surrealism in poetry and life," had had its day. Two weeks later, Breton declared that Symbolism, Dadaism, and Cubism were also spent enthusiasms. He envisaged art as life-changing. Salvation lay in the unconscious, from which Surrealists proposed to "take dictation," like evangelical scribes at the mouth of an inner oracle.

Two years later, shortly before the publication of the movement's new journal, *La Révolution Surréaliste*, Breton issued a long manifesto in which Surrealism was defined as "psychic automatism in its pure state," or a method of freeing thought from the shackles of reason and letting it play innocently, without regard for morality and aesthetics. Its foundation, he wrote, is a belief in "the omnipotence of dream," which, in turn, sustains a belief in "the superior reality of certain forms of hitherto neglected associations."

Although Descartes was the last philosopher with whom Breton wished to be associated, his creed echoes the motto illustrated in Jan Weenix's famous portrait of the philosopher, *Mundus est fabula:* the world is a fable. In Breton's manifesto, the world is not so much a fable as it is our narration of it. Having declared in the manifesto that "man was given language to make Surrealist use of it," he took that thought one step further in *Point du Jour* by contending that "the mediocrity of our world" derives essentially from the way we use our power of speech. "What prevents me," he asked, "from muddling the order of words and thus dealing a blow to the wholly apparent existence of things?"

It was almost axiomatic among young poets of the postwar generation that Victor Hugo, who had made good his promise to put a red bonnet on the French dictionary, and Mallarmé, who proposed to give a "purer sense" to "the language of the tribe," needed radical heirs. Language had become the instrument and warden of the ruling social order. "This hubbub of cars and lorries, these districts housing merchandise or files rather than people, . . . these governments of shopkeepers and money-grubbing politicians, I want out; but no, we are forced to play the game," wrote Francis Ponge, a young poet who later signed Breton's "Second Manifesto." "Alas, this sordid regime speaks *from within ourselves,* for we have at our disposal no other

The cover of the first issue of *La Révolution Surréaliste,* December 1924.

words . . . than those prostituted from time immemorial by daily use in this squalid world."

How to conjure a new world in speaking it? was the question. Their revolt against the commonly understood significance of words, or against the word *as sign,* led Breton and his confrères to insist on the word's *materiality,* to view words as debris erupting from the unconscious and signifying nothing for being self-referential. Louis Aragon proclaimed that he sought the human equivalent of external things.

The paradox of hermetic transcendence was a collective quest. The new evangelists subscribed to Breton's fantasy that the mind in some altered state would no longer be aware of words but, rather, would press them out of itself, like a thing extruding things. When words themselves became objects impervious to logic, the rift between subject and object would vanish. In *Une Vague de Rêves,* one of the first essays about Surrealism and its experiments, Aragon recounts a magical moment when the group discovered that a written image could affect their senses, "shed its verbal aspect" and call into being phenomena they did not think it possible to create. The concrete is the ultimate moment of thought, and the state of concrete thought is poetry, he concluded. Ponge said something of the same thing more engagingly in his celebration of the snail, whose utterance, as he describes it, takes the form of dribble clotting, drying, and leaving a silvery wake: "It does not have many friends. Nor does it need any to assure its happiness. It cleaves so well to nature, revels so perfectly in its clasp; it is a friend of the ground, and kisses it with its whole body."* In the organism absolutely adequate to the earth, "awareness of" or "consciousness of" is otiose.

Ultimately, Surrealism's initiates might have chosen the snail as their emblem for its shell as well as its dribble—for its exquisite self-involvement as well as its organic trail. Breton wrote this about Picasso:

> The plastic instinct, raised here by an individual to the apogee of its development, draws upon the refusal, the negation of everything that may distract it from a sense of itself. With Picasso it is the sum of all these needs, these essays in disintegration, rendered with implacable

---

* Ponge began writing the prose poems, collected under the title *Le Parti Pris des Choses,* in 1924.

Surrealists, with Breton in the center and his wife, Simone, at the typewriter, taking dictation from Robert Desnos's unconscious. Desnos was reputed to have a special talent for entering self-induced trances. In the upper right-hand corner, craning his neck, is Giorgio de Chirico.

lucidity. . . . It [the plastic instinct] is, to suppose the impossible, the spider devoting its attention to the design and substance of its web's polygon more than to the fly; it is the migrating bird peering over its wing in full flight to look at what it has left behind, or the bird seeking to recover itself in the labyrinth of its own song.

The Surrealist poem was to answer the same ideal of a locked, reflexive universe in which language exists on its own terms ("words make love to one another," wrote Breton), conveying no feeling, no experience, no image felt, experienced, or imagined outside itself. It no longer derived from an intention or preconceived idea but, rather, sprang from pure chance. As the product of unconscious mayhem, it was purely necessary in a way that only things can presume to be. Hence Breton's doctrine of "objective chance": the ellipses, the absence of rhetorical connectives, the dislocated clichés, the unforeseen meeting of rationally unjuxtaposable words, or sometimes the loneliness of a single word drumming through the poem, pivoting on itself in puns or disintegrating into its syllables, form a material cryptogram of one's "mental matter"—not a transparent sign dissolving into significance but an irreducible thing. Surrealist gospel envisioned an objective order of concrete metaphors bearing an imprint of the poet's "true life" on their inner face, like a fossilized secret. It remained for him to find his secret within the order he created by chance.

Aragon—Drieu's close friend and Breton's most eloquent apostle—once told an audience of students in Madrid: "I am stranded at your ear." Stranded they all were, insofar as their ideal of creation had the poet looking out and seeing himself look in, or hearing his voice through his ears, like a listener. One is put in mind of André Malraux's comment in *The Voices of Silence* on his novel *La Condition Humaine*. "We know the yearning every man has for omnipotence and immortality," he wrote. "We know that his mind does not grasp itself the way it grasps the world, that each of us is, in his own eyes, a welter of monstrous dreams. I once told the story of a man who fails to recognize his own voice, freshly taped, because he is, for the first time, hearing it through his ears, no longer through his throat. And because our inner voice is conveyed to us through our throat alone, I called this book *The Human Condition*." What the Surrealists abhorred in the end was less the subversive influence of the bourgeoisie than their own human condition. Or perhaps both inseparably. Emerging from the bloody havoc wreaked by men who honored "*le clair esprit français,*" in a country blooming with monuments to the dead, they could not settle for less than the absolutes of omnipotence and immortality. The Great War fostered literary terror.

Equating mind and word in a substantive sense, Breton wished to short-circuit the world. Nowhere is his intention more explicitly stated than in the "Second Manifesto":

> Everything leads one to believe that there exists a certain vantage point of the mind from which life and death, the real and the imaginary, the past and the future, the communicable and the incommunicable, the high and the low cease to be perceived as opposites. One searches in vain for any other motive to Surrealist activity than the hope of determining this point. . . . It is clear . . . that Surrealism is not seriously interested in whatever is being produced next door under the pretext

of art, or of anti-art, of philosophy, or of anti-philosophy, in a word, in anything whose end is not the annihilation of being in a flash, interior and blind. . . . . What could those people who harbor some concern about the place they will occupy *in the world* expect to gain from the Surrealist experiment?

As in the text on Picasso, Breton draws an image of the self, divided in the phenomenal world but recoiling upon itself, thereby gaining the kind of absolute oneness inherent in matter, on the one hand, and divine vessels, on the other. At times the Surrealist would characterize words as matter materializing the self, like dreams of stone, at other times as a solvent dissolving the self (Breton's image of "soluble fish"). Like Baudelaire's private journal *My Heart Laid Bare,* which opens with the pronouncement "The evaporation and the condensation of the *SELF:* there you have it, in a nutshell," the "Surrealist Manifesto" could have been published with two illustrations on facing pages: Magritte's tableau of a petrified man seated at a petrified table within petrified walls, and a blank canvas on a blank page. Surrealist writings everywhere refer to an original unity of which man has been dispossessed but that he can regain in some new Creation, conceived alternately as a plenum and a void: the dreamer's mind being occluded by the hallucinatory object or being absolved of everything that furnishes a personal history. In one of Aragon's early works, a certain Baptiste Ajamais (who, according to the writer's key, is Breton) says, "Above all there is that joy of finding nothing within myself once I've closed my eyes. Nothing. I am empty. Outside nothing fixes onto my sight any longer."

Although Drieu spent much time with Louis Aragon—at music halls, in brothels, on long walks though the beautiful crescent of the Parc des Buttes-Chaumont, high above Paris, and, during summer holidays, at the Cyrano café near Breton's flat in Montmartre—his name mingled with the Surrealists' publicly only once, in a pamphlet they published, largely at his expense, after the death of Anatole France on October 12, 1924. It was entitled *Un Cadavre.*

Not since December 1923, when Maurice Barrès's hearse, drawn by ten black horses and followed by an immense cortège, crossed Paris en route to Notre Dame Cathedral (halting at the Place des Pyramides to bid Jeanne d'Arc a posthumous farewell) had there been a state funeral of such proportions for a revered literary figure. Anatole France's coffin, draped in black and silver, lay beneath a statue of Voltaire overlooking the square of the Institut de France on the Quai Malaquais. Crosses were banished. Musicians played the Andante from Beethoven's Fifth Symphony and the March from Gluck's *Alceste*. Red flags honoring Anatole France's conversion to Socialism outnumbered the tricolor, and a row of them followed his horse-drawn hearse past the Tuileries and the Arc de Triomphe to a small cemetery in Neuilly. Again, from windows and balconies many thousands witnessed the cortège, which reached Neuilly after dark. France was buried by torchlight.*

The funeral procession began so late because so many dignitaries delivered prolix eulogies: the president of the Republic, the premier, cabinet ministers, the president of the Société des Gens de Lettres. Notable was the fact that no one quoted the famous line from France's own eulogy of Émile Zola at the Montmartre cemetery in 1902. Zola was, he had said, *"un moment de la conscience humaine"*—a moment in the history of human conscience. To do so would have revived memories of the Dreyfus Affair at the very portal of the Académie Française, to which France had belonged and whose meetings he had boycotted between 1902 and 1916 as a protest against his colleagues' unanimous anti-Dreyfusism. There were oblique references to this, but what the speakers trumpeted were the author's unobjectionable virtues—his taste, his style, his exemplification of "French genius." Gabriel Hanotaux, who represented the Académie Française, annointed him "the great writer par excellence, the most French in his language, his ingenuity, his wisdom." Having received "the admirable dialect of Paris" as a birthright, France defended it all his life, said Hanotaux, and thus "contributed to our conquests abroad." His works were "pregnant with humanity," declared Paul Painlevé, the minister of education. He was "the very model of the perfect writer," according to Georges Lecomte, president of the Société des Gens de Lettres, "the writer whose language most exactly translated and fit his thought." In *Le Figaro,* another member of the Académie Française claimed that Pierre

---

* Both ceremonies were dwarfed by Hugo's funeral in 1885. His coffin had lain on a catafalque one hundred feet tall under the Arc de Triomphe. Two million people watched the cortège wind its way to the Panthéon, in which he was interred.

André Breton in the 1950s in his Montmartre apartment, after World War II.

Loti, France, and Barrès, all of whom died within fourteen months of one another, formed "a chain of peaks."

A few years later, Breton would be flirting with the French Communist Party, Aragon and other Surrealists would be seeking their salvation in Marxism-Leninism rather than in the id, and Drieu would be waffling between ideological extremes; but in 1924, none was yet sufficiently political to balance Anatole France's civic heroism against the literary ideals they scorned.

Un Cadavre satisfied enemies who wanted only one more piece of evidence to convict its authors of being mad dogs. "Anatole France hasn't died, he will never die," wrote Soupault. "In a few years, a few worthy writers will have invented a new Anatole. There are people who can't do without this comic character, 'the greatest man of the century,' or 'a *master.*' His every last word is anthologized, his most trivial sentences are studied under a magnifying glass. And then one obligatorily bellows: 'How beautiful it is! How magnificent! How splendid!' The eternal *master.*" Breton's smear appeared under the title "Burial Refused."

> Let us commemorate the year that silenced three sinister men, Loti, Barrès, France: the idiot, the traitor, the cop. Gone with France's departure is a bit of human servility. Let there be rejoicing on the day that ruse, traditionalism, patriotism, opportunism, skepticism, realism, and lack of heart are buried! Let us remember that the basest vil-

lains of this age had Anatole France as an accomplice and let us never pardon him for having colored his smiling inertia with the red, white, and blue of the Revolution. Let his corpse be put in a box, all those old books "that he loved so dearly" packed on top of it, and the whole kit and kaboodle thrown into the Seine. Once he's dead, this man must no longer be able to make dust.

Drieu, who, three years earlier, had argued Maurice Barrès's case at the mock trial, was characteristically ambivalent, chiding Anatole France for his ignorance of everything new in art while lauding his conservative virtues. One could not draw a "principle of life" from his works, but neither could the language have done without him. From the moribund body of France the nation, wrote Drieu, war had brought forth a new nation as alien to the old as the Wild West to Europe or Ottoman Constantinople to Byzantium. In an uncouth country swarming with Negroes and "disturbing" foreigners and automobiles and airplanes, Anatole France rescued the "old family" of words. "He exercised the vigilance and the prudence that enables words to live together like a strong, united nation: it is called syntax, which can be like love among citizens." Readers might have mistaken this for a gross parody of eulogies in the provincial press or the *Bulletin de l'Instruction Publique*. It wasn't intended to be.

Still, Drieu's contrary argument did not prevent him from rushing to the defense of Louis Aragon when Aragon's diatribe in *Un Cadavre* cost him the stipend he received from Jacques Doucet, a famous fashion designer who collected modern literary manuscripts. Unbeknownst to Aragon, Drieu pleaded with Doucet to restore his allowance. "You and I, sir, are of the century, while Louis Aragon is not," he wrote. "He has taken vows that exclude him from it. I don't know if they are permanent but for the moment they put him before us in a situation that demands our sollcitude." Aragon, he went on to say, was a seeker of the absolute among timeservers. He kept the torch lit for others improvising existence, and deserved to be treated accordingly. "Wise kings," he concluded, "have always sheltered mad monks."

A year later Drieu and Aragon were no longer on speaking terms. Friends surmised that Aragon's love affair with a woman who had previously been Drieu's mistress accounted for the break. It may well have played a part in it. But the professed cause was an open letter to the Catholic poet and playwright Paul Claudel, France's ambassador to

Japan, in which the Surrealists denounced him for carrying the cross to Asia. Their hope was that revolutions, wars, and colonial insurrections would exterminate Western civilization. "We seize this opportunity to dissociate ourselves publicly from everything French, in words and actions," they wrote, adding that salvation for them lay nowhere. "We understand Rimbaud to have been a man who despaired of his salvation, whose work and life are pure testimonies of perdition."

Despair was Drieu's homeland. He could travel with his Surrealist friends to its far reaches, but not beyond. With the letter to Claudel seeming to imply that they saw a bright star in the east over Moscow and meant to follow it after abandoning their quest for that "absolute vantage point of the mind," he took offense. And he did so flagrantly, in an open letter to Aragon. "I always believed that your movements, Aragon, had the virtue of expressing a despair that flows in my blood and in that of many around us," he wrote. "After more than ten years in Paris—fitful discussions, anxious pacings, long flights toward love. . . . But suddenly I see you relaxing [your sense of the absolute] and at the first crossroad taking a shortcut to the beaten path before the crowd arrives en masse. . . . Suddenly one point on the horizon is more cardinal than another. . . . What are these superstitions? How can one prefer the east to the west?" He dismissed the image of "light coming from the east" as unpardonably trite and their apparent conversion to "neo-Orientalism" as an outright self-betrayal. "While some consider themselves obliged to murmur 'Long live the King' from time to time, or 'Long live Millerand,' which is more prudent, you fall into the trap and shout: 'Long live Lenin!' "*

All he wished to remember of the Surrealists' diatribe against Claudel was a phrase faithful to the conversations Aragon and he had had during the previous decade: "For us, salvation is nowhere." It voiced the spirit of their bond, and it was, to all intents and purposes, his valediction.

In November 1944, Drieu noted that "the years 1924, 1925 were the first pivotal moment of my life." He remembered spending the sum-

---

* Alexandre Millerand belonged to the club of rotating ministers during the Third Republic. A Socialist turned conservative, he had been president of France between 1920 and 1924 and minister of war in 1914–15, when Colette Jéramec, whose father knew him as a friend, obtained special favors for Drieu.

mer of 1924 at Guéthary, near Biarritz on the Basque coast, in the company of Aragon and in the thrall of an American woman named Constance Wash. Tall, blond, and shapely, she embodied his "Doric" ideal. They had a passionate affair, which continued until April 1925, when Constance, unhappily married but determined to stay that way for her child's sake, sailed home with her husband, leaving Drieu stranded in the Midi, contemplating suicide.

In June his mother, Eugénie, the original lost love of his life, died at age fifty-four.

After putting the loaded pistol down, Drieu, never certain of his virility, challenged it by seducing women seriatim. André Malraux, whom Drieu befriended in the late 1920s, said of him that he played a relentless game of hide-and-seek with himself (which biographers have as truly said of Malraux). "He wasn't alone. Take T. H. Lawrence. If one relied only upon his private writings, one would take him to have been impotent and full of complexes. Well, even with allowances made for the legendary and exaggerated, he, Drieu, was a man of uncommon energy." But much of the uncommon energy was invested in the seeking and hiding— in fleeing the bondage of conquest or the humiliation of failure. Brothels were safest; he patronized them wherever his peripatetic life took him. In 1924 and 1925 he was known to be philandering in Florence; to be courting a beautiful Italian princess in Paris; to have followed her to Rome; to have impregnated, betrayed, and abandoned her; to have broached the subject of marriage with a young Jewish art student of good family and, when expectations were raised, left her for a tryst in Nice with the Italian princess, Cora Caetani (who had aborted their child).* Having dissipated much of Colette's endowment, he lived on a modest inheritance from his mother and a retainer from Gaston Gallimard. In 1925, Gallimard published Drieu's novel aptly titled *L'Homme Couvert de Femmes* (The Man Beset with Women), which, like Drieu's two books of war poetry and his brief memoir *L'État Civil,* received scant notice.

---

* Of his tryst in Nice he wrote, "We took walks along a desolate beach, which was Sahara-like in January, when the accursed cold combined with the curse of sand whipped by a bitter wind, between the bubbling rot of marshland and a sea roaring destruction. Did she know what she was doing by leading me there?"

Born to a wealthy family of Tuscan vintners, the Antinoris, Cora married Prince Michelangelo Caetani and bore him a daughter. She cut a wide swath through European society. It would not have displeased Drieu to learn in the 1930s, long after their separation, that the Antinoris had become supporters of Mussolini.

Drieu's reputation as a notable young writer rested principally upon *Mesure de la France,* a small volume of geopolitical essays arguing, among much else, that institutions born of the eighteenth-century Enlightenment were responsible for France's decay, that a new Pan-European arrangement was needed to restore the nation's vitality, and that party politics were anachronistic. The book was published in 1922, soon after Raymond Poincaré, bent upon invading the Ruhr, which he would do on January 11, 1923, replaced Premier Aristide Briand. Two years later he, in turn, fell from power as the ministerial roundabout of the Third Republic continued to turn.

Party politics thrived, at the expense of political reform, in a legislature scored with fault lines. Church and state had been separated for almost twenty years, but not in the National Assembly. Secular Republicans and the Catholic Right remained at daggers drawn over educational policy. Men who had held office before the war closed ranks against a postwar generation wanting to change the way government worked. The upper house tilted one way, the lower another. There were pacifists, the most notable being Aristide Briand, and sword rattlers who insisted that Germany fund France's economic recovery, *manu militari* if need be.*

By 1924, economic realities had spoken loudly against France's continued presence in the Rhineland, and Poincaré, whose campaign to seize German industry was responsible for the occupation, had squandered much of his credit with the public. A plan named after General Charles G. Dawes, the American who drew it up, promoted measures that led to France's withdrawal from the Ruhr. When elections were held in 1924, voters sick of war, of maintaining an army of occupation, of talk about dismembering Germany and of the need for a buffer state, and most especially of higher taxes to cover the cost of reconstruction, empowered leftist parties allied under the title Cartel des Gauches. Their leader, Édouard Herriot, who became premier, accepted the Dawes plan, which also prescribed a rational schedule of German reparation payments. In *L'Action Française,* Léon Daudet cried treason: "The Herriot cabinet has played its cards: evacuation

---

* Briand's name is linked with that of Frank Kellogg, American secretary of state, in the Kellogg-Briand Pact of 1928, renouncing war as an instrument of national policy except in matters of self-defense. It made no provision for sanctions. Winston Churchill said of Briand's supporters that their heads were full of "benevolent wool."

of the Ruhr; trust in democratic Germany; peace in Europe secured by the forfeiture of our rights." It had played other cards of the same suit, he maintained, by inducting Jaurès into the Panthéon (to the sound of trumpets playing the *Aïda* theme) and allowing a Soviet embassy in Paris.* If history should demonstrate that Herriot had facilitated a German war, he would have to be tried before a high court, Daudet blustered.

Herriot's recognition of the Soviet Union in 1924 was in some sense a rejoinder to Poincaré's reestablishment of diplomatic relations with the Vatican in 1921, sixteen years after the breach.† This and bills introduced during Poincaré's second term, in 1923–24, had alarmed secularists, especially schoolmasters fearful that a permissive view of banned religious orders teaching in towns and rural regions would compromise their authority and diminish their enrollments.‡ The kind of local feuds between Dreyfusard civil servants and anti-Dreyfusard clerics described by Émile Zola in his novel *Vérité* would be resumed as if time had stood still.

In the Cartel des Gauches, Socialists had consented to a most awkward marriage of convenience with the far more numerous Radicals, who were radical in name only. "Representative of the attitude of the party were the writings of its chief, almost its only eminent intellectual defender, Alain," writes the Cambridge historian Denis Brogan.

"The Citizen against the Powers that Be"—that was political life as Alain saw it. The unending audacities of elected persons in betraying their electors moved him less to the indignation of Whitman than to an ironical resignation and to a resolve to reduce, as far as possible, their power for evil, as it was impossible to increase their power for good. But the deputies, bad as they were, easily seduced by flattery and

---

* Communists demonstrated against Jaurès's interment in the Panthéon as an act of ideological embezzlement by the state.

† The breach took place under Émile Combes, a fiercely anticlerical premier. When France's president paid a state visit to King Victor Emmanuel III, he was not received by Pope Pius X, who maintained a hostile view of the king for ruling territories confiscated from the Holy See.

‡ The ban, one of the consequences of the Dreyfus Affair, was suspended in 1914. Poincaré's government maintained the suspension. Supporters of Herriot wanted the ban enforced.

by the social poison of Paris, were not as bad as the bureaucrats, the "Tite Barnacles" (for Alain had read Dickens).

Herriot's Radical Party believed that checks were indispensable to hinder the machine of state from entering the twentieth century too precipitously. By and large, Radicals did not like change, notes Brogan. "The Radical was the man who wished to keep to the ideas and practices of 1789; to defend the Rights of Man as interpreted in the pre-machine age; and to ignore the fundamental difficulties of applying the methods of the age of diligences in the age of motor-cars. . . . For the Radical feared that, if the State were strengthened and modernized, the beneficiaries would not be the little men whose interests it was the business of the party to foster, but the powerful lords of business and finance." It was with some contempt for a backward partner ignorant of economics and pledged to a costive ideology that the party joined the Cartel.*

Financial problems with which the Cartel des Gauches could not deal effectively proved its undoing and, in the two years of its administration, condemned cabinets and premiers to brief tenures.† The prospect of measures that might have stabilized the economy—above all, a tax on wealth and the wealthy—caused a flight of capital. Herriot's successor, Paul Painlevé, appointed Joseph Caillaux minister of finance in hopes that the ex-premier disgraced during the war but remembered for his economic sagacity would succeed where five predecessors had failed. He became the sixth failure. A Cartel whose members quarreled among themselves could not prevail against the so-called wall of money. Those powerful lords of finance, enriching themselves even as the debt-encumbered state limped toward bankruptcy, wanted conservatives restored to power, and in July 1926 they got their wish.

Drieu raised hopes of marriage with political factions as well as with women, and so it was that after reading his letter of divorce from

---

* The Socialists called their strategy "support without participation," although they participated to the extent of accepting five ministerial portfolios.

† Presidents of the Republic could dissolve the Assembly but never exercised the right after 1877. Legislators therefore had no threat of a call for new elections to fear by challenging the executive with confidence votes.

the Surrealist group in the *Nouvelle Revue Française* (*NRF*), Charles Maurras, under the pen name "Orion," publicly urged him to seek intellectual companionship at L'Action Française. In an open letter, Drieu replied that he could not rush headlong into a political trap when his recent denunciation of the Surrealists warned poets against that very danger. "The best way of devoting myself to ideas, to ideal institutions many of which we doubtless share in common, is to remain free of personal bonds. I shall cling to the advantages and disadvantages of a certain solitude, not out of pride or prudence, I assure you, but to husband the limited resources allotted me." His salutations were affectionate.

While he sidestepped political traps, Drieu made an avocation of touring them with a friend and fellow writer named Emmanuel Berl, who was to play a conspicuous role in left-wing journalism during the 1930s. Like André Jéramec, Berl belonged to the well-off Jewish bourgeoisie residing near the Parc Monceau. He had survived the war decorated but in poor health, had married a young Catholic woman (for her property, he confessed), and settled on a remote estate in Béarn, near the Basque coast, where he met Drieu one summer. Their friendship blossomed even as his loveless marriage withered. Before long Berl had sprung back to life, mingling in Paris with Surrealists at the Cyrano café and receiving invitations to salons of hostesses who liked to sprinkle bright young men among the duller eminences of French politics and letters.

Another bright light was Berl's former classmate at the Lycée Condorcet, Gaston Bergery, whom Drieu met here and there on his social perambulations. Bergery, a lawyer by training, had set his course for politics after recovering from an injury suffered at the Champagne front and by 1920, at age twenty-eight, was deputy general secretary of the Reparations Commission. When the latter dissolved, he became principal private secretary to the minister of foreign affairs in the Cartel des Gauches.* Berl, Drieu, and Bergery spent much time together, talking politics. Having survived 1914–18 with emotional and physical wounds to show for it, all three agreed that the hands that had drafted the Treaty of Versailles were wooden spatulas, that Germany should not be ostracized, that the only guarantee against future wars would be a united Europe transcending national egos. "How would this Europe look? Oh, of course," Berl recalled. "I was surrounded

---

* Édouard Herriot served simultaneously as premier and minister of foreign affairs.

by Socialists." In 1925, Drieu's "pivotal" year, Bergery left government to become an appeals litigation attorney whose expertise in private international law took him to the United States and the Soviet Union. In 1928, residents of Mantes, roused by his call for the nationalization of monopolies, elected him mayor and a deputy in the National Assembly, where right-wingers, perceiving his political color to be more deeply dyed than that of his Radical colleagues, nicknamed him "the Radical Bolshevik."

In 1927, at their own expense but hoping for subscribers, Berl and Drieu published a small pamphlet of literary and political commentary called *Les Derniers Jours.* It expired after seven issues. Berl described the project as *"casse-cou"*—reckless or daredevil. "We commented on everything and everyone: Lenin, Mussolini, Freud, Einstein, the Paris school of painting. After the first issue, Léon Blum, a cousin of [our friend] Colette Clément and Drieu's bête noire, telephoned, wanting to make our acquaintance. Maurras also called attention to us in *L'Action Française."* It is thought that Bergery had some hope of the magazine becoming an instrument of his political ambitions. Its apocalyptic title would have told him that the editors concerned themselves more with ends and beginnings than the calendar of political life.* Pouring out of Berl were the ideas that inspired his mordant pamphlets, *La Mort de la Morale Bourgeoise* and *La Mort de la Pensée Bourgeoise.* And Drieu's contributions include several articles about Surrealism that by their mere existence argued a stronger attachment to the movement than his public repudiation of it suggested. Politically he had worn as many

---

* *Les Derniers Jours* can be read as a double-entendre meaning "Recent Days" or "The Final Days," but in an autobiographical novel, *Gilles,* Drieu revived it under the title *Apocalypse.*

Bergery was to have a tortuous political career. In 1933 he resigned from the Radical party and founded his own, "The Common Front Against Fascism, Against War, and for Social Justice," on the basis of which he ran for office in 1936 and served as an independent deputy during the Popular Front. After France's defeat in 1940, he became an ardent Pétainist, threw in his lot with the Vichy government, and became its ambassador to Turkey. On July 6, 1940, four days after the rump Parliament granted Pétain unrestricted power to change the Constitution, Bergery heralded "a new Order—authoritarian, national, social, anti-Communist, and anti-plutocratic."

Berl's ideological itinerary also led to Vichy, or at least to Pétain, for whom he wrote speeches during the marshal's premiership. He didn't travel as far in that direction as his cousin Lisette Ullmann, née Franck, who divorced her husband, a Jewish banker, to marry Fernand de Brinon, Vichy's ambassador to Paris. As an "honorary Aryan," she hobnobbed with Joachim von Ribbentrop, among other prominent Nazis, during the Occupation. Brinon was executed in 1947. Lisette served a brief prison sentence.

hats as a well-furnished dandy, never sporting them long enough to wear them out and doffing them left and right to gain attention yet remain impenetrable. But in the deepest part of him, beneath his shifting political personae, was something that didn't change: a yearning for certainty, for a new dispensation compatible with the messianism of Surrealist manifestos. In that deep place he was still the boy bedeviled by failure, marching off to war with Nietzsche in his knapsack. He was still the actor compelled to seduce audiences while dreaming of perfect self-possession in an earthly netherworld. "If one wants to hold a little of the earth in one's arms, one must survive a shipwreck and resign oneself to being the Robinson of some lost island," he wrote, but elsewhere he preached just the opposite, that salvation might lie beyond individuality, in collective existence. No matter. The insular "I" and the collective self were twins. One way or the other, to be was to be reborn in a new world liberated from the dichotomy between inside and outside.

His thinly veiled memoir *Le Jeune Européen,* dedicated to André Breton, enlarges on this theme in a chapter entitled "Ruins." There he wrote that he believed in decadent man because he believed in primitive man. "If man is old, his senescence has lasted so long that it amounts to perdurable youth. Senescence capable of renewals and springtimes is no longer old age; it is life in its alternations." Progress was dismissed as one of those secular myths that legitimized the bourgeoisie's claim to power: "We cannot seek our reasons for existence in history: we must free our era from bonds that tie it to other eras. . . . Being souls outside of time, we must shut our minds to the idea of time. Enough of shop-worn comparisons and superstitious analogies." *Le Jeune Européen* also echos the raptures of Barrès's *Le Culte du Moi:* "Thus, I joyfully cried that I was the forest. The tree was rotting, but I partook of the inexhaustible sap of the forest." The solipsist in Drieu abhorred division: the division of life into units of time, of the mind into consciousness of the "Self" and "non-Self," of government into parties, of Europe into countries. Following Barrès's lead but going well beyond Barresian nationalism, Drieu found shelter for his mind only in visions of a one-man island or an unbounded continent.

On April 12, 1926, he wrote in his diary, "I am thirty-three years old. I am still alone, as I was at twenty-three, as I was at thirteen, as I will be at forty-three. But forty-three is the end."

. . .

Like his twenties, Drieu's thirties were a loneliness crowded with new acquaintances and ephemeral lovers. Notable among the former was André Malraux, whom Drieu met in 1927 at the apartment of Daniel Halévy.* Malraux had just brought out *La Tentation de l'Occident*, an Asian-European correspondence that may have benefited from the stir he had made three years earlier, when French colonial authorities in Cambodia arrested him for attempting to smuggle Khmer temple reliefs out of the country. He would base his novel *La Voie Royale* on that escapade. In the meantime, he made the most of it at Parisian salons, keeping his audience spellbound with virtuosic recitals, all performed at breakneck speed and accompanied by facial twitches. Malraux, who had as much reason as Drieu to heed Pirandello's warning "Woe to him who doesn't know how to wear his mask," found a nimble interlocutor in Drieu.† And in Malraux, Drieu found a younger replacement for Aragon. They took long walks through the city, conversing hectically about their works, about ruins and rejuvenation, about East and West and the multitude of "isms" available to ideological shoppers, about the inevitability of war without the bulwark of a united Europe, about the threat of a Bolshevik hegemony or of conquest by American capitalism. That Malraux eluded definition when so many confrères were rooting themselves in movements, ideologies, schools, and parties made him all the more attractive to Drieu. "His likes are few and far between," Drieu wrote. "He has traversed philosophical and historical speculation, Asia, the Revolution. He will always be adding to his booty in these various provinces, but he will settle in none of them. Politics? Archeology? Business? It's too much or not enough for a man. Being a writer? Again, too much or too little."

---

* Daniel Halévy, the son of Ludovic, Offenbach's and Bizet's librettist, had been a school-mate of Marcel Proust's at Condorcet. They remained friends and active Dreyfusards in the 1890s. In 1927 Malraux was twenty-six, Drieu thirty-four.

† Reviewing *La Voie Royale* in the December 1930 issue of the *NRF*, Drieu wrote of Malraux: "His novels are fast moving, compelling, enthralling, but their scope is narrow and unilinear. . . . One has the impression that the author hardly ever departs from facts with which he is personally acquainted. . . . There is a single line of events, and treading this line is a single character, a hero, who is not Malraux but the mythical figuration of his Self. More sublime and concrete than himself. . . . Search your memory and you will find the greatest, flanked by their heroes: Byron and Manfred, Stendhal and Julien Sorel, Balzac and Rastignac, Dostoyevsky and Stavrogin, etc."

André Malraux, 1920s.

They honed each other's intellects in public as well as in private—or, rather, public may have been all there was. The novelist Jean Giono describes meeting Drieu, Malraux, and André Gide in 1930 or 1931 at the Rôtisserie Périgourdine for a meal that soon became a staged debate between Malraux and Drieu, with André Gide and himself there as the audience. "The subject of the conversation," he wrote, "was an extraordinarily intelligent one—so intelligent that Malraux and Drieu La Rochelle started talking promptly at half past twelve and continued until six in the evening." Cigarettes were chain-smoked, drinks were served, and on they nattered.

> I noticed that Gide was silent throughout. When the conversation ended and we went back outside, I bade farewell to Malraux and Drieu La Rochelle, who walked off in different directions. I accompanied Gide a way and apologized to him, saying: "I kept quiet because I must admit that I understood nothing, not a single word." Gide touched my arm and kindly replied, "If it's any consolation, Giono, I, too, understood nothing."

After a few steps, Gide added a self-consoling postscript: "And I don't think they did either."

What struck Malraux's wife, Clara, more than Drieu's lengthy improvisations was his fin-de-siècle affectation of ennui, which proved irresistible to certain women, though not to her—and not immediately to the woman he married in 1927. It was in fact her resistance as well as her youth that attracted Drieu to Olesia Sienkiewicz, the vivacious twenty-three-year-old daughter of a Polish banker and a mother related to the Hetzels (famous and rich for publishing Jules Verne). Olesia looked nothing like the Junos Drieu generally preferred, but a fire was lit and a determined courtship followed. On August 19 he informed Gide, when they met on a Paris street, that he was soon to marry. "I offered him a glass of port in the nearest bar," Gide noted in his journal. " 'Yes, it's an experiment I want to perform,' he told me. 'I want to know whether I can stick it out. Up to now . . . I have never been able to maintain a love affair beyond six months.' "

Soon came the bondage of conquest. Olesia and Drieu exchanged vows in a Catholic ceremony on September 22, 1927. By March, Drieu had tired of Sundays *en famille* and fled to Athens. The couple's brief life together became an epistolary marriage. And even after his return from Greece, there were more intermittences than intimacies. He dispatched Olesia to the Alps for skiing with friends or found asylum from their apartment in the upper recesses of the immense Hôtel d'Orsay. When a literary journalist interviewed him about his latest book, *Genève ou Moscou* (which moots the case for a Pan-European state), he confided, "I have always had other people's wives. Now I have my own. She's charming. I have somewhat the impression of being her father." Drieu mentioned in passing a recent excursion to England with "a very pretty creature."

The marriage lingered into the summer of 1929, through three unhappy months spent at Talloires in the French Alps, where Drieu read Nietzsche, Conrad, D. H. Lawrence, and Virginia Woolf as he labored to complete his fourth novel, *Une Femme à Sa Fenêtre.**

---

* Benjamin Crémieux, an astute critic who wrote an early essay on Proust—perhaps the earliest—and played an important part in acquainting the French public with Pirandello, also praised young Drieu after the publication of his war poems. Having demonstrated his admiration for the verse, he savaged the novels, which combined—to ill effect, as he saw it—critical analyses of the world situation and the confessions of a "postwar neurotic" reminiscent of such Romantic melancholics as Chateaubriand's René and Senancour's Obermann. Drieu was clearly a master of French prose, but he had yet to prove himself a novelist. "There is nothing in him of the failure or the cripple. It's just that he is incom-

"I have to spend three months with a child who is feverish and supplicating, but also obstinate and sly," he wrote to his new mistress, Victoria Ocampo. "Three months with the corpse of love. Three months of *wary* correspondence with you."

Drieu had met Victoria Ocampo, along with Ortega y Gasset, at the Paris residence of Duchess Isabel Dato, daughter of the assassinated prime minister of Spain. A purposeful, elegant, dark-eyed Argentinian whom Ortega nicknamed "the Giocanda of the Pampas" but who looked more like the intellectual sister of Sargent's *Madame X,* Victoria came from great wealth and spoke French as fluently as Spanish, having been tutored by a French governess. During a two-year sojourn in Paris, her very Catholic family allowed her to study philosophy with Bergson and literature at the Sorbonne. Their liberalism extended no further than that. When she announced her desire to become an actress, they drew the line: Argentinian aristocrats didn't exhibit themselves onstage. Cheated of one theatrical career, Victoria embarked upon another as the wife of a diplomat, Bernando de Estrada, and played the part long after they had ceased to live connubially.* She left Estrada in 1920, at age thirty. Until then, and ever afterward, literature sustained her. Her devotion to the cause of Latin American letters matched her will to flout social convention. She was herself a prolific writer, but the publication for which she was best known in her own day and is best remembered in ours had yet to appear when Drieu met her in 1929: the literary magazine *Sur.* She founded it two years later, flinging the continent open to the work of European writers and nurturing homebred talent, notably Jorge Luis Borges. "Victoria is something above and beyond: she is the founder of a spiritual space," Octavio Paz declared. "Because *Sur* is not merely a publication or an institution. It is a tradition of the spirit."

Months before Drieu wrote to Victoria from Talloires, he had pursued her to London and found her living in lavish quarters at the Savoy Hotel, with a view of Cleopatra's Needle. They spent some

---

plete and partial, like the rest of us. May he just accept himself as he is."

* In 1934 she enjoyed a brief stage career, playing a part in Stravinsky's *Perséphone* (with a libretto by André Gide) at the Teatro Colón and in Rio de Janeiro. Many years later she confessed that it was her most painful memory. "I say painful because I would have wished to continue doing these performances, which were the best thing I have done in my life."

weeks together, often in the company of her future contributors or Drieu's friend Aldous Huxley and Huxley's friend D. H. Lawrence. Much the stronger of the two, Victoria entered the relationship well guarded against fantasies of shaping a future around someone whose entire being, down to his fingertips, bespoke impermanence. "His long, slender hands," she later wrote, "seemed made to let precious sand flow between the fingers." It was an intense affair while it lasted, which was time enough for her to address his vulnerable core. He dissolved in tears when she told him one evening, upon returning from the theater, that one could not be jealous of a man like him. "That evening I saw . . . a very unhappy child always wanting a woman to offer him *the moon*. One always wanted to give it to him . . . as one does with children."

After a dreary weekend on the Normandy coast, they went their separate ways, she to Spain and Argentina. They corresponded as former lovers, developing a transatlantic intimacy that allowed Victoria to upbraid him for his ill treatment of women and he to lay bare the doubts that belied his apparent indifference to the opinion of others or the importance of writing. He would have liked to please even journalists—even his in-laws—all of whom found him unintelligible, at best. Believable were the taunts of "cretins" and dubious the compliments of admirers. Inferiority shadowed him like a sleuth tailing an impostor.

The character Drieu could flesh out most convincingly was his shadow. This he accomplished in *Le Feu Follet* (*Will o' the Wisp*), a short novel describing in painful detail the inner predicament and last hours of a man whose ties to the living have gone slack.* Inspired by the suicide in 1929 of a former Surrealist, Jacques Rigaut, whom he had continued to befriend after 1925, it gave voice to Drieu's obsession with decadence, with the unraveling of the will, with the faintness of vital signs in European civilization, with wear and tear and the depredations of intellect. Alain, the protagonist, is a moribund dandy. Ravaged by drugs, he hangs the remains of his wardrobe on the ghost of his body. Unable to write, he finds solace in the dicta of a literary movement that taught him contempt for literature. The women who supported him have departed. Their largesse is spent, and so are his days on earth. Empty forms people the world. Help is nowhere to

---

* Louis Malle's film *The Fire Within* is based on Drieu's novel.

be found, least of all from the physican treating him, who prescribes willpower. "How could he talk about willpower when the sickness lies at the very heart of the will? . . . The individual will is the myth of another age. A race worn out by civilization cannot believe in will. Perhaps it will take refuge in constraint: the rising tyrannies of Communism and Fascism promise to flagellate drug addicts." Alain's one commanding act is his suicide. He lies on his bed in the posture of a defiant soldier facing execution and presses a revolver to his heart. "A revolver, that's solid, that's steel. To come up at last against an object." It's as if he were returning to the trenches and that narrow border of primitive life where life hinged on a moment. That was real.

Gallimard published *Le Feu Follet* in 1931, the year Drieu's marriage ended. M. Sienkewicz, the banker, had been ruined by the crash, and with Drieu himself begging, Olesia found herself in financial straits. Obviously related to these events was a play Drieu wrote about love, marriage, and money (all irreconcilable). Staged at the Théâtre des Champs-Élysées, *L'Eau Fraîche* had a respectable run for the wordy imbroglio it was, but did not enrich anyone or come near allowing Drieu to repay his debts. Still, his plight may not have been dire. Relying on gifts from his former wife, Colette Jéramec, a stipend from Victoria Ocampo, and a modest inheritance from his mother, he rented a flat on the Île Saint-Louis facing Notre Dame Cathedral, very near Olesia, who had meanwhile set up house with a young friend of Drieu's, the psychiatrist Jacques Lacan.

And he traveled, thanks largely to Victoria Ocampo. In 1932, shortly after launching *Sur,* she asked him to lecture in Argentina. At first the idea of speaking in public unnerved him, but he warmed to it and proposed a series of four lectures on the crisis of European civilization. His intention, he explained, was to study "European anguish" in religion, in war, in love, in philosophy, in politics. It would be "an epic commentary on my generation," a history of Europe since 1914 seen through the prism of his personal experience. Entitled "Is Europe Going to Die?," it would be *Le Feu Follet* writ large.

As his confidence swelled, so did the series, from four lectures to eight. No record exists of what he told his audiences, except for a summary he wrote two years later:

> Young Argentinians, like young Frenchmen, challenged me to declare myself Fascist or Communist, I insisted that as an intellectual I

needed a vantage point on the margin of events, from which to survey the whole scene. I sympathetically analyzed the Italian phenomenon and the Russian phenomenon. The global importance of Fascism emerged more clearly when viewed from the perspective of the past fifteen years. Hitlerism was rumbling toward its goal. I predicted that without a doubt the movement, if not its leader, would one day triumph. The inanity of proletarian parties, which was already apparent to me, had been driven home in a surprising way. To be sure, I stated my broad allegiance to Socialism, but not Socialism as it is now. The Socialism I championed would transcend political parties.

The summary was written in 1934, with the benefit of hindsight. Drieu stayed in Argentina for almost five months, from June into October. Midway through his long sojourn, on July 31, 1932, news reached Buenos Aires that the Nazi Party had won 38 percent of the vote in the German federal elections and become the largest parliamentary bloc. Had Drieu truly predicted Nazism's electoral triumph and Hitler's uncertain future before July 31? Determined to become the ruling party, in order to abolish all but their own and with them the Weimar Republic, the Nazis did their utmost to make government unworkable under the chancellors of minority coalitions, while Hitler, rebuffed again and again by President von Hindenburg, wondered anxiously when or whether his turn would come. It came like doomsday on January 30, 1933, after Gemany had sunk deeper into an abyss of political intrigue and economic mayhem.

Drieu made an excursion to the Indian remoteness of Bolivia with a French ethnologist, but he found companionship of the sort he had enjoyed with Aragon and Malraux in Jorge Luis Borges. They were indefatigable walkers; talking all the while and always at night, they walked through Buenos Aires often to the edge of the pampa. "Everyone was asleep," Drieu recalled. "The cinemas were closed, the cafés twinkled. Every two or three kilometers, the anguishing brightness of a little brothel beckoned. My poet walked and walked, striding like one possessed. He walked me through his despair and his love, for he loved this desolation."

Before the Argentinian interlude, in January 1932, Drieu had written to a friend that "the man in him" who had borne arms in his early twenties and dispensed political advice (presumably to Gaston Bergery) in his early thirties could no longer settle for existence in the "fallen state that gives birth to novelists." When he returned from Argentina, he was determined to retrieve what he had lost during fifteen years of postwar womanizing and intellectual vacillation—to be a warrior, *un homme d'action,* a man with fire in his belly—and he envisaged the transformation as another kind of fall. "The ghost of ambition has an enormous advantage over that of love: once you grab hold of it, it doesn't let you slip free. You must find the stone heavy enough to attach to your neck and help you sink to the bottom. The fall is what gives meaning to a destiny."

Had Drieu attended Charles Dullin's production of Jean-Paul Sartre's *Les Mouches* ten years later, during the German occupation, he might have seen himself in a protagonist tortured by the feeling that he does not weigh enough to leave tracks in life. Sartre's Orestes acquires gravitas—a destiny, as Drieu liked to say—by murdering his father, Agamemnon. For Drieu, intellectual suicide would also do. Manhood demanded only a weight around one's neck and the will to leap. In his preface to a translation of *The Man Who Died,* he claimed that D. H. Lawrence understood the great purpose served by Fascism and Communism in salvaging man's "animality" and "primitiveness."* What made Rome and Moscow admirable, in his view, was "the great rhythmic dance of an entire people gradually reconstituting itself."

In 1933 Drieu stood at the cliff's edge, still unable to step back from it or leap. He wrote a play pitting a dictator, sympathetically portrayed, who declares that freedom is no longer the supreme good it had been in other seasons and centuries against a libertarian intellectual who conspires to assassinate him. He wrote short stories about World War I, collected in *La Comédie de Charleroi,* denouncing modern, industrialized warfare but recalling the intoxication of an infantry charge at Charleroi in 1914. "There I was a leader. I wanted to mass the men around me, grow bigger through them, aggrandize them through me, and advance as one, with me in front pointing forward, across the universe." Malraux sought his support when French intellectuals joined

---

* In the late 1930s, Granville Hicks, among other literary critics in England and America, accused Lawrence of Fascistic thinking. Christopher Caudwell, the author of a book entitled *Studies in a Dying Culture,* denounced him for turning backward "to old primitive values, to mythology, to racialism, nationalism, hero-worship, and *participation mystique.* This Fascist art is like the regression of the neurotic to a previous level of adaptation."

demonstrations protesting the arrest and trial of George Dimitrov, a Bulgarian Communist the Nazis accused of setting fire to the Reichstag. Drieu declined. Less important to him than Dimitrov's fate at the hands of a tyrant was his own at the hands of a self-indulgent, angry, desultory child. He told himself that freedom had undermined him, just as it had made France sluggish. Both needed a master: he for direction and France to awaken from her torpor.

In January 1934, Drieu spent a week in Berlin, observing the Reich soon after the Reichstag fire and the "Strength Through Joy" campaign launched by Hitler to pacify German workers. On February 6, he was present at the Place de la Concorde when extreme right-wing groups demonstrating against government corruption confronted a cordon of police assigned to prevent them from crossing the bridge to Parliament. A riot ensued, leaving fifteen dead, six of them Camelots du Roi.

Drieu sided with the dead, with death.

CHAPTER 9

The Stavisky Affair

The stock market crash of 1929 shook Europe and affected the political fortunes of France's coalition, the "Union Nationale," which had been elected in 1926 to right a foundering ship and succeeded in doing so under the second premiership of Raymond Poincaré. In 1926, bankruptcy had become a very real prospect. Poincaré, chairing a cabinet that included six former premiers, prevailed upon the Assembly to increase revenue with higher taxes on income and property. As a result of more rigorous fiscal policing, devaluation of the overvalued franc, and German reparations payments, investors expecting bankruptcy felt reassured. Capital returned from abroad. In his person, Poincaré—whom one historian likened to an upright, unimaginative, industrious, and intelligent village notary—rallied middle-class spirits. Industrial production increased, markets opened for cheaper French goods, and unemployment fell to unprecedented levels, despite the influx of Italians and Eastern Europeans, many of whom were diverted from the United States by the American anti-immigration law of 1924. Aristide Briand, serving Poincaré as foreign minister, effected a rapprochement with the Weimar Republic (whose economic woes were alleviated in the late 1920s, thanks in large part to large loans from American banks and the financial acumen of Dr. Hjalmar Schacht, president of the Reichsbank). Briand and the German foreign minister Gustav Stresemann shared the Nobel Peace Prize in 1926.

With Poincaré's retirement in 1929, after a long-lived premiership of two years and three months, deputies who had mustered behind him on bipartisan ground retreated to their factional camps. The Union

Nationale collapsed. A technocrat of the Center Right, André Tardieu rose to power and fell from it three times in two years while implementing reforms championed by social progressives—a free secondary school education, social security, a Ministry of Health, rural electrification, the retooling of industry. He couldn't count on favor outside his own party. Radicals inveighed against him for violating the separation of church and state and conferring benefits on the worker and wage earner at the expense of small entrepreneurs. The extreme Right vehemently complained that France's security was put at risk by a government that scanted the military. When André Maginot, the minister of war, addressed the Assembly, *L'Action Française* declared that Tardieu's government had learned nothing from the bloodiest war in history. "This government *devoid of memory, devoid of conscience, devoid of reason,* this *inhuman* government exposes us today to the prospect of waging again what M. Maginot called the war of bare chests, exactly as in 1914, after fifteen years of credits for new matériel being sabotaged, according to the dictates of the Dreyfus party!" Funds were voted to build a line of fortifications along the German border, the so-called Maginot Line.

By 1932 everything was scarce as the world financial crisis visited increasing misery upon France. England's renunciation of the gold standard in 1931 dealt a severe blow to the French economy, which had been buffered from the initial effects of the Depression by its enormous gold reserves and budget surplus. Prices plunged, and the agricultural sector suffered from the collapse even more grievously than the industrial. Hundreds of thousands were thrown out of work. Government revenue fell by a third. In Parliament, Left and Right ganged up on the ruling center, which retained control, but with a shaky hand. Between November 1929 and May 1932, eight governments lost confidence votes. None lasted more than a few months. Tardieu and Pierre Laval served as premier three times each, while in Germany, where over four million were unemployed, Hitler moved inexorably toward the chancellorship.*

Each served for the last time in 1932, before the general elections returned a majority of left-wing candidates, divided, as in the previous decade, between minority Socialists and majority Radicals. Their

---

* Laval is chiefly remembered as Pétain's premier during the Vichy regime; he was tried and executed after the war for "intelligence with the enemy."

failure to deal with the economic crisis soon became apparent. Men and women staged hunger marches all over France. Radicals wanting civil servants to accept a cut in salary despite protests, and Socialists exciting the Radicals' fear of big government by demanding the nationalization of major industries were two of the bones they worried. Reparation payments ceased for good when Hitler came to power and deficits soared. With parliamentary democracy at its most dysfunctional, premiers rose and fell, pursuing no line of policy, and cabinet ministers shuffled around in the same game of musical chairs played by their conservative brethren.* These cabinets were sometimes dubbed "corpse cabinets" by the disillusioned public, consisting as they did of men revived from a fallen administration.

Word spread of German rearmament, but the French budget expressed no urgent need to modernize the army. Nor was Germany called to account. "The history of Europe and of European confabulations in recent weeks may be resumed with three points," wrote Charles Maurras in the October 13, 1932, issue of *L'Action Française.* "Firstly, it is admitted that Germany has rearmed. This is a truth . . . to which no one can raise the least objection, not even our good friends the English, who claim to be as well informed as the French, with their classified and unclassified dossiers. Secondly, no one in Europe can deny that German rearmament flouts treaty law. Thirdly, since no one wishes or dares to repress this violation, we concluded that everyone is of the opinion that *the law should be changed.* Whenever something similar occurs in the civil domain, one calls it an encouragement of crime. . . . We recommend that the professor of literature Herriot, who . . . knows Pascal inside out, consider his famous reflections about the might that makes right and the might that serves justice. It will furnish him with the theme for yet another oratorical topos. As

---

* In a comprehensive view of postwar France, two French historians, Jean-Pierre Azéma and Michel Winock, observe that the public ethos was generally hostile to change. "New" was as feared in France as it was glorified in the Soviet Union, and the myth of the "belle époque," cultivated after 1918, bore witness to this nostalgia for a lost golden age. "The springs of the republican regime, already worn before 1914, lost even more resilience during the war. When the time came to modernize, the spirit of innovation was lacking. After years of hemming and hawing, the gold-backed franc was restored, albeit at one-fifth of its previous value. But more difficult to restore was the republican spirit, which had suffered comparable depreciation. In retrospect, the twenties appear to have been a quagmire."

far as action is concerned, the book on him is closed."* Maurras made much of this admonition in a 120-page plea at his trial for treason in 1945. It was outweighed on the scales of justice in postwar France by his multitude of tirades against Jews and the Republic.

Maurras's trenchant article did not sit well with Herriot, who lost the premiership two months later, but reprimands in *L'Action Française* did not speak as loudly in 1932 as they had a decade earlier. The favor that Maurras, his movement, and his paper had officially enjoyed in Vatican circles did not extend beyond Pius X's papacy.† Pius's successors, who strove to promote world peace, distanced themselves from an ideology whose basic premise was that ends justified means and that all means should be employed to the ultimate end of restoring a monarchy. Maurras's *nationalisme intégral,* which regarded the nation as the sovereign to which individual scruples rendered obeisance and as a higher moral authority than the Holy See, appalled Pius XI. It had also lost the hold it had once had over the French episcopate when, during the Dreyfus Affair, many of its prelates had succumbed to the passion that made bedfellows of the church and the anti-republican Right. In August 1926, Cardinal Andrieu, archbishop of Bordeaux, reproached L'Action Française for being Catholic by design rather than conviction and for bending Catholicism to its political agenda instead of serving the church's mission on earth. Cardinal Andrieu's article and further admonitions in the official Vatican newspaper, *L'Osservatore Romano,* heralded an apostolic decree. It came in December, when seven of Maurras's works and *L'Action Française* (guilty of defending itself against ecclesiastical opprobrium in vitriolic articles signed by Maurras and Daudet) were placed on the *Index Librorum Prohibitorum.* Penalties followed. On March 8, 1927, the Apostolic Penitentiary declared that seminarians loyal to L'Action Française would be deemed unfit for the priesthood; that priests guilty of the same offense would be prohibited from exercising their sacerdotal functions; and that parishioners who continued to read *L'Action Française* would be

---

* Édouard Herriot, leader of the Radical Party, twice premier, and perennial *président de la Chambre* (Speaker of the House), was a graduate of the École Normale Supérieure. He taught advanced classes in literature and rhetoric at lycées in Nancy and Lyon and was awarded a prize by the Académie des Sciences Morales et Politiques for a work on Philo and the Alexandrian school. Among his thirty books are a life of Beethoven and a history of French literature. He entered politics during the Dreyfus Affair, as a Dreyfusard.

† Pius X died in 1914. He was succeeded by Benedict XV and Benedict by Pius XI in 1922.

stigmatized as public sinners and denied the sacraments. To a French Catholic novelist named Henry Bordeaux, Pius XI said of Maurras, "He is one of the best brains of our times; no one knows that better than I. But he is only a brain. . . . Reason does not suffice and never has. Christ is foreign to him. He sees the church from the outside, not from within." L'Action Française refuted the papal decree in an article entitled "*Non Possumus.*" "The reigning pope," it stated, "is not invulnerable to human error where political questions are concerned, and though the church has the power to promise eternal life, men of the church—all of history proves it—can be led astray by dishonest parties, can engage in harmful enterprises. L'Action Française is not a Catholic paper. It was not founded by any specifically Catholic authority; it founded itself."

The papal decree hurt the movement, although a distinguished Catholic thinker, Jacques Maritain, could still note early in 1927 that "without having a single one of its members in Parliament, L'Action Française enjoys among many the prestige of a virtual public authority or principate of opinion." Soon thereafter, circulation of the newspaper began to fall. Many provincial chapters languished. Moving its headquarters in Paris from the Rue de Rome to a building on the elegant Avenue Montaigne belied the fact that its coffers were empty, or would have been if not for patronage from rich aristocratic families.

The number of Camelots du Roi, for whom the sacraments were a trifling consideration, may not have dwindled significantly, but under the conservative governments of 1926–32 they tended to make their presence felt with pranks rather than acts of brutal incivility. The most sensational event took place in May 1927 and involved Léon Daudet, who barricaded himself inside the offices of L'Action Française, behind barbed wire and barred gates, when summoned to serve the prison term imposed on him two years earlier for slandering the cab driver in whose taxi his son Philippe had shot himself. The siege lasted three days. Jean Chiappe, a prefect of police known for his right-wing sympathies, finally prevailed upon Daudet to surrender. He emerged with his praetorian guard of Camelots and was driven in Chiappe's limousine to the Santé Prison, where he endured several weeks of comfortable internment. On June 25, a colleague impersonating an official of the Ministry of the Interior informed the warden that the government, in a gesture of conciliation to extremist parties, wanted Daudet and a Communist leader released immediately. The gullible warden complied. Daudet walked, and slipped across the border into Belgium. He was eventually pardoned by President Gaston Doumergue.

The Camelots du Roi truly sprang to life with demonstrations in February 1931, when the Ambigu theater staged the French adaptation of a German play about the Dreyfus Affair. Intent on shutting it down, they disrupted performances with stink bombs and challenged patrons entering the theater with their heavy canes. Scuffles on the Boulevard Saint-Martin became bloody riots. Shouts of "Long live the army" and "Down with the Jews" revived memories of the furious reaction to Zola's "J'accuse" in 1898. Havoc reigned nightly between the Porte Saint-Denis and the Place de la République for almost three weeks, until performances of *L'Affaire Dreyfus* were suspended by Chiappe, who acceded to a request by the directors of a veterans' association called the Ligue des Croix de Feu that an end be put to the "lamentable exhibition" in whatever way his "professional conscience" dictated.* *L'Action Française* published the letter and added, "All good Frenchmen will congratulate the Croix de Feu for having expressed, with the dignity befitting an association that incorporates glorious veterans of every opinion, its indignation at a national spectacle that has lasted too long. We know that other associations of veterans are preparing to intervene."† It characterized *L'Affaire Dreyfus* as a piece of "German and anti-French propaganda" whose audiences in Berlin mocked the French uniform. *Le Populaire,* a daily, compared the success of the Camelots du Roi and the Croix de Feu in suppressing a play about Dreyfus to that of the "Hitlerians" in having the film adaptation of *All Quiet on the Western Front* withdrawn from German cinemas. "In both countries, the same individuals, animated by the same spirit,

---

* Chiappe also forbade Felix Weingartner's appearances as conductor of the Pasdeloup Orchestra. It is worth noting that Dreyfus himself was still alive to observe the longevity of the myth that bore his name. He died in 1935.

† The *Jewish News Archive* of March 7 reported that Jewish circles were much concerned by the demonstration of anti-Semitic strength in France. "The anti-Semitic passions which ran high during the Dreyfus Affair have been found by this new affair to be still alive in France, the royalist and military circles who contended that the Jew Dreyfus was guilty of appearing to have a strong following still, despite the verdict of history, even to the extent of a woman publicly proclaiming herself Esterhazy's daughter and making an attack in the theater on M. Richepin [the French adapter of the play] because it depicted Esterhazy as the traitor."

pursuing the same goals by the same means, terrorize assemblies and the streets with organized bands. The League of the Rights of Man insists that republican opinion accustom itself to the danger of this nascent Fascism, which is all the graver for going unopposed by the feeble powers that be."

Although the rioters on this occasion were mainly Camelots du Roi, Paris abounded in right-wing "leagues" with paramilitary contingents always ready to parade and brawl. Their numbers increased exponentially in the early 1930s, when the Cartel des Gauches, resuming its fractious career, implemented deflationary measures that made a weak economy weaker. Most numerous were the Union Fédérale des Combattants and the Union Nationale des Combattants. Best known was the aforementioned Croix de Feu, an association of decorated veterans whose membership included general volunteers pledged to the movement's central tenet, that the "spirit of the trenches" should engender "national reconciliation." Its motto was *"Travail, famille, patrie"* (later adopted by the Vichy regime). Everything that caused division, above all class conflict, was objectionable to its leader, Colonel François de La Rocque, who, if judged only by the movement's torchlight parades and military maneuvers, might have passed for a Gallic Hitler. An older generation may also have been reminded of General Georges Boulanger. The colonel did indeed express his repugnance for party politics and internationalist creeds, but, whatever his nebulous language may have shrouded, nothing in it suggests a Fascist alternative to the Republic. Nor did anti-Semitism strongly color his understanding of France's fall from grace.

The same cannot be said of many among his four hundred thousand followers. And passionate anti-Semites had a choice of aggressively bigoted organizations. One of the largest in the early 1930s was Solidarité Française. Financed by the vastly rich perfume manufacturer François Coty, who acquired *Le Figaro* after the war, it proposed to exorcize the demons of parliamentarianism, of rampant bureaucracy, of hospitality to foreigners, of modern art, of Bolshevism, and of the "anonymous, irresponsible, vagabond capitalism" more or less synonymous with international Jewry. Like other such groups, notably "Les Francistes," whose model was Mussolini, it conferred honor and pride upon its members. Also modeled after Mussolini's Blackshirts were the Jeunesses Patriotes, largely recruited from among university students and financed by Pierre Taittinger of the Taittinger champagne house. They wore berets and blue raincoats. They gave Roman salutes.*

What sparked this explosion early in 1934 against the Third Republic was a scandal involving financial skulduggery and political corruption called the Stavisky Affair.

Alexandre Stavisky was the son of Emmanuel Stavisky, a Russian Jewish immigrant. Alexandre received his formal education at the Lycée Condorcet, but by 1912, at twenty-six, he was well on his way to establishing himself as an inveterate swindler. That year, he rented the Folies-Marigny Theater for a summer, staged a play that closed after two weeks, and failed to repay concessionaires their surety deposits. He was brought to book but never tried, thanks to the outbreak of World War I. The war also saved him from prosecution for swindling the munitions firm Darracq de Suresnes of 416,000 francs in the sale of twenty thousand bombs to the Italian government.

Amnestied in 1918, Stavisky took up where he had left off, with ever more ingenious scams, for one of which he served seventeen months in prison. He was by no means alone in robbing French investors during the 1920s. Almost as infamous as he, were Marthe Hanau and her former spouse, Lazare Bloch, who founded a financial journal that drummed up business for shell companies it promoted and fraudulent short-term bonds promising high rates of interest. Brokers drove a thriving trade until banks, at the instigation of a rival financial news agency, looked into the matter more closely. Hanau distributed bribes to quash rumors. But in December 1928, police arrested her, Bloch, and their business partners. Investors had lost millions. Hanau delayed the trial by staging a hunger strike, rappelling down a hospital wall on a rope of sheets to escape being forcibly fed, and resorting to other extremities. When the trial finally took place, in February 1932, she revealed the names of complicit politicians. Freed from prison after nine months, she published an article about the shady side of the financial markets, quoting classified material leaked to her by an employee in the Ministry of Finance. For this indiscretion she

---

* In 1928 Coty bid for working-class support with a newspaper named after Marat's paper of the revolutionary period, *L'Ami du Peuple*. Among other articles of commentary published in it was one entitled "France d'Abord! Avec Hitler Contre le Bolshévisme!"

went back to prison. She escaped, was recaptured, and, at her wits' end, committed suicide. "The founder of the *Gazette du Franc,* who could take pride in her exalted and useful republican collaborations," *L'Action Française* gloated, "was 49 years old, which is to say that she was barely 40 when she conceived one of the most formidable hoaxes of our time."*

No less devious was Stavisky, who entered the 1930s in the shadow of a trial adjourned nineteen times, but mingling prominently in café society, gambling for high stakes, and sporting the accouterments of wealth.† He and his glamorous wife occupied rooms at the Hôtel Claridge. A compulsive illusionist whose main act was the Ponzi scheme (performed under the alias Serge Alexandre or Monsieur Alexandre), he owned two newspapers (of opposite political persuasions), a theater, an advertising agency, a stable of racehorses, and a sty for enablers feeding at his trough. The latter were highly placed policemen, rogue politicians, disgruntled civil servants, crooked lawyers, publicists, and influential journalists. In 1931, undeterred by omens, Stavisky launched the operation that eventually made him the titular villain of an "affair." For quite some time he had had an eye fixed on municipal pawnshops, or crédits municipaux, which were in fact lending institutions recognized by the government as "publicly useful" and authorized to issue tax-free bonds, with the understanding that profits derived therefrom would benefit the municipality. In a fateful meeting at Biarritz, Stavisky inveigled the mayor of Bayonne, who was also a well-connected legislator, into securing the approval of the relevant ministry for a crédit municipal. It served their purpose that Bayonne lies twenty-five miles from the Spanish border. "The month Spain lost its king, April 1931, Bayonne gained its crédit municipal," writes the historian Paul Jankowski. "Revolution in Madrid had come just in time for Stavisky and his hirelings, and had made plausible their fable—of jewels from Alfonso XIII and the royal family, from Countess San Carlo, from rich Antonio Valenti of Barcelona, and from frightened Spaniards reported crossing the border to seek safe haven for themselves or their valuables. Rumors of plunder and flight justi-

---

* Janet Flanner published several long articles about Marthe Hanau in the *New Yorker* in the 1930s.

† Stavisky's father had committed suicide several years earlier, after trying to save him from another financial embarrassment.

Alexandre Stavisky

fied by their proximity to the town's new crédit municipal, launched with a budget that would have been extravagant even in a teeming metropolis." This ur-fable laid a foundation for every subsequent ruse, the success of which depended upon connivance, nonchalance, false assumptions, a double set of books, and the flight of common sense. How Bayonne's crédit municipal could afford to pay high interest rates in a depressed economy and for what purpose it needed huge sums were questions that bondholders didn't pose insistently enough, or at all. It swelled like the frog with delusions of grandeur bloating itself in La Fontaine's fable. Large insurance companies flattered the frog's wish to pass for an ox. La Confiance, L'Avenir Familial, and others poured millions into Stavisky's magic show.* Stavisky himself pocketed 160 million francs.

The frog burst in 1933, when an insurance company sought to redeem its fake bonds. The crédit municipal temporized as Stavisky, having made no provision for the inevitable, frantically rallied cronies to raise funds with a new bond issue. Things did not go his way. Rumors of malfeasance were spread by journalists who delved deeper than government overseers. While the latter continued to shuffle paper from ministry to ministry, a serious investigation was set in motion. The treasury receiver in Bayonne scrutinized the crédit municipal's books on orders from the state comptroller, and revealed a breathtak-

---

* Lloyd's of France had invested 5 percent of its total assets in the crédit municipal.

ing discrepancy between its private records and its public fiction. It had nothing very valuable in pawn, least of all the Spanish crown jewels. Police officers arrested a key executive of the bogus enterprise, one Gustave Tissier. It was December. Everything then began to unravel.

Beneficiaries of pension funds heavily invested in the crédit municipal (with the Ministry of Labor's approval) derived some satisfaction from seeing Stavisky exposed. They would learn long after the fact that the normally suave con artist had lost his composure upon hearing of Tissier's arrest and had fled south to the French Alps. The hunt soon began for the man known in many quarters as M. Alexandre. Reporters caught wind of it and finally bruited his surname. On January 1, 1934, *Paris-Soir* ran an article entitled "Search Continues for Swindler Stavisky." Several days later, the criminal investigation department—Sûreté Générale—received a credible tip. Inspector Marcel Charpentier boarded a train for Lyon and on January 8 met with the owner of a chalet perched on a snowy slope of Mont Blanc in Chamonix. Police entered, knocked on the door of a back room, identified themselves, heard a shot, and found Stavisky mortally wounded. Officialdom ruled it a suicide, leaving half the country convinced that people in high places against whom Stavisky could have testified were assassins.

Blame for the impunity with which Alexandre Stavisky had conducted his criminal operations fell on many heads as the prosecutor's office interrogated a host of witting and unwitting accomplices in government, in the Sûreté Générale, in the judiciary, in the press. Camille Chautemps, France's most recent prime minister, a Radical whose party had much to answer for, promised that neither fear nor favor would sway the hand of justice. The skillful orator acknowledged the lapses of justice (the nineteen adjournments of Stavisky's trial) and of the police, wrote a sardonic commentator in *Le Figaro:* "And this rapturous beating of mea culpas on other people's breasts was punctuated by an oath to exact punishment, once the inquests are complete, without regard for bonds of friendship, affection, or family. . . . The Left seemed to consider this promise a gesture worthy of Brutus." One of the first casualties was the minister of colonies, Albert Dalimier, who, as minister of justice in 1932, had declared Bayonne's crédit municipal a legitimate candidate for the investment of insurance funds. Dalimier resigned when his letter of authorization was leaked to the press. Leaks led to resignations, detainments, and suicides. Thirteen months

Stavisky's widow, Arlette, formerly a Chanel model, being tried in 1936 on a charge of colluding in her husband's swindles. She was acquitted.

after the inquest began, the investigating magistrate gave the public prosecutor two volumes containing seven thousand pages of experts' reports. By then Chautemps had long since fallen from power. Nineteen of Stavisky's associates, as well as his wife, Arlette, were indicted for crimes and misdemeanors.

News other than the Stavisky Affair was forced into cramped quarters. Many daily papers regularly reserved half of the front page for analyses of the nefarious scheme, photographs of the actors, and commentaries suggesting that it would not suffice to chase moneylenders from the temple: the temple itself had to be demolished. Like Dreyfus's treason, Stavisky's machinations told against the Republic. In an article about the Dutch Communist beheaded by the Nazis for burning down the Reichstag, Philippe Barrès, Maurice's son, wrote that a dynamic team was needed in France, as existed in Germany, to purge the homeland and make it stand tall in the eyes of the world.* "While

---

* Marinus van der Lubbe, the alleged arsonist, was active in the unemployed workers' movement in Holland. He moved to Germany in 1933 and joined the Communist underground. The Sturmabteilung, the SA, had been committing particularly brutal murders in a reign of terror since the summer of 1932. The most widely publicized took place in the Silesian town of Potempa on August 10, when SA thugs trampled to death a Communist miner in the presence of his mother and brother.

we blame the harshness of the National regime, it is high time that we react to some of the same disorders that afflict the Reich. . . . We must proceed to investigate the Stavisky scandal exhaustively." The Far Left and the Far Right chanted antiphonies of denunciation. Could anyone doubt any longer the turpitude of the ruling class? asked *L'Humanité*. It was pervasive. "Every day a new name, a new agency of government, a sacred principle of bourgeois democracy is sucked into the whirlwind. Magistrates shielding a swindler. Deputies serving him. High functionaries sharing his booty. A police force of gangsters admitting him into their midst, then shooting him. A minister handing pension funds over to him. . . . Liberal? Conservative? Your alternate displays of morality are nothing but the dustups of rival gangs." Léon Daudet, home from Belgium, hectored the "government of Scum" day after day, surpassing himself in invective. Charles Maurras took the broader view: "Besides the Jewish State, the Masonic State, the immigrant State, the Protestant State, there are several thousand profiteering *clans* whose titles derive from their yeomen work in dismantling the French State after 1793." The battle between parliamentary conservatives and liberals over Stavisky was, he declared, nothing but a preliminary skirmish in the war between the "legal State" constituted by usurpers and the "real State" of true Frenchmen taking up arms against a "judiciary of bandits, a police force of assassins, a government of traitors."

To militant anti-republicans, and particularly to L'Action Française, the Stavisky Affair was revivifying. Its leaders lived for havoc even as they called for the restitution of true social order, and on January 10, a day after several hundred demonstrators, mostly Camelots du Roi and their cousins in the Jeunesses Patriotes, had been repulsed by the Republican Guard near Parliament, they rallied the faithful to gather in greater numbers. "Parisians! This evening, upon leaving your offices and ateliers, when cabinet ministers addressing venal deputies try to hoodwink the French, come shout your scorn for their lies." More than five thousand people heeded the call. In the tradition of Parisian firebrands, they halted traffic near the Palais Bourbon with cast-iron grates, overturned lampposts, and tree branches. Deputies inside Parliament heard shouts of "Down with the sellouts!" coming from the streets. After six hours of confusion, paddy wagons were filled to overflowing. Thirty policemen suffered injuries.

The government suspended performances of *Coriolanus* at the Comédie Française, fearing that Shakespeare's play about a patrician hero pitted against Rome's plebeian tribunate might incite further violence. To no avail. Things went from bad to worse. In his paper *La Victoire*, Gustave Hervé, a right-wing extremist, who was beating the drums for Pétain, declared, "Anything but this filthy anarchy! How many people must be mumbling between their teeth these days: '*Ah! Vive Mussolini et vive Hitler!*' "

Ginned up by the right-wing press, bolstered by paramilitary leagues, and confident that the prefect of police, Jean Chiappe, would refrain from turning water cannons on Camelots du Roi as he did on Communists, L'Action Française grew bolder. No longer content to win minor victories in peripheral neighborhoods, it concerted with the Union Nationale des Combattants and the Jeunesses Patriotes to launch a demonstration from the Place de l'Opéra on January 27. Thousands gathered there in the early evening and swarmed down lamplit streets and avenues leading to the Place de la Concorde, where, within sight of the National Assembly across the Seine, large police vans blocked their advance. The rally became a riot. It lasted until midnight. By that time Chautemps had resigned from office, citing the riots as one reason for his resignation. There were violent clashes at barricades. Police had taken the precaution of having tree grates removed, but the rioters set fires, cut fire hoses, overturned kiosks and benches, ripped up gas lines, smashed shopwindows. Three hundred people were arrested, all of whom soon walked free. Later, a commission of inquiry concluded that "these systematic depredations, the street turmoil, the paralysis of traffic cost the authorities their prestige and exposed the pusillanimity of justice. It paved the way to February 6." Among those wounded on January 27, no one died. Blood would flow ten days later.

High on the agenda of the new premier, Édouard Daladier, was the reform of a police department responsible for allowing Stavisky to operate without let or hindrance, and particularly the removal of Jean Chiappe, who, after years at the prefecture, considered it his fiefdom. Daladier offered the dapper, well-connected, right-wing Corsican a prestigious sop—the governorship of Morocco—lest his eviction appear to have been dictated by Socialists in the coalition, or by hints of involvement in the Stavisky scandal (an investigative report having indicated that the Prefecture of Police had been for some time well aware of Stavisky's mischief and done nothing about it). News of the ministerial shuffle and of Chiappe's rage were a spark to tinder. The paramilitary leagues, loosely confederated, set in motion plans for a monster demonstration. On February 4, they distributed a tract declaring that the country was in danger; that all signs pointed to a "formidable purge in the army, the judiciary, every level of administration"; that the people had to impose their will. Was it not true that the government had equipped the Palais Bourbon with machine guns? (It hadn't.) In the February 4 issue of *L'Action Française,* Charles Maurras wrote:

> The thieves have one enemy and even two: Paris and France. The sustained, repeated demonstrations in Paris . . . testify that our race, sound and upright, will not suffer the crimes of highway robbers, however highly placed, to go unpunished. The cabinet deploys against France like a battalion of Germans. They have taken the police chief hostage.

In an article he had written for the *London Evening Standard,* Léon Daudet declared that the day was fast approaching when the Republic and parliamentarianism could no longer pillage France. His colleague Maurice Pujo called upon Parisians, when summoned, to "shake the Masonic yoke" and topple "this abject regime."*

The editors of *L'Action Française* issued that summons two days later, on February 6, 1934, the day of Premier Daladier's scheduled appearance before Parliament. Another such summons came from Solidarité Française, whose secretary-general warned compatriots that they were being herded to the "fair," like animals branded for sale or slaughter, by politicians "sporting names as un-French as Léon Blum."

He urged that members should demonstrate that evening against "this travesty of a regime." They were to gather on the boulevards between Richelieu-Drouot and the Opéra, and to march "at precisely 7:15."

At the Sorbonne, flyers announced a political epiphany: "The long awaited hour has arrived! The hour of the national Revolution! Every-

---

* A number of men in high public office, representing the moderate Left, belonged to the French Masonic Lodge called the Grand Orient de France. To Solidarité and other elements of the Far Right, Masonry signified devotion to the ideals of the eighteenth-century Enlightenment.

body, show up on the Boulevard Saint-Michel at 6 o'clock." Not to be left behind by events but wary of violence, the Croix de Feu mustered some of its men on the Right Bank at a prudent distance from the Place de la Concorde, where Camelots du Roi and others would challenge police assigned to defend that approach to Parliament, across the river. Eventually many broke ranks and joined a mob flooding the Place de la Concorde from the Rue Royale and other tributaries.

By six-thirty, after sunset, the battle was joined. Buses were burning on the great square, near the obelisk and the American embassy. Fires had been set elsewhere. Several hundred gendarmes, mounted *gardes républicaines,* and detachments of riot police called up from the provinces earlier that day faced a mob of thirty thousand, some armed with guns and razor-tipped sticks to hobble the horses, but many more with weapons of opportunity: chunks of asphalt, stones, hoops torn from the Tuileries Garden, the tree grates removed ten days earlier but since restored.

Rioters and police charged and retreated by turns, while parliamentarians hurled brickbats at one another in the Palais Bourbon (which was being immediately threatened by Camelots du Roi and three thousand members of the Croix de Feu who had begun their rally on the Left Bank in the Faubourg Saint-Germain). Daladier attempted to conduct parliamentary business, citing such critical issues as the industrial and agricultural slump, high unemployment, threatened savings accounts, and national security in a Europe overshadowed by belligerent dictators. "Scandals pass, problems remain," he noted. "We shall defend the regime. Republicans must unite if they want to ensure the survival of one of the very few free political arenas left in the world." Likewise, Léon Blum, the leader of the Socialists, exhorted the opposition to repudiate the campaign discrediting institutions and to appreciate the danger of prolonged debate. Neither Daladier nor Blum could make himself heard above the commotion. Taunts came from Right and Left. A member of Daladier's own Radical Party rose to criticize him for his "insolent refusal" to address the Stavisky Affair, saying, "He invokes preoccupations that weigh heavily on all of us and the need for public order, but he is the first to threaten public order. The premier willingly speaks of Fascism, but the day the executive power forbids the sovereign Assembly to deliberate is the birthday of Fascism." Maurice Thorez, leader of the French Communist Party, denounced Daladier as a "Jacobin dictator." It was the responsibility of proletarians, he said, "to chase Fascist bands from the streets" and to take arms against men who defended a "financial republic" corrupted by venal charlatans. Debate, such as it was, stopped when the Communist delegation began to sing "The Internationale," prompting other deputies to answer with "La Marseillaise." By then, reports of gunfire on the Place de la Concorde and of people fatally wounded had reached the Assembly.

Guests observing the insurrection from the balcony of the palatial Crillon Hotel saw gendarmes beset at a dozen different points by demonstrators hurling torches and spreading lumps of coal over the cobblestones wherever mounted police threatened to charge. Next to the Crillon, flames shot out of the Naval Ministry. Across the square, a fusillade was heard on the riverside approach to the key bridge, the Pont de la Concorde. While reinforcements cleared the Tuileries Garden, bordering the east end, a large column of veterans—five or six thousand men singing "La Marseillaise"—entered from the west, via the Champs-Élysées.* Prominent as well were members of the Union Nationale des Combattants, veterans easily recognized by their battle ribbons and Basque berets. Repeated attempts were made to breach the police line at the Pont de la Concorde, but the line held. There were lesser riots elsewhere in Paris that evening. All told, fourteen civilians and one gendarme had been killed, more than fourteen hundred wounded. The toll increased during Communist rioting the next day, and for days thereafter.

L'Action Française and les Jeunesses Patriotes mourned their dead. The consecrated ground in which Colonel Hubert Henry had lain buried since the Dreyfus Affair became the graveyard of new martyrs. But the temper of the times and of the movements made it difficult to distinguish lamentation from vituperation, especially when, on February 7, the minister of the interior issued orders for the preventive arrest of Maurras and Daudet. "The accursed Chamber of 1932, the Chamber of the Cartel, . . . is doomed, and it were best that it remove itself of its own accord," wrote Daudet in response. "Moreover, parliamentary government, which was moribund even before this drama, cannot recover from the carnage that could easily have been avoided by administering justice instead of sheltering Stavisky's accomplices. . . .

---

* Badgered by young Communists en route, they paraded under a banner that read, "We want France to live in order and propriety."

The Paris street riots of February 1934.

The indictment of Maurras and the seizure of *L'Action Française* in newspaper kiosks are the twitches of imbeciles at their wits' end." Maurras assured the aggrieved families of the dead that "all men and women worthy of the name French" shared the conviction that "the murderous pistols and rifles of democracy" were aimed at a valorous avant-garde. The assassins' bullets were propelled by envy and by the hatred of idle, gluttonous profiteers for workers, savants, artists, "people who actually produce something."

Unworthy of the name French were Jews. It went without saying (but was said anyway, repeatedly, in the pages of *L'Action Française*, whose circulation soared) that one Jew had devised the scheme corrupting government and that another Jew, Léon Blum, had contrived to draw attention away from it by drowning protesters in blood.* Had the Stavisky Affair not been born of the Dreyfus Affair? Had one plot not descended from the other? Daudet declared as much in lectures on "the Jewish question." Like the earlier scandal, the recent one threatened the strength and integrity of France, in which one hundred thousand Germans, many of them Jews, had found refuge from the Third Reich. "I want to draw the attention of our innumerable readers . . . to

---

* Not wanting to bear the same given name as Léon Blum, Léon Daudet took to calling him Béla Blum, with Béla Kun in mind. Kun, born Kohn, led the Hungarian Revolution of 1919 and presided over the Hungarian Soviet Republic.

another aspect of the conspiracy, which ended in a bloodbath," he wrote. "The fact that Daladier appointed Joseph Paul-Boncour [formerly minister of foreign affairs and allegedly Arlette Simon Stavisky's lover] minister of war has great symbolic weight.* For it is certain that Lieutenant Colonel Barthe, who organized the butchery, could not have done so without the authorization of his superior, Paul-Boncour. Léon Blum himself admitted that he told Daladier to 'resist'—in other words, *to accelerate the massacre*—on Wednesday morning, the 7th. But for several weeks, Blum, the real head of the Cartel, had been hectoring Paul-Boncour to disarm, in spite of Germany arming herself to the teeth with the obvious goal of seeking revenge." What amounted to treason, in Daudet's view, was opposed only by extraparliamentary patriotic organizations such as the Croix de Feu, his own Camelots du Roi, students, and the Jeunesses Patriotes. He noted that the protection Stavisky purchased in Parliament coincided with the "shady designs" of Blum and Paul-Boncour, hampering France's ability to defend herself against Germany.

After February 6, 1934, France provided L'Action Française and kindred movements a resonant sounding board for the drumroll of xenophobia. In March, Bernard Lecache, the founder of the Ligue Internationale Contre l'Antisémitisme (LICA), observed that hatred of Jews was flagrant. A report approved by Paris's chamber of commerce on the situation of foreigners in France welcomed immigrants "who bring us their money" but urged that those bred in "ghettos" and "unworthy of living under the sky of France" be deported forthwith. Chamber of commerce reports about the "foreign menace" led to the passage of laws requiring artisans to obtain an identity card and street peddlers to reside in France for five years before plying their trade. In 1935, French physicians would prevail upon the government to pass a law making the practice of medicine by foreigners—especially Jews fleeing Nazi Germany (where, in April 1933, Jewish physicians had been denied government insurance reimbursement for their services)—all but impossible. Even so, the journal of the French medical society would, three years later, denounce "the scandal of excessive naturalizations."

On February 7, 1934, amid violent counterdemonstrations in which

---

* Daladier had appointed Paul-Boncour minister of war only two days before the riots of February 6.

A demonstration of the Vigilance Committee of Anti-Fascist Intellectuals, organized in March 1934 in response to the right-wing riots of February. Marching in the front row is André Malraux, who had recently published *La Condition Humaine.*

eight more people died, Daladier and then his cabinet members, submitted their resignations after only one week in office. *L'Action Française* commented that his regime would preserve from its short and sinister career only the shame of having, for the first time since the war, caused French hands to shed blood. That day, Albert Lebrun, president of the Republic, asked a septuagenarian deputy known for his conservatism and amiability, Gaston Doumergue, to form a "government of national salvation." It was much to ask of him. Doumergue had been in office for less than a week when left-wing parties called for a general strike and a protest rally. The police expected another riot, but on February 12 demonstrators in the hundreds of thousands gathered at the Place de la Nation—Socialists and Communists coming from opposite directions—to hear Léon Blum and Jacques Duclos address them from separate tribunes. "Feburary 12 will henceforth be a historic date," Blum declared. "With dignity and calm you have exhibited to fellow Parisians the strength of democracy. We will reserve that strength for the defense of the Republic."

Doumergue appointed a commission to investigate the Stavisky Affair and got down to business as best he could with a liberal majority in the Chamber and a cabinet that included Pierre Laval and Marshal Philippe Pétain, who was already being hailed in a widely distributed pamphlet entitled *C'est Pétain Qu'il Nous Faut!* as the man chosen by Providence to lead an autocratic state. One solution to the task of reconciling the irreconcilable was to unyoke the executive from the team of factional horses pulling the legislature apart and issue executive decrees, which Doumergue regularly did during his nine-month tenure, shaping an agenda rather like Tardieu's.

For the militant leagues, business as usual was a sobering outcome.* The blood they had shed brought them nothing of the new order they envisioned, only regrets that they had not coordinated their maneuvers and the hope that a truly tactical effort the next time might rouse public opinion to better effect against the "parliamentary and individualist Republic that divides and corrupts." As a result, the Jeunesses Patriotes and Solidarité Française, with the blessings of L'Action Française, announced the formation of a "national front" on May 7, 1935.† They stated that its mission was to marshal all the forces of the nation against the "anti-French red front" and to make common cause should any one of its constituents be threatened or come under attack. "The royalist and Fascist shock troops have experienced their strength, and their audacity will grow," warned Léon Blum, little suspecting that a year later, shortly before he became premier, their audacity would lead right-wing louts to drag him from his car and beat him bloody.

In January 1934, Pierre Drieu La Rochelle spent a week in Berlin, under the auspices of a Nazi youth group eager to promote Franco-German friendship. With uniformed members of the Sturmabteilung and the Schutzstaffel guiding him around the city, he looked like a Parisian swan attended by brown cygnets. The tour proved to be immensely seductive. Reawakened in him was nostalgia for the camaraderie of the trenches, according to Bertrand de Jouvenel, his friend and trav-

---

* It was not altogether business as usual. During the parliamentary session preceding the confidence vote for Doumergue, one deputy, Xavier Vallat—a one-eyed, one-legged veteran who later became the Vichy government's first commissioner of Jewish affairs—proclaimed that he was happy to be hearing the voice of France after having heard "those of Israel and of Moscow."

† Thirty-seven years later, Jean-Marie Le Pen founded the Front National in its second incarnation.

eling companion.* He put Jouvenel in mind of Alfred de Vigny's post-Napoleonic officers marking time in desultory love affairs while longing for mortal combat. He knew what Robert Graves meant by "Death was young again," in the poem "Recalling War":

> Natural infirmities were out of mode,
> For Death was young again: patron alone
> Of healthy dying, premature fate-spasm.
> Fear made fine bed-fellows. Sick with delight
> At life's discovered transitoriness,
> Our youth became all-flesh and waived the mind.

Jouvenel had the impression that war and Fascism were all that brought light to Drieu's pale blue eyes. The previous year Drieu had written a play called *Le Chef,* one of whose protagonists declares, "When one kills freedom, it did not have much life left in it. There are seasons—a season for freedom, a season for authority."

Drieu would not have sought in Berlin an answer to his longings for release from the curse of self-doubt and the anguish of solitude if he had not already found it or concluded that the key was totalitarian authority. On February 6, at the Place de la Concorde, he witnessed what he took to be a spontaneous explosion of French instinct, ardor, and pride. It was *la furia francese* at its most impressively brutish, and brutishness had always entranced him. In a memoir he wrote, "The rugby scrums and boxing matches I saw during my student days at Shrewsbury utterly disconcerted me, but didn't change my fixed habit of only dreaming about sports. I dreamed of the roughest ones, of rugby scrums and boxing matches. . . . I continued to shy away from the thing I knew to be essential, which was that I become a brute capable of holding my own against brutes."† Until February 6 he had been

---

* Bertrand de Jouvenel was ten years Drieu's junior. The son of an old-line aristocrat and a Jewish heiress, he had written several books on economics, most recently *La Crise du Capitalisme Américain.* His love life, which seems to have rivaled Drieu's, included an affair with his stepmother, the novelist Colette (whom he called Phaedra) and, at the time of his voyage to Berlin, with the American journalist Martha Gellhorn, a staunch anti-Fascist, who became an eminent war correspondent and, in 1940, Ernest Hemingway's third wife.

† "In the street I was at the mercy of anyone who crossed my path," he continued in this memoir. "During skirmishes in the student quarter, I took advantage of the mayhem and of the chance to dodge blows that would have destroyed me. . . . I became furtive, elusive, ironical. Erotism served as a compensation, a substitute."

a mere observer, he wrote. His was the "fallen state that gives birth to novelists." Now he decided to join the scrum but, as with everything in life, still debated with himself which colors to wear. Should he follow the examples of Malraux, Gide, and Aragon and turn left instead of right and look to Moscow for salvation rather than Berlin? Did one direction hold greater promise than the other of making him "a new man"?

The spectacle staged by the Nazis at their party congress in Nuremberg in 1935 (and projected beyond Germany in Leni Riefenstahl's film *Triumph of the Will*) seemed to be a decisive event for Drieu. He attended the congress and came away exuberant. "I have never felt such artistic emotion since the Ballets Russes. This nation is intoxicated by music and dance." It was with the same exuberance that he had marched to war in 1914 carrying Nietzsche in his knapsack. "I should only believe in a god who would know how to dance," says Zarathustra. "And when I saw my devil I found him serious, thorough, profound, and solemn: he was the spirit of gravity—through him all things fall."*

The emotional logic that enabled Drieu to reconcile ballet and brutishness was at play in October of that same year, when he and sixty-four compatriots issued the "Manifesto of French Intellectuals for the Defense of the West," justifying Italy's war against "an amalgam of uncivilized tribes" in Ethiopia. Signatories of the manifesto, who eventually numbered a thousand or more, protested that the League of Nations had condemned the invasion and imposed sanctions on Italy in accordance with a fallacious creed of "legal universalism" making no distinction between the superior and the inferior, between the civilized and the barbaric. The slaughter of four hundred thousand Ethiopians had been accomplished in a "civilizing spirit," they insisted. Colonial conquest bespoke Europe's "vitality."

---

* After Nuremberg, Drieu visited Berlin, where he struck up a friendship with the novelist Ernst von Salomon, who had been a member of the postwar paramilitary organization Das Freikorps, had been imprisoned for his role in the assassination of Walther Rathenau, Jewish foreign minister of the Weimar Republic, and had written sympathetically about the social estrangement of many German soldiers after 1918, as in this passage: "They constituted seats of discontent in their companies. The war still inhabited them. It had formed them; it had awakened their most secret penchants; it had given meaning to their lives . . . They were rough beings, untamed men cast out of the world, alien to bourgeois norms, scattered about, who assembled in small bands to make some sense of their combat experience."

CHAPTER 10

The Congress of Writers
for the Defense of Culture

In May 1935, Pierre Laval, France's conservative minister of foreign affairs and future premier, signed a mutual assistance pact with the Soviet Union designed to protect its signatories against German aggression.* Two months earlier, on March 13, Hitler, in flagrant violation of the Versailles Treaty, had decided to reintroduce conscription and increase the size of the German army fivefold. Crowds rejoiced in front of the Reich Chancellery. Newspapers declared that the first great measure had been taken to "liquidate Versailles." On March 17, a day known thenceforth as "Heroes' Memorial Day," General Werner von Blomberg, Hitler's servile minister of defense, told a uniformed audience at Berlin's State Opera House that Germany would again take the place she deserved among the nations. "We pledge ourselves to a Germany which will never surrender and never again sign a treaty which cannot be fulfilled," he declared, with nods of approbation from Hitler sitting in the royal box.

---

* Mussolini, Prime Minister Ramsay MacDonald, and Pierre Laval met at Stresa, on Lake Maggiore, to address the issue of Germany rearming in violation of the Versailles Treaty. Mussolini was anxious to shore up his own imperial ambitions by conquering Abyssinia (Ethiopia), and Laval tacitly bolstered them in order to secure what turned out to be a short-lived and disingenuous alliance against Hitler.

France's pact with the Soviet Union, which Laval inherited, unfinished and unsigned, from his assassinated predecessor in the ministry of foreign affairs, would never include a military convention and remained toothless.

The ink had not yet dried on the Franco-Soviet mutual assistance pact when Ilya Ehrenburg—a prolific novelist and *Izvestia*'s correspondent in Paris—organized the Congress of Writers for the Defense of Culture. Moscow had decided to repudiate pacifist principles and march with Socialists and Radicals against the common foe. Between June 21 and June 25, crowds ebbed and flowed into the Mutualité conference hall on Paris's Left Bank for three daily sessions that addressed topics such as "cultural heritage," "the "role of the writer in society," "the individual," "humanism," "nature and culture," and "the problems of creation and the dignity of thought." Writers came from Germany, the USSR, America, England, Turkey, China, and Holland. Among those who spoke were André Gide, André Malraux, Louis Aragon, E. M. Forster, Isaac Babel, Waldo Frank, Max Brod, Aldous Huxley, Julien Benda, James Strachey, Bertolt Brecht, Robert Musil, Heinrich Mann, Vyacheslav Ivanov, Henri Barbusse, Paul Nizan, Lion Feuchtwanger, Boris Pasternak. Their shades of opinion ran from liberal to Stalinist.

For the Soviet Union, anti-Fascism was a supremely effective propaganda tool. Just as Mussolini extorted tacit approval from foreign minister Pierre Laval for his invasion of Abyssinia by condemning Germany's plan to annex Austria in the *Anschluss,* so Stalin, holding high the torch of anti-Fascism, blinded Western intellectuals to the evil that committed as many as 140,000 slave laborers to a cold grave digging the White Sea Canal and starved almost four million Ukranians in the so-called Holodomor. People who spread the word—who lived by words—were the special object of Soviet ardor. Russia's overtures had begun well before January 1933, but when Hitler took office, promising in the name of race and nation to destroy "individualism and bourgeois culture," the courtship came to include luminaries who qualified for a warm embrace as fellow travelers. Conspicuous among the latter was André Gide, France's most celebrated writer. On March 21, 1933, at a rally of the Association of Revolutionary Writers and Artists (a branch of the International Union of Revolutionary Writers created by Moscow in 1927), he declared, "Why and how I approve today what I reproved yesterday has everything to do with German terrorism, in which I see a reprise of the most deplorable, the most detestable past. In Soviet society I see the opposite—the promise of a bountiful future." *L'Humanité,* characterizing Nazism as "one more atrocious episode in the international saga of class conflict," reported

André Gide speaking at the 1935 Congress of Writers, which he cochaired with Malraux.

that Gide's vow "to stand with the proletariat" excited wild applause. The paper then advertised his solidarity by serializing *Les Caves du Vatican* (*Lafcadio's Adventures*), an odd choice of fiction for apostles of realism. His old friend Roger Martin du Gard, disregarding the guilt born of inherited wealth and the horrors Gide had recently witnessed in the Belgian Congo, urged him to "expunge from your revolutionary vocabulary this 'class struggle,' which does not comport with anything else in your mind." He couldn't imagine Gide "waving the red rag." Gide would come to the same conclusion, but not until he visited Moscow, three years later.

André Malraux, who rose from relative obscurity in 1933 with the publication of *La Condition Humaine* (*Man's Fate*), was a younger star courted by the Soviet Union. In June 1934, a year after receiving the Goncourt Prize, he traveled to Moscow with his wife and Ehrenburg for an international congress held under the auspices of the Union of Writers for the purpose of enshrining realism. They endured hours of lip service to that doctrine in a huge hall whose facade was emblazoned with Stalin's lethal aphorism "Writers are engineers of the soul." In an address verbose even by Soviet standards, Maxim Gorky observed, after meandering from Greek mythology to Cervantes and beyond, that Immanuel Kant would not have cudgeled his brains over the *Ding an sich*—the thing that exists independently of us, unfiltered by the forms of sense—if he had been a primitive man in animal skins. "Primitive man," he concluded, "was a materialist." Hours later, Karl Radek, a Bolshevik warhorse, laid down the line in a more coherent argument entitled "Bourgeois Literature and Proletarian Literature," the burden of which was that the literature of late-stage capitalism displayed the symptoms of "intellectual degeneration."* It was effete, if not senile. It no longer produced the sturdy novels of Balzac's *Human Comedy* but instead issued the sickly ruminations of Marcel Proust (whom he likened to a mangy dog incapable of action, lolling in the sun and compulsively licking its wounds) or the "dung heap" of *Ulysses,* populated by worms whose wriggling Joyce observed under a microscope with evident delight.

What Malraux had to say about literature, after paying homage to the Soviet government for "saving saboteurs, assassins, and thieves" from their criminal lives by having them shovel out the White Sea Canal, did not ingratiate him with the prelates of realism.† To declare that recent Soviet literature faithfully presented "the external facts" of the USSR without touching on its ethics and psychology was considered blasphemous. If writers are "engineers of the soul," he asserted, the engineer's highest aspiration must be to invent—to invent as Tolstoy invented when there was no Tolstoy to imitate. "Art is not a submission, it is a conquest," he said. Marx's lessons explained troubled economics; they did not necessarily promote "cultural progress." Refuting Stalin's dictum, he declared that "there is consciousness of the social and consciousness of the psychological; Marxism is one, culture the other."

For all his waywardness (he also raised a glass to the absent and vilified Trotsky), Malraux was not excommunicated by the Comintern.‡ Nor did dialectical-materialist cant lead him, one year later, to regard

---

* Radek, born Karol Sobelsohn to a Jewish family in Lemberg, Austria-Hungary (now Lviv in Ukraine), participated in the 1905 revolution in Warsaw, became an active Bolshevik functionary in 1917, was one of the passengers on the "sealed train" that carried Lenin through Germany after the February revolution in Russia, and made an unsuccessful attempt to launch a second German revolution in October 1923, before Lenin died. Expelled from the party in 1927 and reinstated in 1930, he helped write the 1936 Soviet Constitution but was accused of treason during the Great Purge of the 1930s and was forced to confess at the Trial of the Seventeen in 1937. He was sentenced to ten years of penal labor and killed in the Gulag on orders from Beria.

† Malraux was by no means alone in lauding the project. George Bernard Shaw, Saint-Exupéry, Edmund Wilson, Sidney and Beatrice Webb, and Harold Lasky, among many other Western writers and intellectuals, hailed it as a Soviet tour de force.

‡ The Comintern was also called the Third International, or simply the International.

a Communist-sponsored congress for the defense of culture as a lure and a derision. To be sure, anti-Fascism spoke much louder than intellectual stringency. It kept odd bedfellows in bed together. But so perhaps did the demon that tormented Malraux with the sense of being an actor, a third person to himself, condemned to ventriloquize and to dream—not unlike Drieu—of transcending his "otherness" in revolutionary action. "Virile brotherhood," a phrase reminiscent of Barrès's "spirit of the trenches," was his ideal. One of the speeches he gave at the Congress of Writers for the Defense of Culture signals a departure from his earlier pronouncement that art is a conquest rather than a submission. By 1935 he was apparently no longer inclined to champion conquest except as conquest over self, or to befriend individualism (which he associated with inner division) except as a collective "I." Being a man, he noted emphatically, "requires each of us to stop playacting." We have heard this before and shall hear it again: to be wholly human was to overcome the breach between self and other, between face and mask, between bourgeois writer and proletarian audience. If the revolution did what it should, men would cease to "live biographically," he declared, implying the possibility of an impersonal rebirth.*

Excluded from a congress that excluded a select few of the Comintern's bêtes noires was André Breton, who had sought, since the late 1920s, when he became a passionate reader of Trotsky's memoirs, to

---

* On the contempt for history and the ideology of newness in Soviet Russia, no one wrote more eloquently than Nadezhda Mandelstam, whose husband, the poet Osip Mandelstam, was sent into internal exile in 1934. In chapter 12 of *Hope Against Hope,* entitled "The Irrational," she wrote, "Our encounter with the irrational forces that so inescapably and horrifyingly ruled over us radically affected our minds. Many of us had accepted the inevitability—and some the expediency—of what was going on around us. All of us were seized by the feeling that there was no turning back—a feeling dictated by our experience of the past, our forebodings about the future and our hypnotic trance in the present. I maintain that all of us—particularly if we lived in the cities—were in a state close to a hypnotic trance. We had really been persuaded that we had entered a new era, and that we had no choice but to admit to historical inevitability, which in any case was only another name for the dreams of all those who had ever fought for human happiness."

One is also put in mind of Jean-Paul Sartre asserting in his later, Marxist years that total transparency between humans was a consummation devoutly to be wished. "I think transparency should always be substituted for what is secret, and I can quite well imagine the day when two people will no longer have secrets from each other, because no one will have any more secrets from anyone, because subjective life, as well as objective life, will be completely offered up, given." There is a historical resonance in all this with Rousseau's boast that he would unashamedly present himself in public if his head were made of glass, with everything inside it open to view. The paranoid Rousseau will also be remembered for denouncing theater as a breeding ground of secrets.

Gide in the middle and Malraux to his left at the Congress of Writers for the Defense of Culture.

persuade skeptical French Communists that Surrealists were reliable henchmen in the struggle for revolutionary change. Ten years earlier, on November 8, 1925, *L'Humanité* had published an article reporting that a symposium hastily organized by "dissident anarchists" to discuss the idea of revolution had elicited a letter from the Surrealists pledging fealty to the French Communist Party (PCF). "The so-called 'Surrealist group' insists on protesting publicly against the misuse of its name," it began. "Some have been led to believe that there is a Surrealist doctrine of revolution. Nothing could be further from the truth.

> Surrealism is first and foremost a method of thought, conferring greater value on certain elements of the mind than on others; it is the violent critique of a certain hierarchy of mental faculties. It far surpasses the artistic and literary applications to which people have sought to reduce it. . . . Because of the morality and method in which Surrealists ground themselves, we have, in the very exercise of Surrealism, come increasingly to count on the fundamental idea of Revolution.

Despite the title of their magazine, Surrealists never believed in a Surrealist revolution, he asserted. "We want *the* Revolution because we want the means of achieving it, and the key to that achievement lies with the Comintern and the PCF, not with individualistic theoreticians . . . who are necessarily counterrevolutionary."

Breton persisted in the illusion that the PCF (unlike Sigmund Freud, to whom he made a futile pilgrimage during the fall of 1921) would embrace a poet preaching revolution of the mind and seat him among its elite.* When he applied for membership in 1927, the party thought that his talents could best be used, and his ideological fiber tested, by assigning him the task of writing a report about the coal industry in Fascist Italy. This humbling ordeal did not result in a report or in membership. Nor did it put an end to his vexed relationship with the party. Three years later, soon after publishing his second manifesto, he founded a new review called *Le Surréalisme au Service de la Révolution,* the first issue of which answered a question telegraphed by the International Bureau of Revolutionary Literature: "Please reply following question what your position if imperialism declares war on Soviets stop." Breton replied, "Comrades if imperialism declares war on Soviets our position will conform to directives Third International position of members French Communist Party stop If you judge better use of our faculties in such case we are at your disposal for specific mission requiring any other use of us as intellectuals stop."

Striving for intellectual heft, Breton favored philosophical and political essays in *Le Surréalisme au Service de la Révolution* but otherwise made his presence felt, as always, with *épater les bourgeois* demonstrations. There was, most notoriously, the screening he organized of Luis Buñuel's film *L'Âge d'Or* at a Montmartre cinema whose lobby was hung for the occasion with scabrous paintings by Max Ernst, Salvador Dalí, Yves Tanguy, Hans Arp, Joan Miró, and Man Ray. Right-wing militants, including an "Anti-Jewish Youth League," took exception to Buñuel's portrayal of Jesus as a Sade-like child molester and trashed the premises, splattering ink over the screen, destroying the projector, hurling stink bombs, attacking spectators with blackjacks, damaging the art, and tearing up copies of *Le Surréalisme au Service de la Révolution* on sale. In a front-page article, *Le Figaro* inveighed against the film as detrimental to everything of human dignity. Not closing it

---

* According to Breton's biographer Mark Polizzotti, he was made to sit in Freud's waiting room, given as much time as the doctor had between patients, and told, courteously no doubt, that they did not have much in common. "The two were clearly speaking at cross-purposes. Freud considered the practical techniques and raw materials of psychoanalysis the means to a therapeutic end, whereas for Breton their primary aim should be 'the expulsion of man from himself.'"

down would be tantamount to official complicity with "the work of intellectual Bolshevism making its mark in the heart of Paris" under cover of "avant-gardism." Hadn't the leagues done what the police ought to have done? Their violent foray was the "instinctive defense" of upright people ("*honnêtes gens*") against a "satanic enterprise." The author, Gaëtan Sanvoisin, praised the high-mindedness of a municipal councillor at whose behest the authorities had made cuts in the film and quoted his letter to Chiappe, the prefect of police:

> I attended a showing on Sunday. The spectators were mostly youths and foreigners. We elected officials are responsible for them. Our responsibility extends to a bookstore next door to the cinema, where a review called *Le Surréalisme au Service de la Révolution* is on sale, along with so-called avant-garde literature. I have several issues for you to peruse. It is because they tore up this garbage that young members of the Ligue des Patriotes were jailed for a night last week. To avoid such incidents, which will unfailingly recur, you have a dozen policemen guarding the cinema, while suffering from a shortage of personnel elsewhere. I won't press you further. Knowing you as I do, I know where you stand. Your men will tire of stifling their just indignation to defend a spectacle conceived by neurotics and an agency of revolutionary propaganda. More of us than ever will no longer put up with the systematic poisoning of society and French youth.

Sanvoisin was certain that Chiappe, if he bothered to peruse the review, would find abundant evidence of Bolshevik sentiment. It declared, among much else, that Indochinese revolutionaries served the oppressed of all nations by fighting to throw off "the French yoke."

Breton's break with Communism followed his break with Louis Aragon. Largely responsible for their estrangement, after thirteen years of literary partnership, had been Elsa Triolet, a Russian novelist better known for her close ties to Ilya Ehrenburg and to the poet Vladimir Mayakovsky than for her own writing.* Tired of his role as the *fidus Achates* of one despot, Aragon fell under the spell of another, who made it her business to unburden him of his Surrealist past and

---

* Elsa Triolet was born Ella Kagan in 1896, the daughter of a wealthy Jewish lawyer, and brought up in Moscow. In 1918 she married a Frenchman named André Triolet. By 1928, when she met Aragon, they had divorced. Her older sister, Lili Brik, had long lived in a ménage à trois with two poets, Osip Brik and Vladimir Mayakovsky.

remodel him along party lines. As labile a personality as Drieu, and as desperate for an ideological home, Aragon lent himself to the remodeling, in the course of which 1930 proved to be a significant year. It was the year that the Congress of Revolutionary Writers took place at Kharkov. Aragon attended it in November, representing the Surrealists, whose review he touted with apparent success and whose grievances against members of the PCF were heard with apparent sympathy. Elsa Triolet (distraught over the recent suicide of Mayakovsky) stood beside him, translating. When the congress ended, five days later, Aragon was prepared to sign a letter drafted by the party demanding that he retract his criticism of Barbusse, repudiate Breton's "Second Manifesto," eschew Surrealist activities, purge himself of Freudianism, and submit all future work for party approval. "This was the first time that I saw open at my feet the abyss that since then has taken vertiginous proportions," wrote Breton.

Soon other long-term companions defected to the Communist camp, notably the poet René Crevel. In 1935, Crevel joined Aragon, Tristan Tzara, Malraux, and Ilya Ehrenburg on the organizing committee of the Congress of Writers for the Defense of Culture. Except for Crevel, Breton was not much loved by any of the above. By Ehrenburg he was hated. In Ehrenburg's study of contemporary French literature, the Surrealists were described as mentally ill or charlatans playing the part of madmen for attention or profit. "These young self-described revolutionists will have nothing to do with work," he wrote. "They go in for Hegel and Marx and the revolution, but work is something to which they are not adapted. They are too busy studying pederasty and dreams. . . . Their time is taken up with spending their inheritances or their wives' dowries; and they have, moreover, a devoted following of rich American idlers and hangers-on. . . . In the face of all this, they have the nerve to call the rag they publish *Surrealism in the Service of the Revolution.*"

Breton was all the more eager to address the congress for having been slandered by its chief impresario. Crevel, despite his defection from the Surrealist movement, persuaded fellow committee members to let Breton speak. The arrangement was canceled a few days later, however, when Breton encountered Ehrenburg on the street and slapped him. The Soviets insisted that Breton be excluded. Breton, in turn, made no apology. Crevel tried to reconcile the parties, shuttling between them frantically, as if life itself depended on the success of his negotiations. And indeed it did. They failed and, four days before the congress opened, he killed himself. "The silly incident was the last drop for René Crevel," wrote Ehrenburg. "Of course a drop is not the whole cup, but it grieves me to recall it."

His suicide succeeded where his mediation had not. The shocked antagonists agreed that Breton should have his say, unofficially and through a proxy. Paul Éluard read his speech late at night on June 24. It was restrained but nonetheless staunch in its opposition to a policy and a doctrine for which the USSR wanted endorsement from European intellectuals: the doctrine being realism and the policy her treaty of mutual assistance with France. Pacifists traumatized by World War I deplored a treaty that might justify the aggressive strategy of French warmongers.* "Is it not true," Breton asked, "that . . . ultra-imperialist France, still stupefied at having hatched a monster in Hitler, invokes the blessing of world opinion . . . to accelerate the arms race? If Soviet leaders regard their rapprochement with France as a matter of harsh necessity . . . let them at least not allow themselves to be guided like blind men or to be swept into making a sacrifice greater than that which is required of them. Beware of faith independent of reason, of lurking fideism! The Franco-Soviet pact may be necessary, but it befits us as intellectuals, now more than ever, not to desert our critical senses. . . . So long as bourgeois France has an interest in it, there is danger." It was very much on his mind that Premier Daladier had agreed to Stalin's demand, as part of the Franco-Soviet pact, that Trotsky be expelled from France, where he had been living in exile.

Breton, who was known to threaten followers with expulsion from the movement for writing fiction, or even for defending a genre he scorned, addressed the issue of realism with as much tact as he could muster. While revolutionary Western writers were urged to survey "the great tableaux of collective life" in Soviet novels (which he dubbed "a school of action"), the Soviet writer was urged to visit "the great provinces of the inner life" reflected in Western literature. "Romain Rolland, describing 'the role of the writer in present-day society,' comes to this lapidary conclusion: 'Lenin said "One must dream"; Goethe said "One must act."'" Surrealism has never aspired to anything else; all

---

* This proved to be immaterial, since the military convention associated with the treaty was never completed.

A photomontage by René Magritte of sixteen Surrealists. It appeared in issue 12 of *La Révolution Surréaliste,* December 1929. Magritte's hermetic caption reads, "I don't see the woman hidden in the forest." Breton is in the middle of the top row. To his right is Louis Aragon, who defected to the Communist Party several months later.

its efforts have tended toward a dialectical resolution of these alternatives."

"Dialectical" rolled off many tongues in the extreme heat of June 1935, like the verily verilies of panting celebrants. It rolled off Breton's again when he came to denounce the mythology of patriotism. "We Surrealists don't love our homeland," he declared.

As writers or artists, we have stated that we do not at all reject the cultural legacy of centuries. It is exasperating that we should be obliged today to recall that it is a *universal* legacy, for which we are indebted to German thought no less than to any other.* Better yet, we can say

* Breton here refers to an article by an editor of the Communist daily *L'Humanité* and, in particular, this sentence: "If, as Marx said, proletarians, being internationalists, 'do not have a homeland,' from now on they have something to defend: the cultural patrimony of

that philosophy written in German is where we have discovered the only effective antidote to the positivist rationalism that continues to ravage us. This antidote is dialectical materialism as a general theory of knowledge.

Reserved for the peroration was a mordant reference to "genuine poets" who had traded "the inner life for the externality of propaganda," meaning their birthright for a mess of pottage. He declared that they would not succeed in "liberating the mind forever" with hackneyed impeachments of Fascism. Everyone familiar with Surrealism's feuds knew that the reference was to Louis Aragon.

If Aragon, who now cut the figure of French Stalinism's tenor voice, had not stayed to hear himself belittled late at night in an almost empty hall, he learned about it soon afterward and made his own speech a diatribe against the movement from which he had divorced himself. Echoing Zola's prosecutorial "J'accuse" with the refrain "I call for a return to reality," he denounced Breton's Marxism as a shell in which the Surrealists smuggled their poetic "baggage." They were impostors bending Marxism to the theories of Sigmund Freud without regard for economic or social truths.* "It's laughable, the scorn these woolgatherers have for the 'baseness' of social reality, and their fear of *the subject* in poems, they who are inspired by a woman's farewell or the flight of time, but who marshal all their abstract energies against the establishment of the new world in poetry."

Aragon's speech chimed with the Soviet party line presented by delegates of the Union of Writers, whose shibboleth was the word "new." The bourgeoisie, proclaimed Ivan Luppol, a professor at Moscow University, had lost its title to the cultural heritage of the past, having shown itself unworthy of it. He averred, "The working class, which is also the creator of a new culture, has been appointed by History as sole heir." Clearly outside the realm of doctrinaire pretensions, if not of revolutionary tropes, were two Russians who had come from the USSR under guard, and only after Gide and Malraux insisted upon it: Boris Pasternak and Isaac Babel. Pasternak received thunderous applause when he rose to say,

---

France, the spiritual wealth accumulated by all that its artists, its artisans, its workers, its thinkers have produced."

* Aragon opened himself to the accusation of shaping Rimbaud and Lautréamont, those icons of Surrealism, to suit the arguments of Marxist dogma.

I wish to talk here about poetry, not about sickness. Poetry will always be at our feet, in the grass. One will always have to stoop to perceive it. It will always be too simple to discuss in assemblies. It will forever remain the organic function of a happy being, brimming over with the felicity of language. It will be clenched in the heart from birth. And the more happy men there are, the easier it will be to be an artist.

He then read a love poem about poetry growing in him from wild melody to words and meter, to "thee are not thee, I am not I," to his face buried in the grass for "nights of the universe" and eyes "dawning to splendid suns."

The last word might have belonged to E. M. Forster, who saw twilight rather than dawn for writers such as himself—writers bred in a liberal tradition and sworn to defend the literary métier against political and religious bondage. "My colleagues probably agree with my account of the situation in our country," he said,

but they may disagree with my old-fashioned attitude over it, and may feel that it is a waste of time to talk about freedom and tradition when the economic structure of society is unsatisfactory. They may say that if there is another war writers of the individualistic and liberalizing type, like myself and Mr. Aldous Huxley, will be swept away. I am sure that we shall be swept away, and I think furthermore that there may be another war. It seems to me that if nations keep on amassing armaments, they can no more help discharging their filth than an animal, which keeps on eating, can stop from excreting. This being so, my job, and the job of those who feel with me, is an interim job. We have just to go on tinkering as well as we can with our old tools, until the crash comes. When the crash comes, nothing is any good. After it—if there is an after—the task of civilization will be carried on by people whose training has been different from my own.

Forster's speech, as far as it was heard, did not sit well with members of the audience who had just heckled the historian Julien Benda for defending a Western tradition that understood the life of the mind to be independent of material or practical ends.* One witness, Katherine

---

* By the end of the year, after Italy's invasion of Ethiopia in October, Benda proved to be more politically militant than many left-wing intellectuals, whom he criticized for con-

Anne Porter, found the scene deeply disturbing: "I think it was just after André Malraux—then as dogmatic in Communism as he is now in some other faith—had leaped to the microphone barking like a fox to halt the applause for Julien Benda's speech, that a little slender man with a large forehead and a shy chin rose, was introduced and began to read his paper carefully prepared for this occasion." Forster paid no attention to the microphone, she remembered,

> but wove back and forth, and from side to side, gently, and every time his face passed the mouthpiece I caught a high-voiced syllable or two, never a whole word, only a thin recurring sound like the wind down a chimney as Mr. Forster's pleasant good countenance advanced and retreated and returned. Then, surprisingly, once he came to a moment's pause before the instrument and there sounded into the hall clearly but wistfully a complete sentence: "I DO believe in liberty!"

The exclamation received polite applause, for which she was thankful. "It covered the antics of that part of the audience near me," she recalled, "a whole pantomime of malignant ridicule, meaning that Mr. Forster and all his kind were already as extinct as the dodo. It was a discouraging moment."

In the April 1936 issue of the *NRF,* Jean Grenier, Albert Camus's professor of philosophy at the University of Algiers, commented upon the congress in much the same spirit as Katherine Anne Porter and E. M. Forster. "One is a Marxist in 1935 as one was a Republican in 1880," he wrote. "We have witnessed the paradox of a Congress for the Defense of Culture initiated by a regime that terrorizes intellectuals, allowing no 'deviation' from established doctrine whether on the Right or the Left, and tolerating scholars and artists only if they remain rigorously 'neutral,' or rather, if they passively adhere to the catechism of the country. They may be honored and revered on that condition, and that condition alone."

In one of the closing speeches, Malraux expressed the hope that in the future, when all the differences at play during the congress were

---

tenting themselves with endless jeremiads against Mussolini but their unwillingness to demand that Fascist aggression be countered with armed force.

At the Congress of Writers for the Defense of Culture, from left to right: André Malraux, Ilya Ehrenburg, and Boris Pasternak.

reconciled in the "fraternal beyond," history would chronicle only the common will that had brought everyone together for five days in June.

His optimistic eulogy could have been repeated, several weeks later, to announce the birth of a political coalition called the Front Populaire—the Popular Front. On Bastille Day 1935, Socialists, Communists, and Radicals stood side by side, under an anti-Fascist banner, with an eye to legislative elections scheduled for April 1936. Communists (whose cues came from the Kremlin), Socialists (whose economic program, for lack of an absolute electoral mandate, was more Rooseveltian than revolutionary), and Radicals (whose constituency was a middle class of entrepreneurs, artisans, doctors, and lawyers generally averse to government regulation) made a motley crowd. Bending more to the left or right than was their wont, they squeezed together on a platform that included the dissolution of paramilitary leagues, the defense of unions and the secular school system, the nationalization of the aviation industry, ambitious public works, unemployment insurance, a forty-hour work week, paid vacations, and an agency charged with protecting the grain trade against speculation.* Their slogan, "Bread, peace, and liberty" required drastic accommodation, especially on the part of the PCF, which had endorsed the Franco-Soviet

---

* Among the young Turks who fought against doctrinal sclerosis in the Radical and Socialist parties were Pierre Mendès France and Claude Lévi-Strauss.

pact and tacitly subscribed to the Stalinist imperative that rearmament proceed apace.

Although the victory of the Popular Front in April 1936 was not overwhelming, it gained a decisive legislative majority, and its leader, Léon Blum, became premier.

Being Jewish and in former days an astute literary critic, Léon Blum resembled no one else in the higher reaches of French politics. Born in 1872, a year after France ceded Alsace, from which his father had emigrated, Blum grew up in bourgeois comfort and distinguished himself at the Lycée Henri IV, one of France's elite institutions, where André Gide was a schoolmate. He gained admittance to the École Normale Supérieure, ranked first in philosophy, but dropped out to study law, despite his literary and philosophical ambitions. Those ambitions persisted. During the 1890s, Blum led a double life, earning his livelihood in government service as a member of the Council of State which exercised judicial review over decisions of the executive branch, while regularly contributing to *La Revue Blanche,* a magazine founded by the Natanson brothers, graduates of the Lycée Condorcet, and destined during its brief run (1889–1903) to mark the literary and intellectual life of fin-de-siècle Paris. In politics, it addressed such issues of the moment as the Dreyfus Affair, from a Dreyfusard perspective, and the massacre of Armenians. It opened its pages to writers as incongruous as Alfred Jarry, Paul Claudel, André Gide, Guillaume Apollinaire, Marcel Proust, and the anarchist Félix Fénéon. It featured the art of the Nabis and the Neo-Impressionists; Bonnard, Vuillard, Toulouse-Lautrec, Vallotton, and Cappiello illustrated books published under its imprint.

As for Léon Blum, *La Revue Blanche* welcomed reviews by the young lawyer, who moved in the wide circle of intellectuals associated with Thadée Natanson. Thus did he meet Jean Jaurès. The year was 1897, two months before Zola published "J'accuse," and the meeting proved fateful. "Léon Blum behaved toward his elder [Blum was twenty-five, Jaurès thirty-eight] like a disciple who would consent to know nothing for the pleasure of learning everything from a master such as he," wrote Natanson. "Their age difference was about the same as that between Socrates and Alcibiades when Alcibiades avidly sought the teaching and favor of the philosopher. As long as Jaurès lived, Blum listened to him. He never thought that he had anything more or better to do." The Dreyfus Affair created new mentors and discredited old ones, notably Maurice Barrès. It clouded Blum's youthful admiration for the author of *Le Culte du Moi,* whom he vainly petitioned to join Zola in righting a scandalous miscarriage of justice.

Blum wrote for *L'Humanité* when Jaurès launched the paper in 1904, one year after *La Revue Blanche* ceased publication. But he wrote much else besides, notably a book entitled *Le Mariage,* which sparked controversy by pleading the case for women's emancipation from the pieties, myths, and legal strictures that assigned them a juvenile role in society. Conservatives bristled. Caricatures depicting a bespectacled old suffragette with Blum's features abounded in the right-wing press and never went out of fashion: Blum the Jew, or Blum the subversive, upon whom Vichyites blamed France's debacle thirty years later, in 1940, was seen as effeminate.*

Having established his expertise in administrative law, he was appointed principal private secretary in 1914 to Marcel Sembat, the minister of public works, and observed at first hand the dysfunction of government in a republic whose executive was constitutionally handicapped. Out of that experience came a book entitled *Letters on Government Reform,* which foreshadowed Blum's commitment to an active political life.

Whether or not an active political life was yet what he had in mind or wanted unambivalently (there were financial and domestic impediments), it was what came to pass. In 1919, he drafted a party program. He then stood for election from Paris and won. A year later, the Socialists convened in the city of Tours to consider the demand of a large delegation that the party cast its lot with the Bolsheviks and accept twenty-one conditions prescribed by Grigory Zinoviev, executive director of the Comintern.† Blum, who did not recognize greater

---

* The book certainly reflected the influence of Blum's mother, a woman devoted to the cause of social justice, with whom he had a loving relationship. It also points to Blum's great admiration for Stendhal, and in some ways takes Stendhal's *De l'Amour* as a model. He may not have been aware of a stirring speech that a great Radical politician of an earlier generation, Jules Ferry, had delivered at the Sorbonne in 1870, when the institution of a republic hung in the balance: "Bishops know perfectly well that whoever controls a wife controls her husband. That is why the Church wants to hold her fast, and why democracy must make her its own. Citizens, democracy must choose, under pain of death. Woman must belong either to Science or to the Church."

† Since the war, membership in the SFIO had increased threefold, with veterans radicalizing the party. As one leader explained, "These new memberships included men severely tried by the bloody tragedy, who had suffered physically and emotionally, in their liveli-

Léon Blum

virtue in the dictatorship of the proletariat than in dictatorship pure and simple, presented the case for social democracy. The SFIO would ultimately achieve social justice, he argued, as a party among parties, subject to universal suffrage within the bounds of a functioning republic. Incompatible with republicanism were the statutes of the Comintern, which threatened to make deputies in Paris straw men answerable to an "occult" central committee in Moscow. Blum said that he could not tolerate "a doctrine that I consider . . . intrinsically false, at odds with the entire theoretical and historical tradition of Socialism, and in any event radically inapplicable to action in France."

---

hoods and in their affective life, in their social situation and in their flesh, small tradesmen whose businesses were extinguished, men of the liberal professions who had lost their clientele, ruined households, sons killed, wounded, mutilated. Among casualties of the great storm, the most quixotic and the most desperate.

The second of the twenty-one conditions specified that "every organization that wishes to affiliate to the Communist International must regularly and methodically remove reformists and centrists from every responsible post in the labor movement (party organizations, editorial boards, trade unions, parliamentary factions, co-operatives, local government) and replace them with tested Communists, without worrying unduly about that fact that, particularly at first, ordinary workers from the masses will be replacing 'experienced' opportunists."

Zinoviev (born Osvei-Gershon Aronovich Apfelbaum) served as a member of the Politburo and first executive director of the Comintern. Under Stalin he fell from grace, and in 1936 was the chief defendant in the Moscow show trial called the Trial of the Sixteen. He was of course found guilty and executed.

He published this credo in *L'Humanité* on October 27 and voiced it two months later at Tours. By then, December 27, it sounded like the parting words of a castaway to his shipwreck. At Tours, the party split in two. After 1920, *L'Humanité* would no longer publish Blum. The newspaper founded by Jean Jaurès had become the organ of a Communist party, the PCF, distinct from the SFIO, which considered itself Jaurès's true heir. At the rump meeting of loyalists at Tours, Blum called upon his colleagues to save another daily, *Le Populaire.* The paper had served him well during the late 1920s, when he became its editor in chief and emerged as leader of the faction in Parliament.

Until the mid-1930s, however, the party's best brain could not help the SFIO resolve the contradiction between its chartered purpose, which was revolutionary, and its modus operandi, which was reformist. While consenting to negotiate successful electoral alliances with the cautiously leftist Radicals in 1924, 1928, and 1932, it would not accept responsibility for executive action by sharing power with them (except briefly, during the "sacred union") or vote on budgets. It thus sacrificed its muscle to its doctrinal virtue. As much may be said of the pacifism a majority advocated in the face of German rearmament, spurning opponents who preached Vegetius's adage *Si vis pacem, para bellum*: "If you want peace, prepare for war."

Hitler's rise, the riots of February 1934, and the Comintern's sudden disposition to befriend parties it had hitherto stigmatized as Fascist or "Social-Fascist" did not immediately raze barriers. Blum hesitated longer than most before yielding to the necessity of creating a common front with the heterogeneous Left and seeking power. By Bastille Day 1935 he had reconciled himself to both. "Short of repudiating parliamentary participation itself, I see no way of absolutely escaping the possible obligation [of ruling]," he wrote. "A proletarian party obligates itself willy-nilly when it gains a majority or is the preponderant element within a majority." The view of some colleagues that an electoral victory should lead right away to the dismantling of the economic and political institutions upon which a capitalist society rested did not comport with his understanding of events. The Popular Front's priority was not to destroy and construct but to defend France against military rule. Fascist coups had succeeded in three countries, and shadows of a fourth hung over republican Spain.

That Léon Blum had his own person to defend against violence became shockingly clear during the electoral campaign of 1936. On

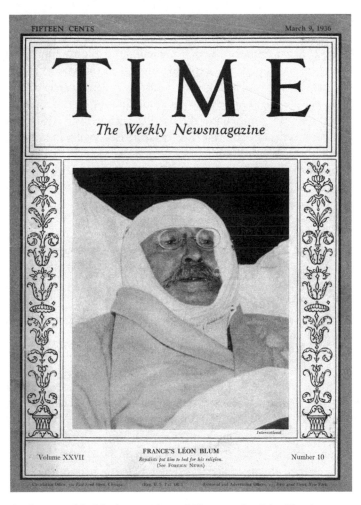

FIFTEEN CENTS   March 9, 1936

TIME

The Weekly Newsmagazine

International

Volume XXVII

FRANCE'S LÉON BLUM
Royalists put him to bed for his religion.
(See FOREIGN NEWS)

Number 10

On the cover of the March 9, 1936, issue of *Time* magazine, Léon Blum is pictured in bandages after a savage beating by right-wing thugs. He became premier three months later.

February 13, the funeral cortège of the historian Jacques Bainville, a pillar of L'Action Française, was proceeding along the Boulevard Saint-Germain when onlookers, widely believed to include Camelots du Roi, recognized Blum caught in a traffic jam. They smashed the windows of his automobile, unhinged the doors, beat him bloody, molested his companions, and shouted, "Finish them off!" They might have done so if not for the intervention of several policemen and construction workers who witnessed the attack from their scaffolding. *L'Action Française*, which made light of Blum's injuries and blamed him for impudently exposing himself to the fury of a crowd paying its last respects to a great royalist, was denounced in Parliament by the premier. On February 16, thousands protesting the attack marched from the Panthéon to the Bastille, with red and tricolor flags held high. Later that year, Maurras was sentenced to eleven months in prison for incitement to murder.

Léon Blum convalesced during an ominous month. Hitler marched into the Rhineland with seventeen infantry battalions, in violation of the Locarno Treaty of 1925, whose other signatories—France, Belgium, England, and Italy—did nothing to oppose him. Keeping faith with his memories of Jean Jaurès in July 1914, and judging prudence to be the better part of valor on the eve of an election, Blum supported nonintervention.

The Popular Front emerged victorious from the election of 1936, which made Socialists the single largest party in Parliament, benefiting from a misguided monetary policy that had crippled production and thrown multitudes out of work. L'Action Française might have regretted the likelihood that outrage at Blum's mugging added votes to the winning margin, if regret ever clouded Léon Daudet's and Charles Maurras's self-righteousness. Their verbal assaults on him in *L'Action Française* became more vicious. They lost whatever they still possessed of a civil tongue after the Popular Front's victory and vented their anti-Semitism when Blum took office. "France Under the Jew" ran across the front page in bold print on June 5, 1936. Two days later it reported the first appearance before Parliament of the cabinet appointed by "Blum the Jew," derisively noting its female and Jewish ministers.

L'Action Française was not the only propagator of virulent anti-Semitism.* Politicians could be relied upon by the right-wing press to provide quotable copy. On June 4, Louis Darquier de Pellepoix, who later reached the acme of his career as Vichy's commissioner for Jewish questions, proposed that the General Council of the Seine, on which he sat, urge unspecified "public powers" to combat

---

* In language common to anti-Semites overt and covert alike, Blum was often portrayed as straining to make himself heard while his parliamentary antagonists spoke in strong, resonant voices.

what he called Jewish tyranny by reconsidering the enfranchisement of Jews and challenging their right to run for office. Given the fact that certain politicians owed their success to an electoral clientele of foreigners imported en masse and hastily transformed into French citizens by a complicit administration, it behooved the state, he argued, to declare null and void all naturalizations approved since November 11, 1918. Unless measures were taken to neuter the alien within, Frenchmen—real Frenchmen, whose "personal destiny" was bound up with that of the nation—faced destruction.

More widely reported was a statement made in the Chamber of Deputies the next day, when Léon Blum presented himself to Parliament for his formal confidence vote and entertained challenges from the Assembly. One such challenge, or *interpellation,* came from Xavier Vallat, representing the Ardèche region, whose tirades against Jews, Freemasons, and foreigners were notorious. Vallat declared that Blum himself was the reason he could not vote for the new administration, and he explained why in a speech frequently interrupted by remonstrances on the Left, applause on the Right, and words of caution from the Speaker.

> Your assumption of power, Mr. Prime Minister, is unquestionably an historic event. For the first time, this old Gallo-Roman land will be governed by a Jew. . . . I say what I think—and bear the disagreeable burden of saying aloud what others only think—which is that this peasant nation would be better served by someone whose origins, however modest, reach into the entrails of our soil than by a subtle talmudicist. . . . The average Frenchman will be uneasy when he considers that M. Blum's decisions were taken in council with the likes of M. Blumel (his general secretary), M. Moch (his general secretary), Messrs. Cain and Lévy (his confidants), and M. Rosenfeld (his penholder).

The Speaker, Édouard Herriot, finally restored order, but not before deputies on the Right and Left had leapt from their benches and invaded each other's quadrant of the amphitheater with fists flying.

During the run-up to Blum's premiership, disgruntled workers were occupying airplane factories, mines, large farms, railroad sheds, construction sites, and department stores throughout France. The slow economy ground to a virtual halt, and the right-wing press stoked fears of revolution. *L'Action Française, Le Figaro,* and other papers suggested that in a scheme devised by the Comintern, Blum had been assigned the role of Kerensky. What credulous deputies thus saw when he delivered his inaugural address was a stooge destined to make way for a Bolshevik despot. If the plot unfolded accordingly, Blum's prudent agenda would prove to have been a Menshevik fable.* Blum haters disposed to suspend disbelief cited a pamphlet entitled *Les Soviets Contre la France,* which read like a well-plotted spy novel, asserting that France's version of the October Revolution would take place on June 12.

By June 12, Blum's government had helped union officials and employers negotiate a settlement, called the Matignon Accords.† Strikes ended and doomsday passed without incident. But alarmists, above all *L'Action Française,* did not want for alternate versions of the apocalypse. Maurras declared that Blum's economic reforms spelled disaster, and especially his proposal to tax the rich. The rich were not wealthy enough to afford additional taxes, as their fortunes were illiquid. They would be compelled to sell property at a loss. And who would profit? Flocks of Jews from all over the world would darken the sky, like buzzards circling carrion. They would acquire whatever it pleased them to own: factories, ateliers, fields, houses, châteaux, historical and art treasures, sacred relics. "Already, thanks to the state-controlled revenue service, established fortunes are no longer renewing themselves, capital is no longer making up its losses. With a Judeo-Socialist tax collector, the residue will soon evaporate."

---

* "The mission of the Party, which is to construct the new society, has not varied, but the task of government is different," said Blum. "We must find out whether we can assure a peaceful, amiable transition from society as it is now to the society whose ultimate realization is and remains our goal. We shall have to be at once bold and wise, to accomplish a long-term project and straightaway take measures that tangibly and effectively affect national life."

† The Hôtel Matignon, on the Rue de Varenne, is the official residence of the premier.

CHAPTER II

Totalitarian Pavilions

Pierre Drieu La Rochelle asserted that the riots of February 6 had been a cure for his infirmity of purpose, that manhood required a weight around one's neck and the will to leap. We last saw him leaping in 1934. We find that he had not yet touched bottom in 1936. Two years in midair had given him ample opportunity to wonder whether bottom would be Fascism or Communism; to court the immensely rich wife of the automobile manufacturer Renault; to write about their affair in the guise of a Persian tale entitled *Beloukia;* to feel liberated by his father's death and imprisoned by his father's ghost; and to write a long short story about a Russian double agent.

"L'Agent Double," as he entitled that story, says much about his own doubleness. Torn between Bolshevism and orthodox czarism, the nameless agent cannot exist except at extremes, and rallies to revolution rather than reaction after falling under the spell of a "leader." In Drieu's phallically charged language, he feels "the sudden power that spurts from a circle of men." What they think matters less than the fact that they think it together and fanatically. Ideology is the bond of a virile brotherhood and, without really believing its articles of faith, the double agent masters its rhetoric. Drieu's character possesses the fluency that served Drieu himself for good and ill throughout his life. It gives him prosthetic muscle. It embellishes a void.* "I had promptly

---

* In Marguerite Duras's brief description of him at a literary salon during the occupation, he is the opposite of glib but nonetheless hollow: "Clearly suffering from pride, he scarcely deigned to speak, and when he did it was as if his voice was dubbed, his words translated, stiff." Guests encountered a similar absentee at Colette Jéramec's receptions during their brief, unhappy marriage.

A demonstration of the Popular Front in June 1937. Banners call for the government to provide old-age pensions.

introduced myself into the ideas proposed to me and argued them to their ultimate consequences. I liked doing that and did it well, too well. . . . Some people were dazzled by my rapid train of thought, which ended up at an absolute that bordered on nothingness." His assignment is to spy on radical czarists led by an orthodox pope.

The evangelist of other men's gospels and the seducer of other men's wives soon transfers his allegiance to the pope on whom he spies, but in whom he finds instead a new source of virility: "I was bigamous. I had two loves. The soul can be completely separated from itself. I served God and the Devil." He becomes a double agent, doubly spellbound, when the Rasputinish pope orders him to befriend and betray a young French Communist named Lehalleur. "From the first I recognized all that was precious in [Lehalleur]. He was a leader. And in calling him a leader, I know whereof I speak. . . . Nothing could be farther from the blurry world of democrats, which reserves high office for musta-chioed sopranos always ready to submit their letters of resignation, to drop their burdens." What makes Lehalleur "precious" is not his wide compass but his narrow focus. For the leader, reason is the servant of action. It doesn't shed light; it burns like a glass that concentrates the sun's rays into a laser. Whether Fascist or Communist, he belongs to that singular race of men whose every word and minute count. They are destined. They are the protagonists of history.

In Jacques Doriot, who founded the French Fascist Party (the Parti Populaire Français) several weeks after Léon Blum took office, Drieu, like the hero of Maurice Barrès's *L'Appel au Soldat,* believed he had found the charismatic leader ordained to save him from the randomness of his life and cast him in a legendary drama.

Doriot was five years younger than Drieu. The son of a blacksmith, he had left the Picardy countryside at seventeen, settled in the populous, working-class Paris suburb of Saint-Denis, joined the automobile workers' union and a youth group before being drafted for service on the eastern front, where he witnessed the Communist revolution in Hungary in March 1919 and D'Annunzio's invasion of Fiume several months later.

Discharged from the army with the Croix de Guerre, Doriot took up where he had left off as a militant member of Socialist Youth, leading his group into the Soviet camp at the Congress of Tours in 1920. This exploit earned him an official invitation to the Third Congress of the Communist International at Moscow, where he rubbed elbows with Lenin and, during a sojourn of fourteen months, conferred with Trotsky on the Commission of Latin Countries. He was twenty-four and intoxicated by his sudden eminence, according to Drieu, who published a biographical essay in 1936: "The young red leader hardly gave a thought to the immense toll of human lives taken by the Bolshevik regime, the material and spiritual wreckage." Two years later he became a member of the executive committee of the Comintern and secretary-general of the Communist Youth, whose numbers quintupled under his leadership, to the consternation of the Poincaré government, which imprisoned him for violently demonstrating against the occupation of the Ruhr. All these credentials served him well in 1924, when Saint-Denis elected him to Parliament, but he continued to distinguish himself in the streets with his bold protests rather than at the Palais Bourbon with his oratory. "Those who saw Doriot back then, alone, defying two hundred policemen, plunging into their midst while twirling a café table over his head . . . know that in France there is at least one political man who is a man," wrote Drieu.

More important than the Republican Parliament was the Comintern, which summoned Doriot to Moscow during the struggle between Stalin and Trotsky and later dispatched him to Shanghai, where he found Chiang Kai-shek and Communists led by Mao Tse-tung locked in civil war. By age thirty, Doriot had acquired as much as he needed of political experience to survive in a world of divided loyalties and to engage in safe transgression, asserting his independence but ultimately toeing the line.

He ceased to toe the line in the early 1930s when his proletarian constituency elected him mayor of Saint-Denis. Greatly admired at home, the burly, stentorian Doriot made himself increasingly objectionable to Moscow with arguments that ran counter to Soviet policy. In 1934, a year before Stalin and his French deputies sanctioned the idea, he championed a popular front. It cost him his membership in the party, but it freed him to form his own, which he did on June 28, 1936. The inaugural meeting of the Parti Populaire Français was held at Saint-Denis. Doriot spoke for almost three hours, promising the thousand people present—among them Pierre Drieu La Rochelle—that their salvation lay in a political model for France akin to Nazi Germany or Fascist Italy. He prosecuted internationalism as a crime subversive of the nation's soul and inveighed against the Soviet Union for holding France hostage to its global designs. The PPF would be national and its program National Socialist.

> To restore the French nation its unity, its prosperity, its security, and its place on the world stage, to give each producer his share of social progress, it is imperative that the country rid itself of foreign influence and vanquish the egoism of the propertied classes. To accomplish this goal, an instrument is needed. Our party will serve that purpose.

"Left" and "right" were insidious distinctions bound up with a history of internecine warfare. If there was to be one France, only one party could unify it.*

Doriot drew one thousand people to the Saint-Denis town hall on June 26.

Before long, the PPF's members numbered 130,000 and its meetings filled the immense Vélodrome d'Hiver in Paris.† It also published

---

* Doriot was of course familiar with the Nazi slogan: *"Ein Volk, ein Reich, ein Führer."*

† Nicknamed the "Vel' d'Hiv,'" it became infamous during the German occupation as the warehouse for thirteen thousand Jews rounded up in July 1942 and subsequently transported to death camps.

a newspaper, *L'Émancipation Nationale,* to which Drieu contributed regularly between 1936 and 1938; its circulation exceeded 200,000. Did he finally have ground under his feet? Did he stand as tall as Aragon? To readers who had never read *Le Feu Follet* or heard of Drieu's novels, he became known for his political enthusiasms. When the Popular Front was passing social legislation in great earnest during the summer of 1936, Drieu, who wore the label "Fascist" as a badge of honor and claimed his place in the line of Maurice Barrès's ideological heirs, was preaching the transcendent virtue of the corporate state. "You have lived too long hidden in your houses, cocooned in your little lives and individual histories," he wrote on August 1. "You no longer know what it is to be together, all together. . . . People everywhere have taken to the streets, have broken the petty chains of the small individual life, have reimmersed themselves in great communions. Sing, shout, squirm, stretch your arms, invoke the Holy Spirit, it will descend upon you. Remember that you are the people who gave Europe its cathedrals, those powerful monuments of collective fervor, of unanimous faith." Membership in the PPF was not a matter of paying dues and subscribing to newspapers but an all-pervasive commitment. At stake was not merely one's political wholesomeness but one's very reason for being. "The Parti Populaire Français will be nothing or it will be the basis for a riotous multiplication of cells and sections. . . . One will no longer belong to it for an hour a day, a day a month, a month a year. One will belong to it at every moment. We must retune our lives to one another. We must rediscover the daily rhythm of communal life." Having witnessed the Nazi Party congress at Nuremberg and likened the spectacle of a human mass animated by the will of a *magister ludi* to Diaghilev's Ballets Russes, which had sent shock waves through Paris in 1913 with the pagan eruption of *The Rite of Spring,* Drieu continued in the same vein. The ideal Fascist society would be harmonious and choreographed. It would make him complete, as the mind had not. "In a Europe where the great, cadenced, reharmonized masses of Fascism, of Hitlerism, of Stalinist Russia have risen, we must quickly breathe in lungfuls of grandeur. If we don't, history will blow away our côteries, our wretched political parties, our crabbed individualities like so much dust." Physical culture obsessed him. Much of what he wrote for *L'Émancipation Nationale* suggests that the self-proclaimed Fascist of 1936 could still recite *Thus Spake Zarathustra* chapter and verse. But also lingering in him

Jacques Doriot addressing members of the Fascist Parti Populaire Français.

was the adolescent hero worshipper besotted with Kipling and Carlyle, who admired his Anglo-Saxon schoolmates romping on the pitches of Shrewsbury. The PPF was the "party of the living body," he wrote. "The most profound definition of Fascism is this: it is the political movement that charts its course most straightforwardly, most radically toward a great revolution of mores, toward the restoration of the body—health, dignity, plenitude, heroism."

Being absolutely devoid of all these virtues, the Jew emerged as their negative exemplar in Drieu's outpouring of journalism and in his novel *Gilles*. Anti-Semitic caricatures were widespread. By the late 1930s, there existed an abundant literature portraying Jews as rootless individualists, neurotic champions of modernism, and foreigners pernicious to the body politic. "The element of disintegration, the element of division, the microbe is the JEW," Darquier de Pellepoix wrote in his journal *L'Antijuif.* "[We] assert that the solution to the Jewish problem is the prerequisite for any French renovation." Drieu may not have had in mind the same solution as Darquier, who eventually played a direct role in the Holocaust, but they quoted from the same text. "In whatever language decadence slavers, whether it be Marxism or Freudianism, the words of Jews inform the drool; biology will have

Jacques Doriot six years after founding the PPF, greeting crowds on the Champs-Élysées during the German occupation.

its way," says the titular hero of Drieu's novel *Gilles.* From the perspective of the aesthete, Jews were ineligible by nature and temperament to participate in France's communal dance. They didn't know the steps for it; they didn't have the legs. Gilles's friend Preuss, for example, "was the most disjointed, the most indecorous, the most ill-assembled Jew ever produced on Christian soil. Wherever he appeared, the senseless disorder of his limbs, of his clothes, and of his statements created a little whirlwind that caught all the Christians or Aryans present in its vortex and dulled their wits."* Hectic in speech and spastic in movement, he is herky-jerky even in his ambitions: "Like many Jews, he wasn't patient or organized in his quest for success. Bolstering him

---

* In an unofficial capacity, Jean Giraudoux, the minister of information in 1939, against whom Drieu fulminated for representing a government that censored *Gilles,* shared his anti-Semitism. Giraudoux described Jews seeking asylum from Nazism in France as "a horde that manages to get stripped of its national rights, to invite expulsion, and whose frail and abnormal constitutions land them in our hospitals, monopolizing wards." He was known to be in favor of establishing a "ministry of race."

were two or three generations who had acquired material security in France, among whom the hunger for wealth was not as sharp as it had once been. Money lust had become an appetite for success, which haunted him episodically, like a recurrent neurasthenia."

Preuss is only a superlative specimen of his kind. Referring to Gilles's Jewish wife, whom Drieu modeled after Colette Jéramec, he writes that in her deracinated milieu "physical experience was unknown, whether it be sport, love, or war." Theirs was a world of abstraction in which bodies didn't couple, clash, weigh, belong here rather than there, and generally accord with nature. Being estranged from the natural world led them, like the potion that deranges Titania, to embrace a Bottom of grotesque images celebrated as modernity. The Jew is modernity incarnate.

Whence Drieu's chimera of a medieval golden age. The obloquy he heaped on rationalism, the Enlightenment, Freemasonry, Jewry, and the "intellectual individualism" fostered by the French school system was bound up with his enthusiasm for the communal spirit that reared churches in which the individual found refuge from his personal history, his conflicts, and daily impostures. "To make a church, there was audacity, risk, the creative expression of faith in the architect's calculations. There was the tree and next to it the church. . . . There was French reason in that furious, proud, passionate 12th century gushing with epic poems, cathedrals, Christian philosophies, sculpture, stained glass, illuminations, crusades." The stone cut from French quarries and the tree rooted in French soil are the stuff of "French reason." Had Drieu been of age in the 1880s to observe the rising of the Eiffel Tower, he would no doubt have joined the protest of writers and artists who denounced it as an insult to the "august proliferation of stone" that is Paris.

Although Drieu's political vow was noted with dismay by friends in the opposing camp—for he still had some there—a greater splash was made in 1936 by André Gide's recantation. At the international congress, which he cochaired, Gide had praised the Soviet Union for marrying nationalism to internationalism in its celebration of the idiosyncratic cultures under its broad sway. He contended likewise that the great literary works of every country—*Don Quixote, Gargantua and Pantagruel,* the theater of Shakespeare and Racine—did the same, expressing the universal in the particular. What reflected badly on French literature was its infatuation with form and appearance. A penchant for abstraction marred even those works that offered the travails of the common man a prominent place in the realm of literature: Hugo's *Les Misérables,* Zola's *Les Rougon-Macquart.* He tipped his hat no higher than that to the creed of realism, but his peroration made up for his restraint. "Only adversaries of Communism can see in it a will to create total uniformity," he said. "What we await from it, and what the USSR has begun to show us after its embattled period . . . is a social state that encourages the greatest possible flowering of every man, the realization of all his possibilities. In our woeful West, we fall far short."

Being France's preeminent fellow traveler earned Gide an invitation from the Soviet Writers' Union, and in June 1936 (after several changes of mind prompted by conversations with his friend Pierre Herbart, who had visited the Soviet Union and peeked behind the facade of Potemkin village), Gide arrived in Moscow. He was carried to an official reception on the shoulders of airport employees, as the novelist Louis Guilloux, the publisher Jacques Schiffrin and other members of his entourage followed on foot. But a dark shadow fell over events the next morning when Mikhail Koltsov, editor in chief of *Pravda,* informed Gide that Maxim Gorky, who had been ailing, had died during the night. Credible rumors, which reached Gide's ear, began to circulate that Stalin, fearful of Gorky's opposition, had had him assassinated. Gide was denied access to Gorky's villa but joined the honor guard at his coffin in the Hall of Columns of the House of Unions. A day later, he stood on a podium overlooking Red Square, beside Stalin, and delivered a funeral oration that might as well have been scripted for him by a party hack. Willful naïveté was the most sympathetic construction placed upon it. Literature of the future, he prophesied, would be "national in form and in content." Writers "of value" had always striven to encourage the ferment of insubordination and revolt in society, but in a revolutionary society, such writers were no longer insubordinate. "The fate of culture is bound in our minds to the very destiny of the USSR," he said. "We shall defend it."

The state set in motion its propaganda machine for Gide's benefit during the nine weeks he spent touring the Soviet Union, from Moscow and Leningrad to Tiflis and Sebastopol. It distributed three hundred thousand postcards with his photograph. He was toasted at an endless round of receptions, housed in large hotel suites, chauffeured in Lincoln limousines. His itinerary was planned to a fare-thee-well

Gide delivering a eulogy to Maxim Gorky on Red Square in 1936, during his tour of the Soviet Union. To the right are Molotov—chairman of the Council of People's Commissars—and Stalin.

and armed against improvisation.* He was taken to model factories and surrounded with smiling workers. He visited Bolshevo, a model labor colony with its own industrial plant, where convicts attended classes in proper Soviet etiquette and recited well-rehearsed accounts of their crimes for the distinguished visitor. Long queues at state stores, uniformly drab clothes, and other depressing sights observed on forays through the streets of Moscow gave him pause, but every respect in which the workers' paradise obviously departed from an ideal narrative had its justification. Did Boris Pasternak and Isaac Babel, who were now prevented from publishing their work, say nothing to disabuse him when he visited their dachas in the writers' colony of Peredelkino, outside Moscow?

Two years earlier, in April 1934, a frightened Pasternak had warned Osip Mandelstam that the walls had ears, and maybe even the benches on the boulevard, after hearing the doomed poet recite his satirical poem "The Stalin Epigram." Babel was not arrested until 1939. Inevitably, he would suffer the same fate as Mandelstam. But Gide, for all his misgivings about the Communist utopia, returned from the USSR clinging publicly to his belief. The Great Purge, which began

---

* "In no country have I seen so many barricades, barbed-wire fences, 'no entry' signs, special passes, guards and sentry-huts," Herbart noted.

soon thereafter, in August 1936, with a show trial of Bolsheviks Stalin wanted to eliminate, including Zinoviev and Lev Kamenev, disturbed him. "[I read] the report about the Moscow trial (which the *Journal de Moscou* of 25 August gives in extenso) with indescribable uneasiness," he wrote in his journal on September 5. "What is one to think about these sixteen defendants accusing themselves, all in almost the same language, while lauding a regime and a man for whose destruction they allegedly risked their lives?" Gide's qualm was by no means the least skeptical reaction among Western Russophiles. In America, Corliss Lamont, Lillian Hellman, and eighty-seven other public figures published "An Open Letter to American Liberals" denouncing criticism of the Moscow trials. Joseph E. Davies, the United States ambassador to the USSR, declared in *Mission to Moscow,*

> Assuming . . . that basically human nature is much the same everywhere, I am still impressed with the many indications of credibility which were obtained in the course of the testimony. To have assumed that this proceeding was invented and staged as a project of dramatic political fiction would be to presuppose the creative genius of a Shakespeare and the genius of a Belasco in stage production. The historical background and surrounding circumstances also lend credibility to the testimony. . . . The circumstantial detail, apparently at times surprising even to the prosecutor as well as to other defendants, which was brought out by the various accused, gave unintended corroboration to the gist of the charges.

L'Humanité served up a report from *Pravda* that the authorities had indisputable proof of the sixteen "Trotskyites" conspiring with the Gestapo to overthrow Stalin. It excoriated *Le Populaire* for wondering whether the defendants, guilty though they may have been, had received legal counsel and other benefits of due process during their trial. Editors of that paper, like Gide, felt "*malaisés.*"

"Malaise" was a euphemism for something much worse. Just as the Socialists could not voice their incredulity without splintering the Popular Front, so Gide could not voice his disillusionment without fearing the clatter of his fall from Marxist grace and the comfort his palinode would give the enemy. He had been placed on a very high pedestal. Still, he wished to make amends for championing a despotic regime, all the more after learning at first hand that it tortured and imprisoned homosexuals.* When word spread of the possibility that he might write critically about the USSR, Louis Aragon and others begged him not to, arguing that the insurrection of Fascist troops in Spain demanded solidarity. Two years later in his novel *Man's Hope*, Malraux would declare that it was necessary in war to cast a blind eye on the abominations of one's ally. War is Manichean, he wrote, anticipating Churchill's famous line, also spoken with the Soviet Union in mind: "If Hitler invaded Hell, I would at least make a favorable reference to the Devil in the House of Commons."

Once Gide made up his mind, with moral support from Schiffrin and Guilloux, who had quit the Russian tour in disgust, nothing could deter him. *Retour de l'URSS* was written quickly and appeared on November 13. In a preface, Gide warned the reader that the short book was not a rebuff but an expression of tough love. His mind, he said, was so constituted as to treat most harshly what he would have liked to approve unreservedly. His calling attention to its flaws was not to be understood as disparagement of the Soviet Union but as concern for a revolutionary order whose prodigious accomplishments had stunned the world. If his guide had wandered off a path that promised salvation for the suffering of the earth, was blame to be placed on the path or the guide?

Gide then proceeded to describe the reign of a despot. "One encounters Stalin's effigy everywhere," he wrote. "His name is on every tongue, praise of him inevitably enters every speech. Especially in Georgia, I couldn't enter an occupied room, however humble and squalid, without noticing a portrait of Stalin nailed to the wall, where an icon formerly hung no doubt. I don't know whether it's out of adoration, love or fear, but he is always and everywhere there." Conformism, or what Gide called "the spirit of submission," was mandatory. Every deviation from the official line was denounced as counterrevolutionary and labeled "Trotskyite." In a country kept ignorant of events and conditions beyond its borders, truth issued from the head of its leader.

> Suppressing the opposition in a State, or simply preventing it from forming, from articulating itself, is a very grave matter. Terrorism is born of it. It would undoubtedly be a great convenience to rulers if all citizens thought alike. But who, in view of such impoverishment,

---

* In 1924, Gide had published a famous apology of homosexuality, *Corydon*.

could still dare speak of "culture"? . . . There is great wisdom, I think, in listening to adversaries, in nurturing the opposition if need be, while preventing it from doing harm: of combating it but not suppressing it. Suppressing the opposition—it's a good thing Stalin is so bad at it.

Gide went on to write that humanity is not simple, that attempts at simplification, unification, or reduction imposed from above were odious, and ultimately futile.

"The Holy Family will always escape Herod" was Gide's way of saying that one purge would never suffice. There would always be partisan voices to silence, as well as inconvenient memories. Like a conscience that convicts by its mere existence, "old Bolsheviks" faithful to the spirit of the revolution had become an unacceptable limit to the will of the tyrant. If there was some one thing that finally convinced Gide to throw caution to the winds in *Retour de l'URSS* it was the show trial of 1936. "The spirit regarded as 'counterrevolutionary' today is the same revolutionary spirit that staved in the half-rotten casks of the old czarist world," he asserted.

One would like to be able to think that an overwhelming love of man, or at least an imperious need of justice filled hearts. But once the revolution triumphed, they were no longer an issue. Feelings of that sort, which spurred the first revolutionaries, became encumbrances. . . . I compare them to the wedges needed to build an arch but superfluous once the keystone has been inserted. Now that the revolution has stabilized, now that it compounds with its conscience and (some would say) has learned to behave, those who regard its successive concessions as so many betrayals are reviled. Would it not be better, instead of playing with words, to recognize that the revolutionary spirit (and even, simply, the critical spirit) is outmoded? Conformism is the order of the day. What the powers that be want is approbation of everything done in the USSR—and sincere, enthusiastic approbation at that. Astonishingly, they get it. Or not so astonishingly, for any protest, however meek, is subject to the most extreme penalties. I doubt if there is any country, even Hitler's Germany, in which the mind is less free, more bowed, more fearful, more vassalized.

When backs were turned, Gide had had dangerous conversations during his tour, in one of which an unidentified interlocutor lamented that the Soviet experiment was remarkably successful at breeding incuriosity. For the most part, Russian youths ignored forbidden fruit. It wasn't necessary to put Dostoyevsky (about whom Gide had written at length) on an index, as the young read only what the state prescribed. "If the mind is so molded that it obeys watchwords even before hearing them, it has lost the very awareness of its servitude," Gide wrote, paving the way for Orwell.

Within a year, almost 150,000 copies of *Retour de l'URSS* had been sold, more than any other book on the best-seller list for 1936–37. It had been translated into fourteen languages and banned in Germany, Italy, and the Soviet Union. Gallimard reprinted it eight times in ten months. Declaring that the book had obviously been written to make money, a Communist youth club informed Gide that he was no longer worthy of being its honorary president. Gide replied that if they could be taken in so easily by that slur, they would not be disposed to believe that he was losing more in the royalties for his collected works that would have come from Russia than he had earned from the sale of this one in France.

Retour de l'URSS generated a multitude of hate mail, but *L'Humanité* refrained from commenting on it for several weeks. During the interval, it published in extenso Stalin's speech on the new constitution of the USSR delivered at the Eighth Extraordinary Congress of Soviets, in which many of Gide's observations were implicitly held to be the criticism of a benighted Westerner.* Likewise, *L'Humanité* countered Gide's depiction of the collective farm, or "kolkhoz," as a microcosm of the larger dystopia with its own portrait of a collective abounding in pride, camaraderie, and produce.

L'Humanité let more than a month go by before addressing *Retour de l'URSS* directly, and, when enough time had passed to demonstrate its contempt, published not its own review but *Pravda*'s long denunciation of the book and its author. Gide, *Pravda* declared, was a character straight out of his novel *The Counterfeiters,* which is to say, a writer who knew whereof he wrote for being himself a prime specimen of the decadent bourgeois intelligentsia. *Pravda* charged:

---

* The freedom to form political parties, for example, is irrelevant: "We Bolsheviks regard the matter from a different point of view. There are different political parties and the freedom to form them only where there are classes whose interests are hostile and antagonistic."

Throughout his literary life, he has kept his distance from the great social ideas, the great social ideals. . . . He is an individualist who delights in his own games. He is one of the "wittiest" French authors and finds perversity irresistibly attractive.*

"Bourgeois" summarized the multitude of Gide's imperfections. It was predictable that Soviet fare would taste insipid to a bourgeois palate dulled by exotic sweetmeats and that Soviet boasting would disconcert an anoxic "bourgeois soul" dying of refinement. "Our society liberated from exploiting classes seemed to his bourgeois soul too 'simple' and 'uniform'" the review posited. "He prefers a society crawling like a swamp with all of the human types spawned by the bourgeoisie. He felt an outsider in a country from which the promiscuous horde of parasites and freaks has disappeared."

The Kremlin organized a campaign against Gide, beginning with Sergei Eisenstein and Boris Pasternak, who were invited to denounce him as "Fascist and Trotskyite." Ilya Ehrenburg followed suit. *L'Humanité* received and published what purported to be the deathbed letter of Nikolai Ostrovsky, a blind, bedridden Soviet writer famous in Communist circles for a realist novel entitled *How the Steel Was Tempered,* whom Gide had visited during his tour. "You have surely read the article in *Pravda* about André Gide's betrayal," he wrote to his mother. "How he betrayed our hearts! Who would have thought that he could act so basely. Shame on this old man. It wasn't just us he betrayed, but our valiant people. Now all the enemies of Socialism will use this book against the working class." Invoking the Synoptic Gospels whenever they served a Soviet purpose, *Pravda* compared the parting kiss that Gide planted on Ostrovky's face to the kiss of Judas.

Retour de l'URSS received favorable notice in *Le Populaire.* What Gide observed of depersonalization in the USSR came as no surprise to the reviewer, who agreed that only malign spirits of the Right would insist on confusing Socialism with Stalin's sinister perversion of it. Socialism doesn't enslave, it liberates, he asserted. The idea of a regime in which the cult of liberty did not flourish was "an absurdity."

These contradictory responses boded ill, and, indeed, the Popular Front, behind which Communists and Socialists masked their differences, proved to be an edifice as short-lived as the national pavilions

---

* In an excerpt published by *Le Figaro,* "perversity" is translated as "perversion."

built for Paris's World's Fairs. It had one season of glory, then deteriorated under pressure from within and without.

Social and economic reforms enacted by the Popular Front during its golden summer induced a bipolar state of euphoria and fear, with one class welcoming the dawn and others brooding over nightfall. For workers, it was a new order; for the bourgeoisie, "petite" and "haute" alike, who regarded Blum as Lenin's Kerensky, Red October lay at hand.

Blum's cabinet had been sitting for less than a fortnight when Parliament passed laws mandating the forty-hour week at undiminished wages, with two weeks' paid vacation, in the hope that workers would live and labor more productively under humane conditions, that industry would be compelled to create additional shifts, that more money thus put in circulation would stimulate the economy. America's WPA inspired a program of large public works. To bolster this legislation, the government appointed an undersecretary of state for sport and the organization of leisure.* But the new dispensation, as it appeared to be, provided for the common man's cultural enrichment as well as his material welfare. "Parallel to the great political and social movement . . . a vast cultural movement is unfolding," Jacques Soustelle wrote in the weekly *Vendredi*. "Its motto could be: 'Let us open the doors of culture. Let us level the wall surrounding it and enter a beautiful park hitherto forbidden to poor people, a culture reserved for an elite.'" Adult education courses proliferated. Amateur theater groups sprang up in Paris and provincial cities. The Théâtre National Populaire, which had been inaugurated after World War I at the Arc de Triomphe in a ceremony honoring the Unknown Soldier, rivaled the Comédie Française.

With the Popular Front, France became once again a country "on the march." The year 1936 was marked not only by legislation that offered the laboring class greater security but by rituals that mobilized Frenchmen en masse. Young people set out in far greater numbers than ever before on treks around France, as youth hostels multiplied under the aegis of a government whose undersecretary for sports and

---

* In 1936, Léo Lagrange, the undersecretary, a square-jawed young Socialist, helped organize the People's Olympiad in Barcelona to counter the official Olympiad in Nazi Berlin.

leisure declared, evangelically, that youth hostels were one aspect of an experiment to transform the human condition. The fortnight's paid vacation called for special trains that conveyed workers at reduced fares to seaside villages where party guides hailed them with close-fisted salutes (this exodus inspiring a counterexodus of bourgeois fleeing the plague sent upon their summer nation).

Even more significant than the movement away from cities was the swarming that took place within them, and particularly within Paris, whenever Communist and Socialist leaders exhorted the faithful to assemble for a show of strength. "France of the Popular Front was, first and foremost, the cortège of militants in all its diversity and anonymity," wrote one historian. The "cortège of militants" resembled nothing so much as a general mobilization for war, with tens of thousands of workers from the *banlieue* jubilantly converging on the capital by metro, by bus, by car, by van, on foot. Several days before a march, *L'Humanité* and *Le Populaire* would have begun to diagram it in detail—its order, the composition of its eight or ten major groups, the site at which each formed up, the roster of leaders—lest chaos ensue, though chaos was there as an ever-present threat. Wherever marchers marched they made themselves heard, singing songs that evoked the revolutionary past and the utopian future. "From the minute we set out to the minute we dispersed (many hours later for those among us who brought up the rear), we would shout and sing ourselves hoarse," wrote Henri Noguères. Mingling with Soviet songs widely heard on Chant du Monde records ("Komintern," "The Partisans," "Long Live Life") were songs of the French Revolution—"La Carmagnole" and "Ça Ira"—in topical variations.

Which direction the crowd took was dictated by circumstances, or by the nature of the event that summoned it. A demonstration against L'Action Française mobilized the Latin Quarter.* Mourning Henri Barbusse, the novelist who had died in Russia, Communists followed his casket up Ménilmontant to Père-Lachaise Cemetery. Commemorating the assassination of Jean Jaurès, Socialists assembled at the Panthéon. Asserting solidarity with Spain's Frente Popular, leftists generally took the royal road of popular vociferation, which led from

---

* It should be noted that the student quarter was not exclusively left-wing. The law and medical schools leaned far enough to the right to justify the conviction of the Camelots du Roi that the Boulevard Saint-Michel was their turf.

the Place de la Nation to the Place de la Bastille. But in any event, the crowd beheld itself as a virtuous army and Paris as the Champs de Mars. "As others reminisce about their campaigns, the veterans among us—who were not necessarily the oldest—would learnedly compare a demonstration which had just taken place with its predecessors, evaluating the number of marchers, enumerating the 'stars' they had seen, appraising the behavior of police (both police in uniform and police in civilian clothes)." Not since 1793 and 1794 had such multitudes gathered on so many occasions. Indeed, one mass demonstration was held to commemorate another as the mass become increasingly self-absorbed and the cortège an end in itself, transcending its pretexts. Demonstrations pullulated, like the logos or acronyms that all by themselves tell the sociopolitical story of France during the leftist coalition's heyday.

Many Parisians remembered that heyday as a radical departure from workaday life, with students roaming the streets, workers occupying factories, Socialists holding rallies in Luna Park, converts to Bolshevism meeting conspiratorially, and everyone marching. It was on an official holiday that Paris of the Popular Front displayed itself at its most exuberant. On July 14, 1936, people were swept up by the passion that informed a million voices singing the "The Internationale" as loudly as the "La Marseillaise" and invoked the names of revolutionaries whose roster dismayed everyone with visions of France revisited by the Terror: Marat, Saint-Just, Robespierre. "We marched, we sang with our comrades," three prominent writers reported. "Marching in one row between two human hedges, underneath windows from which flags were waving, we looked at the faces. And if we are so joyous this evening, we owe our joy to the fraternal spirit borne home by the smiles of unknown men and women. . . . Saint-Just used to say that happiness was a new idea. Today we have breathed, in the air of Paris, the newness and youth of that idea."

Le Populaire described a sea of humanity billowing down the boulevards and submerging the Place de la Nation, where Blum and the Radical leader Édouard Daladier shared a podium.* *L'Humanité* drew upon the same fund of images: "immense swells," "a sea of ban-

---

* Maurice Thorez, leader of the French Communist Party, also addressed crowds. Neither he nor his comrades were members of the government, which his party agreed to support, but in which it refused to participate.

ners." Romain Rolland, who rejoiced with his fellow Socialists, might have used the word "oceanic," as he had done several years earlier to describe his experience of religious rapture in his correspondence with Sigmund Freud.* Rolland's play *Le Quatorze Juillet*—written during the Dreyfus Affair, performed once, and consigned to oblivion—was revived that evening at the Alhambra for crowds who flowed into the huge hall after milling on the streets. With a cast of two hundred, *Quatorze Juillet* featured a march composed by Arthur Honegger and an enormous curtain painted by Picasso.† It played to an ecstatic mob, crowning the old age of the Nobelist whose supreme ambition was—had long been—to replace theater with civic festivities, to make the populace the cast, and its revolutionary history the play. In that self-celebratory state, which presented a utopian model for the life of society, there would be no more acting. Gone would be the division between audience and stage. The inner person would marry the outside world. The individual would have united with his god.

In July and August, hearts were gladdened by the abolition of paramilitary leagues and the passage of more egalitarian legislation, notably a law designed to free the country's central bank from the grasp of an oligarchy called "the two hundred families." But before long, trouble besieged the government from every side, as if to demonstrate that no good deed goes unpunished. Predictably, the extreme Right answered the euphoria of the Left with campaigns of slander. In a relatively mild editorial written soon after Blum announced his cabinet, Charles Maurras declared that the appointment of the Jew Jean Zay as minister of education was a crime against the fatherland, Zay having insulted the French flag twelve years earlier, at age twenty, by calling it a symbol of the perfervid nationalism to which a million and a half young lives had been uselessly sacrificed. "What insolence!" Maurras wrote. "What madness! What a challenge to the fatherland, to the honor and memory of the dead, our protectors and saviors! After an ascent to the summit, the Jewish neurosis has flared up; in thin air, the imprudent climbers have lost their minds." *L'Action Française* reported that Bastille Day 1936 was celebrated by a tenth as many

---

* Freud quotes Rolland's letter at the beginning of *Civilization and Its Discontents* (1930).

† The canvas pictured Fascism as a giant with the head of a predatory bird supporting the bestial, moribund body of capitalism while recoiling from the raised arm of a young guardian spirit wreathed in stars.

people as left-wing papers claimed and hailed with ten times as many red banners as tricolor. Maurras quoted an observation of "the learned Bertillon" (the inventor of the mug shot and a self-proclaimed graphologist whose ludicrous testimony had helped convict Dreyfus at his court-martial in 1894) that "one never knows what is taking place in the head of a Jew." Treason came naturally to creatures opaque by nature, with heads for hiding their true allegiances.

On the other hand, it was not thought that Jews enjoyed an absolute monopoly of treasonable secrets. During the summer and fall of 1936, *L'Action Française* and *Gringoire,* its partner in calumny, took turns accusing Blum's minister of the interior, Roger Salengro, of having crossed enemy lines in 1915, as a uniformed bicycle messenger, and surrendered military intelligence to the Germans. Solid evidence had satisfied a court-martial that he had been captured while trying to retrieve the body of a dead comrade, but his prosecutors, who invoked the testimony of anonymous veterans, were relentless. After studying the dossier, a commission appointed by Blum and chaired by the chief of staff, General Maurice Gamelin, found no substance in the charge of desertion. Its report fell on deaf ears. Two days after the eighteenth anniversary of the Armistice, Henri Becquart, a deputy of the Far Right, and Xavier Vallat, who had distinguished himself five months earlier by questioning the appropriateness of a Jew holding sway over a Gallo-Roman nation, declared that Salengro's record was still suspect. Blum rebutted their argument in exquisite detail, without laboring under the misapprehension that any amount of evidence could change minds in the Chamber of Deputies, and not before a violent scuffle had interrupted parliamentary proceedings. He then called upon the chamber to declare the charges against Salengro groundless, which it did by a large majority.

Four days later, on November 17, Salengro, whose wife had recently died, committed suicide. He could no longer endure the smears, he wrote to Blum, and hoped that "if they hadn't succeeded in dishonoring me, they would bear the responsibility for my death." Sad to say, he was bargaining for posthumous disappointment. Politics had become mortal combat. In *L'Écho de Paris,* a paper to which readers of *L'Action Française* and *Gringoire* might have subscribed, Henri de Kérillis laid the blame at Blum's doorstep, asserting that Salengro would still be alive if the arrogant premier hadn't appointed him minister of the interior and thus put a compromised man in the line of fire. "Roger

Salengro's death turned a page in French political history," writes the historian Serge Berstein. "On the French Far Right, the will to destroy one's political adversary at all costs and by all means had replaced the conflict of ideas, the debate over different ways of resolving national problems." No doubt, other events had turned the page several years earlier, only now there was a ministerial corpse to be reckoned with. That the church—no friend of Socialists and suicides—denounced the campaign as unchristian provides a measure of its violence. "Politics does not justify everything," declared Cardinal Liénart of Lille, Salengro's hometown. According to the cardinal, who spoke ex cathedra, a press "specializing in defamation and slander" found no favor in the eyes of God. *Le Croix* disseminated his pronouncement throughout France.

In substantive matters, papers of the Radical Right echoed the conservative press (*Le Figaro, Le Temps, Le Journal des Débats*), whose fierce opposition to the Popular Front was rooted in its fear of a Communist revolution. Behind Blum loomed Stalin, and economic woes enlarged that specter. A steep rise in the cost of living soon compromised the benefits legislated in June. People bought less, production declined, and capital fled to safe havens abroad when investment was most needed at home. France became an even poorer country, burdened with debt. Its dwindling gold reserves forced Blum, despite promises he had made, to devalue the franc. Then there was the so-called wall of money in the form of France's Banque de France—the bank of issue—which remained the preserve of rich regents bent on bringing Blum to his knees. Inflation bred widespread disenchantment. In turn, disenchantment polarized workers who had chanted for solidarity on Bastille Day. Many were drawn to Jacques Doriot's PPF and to the political reincarnation of Colonel de La Rocque's dissolved Ligue des Croix de Feu (the PSF, or Parti Social Français). Others drifted leftward, from the party to militant Communism, widening the rift within the Popular Front. Widening it still further was the desertion of a middle class that normally voted Radical but felt neglected by Blum and harnessed to a coalition that might, under Soviet influence, drive France across the Pyrenees for what was seen to be a gladiatorial contest pitting Hitler and Mussolini against Stalin. They didn't want entanglements. They didn't want war. And the Frente Popular was itself an imbroglio.

Internal dissension over the Spanish Civil War may have done

Colonel François de La Rocque, leader of the Croix de Feu, which, after the banishment of paramilitary leagues, legitimized itself as a political party, the French Social Party.

more to scuttle the Popular Front than the economic doldrums and the Far Right's campaign of vilification. War broke out on July 18, 1936, when, assisted by Mussolini, rebel troops stationed in Spanish Morocco invaded the mainland. At the behest of Spanish republicans, Blum undertook to supply the besieged government with arms and matériel, but he encountered vehement opposition from all quarters of the Right and from Radicals inside his own coalition. On July 31, the foreign minister, Yvon Delbos appeared before the Chamber of Deputies and denied that the Spanish Republic had requested arms, though it would have been entirely within its rights to do so: "It did not for reasons of doctrine and humanity, lest it furnish those who wish to help the insurgents with a pretext." *Le Figaro*'s commentator quoted this assertion with winks insinuating that the legitimacy of the Spanish Republic might be considered questionable, and the uprising against it lawful.

In Spain, a republic had been established in 1931, after the dictatorship of Miguel Primo de Rivera. Republicans and Socialists drafted a constitution that inspired securalizing reforms and legislation cal-culated to improve the lot of workers and farmers. The Depression hampered their efforts. Popular enthusiasm waned and a conservative government nullified many of the reforms. Left-wing parties narrowly regained power in 1936, amid fears of a military coup on the one hand and a Communist revolution on the other. Violent clashes became commonplace, undermining confidence in the republic's ability to effect economic and social change peaceably. In July 1936 the Spanish Army of Africa invaded the mainland under the command of Fran-cisco Franco, who characterized the civil war that ensued as a struggle between the "red hordes" and "Christian civilization."

Faced with choices every one of which threatened the Popular Front, Blum hoped to find support for intervention from Whitehall but was advised that Britain would neither intervene nor come to France's aid if she went it alone and found herself invaded by Fascist troops. It led him to blindfold himself; in August, he circulated among the Euro-pean powers a pact of nonintervention in Spain, which was accepted but no sooner signed by all than cynically ignored by Germany and Italy. Soviet tanks and planes arrived later, at the end of October.

On November 6, 1936, amid the amusement rides of Luna Park, outside Paris, where the Federation of the Seine was celebrating the anniversary of the Third Republic (with Josephine Baker and Mari-anne Oswald entertaining the crowd between ministerial harangues), Blum offered his anguished explanation of what many in the audience understood to be a betrayal of the anti-Fascist cause. European nations engaging in an arms race on Spanish soil could only spell disaster, he declared. The pact prohibiting it was the only solution he could con-template.

> I would that these words did not weigh heavily on the Spanish people. We thought that securing general neutrality and thus avoiding inter-national complications of an obviously grave nature would be best for them as well. . . . Now all the powers have signed on to our proposal and promulgated appropriate measures. There is no solid basis for pre-suming that these measures have been violated.*

---

* By November, Blum had every reason to know that Germany had sent several thousand troops, panzer tanks, tons of bombs, and planes and had placed submarines at the ser-vice of the insurgents. He himself was doing as much as he could to bulk up the French military.

Factory delegates had demanded that he reverse his position. Three hundred thousand workers in the Paris region staged a strike against the blockade, to no avail.

> How can we tear up a document we have asked others to sign, when their ink is still wet on it and no violations have occurred. . . . In my view, it is impossible at the present time to act otherwise without provoking a crisis whose consequences are unforeseeable.

He persevered above jeers and delivered a Jaurrasian peroration evoking July 1914 and his passionate commitment to peace:

> I must tell you what I shall do and what I shall refuse to do so long as I remain in power. We have friends who consider that our conduct is a concession to foreign powers. They tell us that we must exalt national pride, that peace can best be preserved by the development of patriotic sentiment. This language has a familiar ring. I heard it twenty-four years ago. I am a Frenchman as proud as anyone of his country and its history, despite my race. I shall spare no effort to ensure the security of France. One of the elements of French national honor is a will to keep the peace. Have we forgotten that? I shall never admit that war is inevitable. Until I draw my last breath, I shall do everything to prevent it. War is fatal only when one considers it such.
>
> I had an almost visceral need to talk to you today. For almost three months I have been asking myself whether I have the stuff of a leader. There are times when I am not perfectly sure of myself.

It was reported on the same page of *Le Figaro* that Germany's ambassador to Spain had left Alicante for Berlin, announcing before his departure that he could no longer represent the Reich in a country run by "irresponsible Marxists."

Self-doubt did not visit Maurice Thorez, the French Communist leader, who made a show of allegiance to the Popular Front while expressing his repugnance for the neutrality pact before and after Blum's speech at Luna Park: "Shame mingles with anguish when we receive word of blood flowing in Bedajos and Irun, of heroic combatants being crushed because they lack arms to fight an enemy well provided with airplanes, cannons, machine guns, and ammunition by Fascist dictators." Arguments, pretexts, cavils, and slurs hurled at the

Communist Party all bounced off the iron-clad conscience of "good proletarians." Summoning the ghost of Jean Jaurès to seal his message, as Blum had done to justify neutrality, he asserted that it was imperative to end the arms blockade: "Twenty-three years ago, the working class learned from his flown spirit that the struggle for peace is the most necessary of wars." Eighty thousand party faithful heard him lament the "grave error" of nonintervention at a suburban stadium on October 4, three days after the insurgents proclaimed General Francisco Franco head of state at Burgos.

Thorez addressed another huge assembly in the Vélodrome d'Hiver on November 22, when word of the Luftwaffe bombing Madrid in a raid that anticipated Guernica was reaching Paris. "For the purposes of a politics that leads, alas! to war, we republicans, anti-Fascists, and sincere pacifists are mendaciously accused of wanting war. It was this calumny that made Jaurès, an apostle of peace, the first of the world war's myriad victims. By calumny, the enemies of the people endeavor to sow division. But the masses of the Popular Front won't allow themselves to become a house divided." Not all the blame for nonintervention could be laid at the doorstep of London's financial elite, of Anthony Eden, of France's two hundred families (who did, in fact, retain control of the Banque de France), of the munitions dealer Sir Basil Zaharoff. As we have noted, there was opposition from within. The Popular Front became a threadbare garment in which three contentious parties continued to wrap themselves, tearing at the fabric even as they proclaimed its integrity. An editor of *L'Humanité*, Lucien Sampaix, asked how "our comrade Léon Blum," could ignore the fact that trucks laden with cotton and glycerine for the manufacture of explosives were crossing the Pyrenees to Fascist-held Basque country. *L'Humanité* ran other such comminatory editorials. But unity remained their watchword.

Almost a year after Blum introduced the neutrality pact, *L'Humanité*'s editor in chief, Paul Vaillant-Couturier, declared in a kind of ritual incantation that the bond between Socialists and Communists had never been so tight. How, he asked, could one seriously imagine a divorce between two parties pledged to advance the program of the Popular Front, to dissolve paramilitary leagues, to "save the peace with Spain"? One who could easily imagine a divorce was George Orwell. "Anyone who has given the subject a glance knows that the Communist tactic of dealing with political opponents by means of trumped-up accusations is nothing new," he noted in *Homage to Catalonia*:

Today the key word is Trotsky-Fascist; yesterday it was Social-Fascist. It is only six or seven years since the Russian State trials "proved" that the leaders of the Second International, including, for example, Léon Blum and prominent members of the British Labor Party, were hatching a huge plot for the military invasion of the U.S.S.R. Yet today the French Communists are glad enough to accept Blum as a leader and the English Communists are raising heaven and earth to get inside the Labour Party.

Another who could imagine it was Pierre Drieu La Rochelle. In 1937, he spent two weeks observing the war from Franco's side of the lines and wrote patronizing letters to Victoria Ocampo, whose pro-republicanism he dismissed as a temporary loss of reason.

The death knell of Blum's premiership, and to all intents and purposes of the Popular Front, which lived in name only until October 1938, was sounded not by the Communist Party but by Radical legislators convinced after the summer of 1936 that a New Deal for the proletariat slighted the interests of their own middle-class constituency. Édouard Daladier, their leader and the minister of war, prevailed upon Blum to suspend his program of economic reform and ramp up the manufacture of armaments. France could hardly afford both butter and bullets. By March 1937, when the flight of capital was emptying the treasury and crippling production, malaise had become a full-blown revolt. Radical youth groups organized large demonstrations in the provinces, at one of which Daladier distanced himself from his premier, speaking as a possible successor with an agenda friendlier to entrepreneurs with enough savoir faire to maintain order where chaos threatened. Everyone knew what chaos meant. On March 16, 1937, Communist and Socialist militants had disrupted a rally of the PSF at Clichy. Unable to clear the square, police had opened fire, killing five of the militants and wounding as many as three hundred.*

Early in June, Blum's minister of finance, Vincent Auriol, drafted a bill requesting that Parliament grant the administration plenary

---

* The conservative daily *Le Temps* reported that the left-wing extremists were armed and had shot up the automobile of Marx Dormoy, Salengro's successor as minister of the interior; Dormoy had been summoned to the scene. "We have too often reproached the cabinet presided over by Léon Blum for its dilatoriness in defending republican law against the transgressions and violence of partisans of direct action not to acknowledge that in this instance the police, over which it has supreme control, accomplished its duty impeccably." The Communist leader Maurice Thorez denounced Blum as an "assassin of workers."

financial powers until June 31, to deal as it saw fit with the nation's economic problems. What it considered "fit" went unexplained, and Radical legislators, fearful of measures even more abhorrent than tax increases, chafed at the proposal, which passed through the lower house, the Chamber of Deputies, but twice failed to gain a majority in the Senate. On June 22, Blum, having concluded that he could no longer govern effectively, resigned the premicrship. He was succeeded by a Radical we have already encountered in the premier's office, Camille Chautemps.

There were several grotesque ironies bound up in the Paris World's Fair of 1937, officially known as the International Exposition of Arts and Technics in Modern Life, which opened on May 24, 1937, after five years in the planning. Blum, who had been an adolescent when the Eiffel Tower began to rise above Paris for the hundredth-anniversary celebration of the French Revolution at the 1889 World's Fair, foresaw that his government could use the 1937 fair to present itself as the torchbearer of progress and modernity. He applauded President Albert Lebrun's inaugural speech expressing the hope that "this great assembly would teach mankind yet again that there is no dignity of life but in mutual comprehension of peoples' needs, aspirations, and genius; no prosperity but in an ever more intense exchange of products and ideas." He stood tall beside Lebrun for a military fanfare between the colonnaded wings of the newly built Palais de Chaillot, where Hitler was to have himself photographed three years later looking triumphantly at the Eiffel Tower. He and Lebrun led a cortège across the Trocadéro Gardens toward the dense cluster of pavilions on the Champs de Mars and along the Seine. At the Pont d'Iéna they boarded launches to view the exposition from a riverine perspective. Crowds along the quays were reported in newspapers to have shouted, "Vive Blum! Vive Lebrun!," though not in *L'Action Française,* which acknowledged Blum's presence only once, and then by way of noting his "unsightly Semitic profile." Unsightly as well were the construction sites all over the unfinished fairground. Right-wing journalists cited them as evidence of workers malingering and of trade unions promoting their delinquency. *Le Populaire,* on the other hand, pronounced the fair a brilliant success. Day after day it reported attendance figures on its first page and the completion of new pavilions.

Two pavilions standing opposite each other and dwarfing all the rest competed for visitors walking down the main avenue between the Palais de Chaillot and the Eiffel Tower. They were stone monoliths in which Soviet Russia and Nazi Germany had invested sums out of all proportion to the buildings' brief life span but commensurate with their symbolic value. Both had frontal towers. The Soviet's served as a pedestal for two heroic figures seventy-five feet tall: a male and female worker, he stripped to the waist, she in a swirling peasant dress, thrusting the hammer and sickle skyward like conquistadors setting foot on a new continent and claiming it for the crown and the cross. They might have claimed world supremacy had Hitler's architect, Albert Speer, not obtained their blueprints from a sympathetic French commissioner and subsequently designed a taller, bulkier tower surmounted by a twenty-foot eagle, as imperturbable as the Soviet couple was dynamic, with its wings spread like Dracula's mantle.

It was not widely commented upon that in the Spanish pavilion, a short walk from the German, Picasso's *Guernica* pictured the destruction rained on a Spanish town by the Condor Legion of German bombers.

That Germany had the most prominent pavilion in the exposition's most conspicuous quarter—that it had any pavilion at all—was the result of what Karen Fiss, who has written brilliantly on the subject, calls "the grand illusion." Anticipating Munich 1938, French authorities, duped by Hitler, bought into the idea that Germany's full participation in the World's Fair reflected her desire to be a good neighbor in the community of nations. Lest she withdraw, as she had withdrawn from the League of Nations in October 1933, they met all her demands, however egregious. It seemed to be assumed that European peace itself depended on her staying, and she milked that illusion for all its worth. Jacques Gréber, chief architect of the fair, agreed to buy—among much else—German pumps and projectors for the light displays, German scientific instruments for the Pavillon de la Découverte, and a German planetarium for the Parc des Attractions.* Gréber dropped his stipulation that Germany plan a more modest frontal tower. When the Paris-based German exile newspaper *Das Neue Tage-Buch* alarmed German diplomats by suggesting in an open letter to Thomas Mann that Jewish and German left-wing refugees

---

* Gréber was known in the United States for his design of Philadelphia's Fairmount Parkway.

The Paris exposition of 1937 viewed from the terrace of the Palais de Chaillot, the German pavilion (left) and the Soviet (right), flanking the Eiffel Tower, which had been erected to commemorate the centenary of the French Revolution at the 1889 exposition.

build a pavilion of their own, French organizers assured them that it was absolutely out of the question.

There was more than politics in the magical thinking that characterized France's obsequious courtship. There was also awe of the regime whose rousing pageants transformed its population into a convulsive organism. We have heard from Drieu La Rochelle, but Drieu had equally zealous company. To French visitors overwhelmed by the Nazi Party congress at Nuremberg, who felt that they had experienced a fullness of being unattainable in their republican homeland, the Rhine marked an existential divide rather than a geographical boundary. Crossing it, one left the parched land of French reason and entered a green world of primitive vitality where reason counted for little. The Right Bank offered a new dispensation, beyond the self. "For the French, alas, the synchronized marching of 120,000 men under blazing flags is nothing but the disguised dance of war," wrote Alphonse de Châteaubriant, a novelist and old-line aristocrat who collaborated with the Nazis during the occupation. In his view, the French, being "logicians," could not understand that the marching steps of Germans corresponded to a "metaphysical" feeling. "Frenchmen are reasoners, while Germans are rhythmicians, and it is through the cooperation of each person in unanimous self-effacement that the religion of this rhythm is established, with each consciousness . . . touching the eternal depths."* The French ambassador to Berlin in 1937, André François-Poncet, observed that the Third Reich attributed a social and civic value of the highest order to festivals, for which it obviously had a sinister genius.

> The highlight of all these festivals was the Nuremberg Congress. . . . For eight days, Nuremberg was a city of jubilation, a city gone mad, and practically a city of convulsionaries. This ambience, combined with the beauty of the spectacles presented and the luxury of the hospitality offered, exerted a strong influence on the spirit of the foreigners whom the Nazi government made sure to invite to its annual meetings. The displays were contagious, and the visitors could not resist them; they returned home seduced and conquered, ripe for collaboration, without perceiving the sinister realities hidden behind the deceptive pomp of these prodigious parades.

Presiding over the world's kermesse with a cracked voice, mindful of Nuremberg, beset by feelings of inferiority, and placing hope of salvation in the "fête nationale," the French government devoted an entire pavilion to the "Art of Festivals." Its director, Jacques Viénot, bemoaned the fact that France—the pageant master under Bourbon kings, revolutionary terrorists, and Napoleon—had lost purchase in Europe. "Rome, Moscow, Berlin . . . all know perfectly how to organize gigantic human maneuvers with an imposing flair for decoration, stagecraft, and propaganda. We must therefore revive the past for the future by reclaiming a glorious tradition and renewing it."

Viénot urged that the government sponsor research into the art of the festival and that it establish for that purpose an institution to be

---

* Châteaubriant's glorification of Hitler and Nazism, *La Gerbe des Forces,* published at the time of the 1937 exposition, made a believer out of Cardinal Baudrillart, rector of the Institut Catholique in Paris. According to Henri de Kérillis, a prominent journalist, the novel, in which Châteaubriant championed the idea of "a European salvation through the Teutonic renaissance, since civilization with roots in the late Roman Empire was dead," found an enthusiastic readership in student circles.

called the Academy of Joy—a name probably inspired by the Third Reich's state-controlled leisure organization Kraft durch Freude. Contemporary humanity had to "relearn joy," he asserted. "Let there be no doubt that henceforth France wants to endow its national demonstrations and popular festivals with new dignity." The general commissioner of the World's Fair, Edmond Labbé, concurred, and in a speech inaugurating the Art de Fêtes pavilion told his sympathetic audience that bored youths who had recourse to "Negro-American music" and "Apache rhythms" for excitement needed a patriotic intoxicant. Wise governments offered their people festivals.

Labbé didn't stop there. The World's Fair commission launched a nationwide competition to revive "*les fêtes françaises*," with publicity flyers citing the Nuremberg rallies and Mussolini's maneuvers in the Forum as examples of great civic theater. Contestants were given various themes for embellishment: torchlight parades, Armistice Day commemorations, Olympic marches, funeral processions. It was, indeed, the plan for a state funeral that won first prize. "The pageant featured an immense catafalque in the form of a pyramid, which would be carried by two hundred men," writes Karen Fiss. "The Arc de Triomphe, draped in crepe, would be encompassed by a circle of vertical searchlights forming 'a luminous funerary chapel.' The description of these illuminated elements . . . suggests that the French designers were aware of Speer's *Lichtdom* or 'cathedral of light.' Speer used a ring of 130 powerful searchlights at the 1934 Nuremberg party rallies, which shot eight kilometers into the dark sky, to form a translucent dome." No great man qualified for this extravaganza, but the plan for a Bastille Day pageant came to fruition in July 1937, three weeks after Blum resigned from office. Immense tricolor banners hung vertically, often three together, at every major square, like carpet runners measured for the Hall of Mirrors. Fifteen thousand torchbearers imitated the nocturnal lava flow of Nuremberg across seven miles of Paris. One newspaper announced "the birth of a tradition." *L'Action Française* noted that "a savage horde" of several hundred Bolsheviks shuffled after the military review, spoiling an otherwise impressive spectacle.

The World's Fair had not yet ended when, in November, Hitler laid out to key ministers and military brass his plan for the conquest of Europe. It survives as "the Hossbach Memorandum," named after the colonel who took minutes. *Lebensraum* was its theme—living space. Eighty-five million Germans needed more of it, and everything that soil provides, to preserve the integrity of the race. Colonies were not the answer, only neighbors, he declared, explaining why Czechoslovakia and Austria could be annexed without interference from France, which, with England, would remain aloof until they themselves were ripe for the picking.* He wanted this memorandum to be his last will and testament, should he die an untimely death.

---

* "The Fuhrer believes personally that in all probability England and perhaps also France have already silently written off Czechoslovakia, and that they have grown used to the idea that this question would one day be cleaned up by Germany. The difficulties in the British Empire and the possibility of being entangled in another long-drawn-out European war were decisive factors in the non-participation of England in a war against Germany. England's attitude would certainly *not* remain without influence on France's. An attack on Germany without British support is not probable."

CHAPTER 12

The Hero of Verdun

Camille Chautemps, the Radical ex-premier, succeeded Léon Blum on June 22, 1937, and held office for eight months, presiding over a cabinet in which Radicals susceptible to overtures from the Right outnumbered Socialists sworn to the social and economic agenda of the Popular Front. It would appear that Chautemps regarded himself as an understudy appointed to go through the motions of government until Édouard Daladier came onstage. He governed during that critical period by cunctation: little was done when decisiveness was most needed. The image of a progressive nation projected at the World's Fair belied France's economic futility. The franc tumbled but not enough to make French exports competitive. Factories closed. The budget deficit reached 28 billion francs. Labor strikes reduced government revenue, and military expenditures, inadequate though they were in light of German rearmament, tithed every other program. With France's currency bound to the gold standard and her gold reserves dwindling, the finance minister, Georges Bonnet, an advocate of austerity, arms reduction, and appeasement, could not expand the money supply as Roosevelt had done in the United States, even if he had been disposed to recommend it.*

Strikes, which required government arbitration, were the bane of a waffling premier's existence. Reluctant, on the one hand, to rule in favor of management lest labor prevail upon Socialists and Com-

---

* Bonnet, who had briefly served as France's monolingual ambassador in Washington, made no secret of his aversion to New Deal economics and his hostility to Roosevelt.

munists to end their marriage of convenience with his own Radical Party and fearful, on the other, of ruling in favor of labor lest he alienate the entrepreneurial class, he ruled this way and that. Conciliation was seen as the strategy of an invertebrate born to slither under fences, alternating between Bonnet's orthodox prescriptions on one side and reform on the other. In January 1938, Chautemps, exasperated by strikes, resigned from office after clashing with Communists. One week later he formed a new cabinet, almost entirely Radical (which is to say, centrist) in composition, assuring his left-wing colleagues that he remained loyal to the Popular Front. "No man can possibly pretend to direct other men solely on the basis of the law of property applicable to things," he declared. "A captain of industry must have his authority respected; but he must endeavor every day to merit the position of director conferred upon him by chance." (Conservative deputies loudly objected to the words "by chance," according to *Le Populaire*.) Chautemps continued: "I am not appealing to a new majority. What I would like, much more than tactical votes, is heartfelt allegiance. Those are the words Léon Blum used, and the phrase was a step toward national reconciliation. . . . It is said that this ministry can only be a ministry of transition. Well, if I were one day overtaken by events and trampled in the victory of companions to whom I showed the way, I would be very proud indeed."* France wanted "normal and peaceful relations" with all states and hoped to find common ground "by an effort of mutual comprehension." Chautemps was trampled in the victory parade not of companions but of German soldiers marching down the Champs-Élysées.

Looking back, he might have wondered whether bombs exploding in Paris during the World's Fair only weeks after he became premier had been the clearest portent of all that overtook him. On a Saturday evening in September 1937, two office buildings situated near the Place de l'Étoile had been wrecked by devices powerful enough to hurl masonry across the street. Since both buildings housed manufacturers' associations, *Le Temps* lost no time blaming "foreign revolutionaries" adept at "a form of terrorism that is not native to us." The paper felt certain

---

* In May 1940, when the French army was retreating from the Germans helter-skelter, Georges Mandel said of Chautemps, his fellow minister and vice premier, whom he regarded as a prime specimen of the political class's fecklessness, "He is rehearsing the speech he will deliver as Chief Mourner should France drop dead."

that those revolutionaries came from "milieux in which the 'capital-ist' is seen as a public enemy against whom every 'proletarian' worthy of the name must consider himself permanently at war." *L'Humanité* agreed that foreigners were no doubt responsible for the destruction, but it blamed Fascist agents, citing as a precedent the Reichstag fire of 1933, which the Nazis, who may have been the arsonists, pinned on Bolsheviks to excite public indignation and justify mass arrests. *L'Humanité's* editor, Paul Vaillant-Couturier, ridiculed *Le Temps*. How could a terrorist act benefit the Communist Party in September 1937, when the Popular Front was cohesive and triumphant? he asked. It was a false-flag operation. "There are people inside and outside France who have a vested interest in creating a state of havoc unfavorable to produc-tion, dangerous for freedom, fatal to tourism, subversive of peace. The recent history of Spain, to mention only that, offers sufficient evidence of Hitlerian interference in the affairs of neighboring countries. . . . The guilty parties will be found along the Rome-Paris-Berlin axis."

On September 17 newspapers reported the footprints of a secret society—not foreign but French, and not Communist but right of right-wing—called La Cagoule, or "the Hood." At that point its exis-tence was better known to L'Action Française than to the Bureau of Criminal Investigation, for it had been founded in 1935 or 1936 by men, mostly renegade Camelots, bent on making France ungovernable with strategically compelling acts of terror. Soon the name became com-mon knowledge. *Le Populaire* identified Cagoulards in custody and two traffickers through whom the terrorists purchased German and Italian arms. But a much fuller exposure of their activities awaited the progress of a police investigation. Months passed. Then, in November 1937, a "Fascist plot" began to make daily headlines in the left-wing press, which furnished details of an elaborately organized mafia, its code of honor, its initiation rite, its murders, its impressive arsenals, its staff. On November 23, the Ministry of the Interior condemned the Cagoule as a subversive brotherhood whose structure was, according to documents found in a police raid, patterned after the army's. It included a high command, internal and external military intelligence agencies, safe houses, and a medical service with nurses and doctors on call. A communiqué from the minister of the interior, Marx Dor-moy, noted that the grouping of its members into divisions, brigades, regiments, battalions, and so on pointed to their intention of waging civil war.

Seized documents establish the fact that the guilty had assigned themselves the goal of replacing the freely chosen Republic with a dictatorial regime before proceeding to the restoration of a monarchy. . . . Discovered in the course of house searches were equipment for counterfeiting identity papers, instructions for the conveyance of arms, precise details about the military guard at political venues in departments neighboring Paris, the weaponry of regiments, detailed maps of Paris's sewer system with itineraries leading to the Parliament building, the floor plans of left-wing newspapers and of flats belonging to deputies, a facsimile of the signatures of certain ministers, a list of ministers and legislators to be arrested as soon as the signal was given.

The police apprehended the society's administrative officer, Eugène Deloncle, a naval engineer by training and the wealthy director of large corporate firms. Only later did it come to light that financial support for the Cagoule had been provided by Eugène Schueller, the founder and owner of L'Oréal cosmetics, who offered employment in his Spanish subsidiary to fugitives from French justice.

Right-wing papers made light of incontrovertible evidence and dismissed the false-flag argument as an "odious burlesque" staged by Dormoy to distract attention from Communist intrigue. L'Écho de Paris claimed that Dormoy, who had indulged the Popular Front's many transgressions since succeeding Salengro, saw arsenals and plots in a few rifles exhumed from the cellars of peaceable Frenchmen who feared, as well they might, the prospect of red revolution.

The Cagoule was disbanded before it mobilized, but not before it reinforced the army of hobgoblins undermining confidence in a Republic seemingly unable to govern. "A dirty stream of undifferentiated hate distorted human and social realities," writes one historian. "Myths of pervading evil turned superficial disagreements into haunting fears and political differences into vendettas, and the French body politic became incapable of any kind of unity because all foundation for mutual trust had been shattered during these ruthless and bitter fights, which no one carried on with more asperity than the Right. Serious or childish, the plots of the Cagoule helped to convince both sides that all such plots were real." People old enough to remember were put in mind of the paranoia and messianism of the Dreyfus years. Where evil was pervasive, so was talk of salvation. And where salvation entered political discourse, heroes, saints, and despots were summoned to shame parliamentarians flailing about in a republican morass. *Le Figaro* declared that France needed a "committee of *public safety*" to restore order. On May 9, 1938, it devoted much of its issue to Saint Joan, whom it glorified as the brightest of the stellar figures illuminating France's past. "Can one find in Napoleon's tomb that which is found in the cradle at Domrémy and on the hard, enchanted road that leads to the stake at Rouen? The festival of July 14, though purified by the blood of martyred soldiers, has repugnant origins. The Maid's festival is incomparably splendid. Fidelity, political wisdom, military heroism, and holiness are the immaculate spray of virtues offered to us by the fifteenth century; it perfumes all the ages, and arms the generations in their defense of the country."

Charles Maurras may have been too tired to march with his colleagues in the traditional procession. He had spent a week in Spain as a guest of the insurgent regime, being fêted at Saragossa and at Franco's headquarters in Burgos, and raising a glass to men who exemplified what he called "the natural advantages of organization, intelligence, science, all the moral and mental levers of civilization over the numerically superior forces of Disorder."

In 1889, royalists, Bonapartists, and ultranationalist revanchists had placed their hopes for overturning the Third Republic in General Georges Boulanger, dubbed "the providential man." Half a century later, that title was dusted off by exasperated anti-parliamentarians and conferred upon Philippe Pétain, the marshal glorified for his command at the Battle of Verdun.* Age had not dulled his luster. Pétain turned eighty-three in 1939, the year Premier Édouard Daladier appointed him ambassador to Spain, where Franco's army entered Madrid on March 28, ending a civil war that had cost the country half-a-million lives.

The last remnants of the Popular Front disappeared with the confirmation of Daladier as premier in April 1938. Remembered today as a signatory of the infamous Munich pact of September 1938, endorsing

---

* In his account of the battle, Pétain praised the performance of the turreted guns and the fixed fortification system when in fact conventional field artillery in the open had inflicted much more damage on the enemy. This misrepresentation influenced France's calamitous decision to build the Maginot Line.

Hitler's annexation of a Czech province, the Sudetenland, Daladier, unlike Chamberlain, did not believe that one more slab of Europe thrown to the beast would definitively sate its appetite for *Lebensraum*. He believed quite the opposite: that war lay ahead but that France needed time to modernize her air force and study the proper deployment of her tanks. What he believed mattered less, however, than what he did and didn't do. Chamberlain's cravenness, the daunting prospect of going it alone against Germany (with whose military might he was well acquainted), his own divided party, and a poll that showed 78 percent of the French electorate favoring appeasement all combined to make Daladier Chamberlain's fellow fool without persuading him in his tortured self-abasement that the betrayal of a democratic ally had purchased "peace in our time." A nation still mourning the dead of 1914–18 cheered him when he returned from Munich, only to find itself placed belatedly on a war footing.* (Daladier's response to the cheering was an aside to his aide Alexis Léger: "Ah, the imbeciles [*les cons*]! If they only knew what they are acclaiming." Winston Churchill voiced the same sentiment rather more eloquently in the House of Commons: "England has been offered a choice between war and shame. She has chosen shame, and will get war.")

Intense rearmament required greater productivity, and Daladier overrode the law that crowned Popular Front legislation—the forty-hour work week. On August 21, 1938, he asserted in a radio broadcast that France alone among industrialized countries allowed its plants to idle two days a week. "As long as the international situation remains so delicate, one must be able to work more than forty hours, and up to forty-eight in enterprises that affect National Defense.

---

* On July 12, six weeks before the Munich agreement, Daladier declared in a major speech, portions of which were published in *Le Temps,* that France's commitments to Czechoslovakia were "ineluctable and sacred." Precisely because these commitments existed and France's intention was to respect them scrupulously, he continued, "she is entitled to exert all her influence over the country to which these guarantees have been given to favor conciliation. . . . Her bounden duty is to spare no effort to maintain peace." In England, Chamberlain's foreign minister, Lord Halifax, voiced his sentiments in a letter to the former prime minister Stanley Baldwin: "Nationalism and racialism is [*sic*] a powerful force but I can't feel that it's unnatural or immoral! I cannot myself doubt that these fellows [the Nazis] are genuine haters of Communism, etc.! And I daresay if we were in their position we would feel the same!" Pierre Flandin, a former premier and holder of various portfolios, put it to an interviewer from *Le Petit Parisien* that economic pragmatism should be France's watchword, that the idealistic opposition to dictators and concern with the "Jewish question" worked against the country's essential interests.

Every enterprise needing a longer work week for its operation should be spared useless formalities and interminable discussions." Conservatives were pleased not only by the measure but by the final dismantling of the Popular Front. A general strike in November fizzled after a day. Having stood it down—for that purpose he had nerve—Daladier carried on as head of government without support from Communists and Socialists.

Something of the internecine hatred that had shed rivulets of blood in 1871, after the Franco-Prussian War—when Germans still camping around the capital witnessed French government troops crushing the Paris Commune—made itself felt in March 1939, when Hitler occupied all of Czechoslovakia. The gathering threat of war did not inspire a sacred union. Anti-Fascists and anti-Communists lambasted each other for France's inadequate production of arms, its antiquated plants, its reliance on the United States for airplanes. It was all Édouard Herriot's fault, Maurras claimed in *L'Action Française*. The onus of having withdrawn French troops from the Ruhr in 1925 fell on him and on Briand. "We shall continue to earn the ill humor of politicians who placed all their hope in the waters of Oblivion. . . . They dismiss our righteous evocation of their infamies as the apple of discord."

France owed her present predicament as well, Maurras maintained, to messianic Jews heralding the dawn of a new age with the victory of the Popular Front in 1936. Zion cast an even longer shadow than Hitler. Blum and his coreligionists were the swine who had surrendered France to her mortal enemy. "There is no time to lose; national authority and political policy must be removed from the Sarrauts, the Mandels, the Paul Reynauds, the Dreyfuses, the Rothschilds. This Jewish power needs no more time than it takes to sign an order and the fatal choice will have been made, the iron die will have been cast. The ardor with which the slyest and most suspect of Israel's servants endeavor to bring about a crisis, though it cost France her peace, is the measure of what they expect to gain from it. Beware of the Rothschilds, of the Louis Louis-Dreyfuses and the madmen who serve them."* Provincial

---

* Another of Léon Daudet's favorite targets, Louis Louis-Dreyfus belonged to a rich family of global commodity merchants. He owned the newspaper *L'Intransigeant* and had served for many years as a deputy and senator. The voices raised against Jews for denouncing the Munich pact and thus exposing France to the hell of another war included politicians of the left as well as the right, especially those associated with the bimonthly *La Flèche,* and in particular Drieu's former friend Gaston Bergery. In the anti-Communist

newspapers offered more temperate versions of the same indictment. A Radical daily, *L'Écho de la Nièvre,* brought to book "the men who allowed disorder to reign after the election of May 1936, slowing the industrial production necessary for our national security, above all Léon Blum and Marx Dormoy." That Zion cast a longer shadow than Hitler was borne out in December 1938, after Kristallnacht, when the German and French governments signed a declaration of mutual amity. Hitler's foreign minister, Joachim von Ribbentrop, was fêted by the French foreign office at a grand banquet on the Quai d'Orsay that the two Jewish members of Daladier's coalition cabinet, Georges Mandel and Jean Zay, might have chosen not to attend even if they had been invited. Mandel, like his fellow conservative (and Anglophile) Paul Reynaud, had vehemently opposed the Munich pact.

L'Humanité rebelled against press censorship, accusing Daladier, when the legislature granted him emergency powers, of exploiting Czechoslovakia to muffle his critics:

> How many times in the past 150 years has a French journalist sat in front of a blank page full of vindictive indignation over measures that violate freedom of the press? These arbitrary acts have seldom brought luck to their authors. Charles X, Louis-Philippe, Napoleon III, and recently Doumergue had tales of woe. Now Daladier is trying to bring off a Napoleonic 18 Brumaire without seeing how desperately things will end. But Bonaparte waged the Italian campaign. All you did, Monsieur Daladier, was travel to Munich.*

---

and anti-Semitic paper *Combat,* Maurice Blanchot, a regular contributor, who achieved fame after 1945 as a literary theorist, declared, in response to the furor over Hitler's invasion of the Rhineland in 1936: "There is, outside of Germany, a clan that wants war and, under color of prestige and international morality, insidiously propagates the case for war. It is the clan of former pacifists, revolutionaries, and Jewish émigrés who will do anything to bring down Hitler and put an end to dictatorships." Condemned in this article were "unbridled Jews" who, in a "theological rage," clamored for immediate sanctions against Nazi Germany.

* In the revolutionary calendar 18 Brumaire was the date of Napoleon's coup d'état, overthrowing the Directory and establishing the Consulate. In comparing Daladier to Napoleon, *L'Humanité* obviously had in mind the opening lines of Karl Marx's *Le 18 Brumaire de Louis Napoléon:* "Hegel remarks somewhere that all great world-historical facts and personages appear, so to speak, twice. He forgot to add: the first time as tragedy, the second time as farce."

Le Populaire proclaimed in bold headlines that the premier's intention was, under cover of trouble abroad, to intensify his war against the proletariat at home. "Republicans," it declared, "cannot abdicate in favor of a government whose parliamentary support consists for the most part of minority groups that tend more and more to penalize the working masses." Did Léon Blum see in Daladier, his former minister of defense, an avatar of the "providential man" destined to subvert the Republic? "You are asking for powers which I understand to be more or less unlimited in nature and in time," he argued during a parliamentary debate. "I consider this desperate resolution unwise. You wish to present us with a fait accompli, having consulted [no one]. Do you think it advisable to sow division at a time of grave events? to cast suspicion on Parliament and Republican institutions? and to do so not when you are riding a tide of success but in the wake of a diplomatic fiasco [Munich]?" Blum's foes could have answered his remarks by quoting the column he had written five months earlier, after the Munich pact was signed: "There is not a woman or man in France who will refuse MM. Chamberlain and Daladier their just tribute of gratitude. War is spared us. The calamity recedes. Life can become natural again. One can resume one's work and sleep again. One can enjoy the beauty of an autumn sun."

On the day of the debate, March 15, 1939, there was commotion of a different sort several blocks away from the Palais Bourbon at the Gare d'Orléans, where Marshal Philippe Pétain departed Paris to assume his duties as France's ambassador in Burgos.* A large crowd packed the vaulted hall of the train station and spilled out onto the Quai d'Orsay. Present were admirals and generals, including Maxime Weygand, retired chief of staff of the French army. An honor guard of *gueules cassées*—crippled and maimed veterans of World War I—formed up at the head of the staircase leading down to Pétain's private carriage. A reverent reporter wrote in *Le Figaro* that the "hero of Verdun" presented "the physical image of perfect aplomb, of that imperturbable calm with which his name is synonymous." Men doffed their hats when the engine fired up, and Pétain, at the entrance to his carriage, bade them farewell "with a courtesy and charm that seemed the garland of history." Charles de Gaulle saw in all this the pitiable spectacle of an old man's vanity.

---

* As previously noted, the nationalists would not enter Madrid until March 28.

The scene, though less frenetic, was reminiscent of Georges Boulanger's departure for Clermont-Ferrand in the 1880s, when crowds gathered at the Gare de Lyon shouting, "He will return!" And the parallel runs deeper, for both departures had political implications. As Boulanger's reassignment to a provincial garrison was tantamount to internal exile, prompted by the justified fear of anti-republican conspirators organizing a coup d'état, so Daladier may have sought to marginalize a threat to the Republic by relocating Pétain beyond the Pyrenees.

This was by no means Daladier's only motive. Germany, which had lent Franco a mighty hand in overturning the Spanish Republic, continued to court favor with him and rewarded Spanish newspapers for portraying Hitler in the most advantageous light. Pétain's principal task as ambassador was to keep Spain neutral in the event of war between France and Germany. The marshal who had received the Medalla Militar from King Alfonso XIII fourteen years earlier for subduing the Moroccan Rif tribes in concert with the Spanish army, stood a much better chance of finding favor with the "Caudillo" than a polished veteran of the diplomatic corps. Franco gave him a chilly welcome, but in due course Pétain accomplished his mission, with the help of gold bullion deposited by the Spanish Republic in the Banque de France, confiscated by the French Republic, and made available to the Fascists.

Pétain had no sooner established himself as ambassador than politicians, the best-known of whom was the former premier Pierre Laval, began courting him, much as Bonapartists and royalists had wooed Boulanger into political life. First it was proposed that he stand for election to the presidency in April 1939. The very notion "horrified" him, he wrote to his wife. He would entertain no more overtures. "I can work two weeks, I can't work fifteen. I'm deaf and that troubles me." No matter. He lent his suitors an ear, irritated by their self-interested importunities but pleased to be the object of their courtship.

On September 1, a week after signing a nonaggression pact with the Soviet Union, the Nazis invaded Poland. On September 3, France and England declared war against Germany. The calls for Pétain's return became so insistent that Daladier, as much to thwart suspected conspiracies as to create a government of "national union," offered him the War Ministry. Was he not, according to one of Daladier's confidants, "an old fetish," "the great moral figure of the last war, a humane, reepected leader whose advice could be precious should disagreements arise between the government and the general staff"? Nothing came of discussions in Paris, during which Pétain, at Laval's urging, insisted on an immediate entente with Italy. He did not tell Daladier that he was loath to serve in a cabinet of inept civilians. What he did say was that much remained to be done in Spain. "Certain official milieux are still too obliging to German propaganda," he wrote. "They do not wish to understand that the war in which we are engaged with Hitler's Germany combined with Soviet Russia is but the sequel to that waged by Spain against Communism for the defense of Christian civilization." It was Franco's line, repeated verbatim.

The longer France and Germany temporized on the eastern front, camping opposite each other in what came to be known as the *drôle de guerre* or "phony war," the more Pétain longed to make himself heard in councils of war. His wish was granted in May 1940. By then Paul Reynaud, a conservative finance minister, had replaced Daladier as premier and the phony war had turned all too real, with panzer divisions racing across the Ardennes under scores of German Stukas bombing French defenses, and the French army in full retreat. Panic-stricken officials at the Foreign Ministry made a pyre of diplomatic papers. "It was as if the ineffective past of the Third Republic were being consumed in a vast crematorium," wrote General Edward Spears, Churchill's personal representative to the French government. On September 18, Reynaud appointed Pétain minister without portfolio and vice premier. He announced his decision in a radio broadcast:

> The victor of Verdun, thanks to whom the assailants of 1916 didn't breach the line, thanks to whom the morale of the French army in 1917 was lifted to victory, Marshal Pétain, returned from Madrid this morning where he rendered many services for France. . . . Henceforth he will be at my side, placing all his strength and wisdom at the service of his country.

With few exceptions, the French press joined in a collective panegyric of the hero who eternally performs his epic feat, turning the tide of battle. Pétain, the "vanquisher of Verdun," had in him the stuff of Coriolanus repulsing the Volsces, of Roland at Roncevaux, of Corneille's Cid putting the Moors to flight, of Joan raising the siege of Orléans. *Le Figaro* declared that France felt "an immense impression of security." The Breton paper *L'Ouest-Éclair* incanted the refrain "Verdun revealed him to the world" and informed readers that it was Pétain who, on February 26, 1916, uttered the rallying cry *"Courage! On les aura!"* (Courage! We'll lick them!), breathing life into battle-worn troops. The article noted, "It is reported that at the funeral of King Alexander of Serbia, Marshal Goering, struck by the prestige of Marshal Pétain, walked a step behind him and couldn't take his eyes off the sky-blue silhouette."* Louder than all flourishes was Maurras's in *L'Action Française:* "At last! . . . Necessity proved as wise as reason. At last, the military hierarchy and the political hierarchy coincide. . . . Veterans of Verdun have all told us how faith and hope were restored to the most downcast when, on a frightful early winter morning, word spread from trench to trench: 'Pétain! Pétain! Pétain is taking command!' This memory spares us from having to insist upon the virtue of prestige. But in 1916 it shone only within our lines. In 1940 it will light up the sky and daunt the enemy."†

On June 11, as German divisions approached the capital from the north, the French chief of staff, Maxime Weygand, proclaimed Paris an open or undefended city. One week earlier, the English general Edward Spears had implored Pétain in his office on the Boulevard des Invalides to oppose colleagues—Weygand among them—who demanded that the alliance with England be renounced and a separate armistice negotiated. Pétain demonstrated the hopelessness of France's military situation on a battle map, then proceeded to blame politicians and exonerate the general staff—all except Charles de Gaulle, his protégé, his bête noire, and the author of *La France et Son Armée,* who, he felt, had not fully acknowledged his own contribution to the book. "Not only is he vain, he is ungrateful," Pétain said of the stiff-necked brigadier. When Spears mentioned Joan of Arc, Pétain, apparently more interested in martyrdom than in victory, insisted on reading a

---

* In 1934 King Alexander of Yugoslavia was assassinated by a Bulgarian nationalist during a state visit to France.

† Maurras, who was all for the invasion of the Rhineland in the 1920s, adamantly opposed France's declaration of war in 1939. On August 26, 1939, six days before Germany invaded Poland, he wrote, "Jews, or friends of Jews, these gentlemen are in close contact with the powerful Jewish clique in London. . . . If today our people allow themselves to be slaughtered unsuspectingly and vainly at the behest of forces that are English-speaking Jews, or at the behest of their French slaves, then a French voice must be raised to proclaim the truth."

commemorative speech he had given at Joan's stake in Rouen. The Englishman found him "infinitely pitiable" and parted with the feeling that France was receding behind a glorious past evoked in the quavering voice of an old man.

No sooner did Weygand proclaim Paris an open city than the government moved south and established temporary quarters in the Loire valley. Churchill and Anthony Eden came over from London, circling beyond the range of German anti-aircraft fire but flying into the teeth of a dispute between *résistants,* notably Paul Reynaud, and capitulators who declared that an armistice was indispensable to France. On his return, Churchill described Pétain as a dangerous man "who had always been defeatist, even during the last war."

Churchill conferred with Reynaud for the last time on June 13 in a lightning-quick visit. General Weygand informed the cabinet that German troops were expected to enter Paris the next day, whereupon Pétain read a document originally meant for Churchill's ears stating that a government in exile would be no government at all. Treating separately with Germany was presented as virtue rather than perfidy, as the courageous stand of Frenchmen rooted in French soil rather than cowardice. Surrender would be painful, but the pain would make amends for the delinquency of a Socialist regime and the corrupting influence of internationalism. France would purge herself. She would recover her selfhood, a prisoner but within her own boundaries. "A French renaissance will be the fruit of suffering. . . . I declare, for myself, that I shall refuse to leave native soil, even if it means withdrawing from the political scene. I shall remain among the French, to share their pain and their miseries." Only an armistice could save the life of "eternal France."

The administration moved farther south, to Bordeaux, along with deputies, senators, civil servants, journalists, and petitioners (as in 1870, during the Franco-Prussian War, when the Germans besieged Paris). Ministers and officers hoping to salvage something of the general staff's prestige with an armistice engaged the party of resistance in heated debate. The whole city became a rumor mill. After several days, Reynaud, who had hoped that Roosevelt would come to the rescue, admitted defeat, tendered his resignation, and on June 14 broadcast a final message to the French nation: "All Frenchmen, wherever they are, will have to suffer. May they prove themselves worthy of their country's great past. May they treat one another fraternally. May they

The victorious German army parading down the Champs-Élysées, June 14, 1940.

close ranks around the wounded fatherland. The hour of resurrection will come." His last word as premier, recommending that President Albert Lebrun invite Marshal Pétain to assemble a cabinet, was spoken between clenched teeth. Armistice negotiations began immediately and resulted in a treaty the draconian terms of which avenged those imposed on Germany by the armistice of November 11, 1918.

News that a line of demarcation would slice across France's midsection just north of Vichy in the Auvergne, with enemy troops also occupying the entire Atlantic coast, had not yet been published when Premier Pétain consoled and chastised his countrymen in a speech aired on June 25. His intention was to explain how and why the army had come to grief. The price exacted by Germany would tax everyone's life. But France, he assured them, would not have dishonored herself. Her leaders would remain on French soil, unlike expatriates prating from London and North Africa. Their loyalty to the earth vouched for the truth of their words: "The earth does not lie. It will be your refuge." Moreover, adversity was not without its blessings. Cognizant of his reputation as "the providential man," Pétain insinuated that defeat may have been a fortunate fall. He repeated what he had said on the eve of Germany's victory parade down the Champs-Élysées, that the French had brought defeat upon themselves: "It stemmed from our laxity. The spirit of hedonism leveled all that the spirit of sacrifice had raised. I invite you, above all, to a moral and intellectual housecleaning."* As in the 1870s after the Franco-Prussian War, when the Third Republic was struggling to survive its infancy under the rule of conservatives who promulgated a "Moral Order," so the Republic in its death throes heard its last premier announce "a new order."

The call for mea culpas and self-cleansing was echoed by *La Croix*. "Why did God permit this frightful disaster?" asked the abbé Thellier de Poncheville. "Let us fall to our knees. We have many faults to expiate. An official enterprise of dechristianization which struck the vitality of our fatherland at its very source. Too much blasphemy and not enough prayer. Too much immorality and not enough penitence. The forfeit had to be paid one day. The hour has come to repent of our sins in our tears and our blood." In *Le Figaro*, François Mauriac, Charles de Gaulle's future champion, wrote that France had not heard a mere individual speaking on the radio but "the summons of a great humiliated nation rising from the depths of our History." Pétain spoke for those who had fallen at Verdun. "His voice, broken by sor-

---

* "The capitulation of the government was less dreadful [to those in command] than a military debacle," Raymond Aron writes in *Chroniques de Guerre*. "General Weygand, whose political conservatism dominated his military thinking, feared that pockets of revolutionary resistance would form within the throng of routed troops. This obsession clouded his view of things. He had responded to the setbacks in Flanders by organizing a continuous line along the Somme. When this fragile defense collapsed, he was confounded by the new dimension of warfare and lost all capacity for synthesis and action."

A TOUS LES FRANCAIS

La France a perdu une bataille!
Mais la France n'a pas perdu la guerre!

Des gouvernants de rencontre ont pu capituler, cédant à la
panique, oubliant l'honneur, livrant le pays à la servitude.
Cependant, rien n'est perdu!

Rien n'est perdu, parce que cette guerre est une guerre
mondiale. Dans l'univers libre, des forces immenses n'ont
pas encore donné. Un jour, ces forces écraseront l'ennemi.
Il faut que la France, ce jour-là, soit présente à la victoire.
Alors, elle retrouvera sa liberté et sa grandeur. Tel est mon but,
mon seul but!

Voilà pourquoi je convie tous les Français, où qu'ils se
trouvent, à s'unir à moi dans l'action, dans le sacrifice et
dans l'espérance.

Notre patrie est en péril de mort.
Luttons tous pour la sauver!

VIVE LA FRANCE!

JUIN 1940   GÉNÉRAL DE GAULLE

General de Gaulle in England calls on his compatriots to continue the fight, after the Pétain government signs an armistice with Hitler. "Nothing is lost, because this war is a world war. In the free universe, immense forces have not entered the fray. One day they will crush the enemy. On that day, France must be present at the victory."

row and age, uttered the reproach of heroes whose sacrifice, because of our defeat, had been in vain." *L'Action Française* transmitted its sentiments through a satellite in Bordeaux: "Great fortune has crowned us in our immense misery. God had prepared a great leader for us. Marshal Pétain has gathered up France on the very day of its distress."

On June 29, the peripatetic government evacuated Bordeaux, which became a German port. Deferring to its aged premier it reestablished itself in Vichy, a spa town well supplied with hotel rooms and enough mineral water to purge the diminished nation. On July 9, what remained of Parliament convened in Vichy's casino to consider a proposal that the constitution be changed. Several deputies and senators who would have dissented—Daladier, Pierre Mendès France, Georges Mandel, and Jean Zay, among others—had boarded a ship bound for Morocco three weeks earlier when it was thought that the entire government would embark and continue the fight from North Africa.* On July 10, the National Assembly, with only eighty senators

* They were placed under house arrest in Casablanca. Zay (Blum's education minister) and Georges Mandel (Reynaud's minister of the interior), both Jews, were eventually assassinated by the Vichy militia. Mendès France, another Jew, was imprisoned but

German flags hanging from the terrace of the Palais de Chaillot.

and deputies objecting, authorized Pétain to promulgate new laws. On the following day the Third Republic died, all powers being assigned to Pétain as "chief of state"; the office of president being abolished; and Parliament adjourned.

In his inaugural address, Pétain sang the praises of discipline and work. "The labor of Frenchmen is the supreme resource of the Fatherland. It must be sacred," he declared.

> International capitalism and international Socialism, which exploited and degraded it, played prominent roles in the prewar period. They were all the more sinister for acting in concert while appearing to cross swords. We shall no longer tolerate their shady alliance. In a new order, where justice will reign, we will not admit them to factories and farms. In our warped society, money—too often the servant of lies—was an instrument of domination. . . . In France reborn, money will only be the recompense of effort. Your work, your family will enjoy the respect and protection of the nation.*

---

escaped. Daladier was handed over to the Gestapo and sent to the Buchenwald concentration camp, where, for a time, his fellow inmates included Reynaud and Léon Blum.

* Money, lies, abstraction, and Jews were cognates in Vichy's vocabulary of denigration.

Marshal Pétain greeting schoolchildren in Vichy, 1940.

Laws calculated to "remake" France were drafted in great haste during the summer of 1940. Six days after Pétain's speech, the sons of foreign-born fathers learned that they could neither practice law nor serve in government. On July 22, all naturalizations approved since 1927 became subject to review. On July 30, a Supreme Court was established for the express purpose of finding ministers of the Third Republic guilty of failing in their duties or betraying the public trust. On August 13, secret associations, above all the Masonic Order, were banned. By law, anyone who came under suspicion of "endangering the safety of the state" could be arrested and imprisoned. October marked the beginning of Vichy's anti-Semitic campaign. Decrees excluded Jews from public office and liberal professions; Algerian Jews lost their citizenship; internment camps filled with refugees from Nazi Germany.

The festivities of July 1939 celebrating the 150th anniversary of the French Revolution were still vividly remembered when "Work, family, fatherland" replaced the republican motto "Liberty, equality, fraternity." This brought immense satisfaction to Charles Maurras, who felt that his editorial jeremiads had, like a desert cactus, unexpectedly flowered after growing needles for forty years. "People have spoken about the 'divine element' in the art of war," he wrote. "Well, the divine element in the art of politics has shown itself in the extraordi nary surprises the Marshal has reserved for us."

And where Maurras led, the royal pretender, the Comte de Paris, followed. "This providential man," he wrote of Pétain, "has managed to accomplish a triple miracle: he has prevented the total disappearance of the fatherland; he has by his presence alone enabled the country to stay alive; and he has set France on the path of its great traditional destinies by breaking with the principles of the fallen regime."

The "État Français" became even more the simulacrum of an independent state when, in November 1942, after the Allies landed in North Africa, German troops crossed the line of demarcation to defend against a Mediterranean invasion.

Epilogue

With each week's accumulation of diplomatic news, it becomes increasingly clear that Europe is now permanently divided into two camps of conviction, which differ fundamentally on one thing: war. For historical and material reasons, France and England today consider war a *summum malum;* for biological and material reasons, Germany and Italy consider war a *summum bonum.*

—JANET FLANNER, February 2, 1939, *Paris Was Yesterday*

I hope for the triumph of totalitarian man over the world. The age of divided man has passed. . . . Enough of this dust of individuals in the crowd.

—PIERRE DRIEU LA ROCHELLE, *Journal,* June 10, 1945

Pierre Drieu La Rochelle, who tacked so obsessively between self-hatred and vanity, ended up collaborating with the Germans despite himself and for reasons of literary promotion. His pledge of fealty to Jacques Doriot and the French Fascist Party in 1936 had followed the pattern of all his enthusiasms. It had laid the ground for disillusionment. He came to believe that the movement capable of transcending politics and organizing France around a militant creed had dissipated its energy in political opportunism. Worse still for Drieu, who felt alive only within the radiant circle of a hero, was the dimming of Jacques Doriot's aura. Drieu accused him of failing to "weld into one metal the energy of the many who had entrusted themselves to him" and in January 1939 resigned from the PPF. Doriot, the Vulcan presuming to harden men in the heat of battle, turned out to be an ordinary trimmer. Like Republican France, he was *"mou"*—soft. Not so, Hitler.

The basic vocabulary of an ideologue at war with his own intellect—energy, fire, metal, strength, virility—received full play in *Gilles,* an autobiographical novel Drieu published shortly after his resignation from Doriot's PPF, hoping finally to establish himself as something more than a respectable but minor literary figure and to find consolation thereby for his political orphanhood. It spans the life of Gilles Gambier from the First World War, when he first visits Paris as a wounded young soldier on leave, to 1937, when the soul-sick veteran of Paris society volunteers for service with Franco during the Spanish Civil War. His movements across the intervening years tell a story not unlike Flaubert's *Sentimental Education* in its randomness—a story of wrong turns, dry wells, and impasses. Women flock to him. He has affairs. He marries a rich Jewess and divorces her. His well-connected wife finds him employment in the foreign office, where he languishes dutifully. He shares his loathing of the bourgeoisie with nihilistic young writers who play at revolution. He flees to Algeria, seeking spiritual solace in the desert, but returns to bourgeois Babylon unredeemed and continues his quest for spirituality as the editor of a journal, *Apocalypse,* dedicated to the proposition that France's ultimate well-being lies not in the sterile middle ground of a republic but at the ideal confluence of political extremes. This, too, is an impasse. *Apocalypse* ends up buried in the riot rubble of February 1934, when Gilles converts to Fascism.

Suffice it to say of *Gilles* that Drieu wrote a picaresque novel with the bones of a thesis regularly poking through the flesh of its characters. Irremediably decadent, France has been undermined by modernity and by the assimilation of foreigners alien to her nature. Surrealists, homosexuals, drug addicts, feminists, and *métèques* are all called to account, but the most lethal and comprehensive agent of subversion is the Jew. Like Maurras, Drieu distinguished between the "real" country and its "legal" counterfeit. Jews belong to the latter. Devoid of the organic Frenchness that inheres in roots and soil and physical reality, they are themselves legalisms, personifying the abstract notion of citizenship invented by the Revolution. Only as old as their abstraction, they are yet responsible for France's senility—a paradox Drieu applies to the broad compass of French history. The modern world, which Jews epitomize, is decrepit; the Middle Ages, in which "French reason" made its home, were young and vital. "Gilles had associated his loneliness with the soul of France," writes Drieu.

> On foot or by car he had made pilgrimages to sites the length and breadth of France. He had rested his eyes on mountains and rivers, trees and monuments. He had been moved and arrested by monuments quarried from the matrix of the earth. How often he had jumped out of his car on a country road to visit some forsaken little church, believing that it contained the secret of life. The French once built churches and they no longer could. . . . The reasoning, calculating architect needed audacity. . . . With his church he challenged the tree rooted beside it. Now what did he make? Office buildings, boxes for rent, public conveniences, and monuments that feebly imitate the style of lost youth and creation. . . . French reason was the passionate, proud, furious twelfth century splurging itself in epics and cathedrals. . . . The French had been soldiers, monks, architects, painters, poets, husbands, and fathers. They had sired children, they had constructed, they had killed, and laid down their lives. They had sacrificed themselves and sacrificed.

"Sacrifice" is another word belonging to the vocabulary of the Fascist at war with his intellect. In an epilogue that calls to mind the French Romantics who portrayed Spain as a netherworld of salutary primitivism, Gilles finds on the battlefield of Extremadura, where men untouched by the modern age and careless of their individual fate fight for a cause, what he couldn't find in the Algerian desert. "Almost all the soldiers were young and recruited from the neighboring province of Old Castile. Young peasants, robust and incorruptible in their simplicity. They were born of that eternally primitive race which still populates the depths of Europe and from which we now see emerging the great irresistible movement that astonishes delicately strung minds in cities of the West."

Drieu's paranoia, feelings of inferiority, and melancholy all played a part in making the publication of *Gilles,* by Gallimard in December 1939, a vexed affair. Months earlier, Jean Paulhan, the editorial director of the literary review *NRF,* to which Drieu contributed, had rejected the chapter ridiculing the Surrealists—a rejection at which he would have certainly taken umbrage even if Paulhan had not continued to publish the work of Louis Aragon, by whose flourishing career Drieu always measured his own. In April he vowed never again to set foot in the *NRF* offices, where "Jews, Communist sympathizers, former Surrealists and all manner of people who believe that truth lies on the left call the tune." He protested to Paulhan that his "national sentiment" was not subject to the vagaries of a foreign power. "Aragon is more Communist than ever and obeys the defeatist agenda of the Soviet Union. As for myself, I remain a resolute adversary of democracy, which I consider above all a ruin encumbering us with its debris—and at the same time a patriot. I am the opposite of Aragon—I subordinate my tastes and distastes to the country I belong to. I have asserted this position in the *NRF*, . . . in the PPF's *Émancipation Nationale*, and in *Gilles*."*

But Paulhan was not alone in thinking that with patriots like Drieu, France had no need of potential traitors. Drieu himself couldn't tease apart his allegiances. "I can't think my thoughts through to the point of hoping for a victory of the totalitarians, although they would establish a European union more organic and effective than our League of Nations," he wrote on May 10, 1940, the day Germany attacked France. "I am incapable of stifling my instinctive French reaction. Habit is second nature and second nature is instinct." Yet three days later, when the Germans were crossing the Meuse at Sedan, en route to the interior, he noted in his diary that he and Hitler were made of the same stuff and moved by the same impulses. "I feel Hitler's movements as if I were he himself; I am at the center of his impulsive force. The male and positive side of my work are what make him tick. Strange adventure, these parallels. . . . In Hitler the same weakness and strength. . . . At twenty-five or thirty, I discerned the essence of Fascism in my first works."

The catastrophic events of 1940–41 unhinged Drieu, intensifying both his paranoia and his grandiosity. He fled Paris on June 10 with or without the poison he had threatened to swallow as soon as Germans entered the city, but more fearful of being assassinated by "Jews and Anglophiles." The army was in full retreat. A tide of refugees

---

* The reference to Aragon being a Communist concerns the Stalin-Hitler nonaggression pact of August 1939. In fact, Aragon was drafted early in the war, won the Croix de Guerre for acts of bravery, and, after demobilization, played a significant role in the Resistance.

swept him down to the Dordogne, where he remained until, on July 19, the opportunity to visit Vichy presented itself. By then Drieu had learned that Germany's ambassador to Paris was Otto Abetz, whom he had met six years earlier in Nuremberg.* Drieu offered to cultivate Abetz for whatever intelligence of German plans their acquaintance might yield. Home he came, crossing the line of demarcation with quasi-official credentials. But the powers that be in Paris proved more alluring to Drieu than the geriatric regime in Vichy. Before long he reconciled his differences with Jacques Doriot in hopes of founding a "Socialist-Fascist" party inspired by the Hitler-Stalin pact. "I tell myself (and, alas, confide to all and sundry) that I would like to play the role of gray eminence and am so persuasive that there has been much whispering about it." Otto Abetz, who kept close tabs on Paris's cultural scene, discouraged the idea and proposed that Drieu apply his energies to literature rather than politics as if the two could be distinguished in occupied France. This he did so effectively that in December 1940 the German authorities allowed the *Nouvelle Revue Française,* which had been shut down, to resume publication under Drieu's directorship, and gave him oversight in the affairs of Gallimard, the book publisher. Suddenly the world had turned upside down for Drieu. The great had been made small, impedimenta had been swept away, and France's foremost literary journal, which had added insult to injury by publishing an uncomplimentary review of *Gilles* before its extinction, would be his to revive.

Reviving it was made easier with the help of Paulhan, whom Gaston Gallimard employed as director of the Pléiade collection. The editor who had slighted Drieu became his indispensable adviser at the *NRF* (apparently eschewing politics after several weeks in a Gestapo prison while clandestinely working for the Resistance). But Drieu could not deny the fact that he held sway over a diminished realm. Once his writing was slighted by an editor of note; now his ersatz *NRF* endured slights from notable writers. Malraux, who remained his friend, had advised him against accepting the position. Gide, who had helped launch the *NRF* before World War I, dissociated himself from it after *résistants* taunted him for contributing a piece to the first issue

---

* The Wehrmacht governed the northern zone, but Vichy, or "L'État Français," was allowed to wear a wispy beard of authority, enough to justify the presence of a German "ambassador."

published under Drieu's directorship, in December 1940.* Attempts to herd Gide, Paul Valéry, and Paul Claudel onto an editorial board failed. "Gide, Valéry, Claudel backed out in the weasel ways of the old generation, more despicable than ever," Drieu fumed. "Claudel, the enemy of Voltaire, served the Masonic government and the Jews. Valéry thrived, and Gide was entirely at his ease under a regime that venerated his pederasty, his asocial strutting."

Power and virtue were not easily reconciled at the *NRF*. Having helped to free Paulhan from a German prison, Drieu found himself overshadowed by the éminence grise, whom authors held in high esteem. The arrangement made Drieu acutely uncomfortable. By October 1942, when he traveled to Weimar for the Nazi-sponsored Congress of European Writers, depression was written all over his face. Photographs show it and his journal voices it.† "I can no longer get interested in anything. I've retreated to my lair and feel that I've never left it. Why did I subject myself to this penitence for a year and a half? All the mediocrities I've read and seen. Why this habit of always altering and upsetting the blessed wholeness of my solitude, of my divine sloth?" *Gilles* was not recognized as the masterpiece he hoped it would be, and the *NRF* did not vindicate him.

Drieu La Rochelle had compromised himself fatally, but fraternizing with evil enabled him on at least one occasion to redeem himself. Early in May 1943, his first wife, Colette Jéramec—now remarried,

---

* Gide had ignored the pleas of the book publisher Gaston Gallimard, whose firm was the review's sponsor. Books bore the imprint "NRF" as well as well as "Gallimard." Roger Martin du Gard, an old associate and friend of both, sent Gide a letter containing the kind of retort he might have made to his critics: "I know what I'm doing. Laid out for me at length are the reasons why the NRF (both the review and book publisher) must be resuscitated if we hope to 'save the furniture' and prevent this double enterprise, which has been more or less our child for thirty years, from falling under foreign direction. . . . The fate of the book publisher . . . is inextricably bound up with that of the review: it will be impossible to save one and sacrifice the other. Now, the review is regarded by readers as mine. . . . The absence of my name from the table of contents, especially under present circumstances, would be tantamount to a public disavowal. I would be knifing it in the back by refusing my collaboration."

† Other delegates included Abel Bonnard and Robert Brasillach. Bonnard—a follower of Maurras who converted to Fascism, a prolific novelist and journalist, a member of the Académie Française, a minister of education in the Vichy government—fled to Spain after the war and was sentenced to death in absentia. Brasillach, also a protégé of Maurras's and a convert to Fascism, who edited the collaborationist daily *Je Suis Partout,* was tried shortly before the end of the war and executed.

the mother of two young boys, and a research physician at the Pasteur Institute—was denounced by her concierge for holding suspicious meetings in her flat and arrested by French agents of the Gestapo. Because she had loudly resisted, they arrested her sons as well and transported all three to Drancy, outside Paris, an internment camp from which prisoners, mostly Jews, were sent to Auschwitz.* Upon learning of their predicament, Drieu rushed home from the Midi and promised to help. She smuggled this letter to him, dated May 2, 1943:

> D. I don't doubt that you spend most of your time working on my behalf. But L. [Dr. Legroux, a friend] led me to hope that the little meeting you had on Wednesday was to be followed by another and hearing nothing further about it upsets me. To tell the truth, I don't place much faith in the effectiveness of other approaches; what little hope I have I place only in you, knowing how tenacious you can be in certain circumstances. But what can you do? . . . I'm not suffering too much materially, and am above all happy that the two men [her children] haven't suffered at all. Emotionally, despite appearances which certainly didn't deceive you, you can imagine my thoughts.† Try to meet again, alone or in company. . . . Above all, I know that you will . . . not delude either yourself or me with vain hopes. . . . If you can't speak to me one day put a word in your own writing on the next card, I would prefer it. Or if not, have me informed of your thoughts as minutely as possible. Knowing for sure that the two others can look forward to getting out, even without me, would set my mind at rest.

Drieu spent more time working on her behalf than would have been necessary if his friend Otto Abetz were still the German ambassador. Abetz had fallen out of favor and been replaced by Rudolf Schleier. But the real obstacle was the German security service, the Sicherheitsdienst, whose director distrusted the embassy. Drieu enlisted the help of people he generally avoided, volunteered to lecture at the German Institute, and threatened to stop writing for the Paris press if his petition was denied. As a result of his exertions, Colette and her children

---

* In another version, Colette was asked for identity papers by a German soldier stopping automobiles at a checkpoint in Paris. She complied indignantly, and was later arrested in her apartment by the Gestapo.

† Drieu must have obtained permission to visit her at Drancy.

Pierre Drieu La Rochelle, director of the *Nouvelle Revue Française* during the occupation.

were released after two months at Drancy, unlike sixty-five thousand other internees, who were deported to the east; sixty-three thousand of them died.

Far from taking pride in the rescue, Drieu taxed himself with being soft and blamed the beneficiary of his good deed for subjecting him to the judgment of his conscience. "The Jews tricked me," he groused that summer. "My first wife deliberately got herself imprisoned, it seems, to put me under the obligation of freeing her. I was cowardly enough to whine over her fate and have her chains removed. . . . She has absolutely no idea that I find her insufferable." For the superior man of Zarathustra, mercy is a cardinal vice.

In 1943 he turned fifty, reimmersed himself in Nietzsche, left the *NRF* to Paulhan's management, and questioned his reasons for living any longer as the world order in which he had tried to make his home began to crumble. The Russians had triumphed at Stalingrad and were advancing on Kursk. The Allied forces had landed on Sicily. In July the Fascist Grand Council dismissed Mussolini, who was arrested and imprisoned. "Mussolini has resigned like some vulgar democratic minister," Drieu noted. "It's ludicrous. So Fascism turns out to have been nothing more than that. Fascism was no stronger than I, an armchair philosopher of violence. He will be more grotesque than Napoleon on the *Bellerophon*. By its weakness Fascism demonstrates the weakness of Europe, the decadence of Europe. Will Hitler do any better?" He worshipped *la force* no less than before, but he saw decadence everywhere, and took to quoting Isaiah's images of messianic wrath.

In November, Drieu spent several weeks in Switzerland with his friend Bertrand de Jouvenel, who assured him that cantonal authorities would be disposed to grant him a long-term visa if he chose to remain. He chose instead to return, with the intention, as he later explained, of dying by his own hand "in due course." Living almost reclusively, he studied the great texts of Eastern religion, completed another novel, and reckoned with himself as best he could in a diary. "I would have liked to be just a man, not a writer: talent doesn't excuse the lack of genius. But here I am writing. This journal is graffiti on the wall of a urinal or of a prison cell—even the graffiti writer believes that he will be read. The eternal Crusoe." He was unremitting in his anti-Semitism but occasionally lucid enough to recognize its ignominious source. "I've always been scared to death of Jews, and terribly ashamed of my fear. Not hatred, but repugnance. Horror of Jewesses: almost not slept with them. They've approached, then fled. The Jew succeeding as he has in France has branded me, even more than the Anglo-Saxon, with an impression of French inferiority."

After the Normandy invasion, collaborators went into hiding or fled the country, some to the Swabian town of Sigmaringen, where the Vichy government, rescued and sequestered by Germany, occupied an enormous castle. Drieu could have fled to Spain—he obtained papers —but once again the prospect of living in exile repelled him. He wrote that if any army could have accepted him with his multitude of physical ailments, he would have volunteered to die at the front, on either side, in the uniform of a Scottish Highland regiment or the Waffen SS. To be avoided above all was a trial and judgment. "Should I soon commit suicide?" he asked himself. "I want to avoid being stupidly disemboweled by a mob of concierges or humiliated by Jews."

He wrote a will, letters of farewell (to Malraux, Victoria Ocampo, and Christiane Renault, among others), and on August 12, 1944, swallowed what would have been a fatal dose of phenobarbital if his maid had not found him in time. Three days later, at the American Hospital in Neuilly, he slit his wrists, but was saved again. "Where am I, in any sense?" he wrote to Paulhan. "I don't know and am in no hurry to find out. I eat, I would like to chat with you slowly, after a long, silent walk."

With the battle for Paris impending, Drieu's women friends took him under their collective wing. Colette Jéramec hid him on the Rue de Grenelle in the apartment of a physician, who ministered to him for a month. He then lodged at Orgeval, outside Paris, in the country house of an old American friend, Noëlle Murphy, whose release from an internment camp for foreigners he had helped arrange in 1942. At Orgeval he regained his health and enough inner strength to embark upon a novel about a painter of genius, based on Van Gogh's life but drawing heavily on his own, *Mémoires de Dirk Raspe*. He read as much philosophy as friends made available to him. By January 1945, the discomfort of winter in an unheated country house had put an end to his convalescence. He fell ill, and doubts almost as old as consciousness itself assailed him like reawakened Furies. "I wanted to be a complete man, not only a bookworm but a swordsman, who assumes responsibilities, who absorbs blows and returns them. . . . I shall regret not having filled during these past few years the role that remained available to me, that of dandy—of the unflinching nonconformist who rejects fatuities of every persuasion, who discreetly but firmly displays his impious indifference."

There were also Furies in the shape of informants. Drieu was a wanted man, with his name on a list of collaborationist writers drawn up by the Comité National des Écrivains. Suspecting that locals had rumored his presence at Orgeval, Colette moved him to her own country house, and from there to an apartment in Paris near the Place de l'Étoile. Another collaborator, Robert Brasillach, was executed in February. The trial frightened Drieu—the trial more than the sentence.

On March 16, leaving nothing to chance, he detached a gas pipe and swallowed three vials of phenobarbital. A note insisted that the burial be nonreligious. His brief list of official mourners did not include Colette Jéramec or Christiane Renault. He requested the presence of only two men, one being André Malraux, whom he named his literary executor.

Acknowledgments

I owe a particular debt of gratitude to Donna Sammis of the Frank Melville Library of the State University of New York at Stony Brook. I would also like to thank the staffs of the Butler Library of Columbia University and the Cabinet des Estampes of the Bibliothèque Nationale de Paris.

My thanks go to Paula Deitz for publishing a version of chapter 4 in the Autumn 2012 issue of *The Hudson Review.*

Among the many friends whose conversation and encouragement buoyed me, I must make special mention of Ruth Kozodoy, who perused the manuscript with pencil in hand at various stages of the writing.

My thanks go as well to Georges Borchardt, the kindest and most helpful of agents.

I am indebted above all to Victoria Wilson of Knopf, whose devotion and care made this work possible.

Notes

ix "the tree of liberty grows only when watered": quoted in Wikipédia (the French version of Wikipedia). The statement by Bertrand Barère de Vieuzac was a close variation of one made five years earlier by Thomas Jefferson.

x "The plantings had multiplied": Maurice Agulhon, *Les Quarante-huitards* (Paris: Gallimard, 1992), p. 52. Unless noted otherwise, all translations from French are mine.

x "Alas, Lorraine undertook": Maurice Barrès, *Les Déracinés* (Paris: Plon, 1922), vol. 2, p. 238.

PART ONE

CHAPTER 1 The Coming of War

3 "Nothing collapses more quickly": George Eliot, *Impressions of Theophrastus Such* (London: BiblioBazaar, 2006), p. 85.

3 "the Servian [*sic*] is both by principle": Edmund Spencer, *Travels in European Turkey: 1850* (London: Colburn & Co., 1851), vol. 1, p. 34.

4 "moments of excitement": *New York Times*, June 24, 1903.

4 "The assassination of King Alexander": *Le Petit Parisien*, June 12, 1903.

5 "in a Christian country": *Le Gaulois*, June 12, 1903.

5 "The Serbs change government": *Le Figaro*, June 12, 1903.

5 "There had been a score of opportunities": Winston Churchill, *The World Crisis* (New York: Free Press, 2005), p. 87.

6 "Never has the season": *Le Figaro*, July 29, 1914.

6 "a shade of anxiety": Raymond Poincaré, *The Origins of the War* (London: Cassell, 1922), p. 182.

6 "a blaze of fire and flame": Maurice Paléologue, *An Ambassador's Memoirs* (New York: George Doran, 1923), p. 14.

7 "commonplace assurances": Poincaré, *Origins of War*, p. 190.

8 "the same ideal of peace": Paléologue, *Ambassador's Memoirs*, p. 24.

8 "had decided *in principle*": Luigi Albertini, *The Origins of the War of 1914* (Oxford: Oxford University Press, 1952), vol. 2, p. 591.

9 "unanimity of patriotic resolution": Poincaré, *Origins of War,* p. 206.

9 "Never have I felt so overwhelmed": quoted in Albertini, *Origins of the War,* vol. 2, p. 596.

10 "no disorder, no panic": *Le Temps,* July 30, 1914.

10 "there is no longer any justice": Edward Berenson, *The Trial of Madame Caillaux* (Berkeley: University of California Press, 1992), p. 2.

11 "proceed united as one": ibid., p. 241.

11 "The Serbs are Orientals": Albertini, *Origins of the War,* vol. 2, p. 468.

12 "generous Slav heart": ibid., p. 350.

12 "My thoughts were utterly pessimistic": Paléologue, *Ambassador's Memoirs,* p. 37.

12 "This is the way things": Albertini, *Origins of the War,* vol. 2, p. 489.

13 "Today you are told": Harvey Goldberg, *The Life of Jean Jaurès* (Madison: University of Wisconsin Press, 1968), p. 444.

13 "If all of Europe": *L'Humanité,* June 30, 1914.

13 "Think of what it would mean": Goldberg, *Life of Jean Jaurès,* p. 446.

14 "The ultimatum sent to Servia": *New York Times Current History* (New York: The New York Times Co., 1915–16), vol. 1, p. 401.

15 "Care must be taken to avoid": Jean-Jacques Becker, *1914: Comment les Français Sont Entrés dans la Guerre* (Paris: Presses de la Fondation Nationale des Sciences Politiques, 1977), p. 142.

15 "All civilized people": Becker, *1914,* p. 141.

15 "the conflict became inevitable": ibid.

15 "Your sentence will have no political": *Le Figaro,* March 30, 1914.

15 "Perhaps it meant to affirm": *L'Humanité,* March 30, 1914.

16 "the criminal maneuvers": ibid.

16 "This Wilhelm": ibid., p. 334.

16 "Germany has long been spoiling": ibid.

16 "War had to erupt": ibid., p. 335.

16 "ancestral," "hereditary," "eternal": ibid.

16 "If France is invaded": ibid., p. 410.

16 "The truth of the matter is": ibid., p. 412.

17 "At this tomb, on which": *Le Figaro,* August 5, 1914.

17 "What he would say": *L'Humanité,* August 5, 1914.

18 "What was the psychological phenomenon": Becker, *1914,* p. 407.

19 "legitimate reparations": *Le Temps,* August 5, 1914.

19 "Under siege": ibid.

20 "one of the grandest": *Le Figaro,* August 5, 1914.

20 "Henceforth I know no parties": C.R.M.F. Cruttwell, *A History of the Great War* (Chicago: Academy Chicago, 1991), p. 125.

21 "Even if it involves" Maurice Barrès, *Chroniques de la Grande Guerre* (Paris: Plon, 1968), pp. 123–24.

22 "The task of Christians": Becker, *1914,* p. 471.

22 "We know full well": Modris Eksteins, *Rites of Spring: The Great War and the Birth of the Modern Age* (Boston: Houghton Mifflin, 1989), p. 196

CHAPTER 2 The Making of a Xenophobe

23 "Maurice Barrès": The quote is from Michel Winock, *Le Siècle des Intellectuels* (Paris: Seuil, 1997), p. 149.

23 "educate," "illustrate": article on Barrès in A. K. Thorlby, ed., *The Penguin Companion to European Literature* (Baltimore: Penguin Books, 1969), p. 84.

24 "At this moment": Maurice Barrès, *Mes Cahiers: 1896–1923*, ed. Guy Dupré (Paris: Plon, 1994), p. 6.

24 "*Le juif errant / La corde aux dents*": François Broche, *Vie de Maurice Barrès* (Paris: Jean-Claude Lattès, 1987), p. 27.

27 "Rambunctious kids": ibid., p. 36.

28 "Was I to become": Barrès, *Mes Cahiers*, pp. 10–11.

28 "Those who did not begin": Henri Brémond, introduction to *Vingt-cinq Années de Vie Littéraire*, by Maurice Barrès (Paris: Bloud, 1908), p. xvi.

29 "Well, if not superior": Barrès, *Mes Cahiers*, p. 1025.

30 "You were born with a caul": Broche, *Maurice Barrès*, p. 76.

30 "When one wants to *arrive*": ibid., p. 77.

31 "brain cells": ibid., p. 83.

31 "The important thing": ibid., p. 85.

31 "The young king": Maurice Barrès, *Les Déracinés* (Paris: Plon, 1924), vol. 1, p. 71.

32 "very much the prince": Broche, *Maurice Barrès*, p. 98.

32 "Who are you": ibid., p. 97.

32 "Why did I want": Barrès, *Mes Cahiers*, p. 12.

33 "I have concluded": Broche, *Maurice Barrès*, p. 122.

33 "Raising funds": ibid., p. 111.

34 "You wouldn't believe": ibid., p. 104.

35 "I see how it was Wagner": Barrès, *Mes Cahiers*, p. 701.

37 "fortified, transformed": Broche, *Maurice Barrès*, p. 139.

37 "the artistic glories of the public place": ibid., p. 141.

38 "His was a virgin": Maurice Barrès, *Sous l'Oeil des Barbares* (Paris: Plon, 1921), p. 235.

38 "This night celebrates": ibid.

38 "[It's not that we're heroic]": *The Autobiography of William Butler Yeats* (New York: MacMillan, 1953), pp. 36–37.

38 "The borders of our minds": J. W. Burrow, *The Crisis of Reason: European Thought, 1848–1914* (New Haven: Yale University Press, 2000), p. 231.

38 "a new religion": *The Autobiography of William Butler Yeats*, p. 71.

39 "It is said of the man of genius": ibid., p. 40.

40 "We have intellectual fathers": Zeev Sternhell, *Maurice Barrès et le Nationalisme Français* (Paris: Fayard, 2000), p. 64.

41 "There's something about you": Jean Garrigues, *Le Général Boulanger* (Paris: Perrin, 1999), p. 46.

41 "We have to fear": ibid., 81.

41 "Throughout the whole": James Harding, *The Astonishing Adventure of General Boulanger* (New York: Scribner's, 1971), p. 7.

42 "The renown he craves": Jules-Michel Gaillard, *Jules Ferry* (Paris: Fayard, 1989), pp. 623–24.

43 "For some time": ibid., p. 628.

43 "If I knew something useful": Joseph Dedieu, *Montesquieu: L'Homme et l'Oeuvre* (Paris: Boivin, 1943), p. 22.

45 "You are called upon": Adrien Dansette, *Le Boulangisme* (Paris: Fayard, 1946), p. 132.

45 "Today, most great soul-conquerors": Gustave Le Bon, *La Psychologie des Foules* (Paris: Alcan, 1895), p. 63.

46 "[Boulanger's] program": quoted by Michel Winock in *Nationalisme, Antisémitisme et Fascisme en France* (Paris: Le Seuil, 1994), p. 45.

46 "inexplicable vertigo": Charles de Freycinet, *Souvenirs: 1878–1893* (New York: Da Capo Press, 1973), p. 400.

46 "thousands of young people": Broche, *Maurice Barrès*, p. 150.

47 "For any man of action": ibid., p. 165.

47 "The violence of approbation": Barrès, *Mes Cahiers*, p. 19.

48 "My temperament": ibid., p. 183.

50 "General Boulanger didn't deceive us": Arthur Meyer, *Ce Que Mes Yeux Ont Vu* (Paris: Plon, 1912), p. 97.

51 "You are isolated": ibid., p. 192.

CHAPTER 3 The Nightingale of the Carnage

52 "There I am in a temple": Maurice Barrès, *Les Voyages de Lorraine et d'Artois* (Paris: Émile-Paul Frères, 1916), pp. 407–8.

53 "Madame Barrès really doesn't exist": Broche, *Maurice Barrès*, p. 203.

53 "The pilgrimage to Bayreuth": Max Nordau, *Degeneration* (Lincoln: University of Nebraska Press, 1993), p. 213.

55 "I've never witnessed": Jean Bouvier, *Les Deux Scandales de Panama* (Paris: Julliard, 1964), pp. 106–7.

56 "The principal participants": Maurice Barrès, *Leurs Figures* (Paris: Émile-Paul Frères, 1917), p. 58.

57 "Baron Jacques de Reinach": ibid., p. 123.

57 "It seems that all": *La Libre Parole*, November 26, 1892.

58 "They continue to impose": Sternhell, *Maurice Barrès*, p. 213.

58 "The paper's tendencies": *Études Maurrassiennes* (Aix-en-Provence: Institut d'Études Politiques, 1972), vol. 1, p. 146.

59 "useful variations": Sternhell, *Maurice Barrès*, p. 289.

59 "How is this conscious self": ibid.

60 "eternal war": Sternhell, ibid., p. 288.

61 "He preached the truth": Barrès, *Les Déracinés*, vol. 1, p. 16.

62 "The sands gave way": Maurice Barrès, *Scènes et Doctrines du Nationalisme* (Paris: Félix Juven, 1902), p. 17.

62 "Jews," he wrote: ibid., p. 63.

63 "[Dreyfus] walked": ibid., pp. 134–35.

63 "Dreyfusism was reinvigorated": Alain Pagès, *Émile Zola: Un Intellectuel dans l'Affaire Dreyfus* (Paris: Librairie Séguier, 1991), p. 108.

64 "aristocrats of thought": Barrès, *Scènes et Doctrines,* pp. 45–46.

64 "(B.) is at once": ibid., p. 57.

65 "Let us rejoice": ibid., pp. 208–9.

65 "The laws of our mind": *La Grande Pitié des Églises de France* in *L'Oeuvre de Maurice Barrès* (Paris: Le Club de l'Honnête Homme, 1966), vol. 3, pp. 12ff.

66 "While the Germans deify": Maurice Barrès, *Chronique de la Grande Guerre* (Paris: Plon, 1968), p. 180.

66 "At six in the morning": John Keegan, *The First World War* (New York: Knopf, 1999), p. 72.

68 "radiantly happy": Barrès, *Mes Cahiers*, p. 752.

69 "I am reproached": ibid., p. 769.

69 "These soldiers coming and going": ibid., p. 750.
69 "a new being—the combat unit": ibid., p. 759.
70 "One could spend hours": Barrès, *Les Voyages*, p. 407.
70 "Only by understanding": Eksteins, *Rites of Spring*, p. 307.
70 "National Socialism is, in its truest meaning": ibid., p. 309.
71 "with colors unfurled": Keegan, *First World War*, p. 202.
71 "It is preposterous to talk about reason": Eksteins, *Rites of Spring*, p. 183.
71 "*Le Crapouillot,* the only trench paper": Hugh Cecil and Peter Liddle, eds., *Facing Armageddon* (London: Leo Cooper, 1996), p. 224.
73 "The maneuvers of German agents": Barrès, *Chronique*, p. 421.
73 "It isn't because": Barrès, *Mes Cahiers*, p. 773.
74 "a beautiful marriage": Barrès, *Chronique*, p. 601.
75 "The holy familiarity": ibid., p. 617.
75 "Joan of Arc . . . obeyed": Barrès, *Mes Cahiers*, p. 830.
75 "intelligence is a very small": Barrès, *Les Déracinés*, vol. 2, p. 72.
75 "I don't long": Barrès, *Mes Cahiers*, pp. 23–24

CHAPTER 4 The Battle for Joan

76 "This living enigma": Égide Jeanné, *L'Image de la Pucelle d'Orléans dans la Littéra-ture Historique Française Depuis Voltaire* (Paris: J. Vrin, 1934), p. 64.
77 "Christian sanctity": Jean Cluzel, "Wallon, Jeanne d'Arc et la République" (Session in homage to Henri-Alexandre Wallon, Institut de France, October 11, 2004).
78 "Everyone had something to say": Archives de la Préfecture de Police, Ba460.
80 "This prohibition will enter": *L'Univers*, May 30, 1878.
80 "Better late than never": *La Lanterne*, May 29, 1878.
80 "believers and free-thinkers alike": Rosemonde Sanson, "La Fête de Jeanne d'Arc en 1894": *Revue d'Histoire Moderne et Contemporaine*, June–September 1973, p. 447.
81 "Like her, let us say": ibid., p. 448.
81 "She was the dawn": ibid., pp. 448–49.
82 "May you disappear forever": *La Croix*, May 10 and 16, 1894. Sermons of Canon Brettes at the Sacré-Coeur in Paris.
83 "tenebrous enemies": Sanson, "La Fête": pp. 454–55.
83 "How twisted": "Mythes de Jeanne d'Arc": Wikipédia.
85 "[He] replied": *Montreal Gazette*, December 2, 1904.
85 "I pledge myself," "Camelots du Roi": Wikipédia.
86 "You know my ideas": Michel Winock, "Jeanne d'Arc": in *Les Lieux de Mémoire*, vol. 3, éd. Pierre Nora (Paris: Gallimard, 1984), p. 713.
87 "To Joan of Arc": *New York Times*, May 12, 1907.
87 "Long live Christ": *New York Times*, December 14, 1908.
87 "Yesterday we seemed capable": Maurice Barrès, *Autour de Jeanne d'Arc* (Paris: Champion, 1916), pp. 45–46.
88 "At the feet of": *Le Temps*, May 17, 1915.
88 "Once again Joan is winning": Barrès, *Autour de Jeanne d'Arc*, pp. 77–86.
89 "Alas, how many Frenchmen": *Le Petit Parisien*, May 9, 1921.
91 "By bending to the natural order": Charles Maurras, *Oeuvres Capitales* (Paris: Flammarion, 1954), vol. 2, pp. 299–315.

CHAPTER 5 Royalism's Deaf Troubadour

92 "L'Action Française has acquired": Maurice Barrès and Charles Maurras, *La République ou le Roi: Correspondance Inédite, 1888–1923,* ed. Guy Dupré (Paris: Plon, 1976), p. 585.

92 "Civilization is an effort": quoted by Raymond Aron in *Chroniques de Guerre* (Paris: Gallimard, 1990), p. 438.

93 "[This worldview] oriented itself": Winock, *Nationalisme,* p. 164.

93 "a deaf man": Gide, *Journal,* p. 753.

95 "The most cherished voices": Stéphane Giocanti, *Maurras: Le Chaos et l'Ordre* (Paris: Flammarion, 2006), p. 136.

95 "What evil demon": Charles Maurras, *Sans la Muraille des Cyprès* (Paris: J. Gibert, 1941), pp. 18–19.

96 "The heavens themselves": *Troilus and Cressida,* I.iii.

98 "In spite of weaknesses": Yves Chiron, *La Vie de Maurras* (Paris: Perrin, 1991), p. 61.

98 "You must perceive Jesus Christ": ibid., p. 62.

99 "At the time": ibid., p. 78.

99 "I must admit": Barrès and Maurras, *La République ou le Roi,* p. 18.

100 "Passion, willfulness": ibid., p. 47 (January 23, 1891).

101 "In Drumont's work": ibid., p. 32.

101 "You persist in confusing": ibid. p. 79 (June 9, 1894).

102 "the scourge of nations": Giocanti, *Maurras,* p. 161.

102 "There was no one to say": ibid., p. 162.

102 "Every sacred drop": *La Gazette de France,* September 6, 1898.

103 "nations have a general": from Joseph de Maistre, "Des Souverainetés Particulières et des Nations": in *Oeuvres Complètes* (Lyon: Vitte, 1884), vol. 1, p. 325; quoted in Alain Finkielkraut, *The Defeat of the Mind* (New York: Columbia University Press, 1995), p. 16.

103 "All of us agree": Maurice Barrès, *Scènes et Doctrines,* p. 118.

104 "M. de Bismarck undoubtedly": Maurras, *Oeuvres Capitales,* vol. 2, p. 387.

105 "French unity, which": ibid., p. 398.

105 "exclusive nationalism" and its "deep-rooted hostility": Chiron, *Vie de Maurras,* pp. 218–19.

106 "Our institute": ibid., p. 220.

108 "The lugubrious": *L'Action Française,* July 21, 1913.

108 "I don't hesitate": ibid., August 2, 1913.

108 "General Pau's speech": ibid., August 1, 1913.

109 "So I have brought down": in Eugen Weber, *L'Action Française: Royalism and Reaction in Twentieth-Century France* (Stanford: Stanford University Press, 1962), p. 90.

109 "Fortunate are those whose hearts": *L'Action Française,* August 1, 1914.

CHAPTER 6 Spy Mania and Postwar Revenge

111 "The truth is": Laurent Dornel, *La France Hostile: Socio-histoire de la Xénophobie (1870–1914)* (Paris: Hachette, 2004), p. 301.

112 "Mystifications, forgeries": *L'Action Française,* January 9, 1913.

114 "Had he not, by his own admission": *L'Action Française,* April 24, 1917.

114 "After one year of bloodshed": Nicolas Faucier, *Pacifisme et Antimilitarisme dans l'Entre-deux-Guerres, 1919–1939* (Paris: Spartacus, 1983), p. 35.

115 "He supported the nationalist thesis": *Le Figaro,* July 23, 1917.

116 "M. Malvy is a traitor": Weber, *L'Action Française,* p. 105.

116 "In this overexcited hall": ibid., p. 106.

118 "One can criticize, detest": *Le Temps,* February 25, 1921.

119 "Judging others by themselves": Leopold Schwarzschild, *World in Trance* (London: Hamish Hamilton, 1943), p. 140.

120 "We will know in a few hours": *L'Action Française,* December 27, 1922.

121 "The German rebirth": Ian Kershaw, *Hitler* (New York: W. W. Norton, 1998), vol. 1, p. 192.

123 "I consider that he bore": *Le Figaro,* January 23, 1923.

123 "A German Bullet": *L'Action Française,* January 23, 1923.

123 "Germany, the Soviet Union": ibid.

124 "In the street, in the dock": *L'Action Française,* January 29, 1923.

126 "While revolutionaries": *L'Action Française,* December 25, 1923.

PART TWO

129 "News of the Armistice": Adam Frantz, *Sentinelles Prenez Garde à Vous* (Paris: Legrand Amédée, 1931), pp. 183–88.

129 "We did not cheer": Richard van Emden, *The Soldier's War* (London: Bloomsbury, 2009), p. 365.

130 "To think that I shall not have to": ibid., p. 367.

130 "We have lived": ibid., p. 364.

130 "As night came": Thomas Gowenlock, *Soldiers of Darkness* (Garden City: Doubleday, 1937), p. 206.

130 "Such courage and nerve": van Emden, *Soldier's War,* p. 370.

131 "I cannot say how far I walked": " 'Stand to' on Givenchy Road" from FirstWorld War.com. This passage is also excerpted from *Everyman at War,* edited by C. B. Purdom (London: Dent, 1930).

131 "I would like to send you home": Gustav Regler, *The Owl of Minerva* (New York: Farrar, Straus, and Cudahy, 1959), p. 56.

131 "We seemed, as we moved up the road": van Emden, *Soldier's War,* p. 129.

132 "Your letter finds me": Jacques Vaché, *Lettres de Guerre* (Paris: Au Sans Pareil, 1919), p. 24.

CHAPTER 7 Scars of the Trenches

134 "the dictation of thought": André Breton, *Manifestes du Surréalisme* (Paris: Gallimard, 1963), p. 37.

135 "War is my homeland": Dominique Desanti, *Drieu La Rochelle* (Paris: Flammarion, 1978), p. 111.

135 "endangering the safety": Marguerite Bonnet, ed., *L'Affaire Barrès* (Paris: José Corti, 1987), p. 24.

136 "It wouldn't be worth a trial": ibid., pp. 64–65.

138 "To be sure": Pierre Drieu La Rochelle, *Journal: 1939–1945* (Paris: Gallimard, 1992), p. 76.

138 "To think that this was an infantry officer": ibid., p. 76.
138 "Giraudoux regards the events": ibid., p. 77.
139 "The father was a peasant": Régine Pernoud, *Histoire de la Bourgeoisie en France* (Paris: Seuil, 1962), vol. 2, p. 482.
140 "She counted on me": Pierre Drieu La Rochelle, *L'État Civil* (Paris: Gallimard, 1977), p. 57.
141 "How often I sobbed": ibid., p. 44.
142 "During recess": ibid., p. 94.
142 "My mother had bought me": ibid., p. 96.
142 "There were two good students": ibid., p. 110.
144 "There, something gripped me": ibid., p. 173.
146 "I revealed with brutal candor": Pierre Andreu and Frédéric Grover, *Drieu La Rochelle* (Paris: La Table Ronde, 1979), p. 74.
146 "I have known two or three": ibid, p. 97.
147 "Only leaders count": ibid., p. 102.
148 "No more family": ibid., p. 109.
149 *"Et nous saurons"*: ibid., p. 123.
149 "Violent death": Pierre Drieu La Rochelle, *Correspondance avec André et Colette Jéramec,* (Paris: Gallimard, 1993), p. 200.
149 "Now, God be thanked": ibid., p. 444.
150 "Don't go crazy": ibid., p. 175.
151 "What is that, next to our affection": ibid., p. 342.
151 "I am appalled": Andreu and Grover, *Drieu La Rochelle,* p. 134.
153 "We are drawn to ageless": Gérard Durozoi, *Histoire du Mouvement Surréaliste* (Paris: Hazan, 1997), p. 9.
153 "In old shop signs": Arthur Rimbaud, "L'Alchimie du verbe": in *Une Saison en Enfer* (Paris: Éditions Garnier, 1962), p. 228.
155 "An entire generation's idea": Louis Aragon, *Projet d'Histoire Littéraire Contemporaine* (Paris: Gallimard, 1994), p. 7.
155 "Dada means nothing": "Manifeste Dada," *Dada 3,* Zurich, December 1918.
156 "I tell you": ibid.
158 "Every time a demonstration": Durozoi, *Histoire du Mouvement Surréaliste,* p. 39.

CHAPTER 8 The Rapture of the Deep

161 "psychic automatism": Breton, *Manifestes du Surréalisme,* p. 37.
161 "man was given language": ibid., p. 46.
161 "the mediocrity of our world": André Breton, *Point du Jour,* in *Oeuvres Complètes,* (Paris: NRF, 1992), vol. 2, p. 276.
162 "This hubbub of cars and lorries": Francis Ponge, "Les Écuries d'Augias," in *Oeuvres Complètes* (Paris: Gallimard, 1999), pp. 191–92.
163 "shed its verbal aspect": Louis Aragon, *Une Vague de Rêves* (Paris: Seghers, 2006), p. 17.
163 "It does not have many friends": Francis Ponge, "Les Colimaçons," in *Le Parti Pris des Choses* in *Oeuvres Complètes,* vol. 1, p. 26.
163 "The plastic instinct": André Breton, *Le Surréalisme et la Peinture* (Paris: Gallimard, 1979).
165 "We know the yearning": André Malraux, *Les Voix du Silence* (Paris: NRF, 1951), p. 628.

165 "Everything leads one to believe": Breton, *Manifestes du Surréalisme*, pp. 66–67.

166 "Above all there is that joy": Louis Aragon, *Anicet* (Paris: NRF, 1921), p. 187.

167 "the great writer par excellence": *Le Figaro,* October 19, 1924.

168 "Anatole France hasn't died": Maurice Nadeau, *Histoire du Surréalisme* (Paris: Seuil, 1945), p. 95.

169 "You and I, sir": Andreu and Grover, *Drieu La Rochelle,* p. 174.

170 "We seize this opportunity": Nadeau, *Histoire du Surréalisme,* p. 222.

170 "I always believed that your movements": *Nouvelle Revue Française,* August 1925.

170 "the years 1924, 1925": Drieu, *Journal,* p. 429.

171 "He wasn't alone": Frédéric J. Grover, *Drieu La Rochelle* (Paris: Gallimard, 1979), p. 63.

171 "We took walks": Andreu and Grover, *Drieu La Rochelle,* p. 196.

173 "Representative of the attitude": D. W. Brogan, *France Under the Republic* (New York: Harper and Brothers, 1940), p. 586.

175 "How would this Europe look?" Desanti, *Drieu La Rochelle,* pp. 147–48.

176 "We commented on everything": Desanti, *Drieu La Rochelle,* p. 238.

176 "a new Order—authoritarian": Wikipédia article on Gaston Bergery.

177 "If man is old": Pierre Drieu La Rochelle, *Le Jeune Européen* (Paris: Gallimard, 1927), p. 117.

177 "We cannot seek our reasons": ibid.

177 "Thus, I joyfully cried": ibid.

177 "I am thirty-three years old": Andreu and Grover, *Drieu La Rochelle,* p. 197.

178 "His likes are few": ibid.

178 "His novels are fast moving": Curtis Cate, *André Malraux: A Biography* (New York: Fromm International Publishing Corporation, 1995), pp. 159–60.

180 "I offered him a glass of port," André Gide, *Journal 1889–1939* (Paris: Gallimard, 1951), p. 849.

180 "I have always had other people's wives": Desanti, *Drieu La Rochelle,* p. 258.

180 "There is nothing in him": Andreu and Grover, *Drieu La Rochelle,* p. 205.

181 "I have to spend three months": ibid., p. 219.

181 "Victoria is something above": "Victoria Ocampo's Chronology," www.villaocampo.org.

181 "I say painful": ibid.

182 "His long, slender hands": Andreu and Grover, *Drieu La Rochelle,* p. 73.

183 "How could he talk about willpower": Pierre Drieu La Rochelle, *Le Feu Follet* (Paris: Gallimard, 1959), p. 48.

183 "an epic commentary": Andreu and Grover, *Drieu La Rochelle,* p. 242.

183 "Young Argentinians": ibid., p. 243.

184 "Everyone was asleep": ibid., p. 245.

185 "fallen state that gives birth": ibid., p. 259.

185 "the great rhythmic dance": ibid., p. 249.

185 "There I was a leader": ibid., p. 262.

CHAPTER 9 The Stavisky Affair

188 "This government *devoid of*": *L'Action Française,* December 3, 1930.

189 "The springs of the republican regime": Jean-Pierre Azéma and Michel Winock, *La Troisième République* (Paris: Calmann-Lévy, 1976), pp. 225–26.

191 "He is one of the best brains": Dansette, *Le Boulangisme,* p. 772.

191 "The reigning pope": Yves Chiron, *La Vie de Maurras* (Paris: Perron, 1972), p. 351.

191 "without having a single one": Weber, *L'Action Française*, p. 268.
192 "All good Frenchmen": *L'Action Française,* March 3, 1931.
192 "In both countries": *Le Populaire,* March 7, 1931.
193 "anonymous, irresponsible": Michel Winock, *Histoire de l'Extrême Droite en France* (Paris: Seuil, 1994), p. 173.
195 "The founder of the *Gazette du Franc*": *L'Action Française,* July 20, 1935.
195 "The month Spain lost its king": Paul Jankowski, *Stavisky: A Confidence Man in the Republic of Virtue* (Ithaca: Cornell University Press, 2002), p. 105.
197 "And this rapturous beating": *Le Figaro,* January 12, 1934.
198 "While we blame": *Le Matin,* January 11, 1934.
199 "Every day a new name": *L'Humanité,* January 9, 1934.
199 "Besides the Jewish State": *L'Action Française,* January 9, 1934.
200 "Anything but this filthy": William Shirer, *The Collapse of the Third Republic* (New York: Simon and Schuster, 1969), p. 324.
201 "formidable purge in the army": Serge Berstein, *Le 6 Février 1934* (Paris: Gallimard/ Julliard, 1975), p. 145.
201 "sporting names as un-French": Marcel Le Clère, *Le 6 Février* (Paris: Hachette 1967), p. 124.
202 "Scandals pass": ibid., p. 138.
202 "He invokes preoccupations": *Le Figaro,* February 7, 1934.
203 "The accursed Chamber": *Le Figaro,* February 9, 1934.
204 "I want to draw the attention": *L'Action Française,* February 16, 1934.
205 "who bring us their money": Michel Winock, *La France et les Juifs de 1789 à Nos Jours* (Paris: Seuil, 2004), p. 187.
205 "The scandal of excessive": ibid., p. 188.
206 "February 12 will henceforth": *Le Petit Parisien,* February 13, 1936.
207 "parliamentary and individualist," Berstein, *6 Février 1934,* p. 230.
207 "The royalist and Fascist": Serge Berstein, *Léon Blum* (Paris: Fayard, 2006), p. 395.
207 "those of Israel and of Moscow": Le Clère, *Le 6 Février,* p. 212.
208 "When one kills freedom": Andreu and Grover, *Drieu La Rochelle,* p. 263.
208 "The rugby scrums": Marc Hanrez, ed., *Pierre Drieu La Rochelle,* (Paris: L'Herne, 1982), p. 93.
209 "I have never felt": Andreu and Grover, *Drieu La Rochelle,* p. 311.
209 "I should only believe": Thomas Common, trans., *The Philosophy of Nietzsche* (New York: Modern Library, 1954), p. 40.
209 "an amalgam of un-civilized tribes": *Le Temps,* October 3, 1935.
209 "They constituted": Winock, *Le Siècle des Intellectuels,* p. 240.

CHAPTER 10 The Congress of Writers for the Defense of Culture

210 "We pledge ourselves": Ian Kershaw, *Hitler* (New York: Norton, 1998), vol. 1, p. 522.
211 "Why and how I approve today": André Gide, *Littérature Engagée* (Paris: Gallimard, 1950), pp. 22–25.
211 "one more atrocious episode": *L'Humanité,* March 23, 1933.
212 "expunge from your revolutionary": *Correspondance André Gide et Roger Martin du Gard* (Paris: Gallimard, 1968), pp. 553–54.
212 "Primitive man": Curtis Cate, *Malraux* (Paris: Flammarion, 1995), p. 258.
213 "Art is not a submission": ibid, p. 262.

214 "requires each of us": Wolfgang Klein and Sandra Teroni, eds., *Pour la Défense de la Culture: Les Textes du Congrès International des Écrivains, Paris, June 1935* (Dijon: Presses Universitaires de Dijon, 2005), p. 197.

214 "Our encounter with the irrational forces": Nadezhda Mandelstam, *Hope Against Hope* (New York: Penguin Books, 1975), p. 50.

214 "I think transparency": Jean-Paul Sartre and Michel Contat, "Sartre at Seventy: An Interview," *New York Review of Books,* August 7, 1975.

216 "Please reply following question": Mark Polizzotti, *Revolution of the Mind: The Life of André Breton* (New York: Farrar, Straus & Giroux, 1995), p. 347.

216 "The two were clearly speaking": ibid., p. 162.

217 "the work of intellectual Bolshevism": *Le Figaro,* December 10, 1930.

218 "This was the first time": Polizzotti, *Revolution,* p. 359.

218 "These young self-described": ibid., p. 418.

219 "The silly incident": Ilya Ehrenburg, *Memoirs 1921–1941* (Cleveland: World Publishing, 1964), p. 307.

219 "Is it not true": Klein and Teroni, *Pour la Défense,* pp. 398–99.

220 "We Surrealists don't love": ibid., p. 399.

221 "It's laughable, the scorn": ibid., p. 469.

221 "The working class, which is also": ibid., p. 110.

222 "I wish to talk here": ibid., pp. 109–10.

222 "My colleagues probably agree": P. N. Furbank, *E. M. Forster: A Life* (New York: Harcourt Brace Jovanovich, 1978), pp. 193–94.

223 "I think it was just after": ibid., p. 194.

225 "Léon Blum behaved": Berstein, *Léon Blum,* p. 62.

226 "Bishops know perfectly well": Jean-Michel Gaillard, *Jules Ferry* (Paris: Fayard, 1989), p. 157.

226 "These new memberships": Berstein, *Léon Blum,* p. 210.

227 "a doctrine that I consider": *L'Humanité,* October 27, 1920.

227 "every organization that wishes": *Minutes of the Second Congress of the Communist International, Petrograd, July 19–August 7, 1920.* www.marxists.org/history/interna tional.

228 "Short of repudiating": Berstein, *Léon Blum,* p. 419.

231 "Your assumption of power": Berstein, *Léon Blum,* p. 497.

232 "Already, thanks to the state-controlled": *L'Action Française,* June 7, 1936.

232 "We must find out": *Le Figaro,* June 1, 1936.

CHAPTER 11 Totalitarian Pavilions

233 "the sudden power": Pierre Drieu La Rochelle, *Histoires Déplaisantes* (Paris: Gallimard, 1963), p. 111.

233 "I had promptly introduced myself": Drieu, *Histoires Déplaisantes,* p. 112.

233 "Clearly suffering from pride": Marguerite Duras, *The Lover* (New York: Pantheon, 1985), p. 67.

234 "I was bigamous": Drieu, *Histoires Déplaisantes,* p. 117.

235 "The young red leader": Andreu and Grover, *Drieu La Rochelle,* p. 360.

235 "Those who saw Doriot back then": ibid., p. 361.

236 "To restore the French nation its unity": *Le Petit Parisien,* June 29, 1936.

237 "You have lived too long hidden": Andreu and Grover, *Drieu La Rochelle,* p. 367.

237 "The Parti Populaire Français will": ibid., pp. 367–68.

237 "In a Europe where the great, cadenced": ibid., p. 368.

238 "The element of disintegration": Winock, *La France et les Juifs,* p. 189.

238 "In whatever language": *Gilles,* p. 553.

239 "a horde that manages": Winock, *Le Siècle des Intellectuels,* p. 335.

240 "physical experience was unknown": *Gilles,* p. 61.

240 "To make a church": ibid., p. 561.

241 "Only adversaries of Communism": Klein and Teroni, *Pour la Défense,* p. 187.

241 "national in form": André Gide, *Souvenirs et Voyages* (Paris: Gallimard, 2001), p. 788.

241 "The fate of culture": ibid.

242 "In no country have I seen": Alan Sheridan, *André Gide* (Cambridge: Harvard University Press, 1998), p. 500.

243 "[I read] the report": André Gide, *Journal,* pp. 1254–55.

243 "Assuming . . . that basically": Joseph Davies, *Mission to Moscow* (New York: Simon and Schuster, 1941), pp. 43–44. Note that this is a reference to the subsequent Trial of the Seventeen.

244 "One encounters Stalin's effigy": Gide, *Souvenirs et Voyages,* p. 776.

244 "Suppressing the opposition": ibid., p. 778.

245 "The Holy Family will always": ibid., p. 779.

245 "The spirit regarded as 'counterrevolutionary'": ibid., p. 774.

246 "If the mind is so molded": ibid., p. 682.

246 "We Bolsheviks": *L'Humanité,* November 28, 1936.

247 "Throughout his literary life": ibid., December 19, 1936.

247 "an absurdity": *Le Populaire,* November 24, 1936.

248 "Parallel to the great": Serge Berstein, *La France des Années 30* (Paris: Armand Colin, 2002), p. 125.

249 "France of the Popular Front": Henri Noguères, *La Vie Quotidienne en France au Temps du Front Populaire* (Paris: Hachette, 1977), p. 19.

250 "As others reminisce": ibid., p. 27.

250 "We marched, we sang": ibid., p. 26.

251 "What insolence!": *L'Action Française,* July 16, 1936.

252 "if they hadn't succeeded": Berstein, *Léon Blum,* p. 502.

252 "Roger Salengro's death": ibid., p. 504.

253 "Politics does not justify": ibid., p. 502.

254 "It did not for reasons": *Le Figaro,* August 1, 1936.

255 "I would that these words": *Le Populaire,* September 7, 1936.

256 "irresponsible Marxists": *Le Populaire,* November 9, 1936.

256 "Shame mingles": *L'Humanité,* September 8, 1936.

257 "Anyone who has given the subject": George Orwell, *Homage to Catalonia* (New York: Harcourt Brace Jovanovich, 1980), p. 178.

258 "We have too often reproached": *Le Temps,* March 17, 1937.

258 "assassin of workers": Berstein, *Léon Blum,* p. 508.

261 "For the French, alas": Karen Fiss, *Grand Illusion* (Chicago: University of Chicago Press, 2009), p. 177.

262 "Frenchmen are reasoners": ibid.

262 "The highlight of all these festivals": Fiss, *Grand Illusion,* p. 176.

262 "Rome, Moscow, Berlin": ibid., p. 182.

262 "a European salvation": quoted in Paul Reynaud, *In the Thick of the Fight: 1930–1945* (New York: Simon and Schuster, 1955), p. 36.

263 "Let there be no doubt": Reynaud, *In the Thick of the Fight*, p. 182.
263 "Negro-American music": ibid., p. 183.
263 "The pageant featured": ibid., p. 182.
263 "a savage horde": *L'Action Française*, July 15, 1937.
264 "The Fuhrer believes": "The Hossbach Memorandum," http://avalon.law.yale.edu./
      imt/hossbach.asp

CHAPTER 12 The Hero of Verdun

266 "No man can possibly pretend": *Le Populaire*, January 22, 1938.
266 "a form of terrorism that is not native to us": *Le Temps*, September 13, 1937.
266 "He is rehearsing": Sir Edward Spears, *Assignment to Catastrophe* (New York: A. A.
      Wyn, 1954), p. 208.
267 "There are people": *L'Humanité*, September 14, 1937.
268 "Seized documents establish": *Le Populaire*, November 24, 1937.
268 "odious burlesque": *L'Écho de Paris*, November 25, 1937.
268 "A dirty stream": Eugen Weber, *L'Action Française*, p. 402.
269 "the natural advantages": *L'Action Française*, May 10, 1938.
270 "As long as the international": Berstein, *La France des Années 30*, p. 150.
270 "ineluctable and sacred": *Le Temps*, July 14, 1938.
270 "Nationalism and racialism": Andrew Roberts, *The Holy Fox: The Life of Lord Hali-
      fax* (London: Weidenfeld and Nicolson, 1991), vol. 1, p. 67.
271 "We shall continue to earn": *L'Action Française*, March 18, 1939.
271 "There is no time to lose": ibid., March 17, 1939.
272 "the men who allowed disorder": Berstein, *La France des Années 30*, p. 161.
272 "How many times": *L'Humanité*, March 18, 1939.
272 "There is, outside of Germany": Winock, *Le Siècle des Intellectuels*, p. 329.
273 "Republicans cannot abdicate": *Le Populaire*, March 18, 1939.
273 "You are asking": Shirer, *Collapse*, p. 404.
273 "the physical image": *Le Figaro*, March 16, 1939.
274 "I can work two weeks": Herbert Lottman, *Pétain* (Paris: Seuil, 1984), p. 222.
274 "an old fetish": ibid.
275 "Certain official milieux": ibid., p. 236.
275 "It was as if the ineffective": Spears, *Assignment*, p. 147.
275 "The victor of Verdun": ibid., p. 241.
276 "It is reported": *L'Ouest-Éclair*, May 19, 1940.
276 "Not only is he vain": Lottman, *Pétain*, p. 251.
276 "Jews, or friends of Jews": Shirer, *Collapse*, p. 482.
277 "infinitely pitiable": ibid.
277 "who had always been defeatist": ibid., p. 254.
277 "A French renaissance": ibid., pp. 255–56.
277 "All Frenchmen, wherever they are": *La Croix*, June 15, 1940.
279 "The earth does not lie": Lottman, *Pétain*, p. 270.
279 "It stemmed from our laxity": *La Croix*, June 27, 1940.
279 "Why did God permit": Aron, *Chroniques*, p. 30.
279 "the summons of a great humiliated nation": Lottman, *Pétain*, p. 270.
279 "The capitulation of the government": Aron, *Chroniques*, p. 30.
280 "Great fortune has crowned us": Weber, *L'Action Française*, p. 441.
281 "The labor of Frenchmen": *Le Figaro*, July 12, 1940.

282 "People have spoken about": Weber, *L'Action Française*, p. 447.

283 "This providential man": ibid., p. 446.

Epilogue

284 "weld into one metal": Andreu and Grover, *Drieu la Rochelle,* 371.

286 "Gilles had associated his loneliness": Drieu, *Gilles,* p. 560.

287 "Jews, Communist sympathizers": Andreu and Grover, *Drieu La Rochelle,* p. 432.

287 "Aragon is more Communist": ibid.

287 "I can't think my thoughts through": ibid., p. 434.

287 "I feel Hitler's movements": Drieu, *Journal,* p. 196.

288 "I tell myself": ibid., p. 274.

289 "I know what I'm doing": *Correspondance André Gide et Roger Martin du Gard,* vol. 2, p. 229.

289 "Gide, Valéry, Claudel": Drieu, *Journal,* p. 295.

289 "I can no longer get interested": ibid., p. 293; April 11, 1942.

290 "D. I don't doubt": Drieu, *Correspondance avec André et Colette Jéramec.*

291 "The Jews tricked me": Drieu, *Journal,* p. 348.

292 "in due course": ibid., p. 354.

292 "I've always been scared to death": ibid., p. 396.

292 "Should I soon commit suicide": ibid., p. 310.

292 "Where am I, in any sense?" Andreu and Grover, *Drieu La Rochelle,* p. 547.

293 "I wanted to be a complete man": Drieu, *Journal,* p. 447.

Principals

Louis Aragon: 1897–1982

Maurice Barrès: 1862–1923

Léon Blum: 1872–1950

André Breton: 1896–1966

Aristide Briand: 1862–1932

Édouard Daladier: 1884–1970

Léon Daudet: 1867–1942

Jacques Doriot: 1898–1945

Pierre Drieu La Rochelle: 1893–1945

André Gide: 1869–1951

Jean Jaurès: 1859–1914

Colette Jéramec: 1896–1970

Joan of Arc: 1412–1431

André Malraux: 1901–1976

Charles Maurras: 1868–1952

Philippe Pétain: 1856–1951

Raymond Poincaré: 1860–1934

Alexandre Stavisky: 1886–1934

Chronology

1870

July: France declares war against Prussia and her German allies.

September 1: Defeated at the battle of Sedan, Napoleon III abdicates. Three days later, on September 4, the empire is supplanted by a Government of National Defense, whose animating spirit is Léon Gambetta.

September 19: The German army besieges Paris.

1871

January: An armistice is declared. The siege lasts four months and results in mass starvation. It ends when, on Bismarck's command, shells from Krupp cannons are lofted into the city.

February: Nationwide elections of a National Assembly are held, to form a government with which Germany can treat.

March: The National Guard regiments in Paris elect a commune, repudiate the armistice, and induce Adolphe Thiers, the effective head of government, to withdraw regular army troops and batteries from the city.

May: France cedes Alsace and part of Lorraine to Germany in the Treaty of Frankfurt.

May 22–28: Adolphe Thiers unleashes the French army on the Paris Commune in a bloody campaign known as *la semaine sanglante.*

La Réforme Intellectuelle et Morale, Ernest Renan.

1874

Frémiet's statue of Joan of Arc is unveiled at the Place des Pyramides.

La Tentation de Saint-Antoine, Gustave Flaubert.

1875

After prolonged resistance from Bonapartists and Royalists, the government is officially declared a republic. The First Republic had followed the dethronement of Louis XVI in 1792, and the second, the dethronement of Louis-Philippe in 1848.

1877

Gambetta pronounces a famous indictment of the church for meddling in political affairs: "*Le cléricalisme, voilà l'ennemi!*" (Clericalism, there is the enemy!).

President Patrice MacMahon (a general promoted to marshal after distinguishing himself during the Crimean War), thwarted by a republican premier and Chamber of Deputies, dismisses the former and dissolves the latter in what is seen as a threat to overthrow the Republic. In the October elections, the public returns a decisive republican majority. MacMahon will resign the following year. No future president will dissolve the Chamber of Deputies, resulting in a government dominated by the legislature.

L'Assommoir, Émile Zola, the seventh volume of his saga *Les Rougon-Macquart.* It is his "breakthrough" novel, scandalizing critics with its use of working-class argot.

Le Tour de la France par Deux Enfants, Augustine Fouillée.

1878

June–July: The Congress of Berlin, hosted by Bismarck in the aftermath of the Russo-Turkish War, remaps the Balkan states.

May–November: The Paris World's Fair, inaugurating the Trocadéro Palace, which will be replaced by the Palais de Chaillot in 1937.

Leo XIII, a liberal pope, succeeds Pius IX, author of *The Syllabus of Errors,* condemning modern science, among much else of the modern world.

Trois Contes, Gustave Flaubert.

1879

Léon Gambetta is overwhelmingly elected president of the Chamber of Deputies, an event that signals the beginning of an era of liberal reform, under the leadership of Gambetta and Jules Ferry.

The National Assembly moves from Versailles, where it had convened since 1871, to its traditional home at the Palais Bourbon in Paris. "La Marseillaise" becomes the nation's official anthem.

1880

June–July: The Jesuits are expelled from their residences and schools. Other "nonauthorized" teaching orders are under threat of expulsion.

July 14 is decreed a national holiday, and the law prohibiting commerce on Sunday is repealed.

Nana, Émile Zola.

1881

A law is passed abolishing tuition in public primary schools. It will be followed by laws making primary school education compulsory and secular.

1883

The pretender, Henri, Comte de Chambord, whom Charles Maurras will describe as "the priest and pope of royalty rather than a king," dies at his castle in Austria.
The Catholic newspaper *La Croix* is founded.

1884

Divorce is legitimized.
Tonkin (Indochina) becomes a French protectorate.
Public prayers opening parliamentary sessions are suppressed.

À Rebours (Against Nature), J. K. Huysmans.

1885

Jules Ferry is voted out of office after a military defeat at the hands of China in Tonkin. There is rioting in Paris.
May: Two million people follow Victor Hugo's funeral procession from the Arc de Triomphe to the Panthéon. He is the first *grand homme de la patrie* to be interred there.

Germinal, Émile Zola, a novel inspired by the miners' strike at the Anzin coal fields of northern France.

1886

General Georges Boulanger becomes minister of war.

Édouard Drumont's violently anti-Semitic tracts *La France Juive* and *La France Juive Devant l'Opinion* appear, months apart. The former will run through 150 editions by the end of the year.

1887

General Georges Boulanger loses his portfolio as minister of war and is assigned to an obscure command in central France. His departure from Paris provokes a tumultuous demonstration of hero worship at the Gare de Lyon. Boulanger will hold secret talks first with representatives of the royalist party, then with Bonapartists.

1888

March: Boulanger is discharged from the army. The Boulangist newspaper *La Cocarde* begins publication. Maurice Barrès will serve briefly as editor in chief.

April: Boulanger is elected to the Chamber of Deputies from the industrial north. He will subsequently be the victor in three by-elections, affirming his national stature.

The first volume of the trilogy *Le Culte du Moi,* by Maurice Barrès, appears under the imprint of Plon.

The Pasteur Institute is founded.

1889

March: Eiffel unfurls the tricolor flag atop the tower named after him, celebrating the centenary of the French Revolution and inaugurating the Universal Exposition.

April: Georges Boulanger flees to Belgium when word spreads that plans are afoot to try him for high treason.

Plon publishes the second volume of Barrès's trilogy, *Un Homme Libre.*

Thadée Natanson founds the short-lived but important avant-garde magazine *La Revue Blanche.*

1891

May: Leo XIII promulgates the encyclical *Rerum Novarum,* defining the church's view of the relationship between capital and labor and refuting the basic premises of Socialism.

1892

February: Leo XIII promulgates the encyclical *Au Milieu des Sollicitudes,* addressed to French bishops, the clergy, and the faithful, urging all concerned to accept the legitimate authority of the Republic but to resist the onslaught of anticlerical legislation.

Édouard Drumont founds *La Libre Parole.* Its first issues feature an exposé of fraud perpetrated by executives and financiers of the defunct Panama Canal Company. It will later bring to light the secret court-martial and conviction of Captain Alfred Dreyfus and will relentlessly argue the case against his retrial in 1899.

1894

France and Russia sign a secret military convention.

December: Alfred Dreyfus is tried and convicted of treason.

Anarchist violence. Auguste Vaillant, who had hurled a bomb into the Chamber of Deputies, is executed. In June, the president of the Republic, Sadi Carnot, is assassinated by an Italian anarchist, Sante Geronimo Caserio.

1895

The major French workers' union, the Confédération Générale du Travail (CGT), is founded.

Félix Faure is elected president of the Republic.

La Psychologie des Foule, by Gustave Le Bon, a work of seminal importance in the literature of crowd psychology, is published. Hitler will draw upon it for his theory of propaganda techniques in *Mein Kampf.*

The Lumière brothers invent the movie camera.

1897

A year after Alfred Jarry's five-act play *Ubu Roi* appears in Paul Fort's review *Le Livre d'Art,* Maurice Barrès publishes *Les Déracinés* (the first volume of *Le Roman de l'Énergie Nationale*), a novel whose title becomes an ideological argument for the stigmatization of Jews, foreigners, and proponents of Kantian universalism.

André Gide achieves fame and iconic status among the young with the publication of *Les Nourritures Terrestres (Fruits of the Earth)*, a prose poem strongly influenced by *Thus Spake Zarathustra,* preaching liberation from the family and its moral confinements.

1898

January: "J'accuse," Zola's brief accusing the army of framing Alfred Dreyfus, is published on the front page of Clemenceau's paper *L'Aurore.* Rioting against Jews erupts throughout France and the Maghreb, with particular ferocity in Algiers.

February: Zola is found guilty of libel. The conviction will be upheld on appeal, prompting him to seek asylum in England.

August. Colonel Hubert Henry who forged documents used against Dreyfus, commits suicide in his jail cell at the Mont-Valérien military fortress. He becomes a martyr of the extreme right.

October: The High Court accepts a plea by Dreyfus's defenders for a new trial.

1899

The ultranationalist Ligue de la Patrie Française is founded. Barrès will later preside over it.

August–September: Dreyfus's second court-martial commences in the city of Rennes. The conviction is upheld. Upon appeal, he is pardoned by the president of the Republic.

Charles Maurras founds *La Revue de l'Action Française*. He will be a contributor during the next half decade to *Le Figaro* and *La Libre Parole*.

1900

Dissolution of the Assumptionists, a Catholic order active in the campaign against Dreyfus.

The World's Fair, organized around the theme "An Assessment of the Century," opens on April 15. The Palace of Electricity is its most impressive pavilion.

Charles Péguy founds *Les Cahiers de la Quinzaine*.

L'Appel au Soldat, Maurice Barrès: the second volume of his trilogy *Le Roman de l'Énergie Nationale*. It chronicles the rise and fall of Georges Boulanger.

1902

September: Émile Zola dies of carbon monoxide poisoning and is buried in the Montmartre Cemetery, from which his remains are later transferred to the Panthéon.

The Radicals soundly defeat the Socialists in the national elections. Émile Combes, a militant anticlerical, accedes to the premiership and wages war against Catholic orders involved in education. Two years later they will be prohibited from teaching.

Leurs Figures, the last volume of Barrès's trilogy, is based on the Panama Scandal.

1904

Jean Jaurès, French Socialism's great orator, founds the newspaper *L'Humanité*.

On an official visit to Rome, Émile Loubet, president of the French Republic, is rebuffed by Pope Pius X, Leo XIII's successor. France and the Vatican suspend diplomatic relations.

The Entente Cordiale between France and England settles a number of outstanding issues, including England's control over Egypt and France's over Morocco.

1905

December: The National Assembly passes a law decreeing the separation of church and state. Religious orders continue to be expelled or denied a pedagogical function, and France severs diplomatic relations with the Vatican.

Wilhelm II challenges France's intention of establishing a protectorate in Morocco by paying a state visit to Tangiers.

The Ligue de l'Action Française is founded around a review of that name.

1906

July: The High Court reverses Dreyfus's conviction and reinstates him in the army.
July: The Radicals remain in power after state elections.
October: Clemenceau becomes premier.
December: The papal nuncio is expelled.

Paul Claudel's play *Partage de Midi* is staged in Paris.

1907

Major strikes and demonstrations take place throughout France. An infantry regiment sent to disband 700,000 demonstrators in Montpellier disobeys orders.

Alcan publishes Henri Bergson's *L'Évolution Créatrice,* a canonical work in the literature of vitalism. It introduces the term "élan vital."

1908

The bimonthly *La Revue de l'Action Française* becomes a daily, its name shortened to *L'Action Française.* Its student hawkers, known as Camelots du Roi, evolve into a body of toughs who will play a conspicuous role in political violence on the streets of Paris.
Austria-Hungary annexes Bosnia-Herzegovina, former Ottoman provinces it had occupied and administered since the Berlin Treaty of 1878.
Georges Sorel's *Réflexions sur la Violence* argues that the proletariat, to succeed, must create a violent, catastrophic revolution. Violence is equated with life, creativity, and virtue. He finds disciples on the right as well as the left, in Charles Maurras and Mussolini. Sorel's contention that myths are important as "expressions of a will to act" comports with a basic premise of L'Action Française.

1909

The Vatican beatifies Joan of Arc.

André Gide and two colleagues found the literary review *La Nouvelle Revue Française.*

1911

July: Germany challenges Morocco's unofficial status as a French protectorate and England's maritime supremacy by sending a gunboat to Agadir. War fever runs high in Paris.
November: France and Germany negotiate an agreement whereby France surrenders part of the Congo in exchange for a free hand in Morocco.

1912

Raymond Poincaré becomes premier, a post he will occupy for a year before acceding to the presidency and remaining president for seven years.

France imposes a protectorate on Morocco.

The First Balkan War pits Serbs, Bulgars, and Greeks against the Ottoman Empire.

France's principal trade union, the CGT, stages a general strike against war preparations.

1913

January: Poincaré is elected president of the Republic.

May–June: No sooner does the First Balkan War end than Bulgaria attacks her recent allies.

July: Strongly endorsed by Poincaré, a law is passed increasing the period of obligatory military service from two years to three. It is opposed by the Left.

August: The Second Balkan War comes to an end.

The premiere performance on May 29 of Stravinsky's *Sacre du Printemps* at the Théâtre des Champs-Élysées shocks a French audience devoted to the conventions of classical ballet.

Gallimard publishes *Du Côté de Chez Swann,* the first volume of Proust's *À la Recherche du Temps Perdu.*

1914

January–March: *Le Figaro* conducts a campaign against Joseph Caillaux, a likely successor to the premiership and a political liberal.

March: Enraged by the publication of a love letter written by Caillaux during his adulterous affair with her years earlier, Henriette Caillaux kills Gaston Calmette, editor in chief of *Le Figaro.*

June: René Viviani, an independent, becomes premier, succeeding Poincaré.

June 28: Archduke Ferdinand, heir to the Hapsburg Empire, is assassinated in Sarajevo by a Bosnian Serb.

July 28: Austria-Hungary declares war on Serbia.

July 30: Russia mobilizes.

July 31: Germany delivers an ultimatum to France. She will declare war three days later. Jean Jaurès is assassinated.

August 1: The French government orders general mobilization.

August 4: After the declaration of war, political parties agree to suspend partisan disputes and bond in a "Union Sacrée," which will prove to be only nominally united and sacred.

August 20–23: The French army suffers 40,000 dead in three days of fighting along the Sambre, near Belgium. By the end of the year, 300,000 French soldiers will have perished.

September 6–9: The headlong German advance is halted in the Battle of the Marne, which leads to a stalemate of four years in trenches scoring the hills and valleys of northeastern France.

1915

May: Italy enters the war on the Allied side.

September: The Zimmerwald Conference in Switzerland, attendance at which is regarded as treasonous by the French government, initiates an international pacifist movement.

1916

February–December: The yearlong Battle of Verdun results in no strategic advantage but in more than 800,000 casualties, the spending of forty million artillery shells, the glorification of French steadfastness, the lionization of General Pétain, and an account of the battle in which Pétain vastly exaggerates the effectiveness of turret guns and fixed fortifications, one consequence being France's disastrous investment in the Maginot Line fourteen years later. He obstinately champions systematic, defensive warfare.

July 1–November 11: The British and French mount an offensive at the Somme River in Picardy, rivaling Verdun in bloodshed. The opening day of the battle sees the British army suffer the most costly military defeat in its history, with 60,000 casualties. After four months it has advanced six miles. The French army is decimated. In three days of fighting, between September 5 and 8, its death toll surpasses 100,000.

Henri Barbusse's antiwar novel *Le Feu* is serialized, causing violent controversy.

More controversy is stirred by *Les Demoiselles d'Avignon,* exhibited nine years after Picasso painted it.

1917

February–March: The Russian Revolution erupts in Petrograd, where imperial regiments disobey orders to fire on crowds protesting the dire conditions created by war. A provisional government is formed. Nicholas II, held captive in the Alexander Palace at Tsarskoe Selo, is forced to abdicate.

April 6: The United States enters the war.

April 16–25: The French army under General Robert Nivelle attempts to dislodge German troops entrenched along a ridge overlooking the Aisne valley in Champagne. The assault fails, and the name of the ridge road, the Chemin des Dames, becomes a byword for carnage.

April–June: An estimated 40,000 troops mutiny, of whom 49 are executed.

November (October 25 in the old-style Julian calendar): The Bolsheviks seize power in Russia.

November: Georges Clemenceau becomes premier.

1918

January 8: President Woodrow Wilson delivers the "Fourteen Points" address to Congress; it will become the basis for terms of the German surrender and the disposition of international relations after World War I.

March 3: Germany and Russia sign separate peace agreements at Brest-Litovsk.

March-July: Germany launches five major offensives, prompting an exodus of Parisians.

November: The German emperor abdicates and a republic is proclaimed, with its capital in Weimar.

November 11: Germany signs an armistice agreement at Rethondes, a small village north of Paris, near Compiègne.

The Spanish influenza pandemic claims the lives of 30,000 French soldiers and as many as 250,000 civilians.

1919

March: Foundation of the Third International, or Comintern, the central body of world Communism.

June: A peace treaty is signed at Versailles, imposing harsh reparations on Germany, a buffer territory in the Rhineland, and the cession of Alsace-Lorraine to France.

July 14: Allied troops parade down the Champs-Élysées.

Between 1919 and 1927, Gallimard publishes the remaining volumes of Proust's *À la Recherche du Temps Perdu.*

The Protocols of the Elders of Zion, a bogus document drafted earlier in the century by the czarist police, purporting to reveal a Jewish plot to gain world domination, circulates in various translations. Henry Ford funds the printing of 500,000 copies in the United States.

1920

January 10: The League of Nations is created.

May: Joan of Arc is canonized.

December: The congress of the SFIO (Section Française de l'Internationale Ouvrière) is held at Tours. A majority votes to join the Third International and founds the French Communist Party (PCF). The minority maintains itself as the SFIO.

Tristan Tzara arrives in Paris, joins the literary group assembled around André Breton, and, with Francis Picabia, orchestrates events that publicize the Dada movement in Paris. Dada had originated among young expatriate writers in 1916 at the Cabaret Voltaire in Zurich.

The first results of automatic writing appear in Breton and Soupault's *Les Champs Magnétiques.*

1922

January: Premier and foreign minister Aristide Briand is forced to resign his offices for showing Germany a conciliatory face. He is replaced by Poincaré.

July: Germany requests a moratorium of four years for the payment of war reparations. The request is denied by England and France.

October: Mussolini seizes power in Rome.

1923

January: French and Belgian troops occupy the industrial Ruhr by way of holding Germany hostage for the defaulted reparations and exacting payment in shipments of coal.

January 22: The young anarchist Germaine Berton assassinates Marius Plateau, a colleague of Charles Maurras's at L'Action Française.

October: Poincaré agrees to abide by the recommendation of a committee of experts, known as the Dawes Commission, appointed to settle the vexed issue of reparations.

November: Adolf Hitler becomes a nationally recognized name after his failed putsch in Munich.

1924

April: France accepts the recommendation of the Dawes Commission.

May: The Left (Radicals and Socialists) gain a majority in parliamentary elections. Édouard Herriot, the Radical leader, becomes premier.

Right-wing leagues are founded or revived, notably the Ligue des Patriotes.

The first issue of *La Révolution Surréaliste* appears in December.

André Breton publishes the "Surrealist Manifesto."

1925

February: Establishment of the Fédération Nationale Catholique, an anti-republican movement.

April–October: The Exposition Internationale des Arts Décoratifs et Industriels Modernes enshrines the aesthetic of "Art Deco."

April 23: An uprising in Morocco led by Abd el-Krim is crushed by French colonial troops under the command of Pétain.

July: Belgian and French troops evacuate the Ruhr.

July: Hitler publishes the first volume of *Mein Kampf,* written during his internment at Landsberg Prison for an attempted putsch in 1923. The second volume will be published in 1926 and a French translation in 1934.

October: At the Locarno Conference, France's boundaries with Germany are guaranteed and the Rhineland, which had been designated a demilitarized zone in the Treaty of 1919, is reaffirmed as such.

1926

May–July: Speculation; financial panic; the fall of the franc; the parade of several liberal governments and Poincaré's return to power. France's economy is stabilized with the passage of a draconian finance law.

September: The pope condemns L'Action Française.

Abel Bonnard—novelist, future member of the Académie Française, and Nazi collaborator—publishes *Éloge de l'Ignorance* (In Praise of Ignorance).

1927

In Paris, major demonstrations are held in support of Sacco and Vanzetti, two anarchists accused of murder and brought to trial in a Massachussetts court. They will be executed on August 23.

May: The Third International endorses open warfare against the bourgeoisie, "class against class."

October: Daladier is elected chairman of the Radical Party, replacing Édouard Herriot.

Julien Benda publishes *La Trahison des Clercs* (*The Treason of the Intellectuals*).

1928

April: Moderate conservatives gain a majority in parliamentary elections.

August: The Kellogg-Briand Pact is signed by forty-one nations, outlawing military aggression as a means of settling international disputes. The following decades will make a mockery of it, but its terms will be reiterated in the United Nations Charter.

December: Marthe Hanau, publisher of *La Gazette du Franc,* is found guilty of defrauding French financial markets. The fact that she is Jewish provides grist for the mill for anti-Semites.

1929

June: French Communists are under attack. André Tardieu, minister of the interior, initiates legal action against *L'Humanité.*

July: Poincaré resigns in poor health and is replaced by Aristide Briand, who sits as premier for the fifth time in his long career.

August: The Young Plan definitively establishes the amount of reparations and a schedule for payments.

Allied troops evacuate the Rhineland.

October: The Wall Street crash shakes European financial markets.

December: A decision is made to construct fortifications along the border with Germany—the ill-fated Maginot Line.

Ullstein publishes Erich Maria Remarque's *All Quiet on the Western Front.*

1930

February: Vietnamese soldiers in the French colonial army mutiny.

November: The banker Albert Oustric joins Marthe Hanau in the postwar rogue's gallery of swindlers. Prominent politicians are compromised.

The book publisher Arthème Fayard launches a weekly paper, *Je Suis Partout,* which will become infamous during the German occupation as a prominent organ of the collaborationist press.

1931

May: Having celebrated the centenary of the conquest of Algeria a year earlier and quelled a revolt of nationalist soldiers in its Vietnamese army, the state opens the Museum of Colonies in conjunction with its Colonial Exposition.

June: Gravely affected by the world economic crisis, Germany ceases to pay reparations. This deals another severe blow to the French economy.

Pierre Drieu La Rochelle publishes *Le Feu Follet,* his novel about the unraveling and suicide of an ex-Surrealist, based on the life of Jacques Rigaut.

1932

May: The president of the Republic, Paul Doumer, is assassinated. He is succeeded by Albert Lebrun.

June: Reparations are officially abandoned at the Lausanne Conference. Germany had paid most of her reparations with money borrowed from the United States. She will repudiate those loans.

August: A Congress for Peace is held in Amsterdam on the initiative of the Third International.

December: Germany secures arms equality with the former Allied powers.

Louis-Ferdinand Céline's *Voyage au Bout de la Nuit* (*Journey to the End of the Night*), published by Éditions Denoël, is a literary sensation.

1933

January: Hitler is appointed chancellor by President Paul von Hindenburg.

June: A Congress for Peace is held at the Salle Pleyel in Paris.

August: Hitler names Nuremberg the "City of Reich Party Congresses." Torchlight parades will be held there annually, in September.

October: Germany withdraws from the League of Nations.

Two leagues are founded that will play a significant role in the rise of right-wing extremism during the 1930s: the Francisques and La Solidarité Française Patronnée.

Alexandre Stavisky's Ponzi scheme is exposed, with enormous repercussions in the political world. Much is made in the anti-Semitic press of his being a Russian Jewish immigrant.

Gallimard publishes André Malraux's novel *La Condition Humaine* (*Man's Fate*).

1934

The Tribunal de Commerce rules in favor of a suit to allow a French translation of Hitler's *Mein Kampf.*

January: Alexandre Stavisky commits suicide. *L'Action Française* and other right-wing papers assert that he was murdered by the police at the behest of politicians who would have been compromised in a Stavisky trial.

February 6: At least fifteen people die in right-wing rioting over the Stavisky Affair while Daladier is seeking legislative confirmation of his appointment to the premiership. Camelots du Roi in the front rank of rioters suffer numerous casualties.

Lacking support, Daladier resigns and is replaced by Gaston Doumergue, leading a conservative coalition, which grants him extensive financial powers.

February 9: The French Communist Party and a major union stage a counterdemonstration, in which six demonstrators are killed.

February 12: The major confederation of trade unions, the CGT, calls a general strike "against Fascism."

April: The conservative Parliament grants the premier the power to issue "decree laws."

September: The USSR enters the League of Nations.

October: Alexander I of Yugoslavia and the French foreign minister, Louis Barthou, are assassinated by a Bulgarian nationalist in Marseille.

The Radicals split from Doumergue, ending his premiership.

After the riots of February 6, intellectuals exasperated by the ineptitude of parliamentary government and repelled by dictatorships of the Right and Left spawn a profusion of ideas for a society based on technocratic principles. "Planification," as they are collectively known, harks back to the ur-text of modern technocracy, Auguste Comte's *Discours sur l'Esprit Positif.*

1935

May: France and the USSR sign a mutual assistance pact.

June: The conservative premier, Pierre Laval, who will hold that position in the Vichy government, is granted virtually unrestricted power over French finances in the depressed economy, to no avail.

June 21–25: The International Congress of Writers for the Defense of Culture, chaired by Malraux and Gide and attended by literary luminaries from the USSR, England, Europe, and America, takes place at the Mutualité conference hall on the Left Bank. It is sponsored by the Comintern.

July 14: A republican anti-Fascist rally in Paris draws 500,000 demonstrators.

October: Italy attacks Ethiopia with its greatly superior arsenal of weapons. The following June, Emperor Haile Selassie, speaking at the League of Nations, which had stood by impotently, will declare, "It is us today; it will be you tomorrow."

November: The shifting Radical Party, recently allied with Doumergue's conservatives, decides to form a coalition with Communists and Socialists in what comes to be known as the Popular Front.

Gallimard publishes Louis Guilloux's novel *Le Sang Noir* (*Bitter Victory*), one of the most eloquent and scathing condemnations of militarism to emerge in the gathering storm of World War II. Guilloux, an active Socialist, will accompany Gide to the Soviet Union in 1936.

1936

February: L'Action Française descends to the nadir of its incivility when members attack the leader Léon Blum in the street and beat him savagely. As many people as had celebrated Bastille Day gather to express their outrage.

February: The Franco-Soviet Mutual Assistance Pact, initiated by Louis Barthou before his assassination, is finally ratified by the National Assembly, its purpose being to counter the increasingly bellicose temper of Nazi Germany. It is toothless, but it furnishes Hitler with a pretext to occupy and militarize the Rhineland. This he does in flagrant violation of the Locarno Treaty and with no interference from its signatories.

April–May: The Popular Front wins a majority of seats in legislative elections. Socialists outnumber Radicals. Communists, the least numerous party in the coalition, have six times as many seats as after the previous election.

June: Léon Blum assumes the premiership. He is received at his inaugural appearance in the chamber with an anti-Semitic speech by the right-wing deputy Xavier Vallat, whose sentiments are echoed in *L'Action Française, Gringoire, L'Écho de Paris,* and other dailies.

June: Jacques Doriot founds the French Fascist Party, the Parti Populaire Francais (PPF).

June–July: Parliament passes many of the laws for which the Popular Front achieves lasting fame, if not long life, as the agent of a new dispensation in the lives of the working class: paid vacations, the forty-hour week, and so on. In addition, paramilitary leagues, notably the Croix de Feu, consisting mainly of World War I veterans, are disbanded.

July: Insurgents occupy Spanish Morocco and obtain a foothold on the Iberian Peninsula at Seville, launching the Spanish Civil War.

August: In Moscow, the purge of old-time Bolsheviks begins with the Trial of the Sixteen, including Grigory Zinoviev and Lev Kamenev, charged with plotting to assassinate Stalin, to dismantle the Soviet Union, and to introduce capitalism. False confessions are extracted from them. They and their relatives will be shot. Other "show" trials and executions will soon follow.

August: Discouraged by England from helping the Spanish republicans militarily, the Blum government opts for a policy of nonintervention.

August–September: The Blum government nationalizes the armaments industry and greatly increases its budget. The franc is devalued, to the chagrin of Blum's radical allies. The Popular Front fares poorly at the Radical Party congress in October.

November: Roger Salengro, the minister of the interior, who had been taken prisoner during the war, commits suicide after repeated accusations by *L'Action Française* of having surreptitiously crossed enemy lines to surrender.

November: Italy and Germany recognize Franco as Spain's ruler.

November: On his return from the USSR, where he was treated with great deference, André Gide publishes an open-eyed account of the Stalinist tyranny, *Retour de l'URSS,* which runs through many editions.

Denoël publishes Céline's second major novel, *Mort à Crédit (Death on the Installment Plan).*

1937

March: In a riot at Clichy, six Socialists and Communists confronting a demonstration of members of the former Croix de Feu (now transformed from a paramilitary legion into a political party) are killed by police.

May: The World's Fair, notable for the immense Soviet and Nazi pavilions framing the Eiffel Tower, opens on May 25, a month after the bombing of Guernica by Germany's Condor Legion. It will stay open for six months, beyond Léon Blum's first premiership, the show trial in Moscow of Red Army generals, and the disastrous defeat of Spanish republicans in the Battle of Brunete.

Picasso's painting *Guernica* is displayed in the Spanish pavilion, having been commissioned by the Spanish republican government. It will go on a world tour to publicize the brutality of the insurgents and their German allies.

June: Blum is unseated and replaced by the radical Chautemps, during whose premiership the French railroad system is nationalized (SNCF) and the franc devalued a second time as capital flees the country.

September: An organization of former Camelots du Roi, the Cagoule, launches a terrorist campaign by bombing two buildings that house a major employers' association. Their strategy is inspired by the Nazis' burning of the Reichstag in Berlin and framing of German Communists.

November 5: At a meeting in the Reich Chancellery, the so-called Hossbach conference, Hitler reveals his plans for European conquest.

December: Italy quits the League of Nations.

Malraux, who fought with the republicans in Spain, publishes his novel about the Spanish Civil War, *L'Espoir (Man's Hope)*.

Jean Renoir makes a powerful case against war with his film *La Grande Illusion*.

Louis Aragon, a founder of the Surrealist movement and the author of novels that dramatize his conversion to Marxist-Leninism, becomes the effective director of *Commune*, a journal committed to mobilizing intellectuals in the war against Spanish Fascism.

Céline writes the first of several virulently anti-Semitic tracts, *Bagatelles pour un Massacre* (Trifles for a Massacre).

1938

January–April: Political instability is the rule, with Chautemps and Blum each briefly revisiting the Hôtel Matignon before Daladier establishes residence there for the third time, supported by a large majority of conservatives. For the third time, as well, the franc is devalued.

March: Hitler absorbs Austria in the *Anschluss*.

September: At the Nazi Party congress in Nuremberg, Hitler announces his intention to "rescue" Germans living in Czechoslovakia's westernmost province, the Sudetenland. France (Daladier) and England (Chamberlain) sanction the annexation at a conference in Munich, to which no Czech representative is invited.

October: Daladier's minister of finance, Paul Reynaud, prepares executive decrees the effect of which will be the annulment of several key Popular Front reforms. The decrees also provide for the arrest of foreigners.

November 9–10: Kristallnacht in Germany and Austria. After the assassination of a German embassy official in Paris by a young Jew whose family had been evicted from their house in Hanover, Jews are killed and Jewish shops and synagogues burned and vandalized in a series of coordinated attacks which leave streets littered with broken glass, giving the event its name—Kristallnacht, the Night of Broken Glass. On November 11, the twentieth anniversary of the Armistice, *Le Figaro* reports, "A kind of madness seized the German population and hatred of the Jewish race reached its peak today, convulsively. Jews of every age, men and women alike, have been set upon, in their houses as well as on the street. Only two have been killed, but in Vienna a wave of deep despair has led to twenty suicides." Far from commenting on the event, Charles Maurras's daily column is a rant against the Jewish minister of education, Jean Zay.

In an official communiqué, Mussolini laments the hospitality France offers Jews and other "parasites." In France a wave of refugees, mainly from Germany and Spain, provokes xenophobic outcries.

December: Joachim von Ribbentrop, the German minister of foreign affairs, arrives in Paris to sign an agreement of "mutual understanding" with the Daladier government, only a month after Kristallnacht.

The French Communist Party launches an evening daily, *Ce Soir,* and appoints Louis Aragon its editor in chief.

George Orwell publishes *Homage to Catalonia,* an account of his experiences in the Spanish Civil War.

Jean-Paul Sartre publishes his first novel, *La Nausée.*

1939

January: The first internment camp for refugees opens in the mountainous region of central France.

February: France officially recognizes Franco Spain, although nationalist troops will not occupy Madrid until late March. Franco thereupon subscribes to the Anti-Comintern Pact.

March: Germany annexes Bohemia and Moravia.

April–May: Germany renounces the nonaggression treaty signed with Poland in January 1934. Italy and Germany form a military alliance dubbed the "Pact of Steel."

Countries are scrambling to make preparations for war. A Franco-British mission visits Moscow to discuss military aid but fails to read Stalin's ulterior design. On August 23, to the shock and dismay of European Communists, he signs a nonaggression pact with Hitler, which includes a secret protocol mapping the division of spoils in Eastern Europe. *L'Humanité* declares in a front-page headline that the pact serves the cause to which the USSR has always devoted itself: world peace. The paper is suppressed after August 26. In September, Communists will be banished from France's confederation of trade unions, the CGT.

September 1: Germany invades Poland. France mobilizes and declares its intention to honor its commitments to Poland but conducts no serious military operation at its frontier with Germany.

September 26: The French Communist Party is dissolved. Communist deputies who have defended the Hitler-Stalin pact will soon be arrested and brought to trial.

November 30: The USSR invades Finland, where fighting will continue until March. The Finns have the better of it in every respect but numbers, which finally prevail.

Gallimard publishes Pierre Drieu La Rochelle's pro-Fascist novel *Gilles*.

1940

March: Daladier is unseated and replaced by Paul Reynaud, vice president of the center-right Democratic Republican Alliance. Reynaud is one of the few French politicians who will later endorse Winston Churchill's proposal that France and the United Kingdom combine their governments in the war against the Axis powers.

May 10: The eight-month "phony war" of German and French troops stalling one another at the border ends when Germany attacks the Netherlands, Belgium, and France. Immense numbers of civilians flee south, toward the Loire and beyond. A French counteroffensive fails.

June 13: Pétain calls for an armistice, opposing Reynaud, who has brought him into the government as vice premier. Three days later Reynaud resigns and Pétain is appointed premier by the president of the Republic.

June 17: Pétain requests an armistice, which is signed four days later at Rethondes, where the same enemies signed an armistice on November 11, 1918. In the meanwhile, General Charles de Gaulle has broadcast a message of resistance on the BBC from London.

July 10: Deputies and senators who had fled from Paris to Bordeaux and then to Vichy confer upon Pétain (now entitled chief of state) full power to revise the constitution. Only 80 in an assembly of 667 vote against the measure. It marks the death of the Third Republic.

Index

Page numbers in *italics* refer to illustrations.

ALSO BY FREDERICK BROWN

FOR THE SOUL OF FRANCE

Culture Wars in the Age of Dreyfus

In the aftermath of the Franco-Prussian War of 1870–71, a defeated and humiliated France split into cultural factions that ranged from those who embraced modernity to those who championed the restoration of throne and altar. This polarization—to which such iconic monuments as the Sacre-Coeur and the Eiffel Tower bear witness—intensified with a succession of grave events over the following decades: the crash of an investment bank founded to advance Catholic interests; the failure of the Panama Canal Company; and the fraudulent charge of treason brought against a Jewish officer, Alfred Dreyfus, which resulted in a civil war between his zealous supporters and fanatical antagonists.

In this brilliant reconsideration of what fostered the rise of fascism and anti-Semitism in twentieth-century Europe, Frederick Brown chronicles the intense struggle for the soul of a nation, and shows how France's deep fractures led to its surrender to Hitler's armies in 1940.

History

ANCHOR BOOKS
Available wherever books are sold.
www.anchorbooks.com

CITIZENS

A Chronicle of the French Revolution
by Simon Schama

In this *New York Times* bestseller, Schama presents not
a dying Old Regime, but an ebullient country, vital and
inventive, infatuated with novelty and technology—a strik-
ingly fresh view of Louis XVI's France.

History

LA BELLE FRANCE

by Alistair Horne

Beginning with Julius Caesar's division of Gaul into three
parts, Horne leads us through the ages from Charlemagne
to Chirac, touring battlefields from the Hundred Years'
War to Indochina and Algeria, and giving us luminous portraits of the nation's leaders, philosophers, writers, artists,
and composers. This is a captivating, beautifully illustrated,
and comprehensive yet concise history of France.

History